Stories on a String

STORIES ON

Candace Slater

A STRING

The Brazilian *Literatura de Cordel*

University of California Press Berkeley/Los Angeles/London

University of California Press
Berkeley and Los Angeles, California

University of California Press, Ltd.
London, England

Library of Congress Cataloging in Publication Data

Slater, Candace.
  Stories on a string.

  Bibliography: p. 275
  Includes index.
  1. Chap-books, Brazilian—History and criticism.
I. Title.
PQ9621.S5   869.1'03   80–29091
ISBN 0–520–04154–2

Printed in the United States of America

1   2   3   4   5   6   7   8   9

For the people who answered my questions

Why do all these professors come around here now asking us questions? Well, I don't know for sure, but I suppose it's because there are so many people in this world who have an education and all the money they need and yet who still can't write a single verse. Then you have the poet, a poor devil who never went to school, who has trouble scraping together a few coins for bread or busfare, and he sits down and writes a story that leaves everybody marveling. So to my way of thinking, all these people want to understand just how the poet makes his stories. They are all itching to know how such a miracle occurs.

Francisco de Souza Campos,
popular poet

The popular poet touches feelings deep within himself; he draws on his own sense of humor and love of drama whenever he writes. And the persons who read his stories find in them those very feelings which they too nourish deep inside them but are unable to express. Well then, I too am a poet, so I understand this. And I read *folhetos* because they are poetry.

Carlos Drummond de Andrade

Contents

Acknowledgments

T he research for this study was conducted between 1977 and 1979 under a grant from the Tinker Foundation. I am particularly grateful to the Center for Latin American Studies at Stanford University and to its director John Wirth for providing office space as well as library and computer privileges. The Brazilian National Institute of Folklore, the Casa de Rui Barbosa, the Joaquim Nabuco Institute, and Braulio do Nascimento, Adriano da Gama Kury, and Mário Souto Maior also aided me in many ways.

This book would not have been possible without the help of the popular poets and educated writers and artists listed in Appendices A and B. In addition, I owe thanks to Ruy Gesteira, Edgar and Zelma Hallock, David Parker, Tony and Judy Seeger, and Luís and Marisa Velho in Rio de Janeiro; Brian Head and family in Campinas; the Cerqueira Beão family in Salvador; the Barros de Carvalho family, Linda El Deir, Ana Elisa Latache and family, Henrique and Tereza Levy, Roberto Mota, Djalma and Virgília Peixoto, Parry Scott, and Suzanne Mary Williams in Recife; Nancy Loy in Campina Grande; and the Dantas Villar family in Taperoá; and to my colleagues Samuel Armistead and Dan Ben-Amos at the University of Pennsylvania. I have special debts to Ariano Suassuna, who first opened the door to Northeastern popular poetry to me; to José de Souza Campos, who helped make the *folheto* part of my own experience; and to Alan Dundes for his guidance and support. I am also indebted in many ways to Agnes Robinson and her family and to my parents and my husband Paul for their unfailing aid and encouragement.

This study also owes much to several hundred *folheto* buyers. I have often thought back on one particularly sunny afternoon in the Recife market when I got into a conversation with a would-be customer, who, questioned about his attitude toward films, replied, "Oh yeah, movies, I'm crazy about them. You know, there's a great one playing right now, how about it?"

Hot and weary, I told him, "Look, friend, you don't understand. I am a university professor, and I ask everyone these questions because I am writing a book about these stories and people who read and write them."

The man looked taken aback for a moment but then winked and grinned. "Oh sure, baby," he said, "sure you're a professor! But look here, even if *you* were crazy enough to run around in the blazing sun asking people like me silly questions, who would ever pay you to write a book about us? And what is more, who the devil would ever want to read it?"

I am grateful to many people in the numerous markets I visited for their good humor and forbearance. I hope their voices remain audible in the following pages.

Preface

The Brazilian stories in verse called *folhetos* or *literatura de cordel* are today the world's richest and most varied heirs to a centuries-old ballad and chapbook tradition once embracing most of Europe. Many of the themes that their poorly educated authors continue to rework date back to long before Cabral laid eyes on Brazil in 1500.[1] This pamphlet literature is, however, also a distinctly national legacy. For almost a century, these stories have been the principal reading matter of the lower classes in the Brazilian Northeast, an area

1. Most scholars divide the nation's history into three major periods: the Colony (1500–1821), the Empire (1822–1889), and the Republic (1889 to the present). The last period may be subdivided into the Old Republic (1889–1930) and the New Republic (post-1930).

In 1494, the papal Treaty of Tordesillas split a yet-undiscovered South America between Spain and Portugal. Six years later, Pedro Alvares Cabral discovered and claimed Brazil for the Portuguese crown. (The country's name comes from a kind of dyewood, which was exported in great quantity.) The first actual colony was established in 1532. Shortly after, the captaincy system, whereby the country was established into hereditary captaincies granted to a dozen donatories, was instituted.

The Northeast of Brazil quickly became a sugar-producing area. As the coast became more developed, settlers began entering the dryer, sparsely populated backlands where they set up cattle ranches on land grants from the crown known as *sesmarias*. The capture of Pernambuco by the Dutch in 1630 made the region more important to the Portuguese crown. The first imperial viceroy was appointed to Brazil in 1640.

Brazilians represent a mixture of African and Tupi Indian as well as Iberian cultures. Events in Europe directly affected the course of the nation's history. After Napoleon emerged triumphant in France toward the end of the eighteenth century and began extending his influence throughout the continent, the Portuguese court found itself compelled to move from Lisbon to Rio de Janeiro, which became the capital of the Empire for some thirteen years. When King João VI returned to Portugal, he left his son, Pedro I, as regent. The young man declared Brazil's independence in 1822 and became the country's first emperor.

The Brazilian Empire lasted until 1889, when the army, under Marshal Deodoro da Fonseca, overthrew Pedro II. The immediate cause of the declaration of a republic was a debate over slavery, which had been abolished by the Golden Law a year before. In reality, the nation was experiencing a series of social and economic changes in which the old plantation oligarchy was being replaced by a new industrial class.

During the first four decades of the Republic, the administration candidate was invariably elected. Then, in 1930, Getúlio Vargas came to power through a coup d'état. Vargas ruled Brazil until 1945, when he was deposed by the military, then returned to the presidency in the 1950 elections, governing until his suicide in 1954. After Vargas, Brazil was ruled by a series of civilian presidents for ten years. In 1964, the military assumed control of the nation and remains in power today.

spanning at least seven states and containing approximately a third of the country's 120 million people. They provide a document of actual historical events and, even more, of people's often ambivalent attitudes toward the forces shaping their lives. While the average erudite edition in Brazil is generally no more than two thousand copies, many *folhetos* go through ten or twenty thousand; sometimes "best sellers" and particularly sensational news stories top the one hundred thousand mark.

The *cordel* is important not only in its own right but also for its wider influence on twentieth-century Brazilian culture. Psychologists, historians, doctors interested in publicizing health measures, politicians, and religious leaders may seek out popular poets. Playwrights, painters, actors, and musicians often base their work on *folhetos*. Internationally known authors such as José de Alencar, João Guimarães Rosa, Jorge Amado, João Cabral de Melo Neto, and Ariano Suassuna have drawn heavily on these stories. Others who at first glance appear to have little or no relation to the *cordel* tradition (Antônio Callado, Jorge de Lima, Ferreira Gullar) often reveal unexpected ties. Today not only intellectuals and artists but a larger middle class looks to popular art forms such as the *folheto*. For some, these stories are simply a novelty. For others, they are indicators of profound social and economic changes within both the Northeast and Brazil as a whole.

Consideration of the *cordel* poses important theoretical questions about the relationship between popular art forms and daily life. This book introduces a subject whose true significance is only now becoming apparent. Providing an overview of the tradition, I devote special attention to contemporary *folhetos*, examining both the texts and their immediate setting. Wherever possible, I have attempted to incorporate the words of popular poets and members of their increasingly heterogeneous audience. Translations of these comments, as well as of all written material unless otherwise indicated, are my own.

My primary focus is the process of writing *folhetos*. I am concerned above all with the dynamics of individual stories. These stories cannot, however, be fully appreciated without understanding how poets and their readers or listeners perceive the act of composing and selling *cordel* tales and, in turn, how these tales do and do not reflect a particular community. There is no doubt that the *folheto* presents an idealized, and for that reason distorted, vision of reality. Nevertheless, in less direct ways the *folheto* also draws on poets' and buyers' experiences.

The term *literatura de cordel* was for centuries a Portuguese rather than a Brazilian expression. The name refers to the way booklets were often suspended from lines (*cordel* means "cord" or "string") stretched between two posts. In Brazil popular poets called their stories *folhetos* or, more colloquially, *folhetes* ("pamphlets") until a decade ago, when use of *lite-*

ratura de cordel by a growing number of middle-class visitors prompted the poets to adopt the term as their own. "It took me a while to figure out that *cordel* was just another word for the stories we had always written," says one poet, "but then I started to use it myself since it's a much prettier name."

The title *Stories on a String* is a more-or-less direct translation of *literatura de cordel*. However, the "string" is also meant to suggest the shoestring on which most poets live. It hints at the "stringing together" of bits and pieces of dissimilar material that results in a *folheto*. The term *cordel* also brings to mind the long if elusive tradition, extending back to the Middle Ages, on which these stories draw. Finally, few things are as homely—or as useful or strong—as ordinary cord.

The following study has three major sections. The first provides a literary and historical context for the tradition as it evolved in Brazil. The initial chapter traces the production and distribution network within which the *cordel* grew; the second focuses on current changes in this system and presents the *folheto* in a national arena.

The next section begins with an overview of theoretical approaches to the tradition. In Chapter 3, I summarize scholarship to date, pointing out its primarily theme-oriented nature and then suggest an essentially structural approach to the *cordel*, arguing that a six-step sequence can be found in virtually all *folhetos*. Chapters 4, 5, and 6 present case studies of one variant on this six-step sequence. The three *folhetos* presented for examination appear very different. One is about a Buddhist king, another deals with an actual kidnapping, still another focuses on a prostitute who is the heroine of a best-selling novel. Nevertheless, all three obey the same underlying pattern, thereby demonstrating both the range and flexibility of the *cordel* and its essential unity.

In the third and final part of the study, I consider the poet's vision of his stories, emphasizing his sense of himself as spokesman versus his identity as individual artist, and then I suggest the *cordel*'s significance for the traditional buyer. In the last chapter I show how the *folheto* draws on experience and how the six-step design evident in *cordel* stories compares with other, broader social patterns outlined by researchers working in Northeastern Brazil. Appendices A and B give brief descriptions of the educated writers and observers and the popular poets who have contributed to this study; Appendix C is a statistical analysis of *folheto* buyers in two sites in Rio de Janeiro; and Appendix D is a glossary of frequently used terms.

This discussion utilizes some one thousand *folhetos* in my own collection as well as others found in various public and private libraries. It also draws heavily on a year of fieldwork in Rio de Janeiro and the Brazilian Northeast sponsored by the Tinker Foundation. This fieldwork included interviews with approximately seventy-five popular poets, close to one hundred educated artists and intellectuals, and over three hundred typical buyers in fairs and open-air markets. I used questionnaires designed specifically for each of these three groups, varying my approach when it seemed necessary.

For educated persons in both the South and Northeast, I used a mimeographed form, which could be filled out but which more frequently served as the basis for a tape-recorded conversation. Because the *cordel*'s future is of such widespread concern today, it was possible to interview persons as diverse as the musicians of the electronic folk group called the Quinteto Violado and Brazil's most famous contemporary poet, Carlos Drummond de Andrade.

The questions I asked popular poets varied somewhat depending on the setting. However, my basic concerns remained the same. Because most poets are extremely hospitable, I frequently spent two or three days at a time in individual homes talking with the author, his family, and friends; and I often returned for a second and third visit. Therefore, much of the information in this study comes not only from outright questions but also from observations made during evenings spent peeling manioc in a smoky farmhouse or listening to neighbors crowd before a television set while the poet sat off in a corner hunched over a stack of paper.

My approach to traditional buyers varied more than my dealings with any other group. In the Rio area, a crowd almost always surrounded the poet-singer Azulão at the São Cristóvão fair. I was therefore able to interview large numbers of persons by using a tape recorder and a standard twenty-question form, which I memorized and tried to make as conversational as possible. At first, people were hesitant to talk, but as they came to see me week after week at the fair, they became more at ease, to the point of objecting when an official later tried to convince me to stop my recordings. ("She has a right to ask us questions; aren't we people like anyone else?")

In the Northeast, however, where I worked primarily in Recife and small cities in the states of Pernambuco, Paraíba, and Ceará, the reduced number of live performances and people's adverse reaction to the tape recorder made this method unfeasible. Generally, individuals either became shy or else displayed such overwhelming interest that the crowd would abandon the poet in order to swarm about me. Needless to say, this did not endear me to the would-be vendor, and I therefore had to seek another strategy.

Longer, less structured conversations with a smaller number of persons proved to be the answer. I recorded my findings either on tape as I went along or on paper immediately afterward. My friendship with one Recife-based poet, José de Souza Campos, resulted in my actually selling *folhe-*

tos, sitting beside him on a rickety stool morning after morning or, not infrequently, taking over the stand while he attended to other matters. ("Why don't you keep an eye on things for a while now? You love to talk, but you always ask the same questions! As if I hadn't told you the answers at least a hundred times!") Though my sales were never astronomical, would-be buyers were willing to tell me their ideas about *folhetos* as well as much about themselves. Because Recife is today as always a focal point for poets and publishers throughout the Northeast, I was able to listen in on numerous conversations between authors as well as between authors and buyers. I also had the good fortune to become friends with Joel Borges, a poet-vendor, who still sings in local marketplaces and who encouraged initially reticent members of his audience to talk with me at the weekly fair in Bezerros, a representative, largely rural community some two hours from Recife.

When I first began reading *literatura de cordel*, the enchanted princes and awful giants who spoke backlands Portuguese struck me as cardboard figures. I therefore turned to the poet and buyer as more promising subjects, and though I read hundreds of *folhetos* throughout my fieldwork, I did so largely at random. Only when I began a systematic structural analysis of the *cordel* almost a year later did I realize not only to what extent these stories represented a series of largely predictable patterns but also the degree to which these very patterns could be seen as an irregular, and for that reason all the more interesting, reflection of the poets' and buyers' daily existence. This study therefore presents the *folheto* as both a centuries-old and a distinctly contemporary and Brazilian art form. By examining the dynamics of the poetic process, the reader unfamiliar with the Northeast can appreciate the often contradictory ways the *cordel* author and his public think and act. "The *folheto*," says a historian and friend, "smells like Brazil." The following pages should provide a whiff of that complex and powerful country.

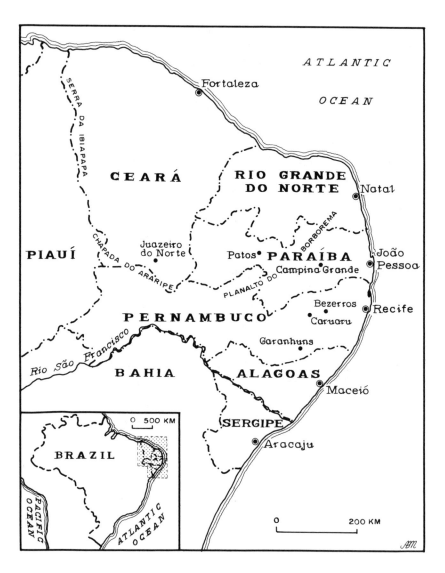

ATLANTIC

OCEAN

Fortaleza

SERRA DA IBIAPAPA

CEARÁ

RIO GRANDE
DO NORTE

Natal

PIAUÍ

CHAPADA DO ARARIPE

Juazeiro
do Norte

Patos

PARAÍBA

BORBOREMA

Campina Grande

João
Pessoa

PLANALTO DO

Bezerros

Recife

PERNAMBUCO

Caruaru

Rio São Francisco

Garanhuns

BAHIA

ALAGOAS

Maceió

O   500 KM

SERGIPE

BRAZIL

Aracaju

PACIFIC OCEAN

ATLANTIC OCEAN

O   200 KM

Northeastern Brazil, including the traditional heartland of the folheto, *the
states of Pernambuco, Paraíba, Rio Grande do Norte, and Ceará.*

I. Background for the
Literatura de Cordel

A sk any educated Brazilian about the pamphlet stories in verse known as *folhetos* or *literatura de cordel*.[1] "Oh yes,"·he or she will often say after a moment's hesitation, "those funny little books!" Individuals who have traveled through the vast, dry, and poor Northeastern backlands or poked about emigrant workers' quarters in major Southern cities such as Rio de Janeiro, Brasília, or São Paulo may describe how the poet chants his stories about Charlemagne or the latest moon shot. Some have seen stacks of *cordel* at culture fairs or art galleries, others at the more workaday open-air markets still found in most cities. The ever-increasing number of books and articles on this kind of narrative poetry and on Brazilian folk and popular traditions as a whole has created a national interest in the *literatura de cordel*. Once found primarily in public squares and the poorest Northeastern houses, these stories now appear on desks and coffee tables from Porto Alegre to Belém as well as in Europe, Japan, and the United States.

To be sure, Northeasterners in general have long been aware of the *folheto*'s existence. Someone's uncle would inevitably leave a drawer crammed full of the *"folhetes"* he had collected over the years. Routinely called on to read these booklets to their largely illiterate workers, more

---

1. The term *literatura de cordel* is an Iberian invention. Its use was restricted to scholars in Brazil until recently. Book-length studies and collections of a general nature on the Brazilian *literatura de cordel* include Átila de Almeida and José Alves Sobrinho, *Dicionário bio-bibliográfico de repentistas e poetas de bancada*, 2 vols. (João Pessoa/Campina Grande: Editora Universitária/Centro de Ciências e Tecnologia, 1978); Sebastião Nunes Batista, *Antologia da literatura de cordel* (Natal: Fundação José Augusto, 1977); Luís da Câmara Cascudo, *Vaqueiros e cantadores* (Porto Alegre: Livraria do Globo, 1939); Mark J. Curran, *Literatura de cordel* (Recife: Universidade Federal de Pernambuco, 1973); Manuel Florentino Duarte et al., *Literatura de cordel: Antologia*, 2 vols. (São Paulo: Global Editora, 1976); *Literatura popular em verso: Antologia*, 4 vols. (Rio de Janeiro: Fundação Casa de Rui Barbosa/MEC, 1964–1978) (hereafter cited as *Antologia*); *Literatura popular em verso: Catálogo* (Rio de Janeiro: Fundação Casa de Rui Barbosa/MEC, 1962); *Literatura popular em verso: Estudos* (Rio de Janeiro: Fundação Casa de Rui Barbosa/MEC, 1973) (hereafter cited as *Estudos*); Liêdo Maranhão de Souza, *Classificação popular da literatura de cordel* (Petrópolis: Vozes, 1976).

privileged individuals maintained a controlling hand in production and an unofficial censorship. Some of the best-known *folheto* writers clearly made use of their ties to the land-owning class. And yet, notwithstanding the interest of a small group of educated persons, the *cordel* was more a routine part of most individuals' existence than an object of serious study. Most tales were written as well as read or heard by members of the lower classes. Even today, despite far-reaching changes associated with industrialization, poets strive to say what their traditional buyers want to hear. New developments in the *cordel* therefore suggest important shifts in the ways ordinary people think. "The future of the *folheto*?" asks one present-day filmmaker. "Ah, the answer lies in the future of Brazil."[2]

Literary Forebears

Although I will refer to the *cordel* in this study as "popular" rather than "folk" literature, it should be evident from the outset that neither of these terms, as usually defined, is adequate.[3] Even if recent folklore research had not so thoroughly challenged the old concepts of folk literature as oral, anonymous, and time-honored, while categorizing popular literature as the written work of identifiable authors, *folhetos* would still pose problems that will become clearer in the course of this discussion. The term *popular* as used here means above all "non-elite" and is for this reason close to what other writers might label *folk*.

The *folheto* is, as people say, a "little book." Customarily measuring four by six-and-a-half inches and numbering eight, sixteen, thirty-two, or (less commonly) sixty-four pages, it is printed on newspaper-weight paper. The fourfold pages, sold uncut, fall into stanzas usually of six or seven lines. The cover, generally in pastel, bears a photograph or engraving not necessarily related to the text. The frequently illiterate reader will recognize a favorite story or be tempted to take home a new choice depending on the design on the cover. The author's or publisher's name or both usually appear above the title. A likeness of the poet, together with

2. Interview with Geraldo Sarno, Rio de Janeiro, November 24, 1977. For identification of persons cited in this study, see Appendix A for educated writers, artists, and observers; and Appendix B for popular poets.

3. For a discussion of some of the problems associated with traditional definitions of "folk" and "popular" art, see Dan Ben-Amos, "Toward a Definition of Folklore in Context," in *Towards New Perspectives in Folklore*, ed. Américo Paredes and Richard Bauman (Austin: University of Texas Press, 1971), pp. 3–15. I believe that the *cordel* is as much a "folk" as a "popular" art form, at least according to how these terms are usually defined.

various announcements of a commercial nature, often appears on the back.[4]

This physical description is helpful in situating the *cordel* within a larger chapbook tradition. Nevertheless, the limited number of references to forms such as the *folheto* before 1900 makes its evolution hard to trace although future research may unearth new information about popular literature in sources such as diaries and letters. The subject of popular literature interested few educated persons until the impact of the Romantic movement around the middle of the nineteenth century. The Brazilian elite customarily studied in or toured Europe, and few of its members knew or cared about the isolated regions of their own country before that time. Because the first available Northeastern *folhetos* date back only to the 1890s, it is not possible to draw on the considerable backlog of texts available to the student of European or North American pamphlet literature. Most discussions of its origins are therefore sketchy and repetitive.[5]

A detailed consideration of sources is beyond the scope of this study. Nevertheless, it is worth briefly mentioning a half-dozen separate if interrelated traditions that contribute to the *folheto*. Among the most important are oral balladry, the European as well as more specifically Portuguese chapbook (which includes written ballads and astrological almanacs), and the Brazilian improvised verse dialogues or contests (*desafios* or *pelejas*), which go back to the *tenzone* of the troubadours and through them to antiquity. Other principal sources include religious material such as biblical stories and the exemplum, the folktale known as the *trancoso* in Brazil, and a variety of African and indigenous (Brazilian-Indian) elements.

Writers concerned with the *cordel* frequently identify these stories as descendants of the centuries-old Iberian *romanceiro* or ballad tradition. This tradition, however, incorporates multiple strands. The term *romance* itself may be applied to either oral or printed compositions. It means not

---

4. The blockprint or *xilogravura* is an important aspect of the *folheto* and is often responsible for whether or not a particular story sells. For examples of blockprints by major popular artists, see *Xilógrafos nordestinos* (Rio de Janeiro: Fundação Casa de Rui Barbosa, 1977). For a discussion of this art form, see Mário Souto Maior, "A xilogravura popular na literatura de cordel," *Brasil Açucareiro*, 75 (1970): 45–53; Thelmo de Jesus Pereira, "A expressão gráfica da literatura de cordel nordestina," *Remag: Revista Métodos de Artes Gráficas* (Rio de Janeiro), 15 (1965): 18–23; Roberto Pontual, "Notas sobre a xilogravura popular," *Revista de Cultura Vozes*, 64 (1970): 53–59. Also see the notes by Ariano Suassuna, in José Costa Leite, *Vinte xilogravuras do Nordeste* (Recife: Companhia Editora de Pernambuco, 1970), and Suassuna's *Xilogravura popular do Nordeste* (Recife: Museu de Arte Popular, 1968). For a study of the back covers of *folhetos*, see Mark J. Curran "A 'página editorial' do poeta popular," *Revista Brasileira de Folklore*, 12 (1972): 5–16.

5. The single most comprehensive overview of the *cordel*'s origins to date is Manuel Diégues Júnior, "Ciclos temáticos na literatura de cordel," in *Estudos*, pp. 1–150.

only "ballad" but also "novel," "tale," "fable," and "story," as well as a *folheto* numbering thirty-two or more pages.

Although the *cordel* is close to the *corridos* or *corrido*-like compositions found in Spanish-speaking countries such as Mexico, Nicaragua, Venezuela, Colombia, Chile, and Argentina, its relationship to the Iberian ballad appears somewhat less direct. *Corridos* tend to be shorter and closer to the oral tradition than the *cordel*. Though they may be printed as broadsides or folded into booklets, they are generally sung to melodies. Though I have followed the popular poets' lead in using the verb *sing* throughout this study for the chanting style in which they recite their verses in marketplaces, the *cordel* is a collection of stories designed to be read. The *folheto* vendor, unlike the *corrido* seller, does not use a guitar because his music is different and also because he needs his hands to turn the pages of these generally much longer compositions. Then, too, whereas the *corrido* singer begins with an initial call to the public in which he summarizes his subject, the *folheto* writer normally starts out with a distinctly literary invocation to the muse, a saint, or God.[6]

Although many *folhetos* reveal the same themes as Spanish-American *corridos* and their Iberian forebears, they draw upon a whole narrative corpus that the latter do not. There are *cordel* versions of news events, the exploits of famous bandits, and religious topics, but there are no *corridos* about Romeo and Juliet or Sleeping Beauty. If this study stresses the *folheto*'s often neglected performance aspect, it would be a mistake to underrate its equally important written character. The *cordel*'s relationship to the Iberian ballad is less direct than the *corrido*'s, in part, because the ballad, though often recorded in writing and cultivated as a literary genre, retains such strong oral roots.

Turning to a discussion of the sources for the *folheto*, we may begin

---

6. For a detailed listing of works on *corridos* and *corrido*-like compositions, see Merle E. Simmons, *A Bibliography of the Romance and Related Forms in Spanish America* (Bloomington: Indiana University Press, 1963); and for updating by Simmons, see his annual folklore bibliographies, the most recent of which is *Folklore Bibliography for 1975* (Philadelphia: ISHI, 1979). The best single introduction to the Mexican *corrido* remains Vicente T. Mendoza, *El corrido mexicano: Antologia* (Mexico City: Fondo de Cultura Económica, 1954), and his *El romance español y el corrido mexicano*, 2nd ed. (Mexico City: Fondo de Cultura Económica, 1959). For book-length works in English, see Merle E. Simmons, *The Mexican Corrido as a Source for Interpretive Study of Modern Mexico, 1870–1950* (Bloomington: Indiana University Press, 1957); and Américo Paredes, *"With His Pistol in His Hand": A Border Ballad and Its Hero* (Austin: University of Texas Press, 1958). For an introduction to the ongoing debate about the *corrido*'s origins, particularly interesting to students of the *folheto*, see Merle E. Simmons, "The Ancestry of Mexico's Corridos," *Journal of American Folklore*, 76 (1963): 1–15; and Américo Paredes, "The Ancestry of Mexico's *Corridos*: A Matter of Definition," *Journal of American Folklore*, 76 (1963): 231–35.

with a few words about oral Iberian ballads. Variants of these anonymous compositions appear today in regions of Spain, Portugal, and their former colonies, as well as in scattered Sephardic Jewish communities. Some of these traditional ballads (*romances velhos*) are still sung in parts of Brazil.[7]

A more general tradition of oral balladry and storytelling dating back to colonial times no doubt prepared the inhabitants of the interior for the emergence of the *literatura de cordel*. One can, for instance, identify common features in Northeast Brazilian ballads and later *folhetos*. These features do not necessarily imply a direct link between the forms since folktales, puppet plays, and circus presentations may also reveal nearly identical characteristics, but a common mentality is definitely at work. The carefully drawn battle between good and evil, in which the former wins a resounding triumph, is, for instance, a constant in these narratives. Although one can find a number of Iberian variants of the "Silvana / Delgadinha" story, in which the wronged daughter goes to heaven and the tempter-father to hell, this conclusion is far more widespread and emphatic in Brazilian versions. There is a tendency in the ballad as well as

7. The classic overview of the ballad tradition remains William Entwistle, *European Balladry* (Oxford: Clarendon Press, 1939). One gets a feel for the vast scholarship on Iberian balladry by consulting the works of Ramón Menéndez-Pidal, especially his monumental *Romancero tradicional de las lenguas hispánicas: Español-portugués-catalán-sefardí* (Madrid: Gredos, 1957, 1963, 1969, 1971–1972). Major book-length works on the Luso-Brazilian tradition include José de Alencar, *O nosso cancioneiro, Cartas ao Sr. Joaquim Serra* (Rio de Janeiro: Livraria São José, 1962); Lucas Alexandre Boiteux, *Poranduba catarinense* (Florianópolis: Comissão Catarinense de Folclore, 1957); Teófilo Braga, *Romanceiro geral*, 3 vols. (Coimbra: Imprensa de Universidade, 1867); Francisco Pereira da Costa, *Folclore pernambucano* (Rio de Janeiro: Imprensa Nacional, 1908); Almeida Garrett, *Romanceiro*, 2 vols. (Lisbon: Imprensa Nacional, 1875); Jackson da Silva Lima, *O folclore em Sergipe: Romanceiro* (Rio de Janeiro: Liv. Cátedra/INL/MEC, 1977); Rossini Tavares de Lima, *Romanceiro Folclórico do Brasil* (São Paulo: Irmãos Vitales Editores Brasil, 1971); Antônio Lopes, *Presença do romancero* (Rio de Janeiro: Civilização Brasileira, 1967); Celso de Magalhães, *A poesia popular brasileira*, rev. ed. (Rio de Janeiro: Divisão de Publicações e Divulgação da Biblioteca Nacional, 1973); José Leite de Vasconcellos Pereira de Mello, *Romanceiro português*, 2 vols. (Coimbra: Universidade de Coimbra, 1958–1960); Sílvio Romero, *Cantos populares do Brasil*, 3rd ed., 2 vols. (Rio de Janeiro: José Olympio, 1954); Sílvio Romero, *Estudos sobre a poesia popular de Brasil, 1879–1889*, 2nd ed. (Petrópolis: Vozes/Governo do Estado de Sergipe, 1977); and Carolina Michaelis de Vasconcellos, *Estudos sobre o romanceiro peninsular: Romances velhos em Portugal*, 2nd ed. (Coimbra: Imprensa da Universidade, 1934). For an excellent descriptive summary of ballad research in Brazil, see Braulio do Nascimento, "Pesquisa do romanceiro tradicional no Brasil," in *Romancero y poesia oral: El romancero en la tradición oral moderna*, ed. Diego Catalán and Samuel G. Armistead (Madrid: Gráficas Condor, 1972), pp. 65–83; and Braulio do Nascimento, "Um século de pesquisa do romanceiro tradicional no Brasil," *Revista Brasileira de Cultura*, 17 (1973): 37–54.

the *folheto* to do away with the ambiguity marking many Iberian variants and to stress or, in some cases, to introduce an underlying moral.[8]

The *cordel* as we know it is not, however, a written transcription of time-honored ballads. Granted, there are enough significant similarities between orally transmitted narratives about cowboys and mysterious bulls and *folhetos* on the same theme to suggest that poems on these particular subjects may provide one of a number of missing links.[9] Today, however, the two traditions are quite separate. While one can pick out a number of common themes such as "father sets out to seduce daughter" in ballads and *folhetos*, such themes are also found in the culture at large. *Cordel* stories do not normally draw directly upon Iberian narratives of the "La Condessa" or the "Jorge and Juliana" type.

This division owes in part to the fact that men do not usually sing oral ballads in public places. The performance of ballads, which is less common than the sort of storytelling associated with *folhetos*, is largely reserved for women in the home, and thus a look at the standard ballad collections will reveal a preponderance of female informants.[10] These women, who are usually old and found more often in the countryside than in cities, may sing pieces of *folhetos* as well as these anonymous ballads, but *cordel* authors seldom incorporate the ballads into their work. Instead, they tend to draw on themes associated with a larger chapbook tradition, which also has European roots.[11]

In some respects, *folhetos* are much like other "little books" available at one time or another not only throughout Europe but in various parts of Africa, Asia, and the Americas. Pamphlet literature can be found in Western Europe, Gold Rush San Francisco, eighteenth-century Japan, and present-day Nigeria. Indeed, booklets in Portuguese were printed in Oak-

8. Compare, for instance, these versions of the "Silvana" ballad found in Braga, *Romanceiro geral*, I, 447–83, with those included in Lima, *O folclore em Sergipe: Romanceiro*, pp. 61–85.

9. For a discussion of these cowman ballads, see Alencar, *O nosso cancioneiro*; Theo Brandão, "Romance do ciclo do gado em Alagoas," in *Anais do primeiro congresso brasileiro de folclore* (Rio de Janeiro: Publicações do Ministério das Relações Exteriores, 1953), II, 113–49: Jackson da Silva Lima, "O boi no romanceiro tradicional," *Momento*, 1(9) (1977): 5–20; Lima, *O folclore em Sergipe*, pp. 452–74; and Braulio do Nascimento, "O ciclo do boi na poesia popular," in *Estudos*, pp. 165–232.

10. As for the preponderance of female singers, in the most recent published collection of Brazilian ballads, Lima's *O folclore em Sergipe*, only five of fifty-seven informants are men. Female singers dominate earlier collections as well.

11. Traditional ballads in *folheto* form are generally the work of educated authors. The Folklore Commission of Espírito Santo has, for example, sponsored publication in *cordel* form of anonymous ballads such as "Juliana e Dom Jorge," "Cego Andante," "Conde Elado," and "Bernal Francês." I am indebted to Braulio do Nascimento for calling my attention to one ballad-based *folheto* by a popular author, Francisco Bandeira de Melo's *História de Antonino e o Pavão do Professor*.

land, California, in the early part of the twentieth century because a sizable Luso-American community existed there.[12]

Chapbooks (the English term comes from the "cheap books" offered by itinerant peddlers called chapmen) and *folhetos* serve similar needs. Though representing different periods and places, their authors provide news, entertainment, and instruction. Most rely heavily on oral traditions as well as on the work of other popular and erudite writers in devising their stories. They cater to illiterate or semiliterate individuals in city streets and country markets who appreciate the simple language, decorative cover, and accessible price of the leaflets, as well as their appealing subjects.[13]

The stories in Brazilian pamphlets recall others brought from Portugal,

12. Claude Hulet of the University of California, Los Angeles, referred to a pamphlet version in his possession of "João de Calais" published in Oakland, California, in 1915, in a summary of a paper, "Two *Folheto* Versions of João de Calais," at the Second Symposium for Portuguese Traditions, University of California, Los Angeles, May 8, 1978. For a general study of the Luso-American community in California, see Walter J. Brown, *The Portuguese in California* (San Francisco: R & E Research Associates, 1972).

13. Aside from a short study by Fernando de Castro Pires de Lima, "Literatura de cordel," in *Ensaios etnográficos* (Lisbon: Fundação Nacional para a Alegria do Povo, 1969), II, 111–34, and Arnaldo Saraiva's "Literatura marginalizada" in *Literatura marginalizada* (Porto: n.p., 1975), pp. 109–21, there are few general studies of Portuguese chapbooks. One can find a growing number of collections such as *Histórias jocosas a cavalo num barbante* (Porto: Editora Nova Crítica, 1980) but much remains to be done. For representative studies of related European pamphlet literature, see, for Spain, Julio Caro Baroja, *Ensayo sobre la literatura de cordel* (Madrid: Editorial Revista de Occidente, 1969); María Cruz García de Enterría, *Sociedad y poesia de cordel en el barroco* (Madrid: Taurus Ediciones, 1973); and Joaquín Marco, *Literatura popular en España en los siglos XVIII y XIX* (*una aproximación a los pliegos de cordel*), 2 vols. (Madrid: Taurus, 1977). For France, see Geneviève Bollème, *La Bibliothèque bleue: Littérature populaire en France du XVIIe au XIXe siècle* (Paris: Juilliard, 1971); Geneviève Bollème, *La Bible bleue: Anthologie d'une littérature "populaire"* (Paris: Flammarion, 1975); and Robert Mandrou, *De la culture populaire aux 17e et 18e siècles* (Paris: Stock, 1964). For Germany, see Richard Edmund Benz, *Geist und Gestalt im gedruckten deutschen Buch des 15. Jahrhunderts* (Mainz: Gutenberg-Gesellschaft, 1951); and William Coupe, *The German Illustrated Broadsheet in the Seventeenth Century: Historical and Iconographical Studies* (Baden-Baden: Heitz, 1966–1967). For England, see John Ashton, *Chap-books of the Eighteenth Century* (London: Chatto & Windus, 1882); Robert Collison, *The Story of Street Literature: Forerunner of the Popular Press* (Santa Barbara, Ca.: Clio Press, 1973); Leslie Shepard, *The Broadside Ballad: A Study in Origins and Meaning* (London: H. Jenkins, 1962); and Leslie Shepard, *The History of Street Literature* (London: David & Charles, 1973). For a listing of further references to English-language chapbooks, see Victor E. Neuberg, *Chapbooks: A Guide to Reference Material on English, Scottish, and American Chapbook Literature of the 18th and 19th Centuries*, 2nd ed. (London: Woburn Press, 1972). For an interesting contrast, see the study on Nigerian chapbooks by Emmanuel N. Obiechina, *Onitsha Market Literature* (New York: Africana Publishing Corporation, 1972); and on Japanese chapbooks by Leon M. Zolbrod, "Kusazōshi: Chapbooks of Japan," in *Transactions of the Asiatic Society of Japan*, 3rd series, 10 (1968): 116–47.

and in many cases both plot and title are the same. Luís da Câmara Cascudo's classic study of five of the best-known *folhetos* and their sources confirms the extent of this borrowing.[14] Nevertheless, the two pamphlet literatures are not identical. Whereas religious plays and short dramatic pieces are found in many Portuguese chapbooks, they are not found in the Brazilian stories that began appearing around the turn of the nineteenth century.[15]

The Iberian chapbook flowered in the sixteenth century when the ties between Spain and Portugal were particularly close. (Between 1580 and 1640 Portugal was part of Spain.) Those printed compositions—known as *pliegos sueltos* in Spain, *folhas volantes* in Portugal—were originally a catchall for traditional and new ballads by known authors (*romances vulgares*) as well as other forms such as *bailes*, *xácaras*, and *villancicos*. Many of the first booklets to appear in the streets of Madrid and Lisbon dealt with historical subjects. Toward the beginning of the seventeenth century, however, the number of nontraditional themes increases. Some stories are pirated editions of ballads by well-known poets and playwrights such as Góngora or the Portuguese Gil Vicente. Others are clearly imitative "Moorish" stories, exotic adventure ballads, or burlesque treatments of assorted rogues and ruffians.[16]

The use by popular authors of satire and bawdy humor as well as their cheerful plagiarism of educated writers irked the elite, leading the Spanish monarch Charles III to forbid (without effect) further publication of these pamphlets because of their "harm to public morals." In Portugal the *literatura de cordel* quickly became associated with "a base, plebeian order."

14. Luís da Câmara Cascudo, *Cinco livros do povo* (Rio de Janeiro: José Olympio, 1953).

15. See Albino Forjaz de Sampaio, *Teatro de cordel* (Lisbon: Imprensa Nacional de Lisbon, 1922); the *Catálogo da Coleção de Miscelâneas*, 6 vols. (Coimbra: Biblioteca de Coimbra, 1967); and *Literatura de cordel* (Lisbon: Biblioteca Geral de Fundação Gulbenkian, 1970). See also José Daniel Rodrigues da Costa, *6 entremezes de cordel* (Lisbon: Editorial Estampa, 1973).

16. For an extensive catalogue of sixteenth-century Spanish *pliegos sueltos*, see Antonio Rodríguez-Moniño, *Diccionario de pliegos sueltos poéticos: Siglo XVI* (Madrid: Castalia, 1970). For a further sampling of Spanish pamphlet literature, see some of the many collections such as María Cruz García de Enterría, *Catálogo de los pliegos poéticos españoles del siglo XVII en el British Museum de Londres* (Pisa: Giardini, 1977); María Cruz García de Enterría, *Pliegos poéticos españoles de la Biblioteca Ambrosiana de Milan*, 2 vols. (Madrid: Joyas Bibliográficas, 1973); *Pliegos poéticos españoles de la Biblioteca del Estado de Baviera de Munich*, 2 vols. (Madrid: Joyas Bibliográficas, 1974); Henry Thomas, *Early Spanish Ballads in the British Museum*, 3 vols. (Cambridge: Cambridge University Press, 1927); and Edward M. Wilson, "Tradition and Change in Some Late Spanish Chapbooks," *Hispanic Review*, 25 (1957): 194–216. For one well-known playwright's reaction to a pirated version of his work, see María Cruz García de Enterría, "Un memorial, casi desconocido de Lope de Vega," *Boletín de la Real Academia Española*, 51 (1971): 139–60.

The stories became increasingly known as *literatura de cego* or "blind-man's literature" after the Brotherhood of the Child Jesus of the Blind Men of Lisbon obtained exclusive sales rights to them in 1789.

No one knows exactly when, in what quantity, and under what conditions these booklets entered colonial Brazil. It is probable that they, like their Spanish counterparts, arrived with the first settlers, but that is difficult to prove.[17] There is evidence that the Rio de Janeiro branch of the Livrarie Garnier, one of the important publishers of the French chapbooks known as the *littérature de colportage*, began importing quantities of Portuguese pamphlet literature toward the middle of the nineteenth century. The old stories about Charlemagne, the Princess Magalona, and the Gambler Soldier were therefore readily available to Brazilian readers at that time. Although it is likely that both oral and written versions of these stories circulated in Brazil much earlier, it is certain that the Northeastern *folheto* draws heavily on these nineteenth-century imports.[18]

The *cordel* clearly draws on a European chapbook tradition but is somewhat different in form. Although a number of Portuguese pamphlets were written in prose, the *folheto* is, with the exception of a small number of prayers in prose, an almost exclusively poetic form. The influence of poet-improvisers known as *cantadores* or *repentistas*, famous throughout the backlands for their on-the-spot compositions and spirited exchanges in verse, may explain many of the *cordel*'s relatively original features.[19]

17. Figures for Spanish America indicate a steady influx of pamphlet literature. We know, for example, that in 1600 some ten thousand copies of "Pierres y Magalona" entered Mexico; see Francisco Rodríguez Marín, *El Quijote y don Quijote en América* (Madrid: Librería de los Sucesores de Hermano, 1911), pp. 36–37. There are, however, no comparable figures for Brazil.

18. Portugal was ruled by France from 1808 to 1821, when Brazil served as the capital of the exiled court and French influences are apparent in Luso-Brazilian popular as well as erudite literature. See Luís da Câmara Cascudo, *Motivos da literatura oral da França no Brasil* (Recife: n.p., 1964), for a general overview of the French presence in the Brazilian oral tradition. See also Roberto Câmara Benjamin, "Breve notícia de antecedentes franceses e ingleses da literatura de cordel nordestino," *Revista Tempo Universitário*, 6 (1980): 171–188.

19. The tradition of verbal dueling appears to date back to the Greeks and Romans. See J. Wickersham Crawford, "*Echarse Pullas*: A Popular Form of *Tenzone*," *Romanic Review*, 6 (1915): 150–64. For a detailed general discussion of the Iberian minstrel tradition, see Ramón Menéndez-Pidal, *Poesía juglaresca y juglares*, 6th ed. (Madrid: Austral, 1964). Now-classic works on Brazilian poet-singers include Gustavo Barroso, *Ao som da viola* (Rio de Janeiro: Livraria Editora Leite Ribeiro, 1923); Francisco das Chagas Batista, *Cantadores e poetas populares* (João Pessoa; Editora F. C. Batista Irmão, 1929); José Rodrígues Carvalho, *Cancioneiro do Norte*, 3rd ed. (Rio de Janeiro: MEC, 1967); Francisco Coutinho Filho, *Repentistas e glosadores* (São Paulo: A. Sartoris & Bertoli, 1937); Francisco Coutinho Filho, *Violas e repentes*, 2nd ed. rev. (São Paulo: Editora Lectura/INL, 1972); Leonardo Mota, *Cantadores*, 2nd ed. (Fortaleza: Imprensa Universitária do Ceará, 1961); Leonardo Mota, *Violeiros do Norte*, 2nd ed. (Fortaleza: Imprensa Universitária do

While *cantador* ("singer") is technically a wider term than *repentista* (a singer specializing in on-the-spot verse exchanges), most popular poets use the two words interchangeably. Unlike a *poeta de bancada* (*bancada* means "bench" and refers to the act of sitting down to write), these individuals specialize in improvisation and may be illiterate.

Historical as well as textual evidence suggests the poet-singer's (*repentista*'s) role in the *folheto*. A descendant of the Iberian singers called *juglares*, the Brazilian *cantador* had counterparts throughout Spanish America. (The Argentine and Chilean *payador* is probably the best known.) Associated above all with the court in medieval Europe, improvised versifying thrived in New World frontiers such as the Northeastern backlands. Though the tradition seems to have begun to wane toward the end of the nineteenth century, some ranchers still reserved a place of honor at their table for the poets who not only entertained the inhabitants but passed on bits of local, national, and international news. Earlier, when the almost total absence of roads and the dangers posed by hostile Indians and bandits made these ranches virtual islands, the arrival of the poet, like that of the peddler or priest, must have been an especially welcome occasion.[20]

The first great school of *cantadores*, the Escola do Teixeira, emerged toward the end of the eighteenth century in the Paraiban interior. Although there may have been clusters of poets elsewhere, the Teixeira group is undoubtedly the best known. Its members were largely responsible for substituting the *repente* (*sextilha*), six lines of seven syllables following a consonantal ABCBDB rhyme scheme, for the then-prevailing four-line *quadra* or *redondilha maior*.

The *sextilha* is the prevailing metrical pattern in the Brazilian *cordel*. Portuguese chapbooks, which were written in verse rather than in prose, inevitably employed *quadras*, but the Northeastern *folheto* eschews this form. Not only the *sextilha* but all metrical patterns found in the *folheto* also occur in improvised poetry. The existence of printed *décimas* and *martelos*, as well as ABCs in which each stanza begins with the same one- or two-line refrain, suggests direct ties between the *folheto* and this form

---

Ceará, 1962); Leonardo Mota, *Sertão alegre*, 2nd ed. (Fortaleza: Imprensa Universitária do Ceará, 1963). An English translation of one poetic contest is available in *The Warriors: Peleja Between Joaquim Jaqueira and Manoel Barra Mansa*, tr. Ernest J. Barge and Jan Feidel (New York: Grossman, 1972). For works on the *payador*, see Simmons, *A Bibliography of the Romance*.

20. Geraldo Ireneu Joffily, *Um cronista do sertão no século passado: Apontamentos à margem das "Notas sobre a Paraíba"* (Campina Grande: Comissão Cultural do Município, 1965), pp. 159–60, mentions the disappearance of the *cantador*. I am grateful to Linda Lewin for indicating this source to me. The information about the chair reserved at the rancher's dining table comes from Ariano Suassuna, interview, Recife, February 16, 1978.

of oral poetry derived from the Teixeira group. So does the existence of a number of literary *pelejas* within the *cordel*, as well as the sporadic use of formulas first associated with the *cantador*. This minstrel heritage is also apparent in Spanish America where we have written accounts of famous duels such as that between the Chilean Taguada and Don Javier de la Rosa. We do not, however, find a fusion of the verbal dueling with the folktale tradition in any country but Brazil.[21] Only in the Northeast do poet-singers play a major role in the evolution of chapbook literature, which, although distinct from oral poetry, continues to bear its stamp.

In reality, Brazilian poets and poet-singers have always been closely associated. The first great *folheto* writer, Leandro Gomes de Barros (1868–1918), grew up in Teixeira, where he had close ties with the Nunes Batistas, a family of *cantadores*. Popular poets attribute various now-classic stories such as *The Sultan's Revenge* or *The Sea Captain*, which bear Leandro's signature, to the well-known poet-singer Silvino Pirauá Lima. Moreover, many of the great *folheto* writers of the first half of the twentieth century were also professional singers. José Camelo de Melo Resende, José Galdino da Silva Duda, and Francisco das Chagas Batista are only a few of the most obvious examples. In addition, even those poets such as Leandro, who did not participate in competitions, inevitably knew how to improvise. Since poet-singers were routinely called upon to recite particularly popular thirty-two-page *romances* at gatherings throughout the interior, they were naturally familiar with individual writers and their work. Some of the older *folheto* vendors report passing the night in homes of singers who lived along their sales routes. As a token of appreciation, they would frequently leave a small bundle of booklets for their host to memorize.[22]

21. For a good overview of metrical patterns found in both improvised and written poetry, see Ariano Suassuna, "Notas sobre o romanceiro popular do nordeste," in *Ariano Suassuna: Seleta em prosa e verso,* ed. Silviano Santiago (Rio de Janeiro: José Olympio/INL/MEC, 1974), pp. 162–90. I am using the term *formula* in the sense of a group of words that is regularly employed under the same metrical conditions to express a given essential idea. See Albert B. Lord, *The Singer of Tales* (New York: Atheneum, 1976). For a bibliography of formula-related studies, see Edward R. Haymes, *A Bibliography of Studies Relating to Parry's and Lord's Oral Theory* (Cambridge, Mass.: Harvard University Press, 1973). For a helpful list of additions, see Samuel G. Armistead, "Edward R. Haymes, *A Bibliography of Studies Relating to Parry's and Lord's Oral Theory,*" *Modern Language Notes,* 90 (1975): 296–99. For the text of the verse duel in question, see Nicasio García, *Contrapunto de Taguada con don Javier de la Rosa: En palla a cuatro líneas de preguntas con respuestas* (Santiago: Imprenta La Victoria, 1886). A version also appears in Antonio Acevedo Hernández, *Los cantores populares chilenos* (Santiago: Nascimento, 1933), pp. 48–55; and a section is repeated in Fernando Alegría, *La poesia chilena: Orígenes y desarrollo del siglo XVI al XIX* (Berkeley: University of California Press, 1954), pp. 142–48.

22. I am grateful to José Alves Sobrinho (interview, Campina Grande, Paraíba, March

The poets' unions, which began emerging after World War II, included not only writers but improvisers. Owing largely to the *cantador*'s present involvement with the radio, where *folheto* recitation would be impractical, the two traditions are more autonomous now than in the past.[23] Nevertheless, *cordel* authors, who can still usually string along a few verses (*glosar*) if prompted, may sell their own short songs along with texts of others by poet-singers. Some singers also turn out *cordel* stories. The emergence of songs called *canções* written for the radio by either *cantadores* or *folheto* poets constitutes another link between the two traditions. Printed on *cordel* presses, these *canções* are then sold in open-air markets by *folheto* vendors.

As the following chapters will make clearer, the majority of these stories can be read as a series of trials. Most *folheto* personages are either this-world saints or sinners. The hero or heroine is most often presented with a test of character, which he or she either passes or fails. Thus, while many *folhetos* are funny and a few are obscene or pornographic, almost all have an explicit message that is both solemn and unambiguous.

This underlying seriousness emphasizes the *cordel*'s links to religious tradition. *Folhetos* draw heavily on biblical material and the lives of saints, suggesting certain parallels to the medieval exemplum.[24] Although exempla, short stories used to illustrate moral and didactic treatises as well as

5, 1978) and Manuel d'Almeida Filho (interview, Aracaju, Sergipe, June 7, 1978) for this information about relationships between *folheto* vendors and poet-singers. The titles of the two *folhetos* in Portuguese are *A Vingança do Sultão* and *O Capitão de Navio*.

23. According to José Alves Sobrinho, the first Poets' Union was established in Fortaleza, Ceará, in 1950, with Domingos Fonseca as president. However, the best-known poets' association of all time was probably Rodolfo Coelho Cavalcante's ANTV (Associação de Trovadores e Violeiros), which was founded in 1955 and lasted three years. Since then, there have been a number of such (generally short-lived) groups established in various parts of Brazil. The first poet-singer radio programs, once again according to José Alves Sobrinho, date back to the 1940s. In Rio de Janeiro, Almirante later started a well-known program, which was later discontinued.

24. For an overview of religious themes in the *folheto*, see Alice Mitika Koshiyama, *Análise de conteúdo da literatura de cordel: Presença de valores religiosos* (São Paulo: Universidade de São Paulo, Escola de Comunicações e Artes, 1972); and Roberto Câmara Benjamin, "A religião nos folhetos populares," *Revista de Cultura Vozes*, 64 (1970): 21–24. For more specialized studies, see João Dias de Araújo, "Imagens de Jesus Cristo na literatura de cordel," *Revista de Cultura Vozes*, 68 (1974): 41–48; Carlos Alberto Azevêdo, *O heróico e o messiânico na literatura de cordel* (Recife: Edicordel, 1972); Eduardo Campos, "Romanceiro do Padre Cícero, *Boletim da Comissão Catarinense de Folclore*, 2 (1951): 30–33; Mário Pontes, "O diabo na literatura de cordel," *Revista de Cultura Vozes*, 64 (1970): 29–35; Mário Pontes, "A presença demoníaca na poesia popular do Nordeste," *Revista Brasileira de Folclore*, 12 (1972): 261–85; Luís Santa Cruz, "O diabo na literatura de cordel," *Cadernos Brasileiros*, 5 (1963): 344; and Mário Souto Maior, "O diabo na literatura de cordel," in his *Território da Danação* (Rio de Janeiro: Livraria São José, 1975), pp. 35–42.

sermons, had their heyday in the twelfth and thirteenth centuries, they have much older roots. The Dominican and Franciscan friars who compiled and adapted them drew on a wide range of sources including myths, chronicles, saints' legends, animal fables, and tales of varied, often Oriental, origin, as may be found in the Iberian *El libro de los enxemplos* (Book of Examples) and *El libro de los gatos* (Book of the Cats), jest books and anecdotes from daily life.[25]

These stories, which might be either in Latin or the vernacular, in prose or poetry, were designed to edify as much as to entertain. They were inevitably followed by a practical application in which each character or object would be equated with a greater reality, thereby giving the tale an allegorical quality, which might otherwise escape even the listener accustomed to looking for hidden meanings. Although some of these tales are solemn, others are very funny. The preacher is quite capable of describing in great detail how a wife and mother hide a lover behind a sheet, before informing his flock that the sheet is Vanity, the mother Earthly Deception, and the unhappy husband a Pilgrim in this Vale of Tears.

The exemplum had long since passed its prime by the time that chapbooks began appearing. Nevertheless, they continued to pepper a number of sermons.[26] This is not the place to do more than suggest a possible relationship between these tales and other chapbook stories, but it is tempting to see a number of pamphlet tales as secular exempla. Like the

25. *El libro de los enxemplos* and *El libro de los gatos* are both included in *Escritores en prosa anteriores al siglo XV*, ed. Pascual Gayangos, *Biblioteca de autores españoles*, vol. 51 (Madrid: M. Rivadeneyra, 1860), pp. 493–542, 543–69. Thomas Frederick Crane mentions a similar short collection of edifying stories in Portuguese manuscripts in the Torre do Tombo in his *The Exempla or Illustrative Stories from the Sermones Vulgares of Jacques de Vitry*, Publications of the Folklore Society, No. 26, 1890 (Nedeln, Lichtenstein: Kraus Reprint Ltd., 1967), p. cvii. For a sampling of general works on the exemplum, also see *Gesta Romanorum*, tr. Charles Swan (London: George Bell & Sons, 1906); Joseph Albert Mosher, *The Exemplum in the Early Religious and Didactic Literature of England* (New York: Columbia University Press, 1911); Fredric C. Tubach, *Index Exemplorum*, Folklore Society Communications, No. 204 (Helsinki: Suomalainen Tiedakatemia, 1969); and J. Th. Welter, *L'exemplum dans la littérature réligieuse et didactique du Moyen Age* (Paris: Occitana, 1927). Of special relevance to this study are Charles F. Altman, "Two types of Opposition in the Structure of Latin Saints' Lives," in *Medieval Hagiography and Romance*, ed. Paul Maurice Clogan (*Medievalia and Humanistica*, n.s. 6) (Cambridge: Cambridge University Press, 1975), pp. 1–11; and Fredric C. Tubach, "Struktur analytische Probleme: Das mittelalterliche Exemplum," *Hessiche Blätter für Volkskunde*, 59 (1958): 25–29. Although there is a special class of *folhetos* which bear the name "exemplum" (*exemplo*) in the title, I believe that the entire tradition grows out of a broader moralizing literature. In this vein, it is interesting to note that Spain and Portugal, more than any other country, appear to have had a practice of casting exempla in the vernacular; see Crane, *The Exempla*, p. cv.

26. See Hilary Dansey Smith, *Preaching in the Spanish Golden Age* (Oxford: Oxford University Press, 1978).

preacher who appealed to the largely illiterate masses, the chapbook author tends to rely upon a wealth of heterogeneous material that he too draws together with a final, explicit statement of an underlying moral not always apparent in the text itself.

The influence of the exemplum is obvious in the work of secular authors such as Chaucer and Boccaccio. In Portugal, the prime example of the exemplum-related narrative is a collection entitled *Tales and Stories of Moral Counsel and Example* written in 1585 by Gonçalo Fernandes Trancoso, who had lost most of his family in a plague.[27] As the title suggests, these stories drawn from both Portuguese oral tradition and chiefly Italian (via Spanish translation) literary sources present a series of positive and negative behavior models in a vibrant, colloquial, and often humorous style. The book enjoyed great success not only in Portugal but in Brazil where there is a reference to its presence as early as 1618. Many of the themes and titles of these stories, like "The Disobedient Daughter," "The Greedy Man Punished," "A Moral ABC," and "The King's Three Questions," suggest later *folhetos*. Significantly enough, although the word *trancoso* originally referred to these moralizing stories in particular, it gradually came to encompass folktales of all sorts.

Many folktales told in Brazil provide the basis for *cordel* stories. *Folhetos*, particularly those sixteen pages and longer, are full of standard tale types and motifs. Many draw on well-known stories such as "Beauty and the Beast," "The Wild Swans," and "The Fisherman's Three Wishes," all of which can be found in both oral and written versions in Northeastern Brazil. Often, the *folheto* makes a number of radical transformations in its source material. The *cordel* version of "Beauty and the Beast," for example, devotes fourteen of sixteen pages to the relationship between the heroine and her father, the beast only lumbering in at the very end.[28]

Then too, a careful look at fairy tale-related *folhetos* reveals that most involving children have been excluded. Although a hero or heroine may first appear as a child, he or she inevitably grows up within the course of the tale. There are thus no *cordel* versions of "Hansel and Gretel," "Goldilocks" or "Little Red Riding Hood" even though these stories can be found in standard Luso-Brazilian collections. This fact suggests that even though children may enjoy these stories, the *folhetos* are primarily destined for adolescents and adults.

Furthermore, while enchanted rings, flying horses, and birds with fiery

27. Gonçalo Fernandes Trancoso, *Contos e histórias de proveito e exemplo* (Paris: Aillaud & Bertrand, 1921).

28. Antti Aarne and Stith Thompson, *The Types of the Folktale*, 2nd ed. rev., Folklore Fellows Communications, No. 184 (Helsinki: Suomalainen Tiedakatemia, 1961). The Beauty and the Beast story is João Martins de Ataíde's *A Bela e a Fera* (Recife, 1944).

feathers appear in certain *folhetos*, the magic elements routinely found in many Luso-Brazilian fairy tales are kept to a minimum. As in many Carolingian tales of adventure, the notion of enchantment is generally tinged with moral overtones.[29] When talismen crop up in the *cordel*, for instance, they are usually seen more as extensions of persons with particular (admirable) qualities than as objects with autonomous, nontransferable powers. Thus, the *folheto* has no coaches that turn into pumpkins and no gingerbread houses. Once the magic actor or article has served the poet's purpose, he or it tends to either vanish or take on human form.

Other *folhetos* draw on different sorts of folktales. Some of these ties are more or less clear. The *cordel* story about a cowman who kills his employer's favorite steer, *O Boi Leitão*, is, for example, clearly related to a Brazilian folktale called "Quirino, the King's Cowman," which is told on the Iberian peninsula as "Boi Cardil e Rabil" (Portugal) or "Boi Barrozo" (Spain). Many of these stories are, however, less directly related. One can, for instance, see the seeds of the *folheto* story *The Prince Who was Born Destined to Die by Hanging* in the Brazilian folktale "Maria de Oliveira," known as "Maria da Silva" in Portugal, but the *folheto* deals with only one of many incidents in the narrative. Conversely, one of the many incidents frequently found in *folheto* versions of John Cricket stories appears in a Brazilian folktale with roots in the Iberian story of "The Wise Child and the Priest."

Poets, who have generally heard these tales as children, are less interested in faithfully reproducing the original tale than in coming up with a good story of their own. The relationship between this oral material and the *folheto* may, therefore, be tenuous or jumbled. Often, the poet simply borrows part of the title or a single section of the plot. Thus, while the *cordel* tale *Evil in Payment for Good* clearly owes something to the folk narrative "Good in Payment of Good," they are not the same story. The poet who wrote *The Princess of the Kingdom Stone-Without-End* had almost certainly heard stories about "The Princess of the Dream Without End," but the two heroines, while related, are hardly identical. Although it is likely that the writer of the *folheto The Mysterious Parrot* was influenced by a tale that can be traced back to the ancient Indian *Panchatantra*, it is difficult to gauge the exact relationship between this story and the oral tradition.[30]

29. For an excellent study of links between Carolingian material and the *cordel* tradition, see Jerusa Pires Ferreira, *Cavalaria em cordel: O passo das águas mortas* (São Paulo: Hucitec, 1979). See also Sebastião Nunes Batista, "Carlos Magno na poesia popular nordestina," *Revista Brasileira de Folclore*, 30 (1971): 143–70.

30. These and other connections rapidly become apparent if one leafs through standard collections of Luso-Brazilian folktales, such as Teófilo Braga, *Contos tradicionais do povo*

The majority of stories retold by *cordel* authors can be found in some form on the Iberian peninsula. Thanks to that region's peculiar history, many of these tales reached Brazil already laced with Oriental and African sources. However, even the most "European" tales inevitably acquired new shadings as they were repeated in the New World. Thus, one can find Afro-Brazilian and Brazilian-Indian terms within oral narratives and *folhetos* that clearly came to the Northeast from Portugal.

Furthermore, some *folhetos* draw more directly on Afro-Brazilian and native sources. The well-known *cordel* story of the two lovers known as *Green Coconut and Watermelon (Coco Verde e Melancia)*, by José Camelo de Melo Resende draws upon an African tale collected by Sílvio Romero. Many of the *folhetos* which feature animals (*The Marriage of the Monkey and the Mountain Lion*) and supernatural monsters (the cross-eyed boar, the headless jackal) may take their models from non-European sources. Some educated observers suggest that the *cordel* may have been influenced by the African narrative tradition known as the *akpalô*, which was brought by slaves to the Brazilian Northeast.[31]

Be this as it may, Indians and blacks tend to be pictured negatively

---

português, 2 vols. (Porto: Livraria Universal, n.d.); Luís da Câmara Cascudo, *Contos tradicionais do Brasil*, 2nd ed. rev. (Rio de Janeiro: Tecnoprint Gráfica, 1967); Luís da Câmara Cascudo, *Trinta estórias brasileiras* (Lisbon: Portucalense Editora, 1955); Francisco Adolfo Coelho, *Contos populares portugueses* (Lisbon: P. Plantier, 1879); and Sílvio Romero, *Contos tradicionais do Brasil*, 4th ed. rev. (Rio de Janeiro: José Olympio, 1954). For a detailed list of other, more specialized regional collections, see Braulio do Nascimento, *Bibliografia do folclore brasileiro* (Rio de Janeiro: Biblioteca Nacional/MEC, 1971). In English, see Zophimo Consiglieri Pedroso, *Portuguese Folk-Tales*, tr. Henriquetta Monteiro (New York: B. Blom, 1969). The texts in question are Francisco Firmino de Paula: *História do Boi Leitão ou o Vaqueiro que não Mentia* (Guarabira: José Alves 1973), and "Quirino, o Vaqueiro do Rei" (Cascudo, *Contos*, pp. 207–11); João Martins de Ataíde: *O Príncipe que Nasceu com a Sina de Morrer Enforcado* (Recife, n.d.), "Maria Oliveira" (Cascudo, *Contos*, pp. 195–202), and "O Menino Sabido e o Padre" (Cascudo, *Contos*, pp. 352–55); Leandro Gomes de Barros: *O Mal em Paga do Bem ou Rosa e Lino de Alencar* (Recife, 1937), and "O Bem se Paga com o Bem" (Cascudo, *Contos*, pp. 212–16); Manoel Pereira Sobrinho: *A Princesa do Reino da Pedra Fina* (São Paulo, 1957), and "A Princesa do Sono sem Fim" (Cascudo, *Contos*, pp. 57–63); José Costa Leite: *O Papagaio Misterioso* (Condado, n.d.), and "A História do Papagaio" (Cascudo, *Contos*, pp. 24–27). As noted elsewhere, *folhetos* attributed to João Martins de Ataíde are published in Recife, and those attributed to José Bernardo da Silva are published in Juazeiro do Norte unless otherwise indicated.

31. See Diégues, "Ciclos temáticos," p. 11. For a description of the *akpalô* and other African narrative traditions, see Arthur Ramos, *O folk-lore negro do Brasil* (Rio de Janeiro: Civilização Brasileira, 1935). The texts referred to here are José Camelo de Melo Resende: *História de Coco Verde e Melancia* (Juazeiro do Norte, 1976), and "Melancia e Coco Molle" (Romero, *Contos tradicionais*, pp. 25–29); and João José da Silva, *O Casamento do Macaco e a Onça* (Recife, n.d.).

within the *folheto*. Those few heroes and heroines whom the poet allows to die are almost always black (Pai João in *The Indian, the Child, and the Monster*), Indian (José de Alencar's *Iracema*), or Gypsy (Kira in *A Night of Love*). When black *repentistas* compete against whites in *cordel pelejas*, they inevitably lose. Even though a glance at the photographs in books by Leonardo Mota and Francisco das Chagas Batista reveals that a number of popular poets have always been recognizably mulatto, mestizo, or black, *folhetos* remain full of racist slurs.[32]

The poets' choice of blacks or Indians as villains provides a convenient scapegoat for the majority of *folheto* buyers, who, though few are wholly white, do not think of themselves as "other." The threat represented by these "different" individuals often leads to their association with black magic. Thus, the animal known as the "sorcerer" or the "*mandingueiro*" bull, who appears in various *folhetos*, is an almost supernatural being whom only an Indian with uncanny powers refuses to pursue. The tale takes its title from the word *mandinga*, meaning "witchcraft," which comes from the name for a number of West African tribes said to be powerful sorcerers.

If anything, black influence within the *folheto* grows as the *cordel* becomes an increasingly urban phenomenon. Many *folheto* authors live literally next door to *terreiros* (Afro-Brazilian cult sites), where drums may play all night. Although most scoff at these rites, many have attended them out of curiosity. In Rio de Janeiro, virtually all of the non-Northeastern *cordel* authors have dabbled in *umbanda*, a kind of spiritism with a distinctly African flavor.[33]

Even when indirect, this experience tends to creep into the *folheto*. Though generally denouncing these cults as the work of the devil, an increasing number of popular poets choose to write about them, and this fact indicates their impact on many buyers. Particularly in Bahia, one can find a number of stories on the order of *The One-Breasted Negress*.[34]

32. See Jeová Franklin, "O preconceito racial na literatura de cordel," *Revista de Cultura Vozes*, 64 (1970): 35–39; and Clóvis Moura, *O preconceito de cor na literatura de cordel* (São Paulo: Editora Resenha Universitária, 1976). The texts are Manuel d'Almeida Filho, *O Monstro, o Índio e o Menino* (Juazeiro do Norte, n.d.); José Martins de Ataíde, *Iracema, a Virgem dos Lábios de Mel* (Juazeiro do Norte, 1978), and João Martins de Ataíde, *Uma Noite de Amor* (Juazeiro do Norte, 1974).

33. Poets from both the Northeast and the South have written on *umbanda*. See, for example, Flávio Fernandes Moreira, *Umbanda em Versos* (Rio de Janeiro, 1978). I have also recorded a manuscript version of an account by Apolônio Alves dos Santos, November 3, 1977. For an introduction to *umbanda* itself, see B. Freitas and T. da Silva, *Fundamentos da umbanda* (Rio de Janeiro: Editora Souza, 1956).

34. The "one-breasted Negress" story is by Rodolfo Coelho Cavalcante, *A Negra de um Peito só, Procurando Tu* (Salvador: n.p., 1973).

The Historical Setting of the *Folheto*

Historical factors not only help explain the rise of the Brazilian *literatura de cordel* but furnish a number of recurrent themes. Specific bandits, messianic leaders, and political figures crop up regularly in its pages. Those droughts that still periodically ravage the interior often provide the backdrop for tragedy or adventure. Figures of not only regional but national importance appear in *cordel* stories. The suicide of President Getúlio Vargas in 1954 triggered the best-selling single editions in *cordel* history with at least a half-dozen versions clearing the one hundred thousand mark. Wars, elections, and spirited outcries against unpopular taxes make *folhetos* interesting to the historian. Real-life outlaws and contemporary politicians rub shoulders with mermaids and medieval kings.[35]

Both poet-singers and a type of *literatura de cordel* in *quadras* could once be found in the extreme south of Brazil. The *folheto* as we know it, however, is intimately associated with the Northeast, especially the states of Paraíba, Pernambuco, Ceará, and Rio Grande do Norte. Although cities have played an indispensable role in the *folheto*'s success, it is first and foremost an expression of the interior.[36]

35. The outlaws Lampião and Antônio Silvino, religious leader Padre Cícero, and President Getúlio Vargas are the most obvious examples. For specific studies of these figures within the *literatura de cordel*, see Mário de Andrade, "O romanceiro de Lampeão," *O baile das quatro artes: Obras completas de Mário de Andrade* (São Paulo: Martins/MEC, 1963), vol. 14, 83–119; Ronald Daus, *Der epische Zyklus der Cangaceiros in der Volkspoesie Nordostbrasiliens*, Biblioteca Ibero-Americana, No. 12 (Berlin: Colloquium Verlag 1969); Orígenes Lessa, *Getúlio Vargas na literatura de cordel* (Rio de Janeiro: Editora Documentário, 1973); Veríssimo de Melo, *O ataque de Lampeão a Mossoró através do romanceiro popular* (Natal: Departamento de Imprensa, 1953); Mário Souto Maior, "Antônio Silvino no romanceiro do cordel," *Revista Brasileira de Folclore*, 10 (1970): 45–53. The figure of Antônio Conselheiro, leader of the messianic community of Canudos wiped out by government forces just before the turn of the century, is examined by José Calasans in *Os ABC de Canudos* (Bahia: Comissão Baiana de Folclore, 1965); José Calasans, *Achegas ao estudo do romanceiro político nacional* (Bahia: Centro de Estudos Bahianos, n.d.); José Calasans, *Ciclo folclórico do Bom Jesus Conselheiro* (Bahia: Tipografia Beneditina, 1950); José Calasans, "A Guerra de Canudos," *Revista Brasileira de Folclore*, 6 (1966): 53–64; and José Calasans, *No tempo de Antônio Conselheiro* (Bahia: Aguiar & Souza, n.d.). For good general introductions in English to Lampião, Getúlio, Antônio Conselheiro, and Padre Cícero as historical figures, see Billy Jaynes Chandler, *The Bandit King: Lampião of Brazil* (College Station: Texas A & M University, 1978); John W. F. Dulles, *Vargas of Brazil: A Political Biography* (Austin: University of Texas Press, 1967); René Ribeiro, "The Millenium That Never Came: The Story of a Brazilian Prophet," in *Protest and Resistance in Angola and Brazil*, ed. Ronald Chilcote (Berkeley: University of California Press, 1972.)

36. For a discussion of the Southern *cordel*, see V. J. Simões Lopes Neto, *Cancioneiro guasca: Coletânea de poesia popular rio-grandense* (Porto Alegre: Liv. Universal, 1910). The following section draws heavily upon Manuel Correia de Andrade, *A terra e o homem no nordeste* (São Paulo: Editora Brasiliense, 1963); Roger Lee Cunniff, "The Great

Colonization of the vast, periodically parched backlands—the *sertão*—was gradual and uneven. Missionaries bent on converting the local Indians, criminals, and runaway slaves were among the *sertão*'s first Portuguese settlers. They were followed by cowmen who began moving inland along riverbeds from northern Bahia to Ceará in the second half of the sixteenth century. This movement reflected the growth of the coastal plantation economy. Though the sugar mills continued to need oxen as beasts of burden as well as for food and leather, land once used for pasture was rapidly converted into cane fields, forcing ranchers to move into the interior.

The Dutch presence in the Northeast (1630–1654) slowed settlement of the interior but prompted the appearance of bands of guerilla fighters, many of whom went on to make the backlands their home. Generally, when the colonial authorities discovered that a sufficiently large number of bandits or squatters had peopled a given area, they granted the land in question to a powerful cattleman. These grants, called *sesmarias*, ranged from four or ten, to two hundred square leagues. The recipient was expected to enforce the dictates of the Portuguese crown, but given the distance of these holdings from official centers, he himself made most major decisions.

Throughout the early colonial period, the population of this largely isolated and forbidding region remained small. "Except on the most heavily traveled routes," asserts one writer, "ranches and villages were seldom less than a day's journey apart, and in much of the *sertão* they were even more widely dispersed."[37] Although by the beginning of the eighteenth century a traveler in the São Francisco valley could ride more than fifteen hundred miles to the minefields without spending a night out of doors, the northern or high *sertão* remained sparsely settled.

Drought: Northeastern Brazil, 1877–1880," Ph.D. diss., University of Texas, Austin, 1971; Irineu Joffily, *Um cronista*; Robert M. Levine, *Pernambuco in the Brazilian Federation, 1889–1937* (Stanford, Ca.: Stanford University Press, 1978); Rollie E. Poppino, *Brazil: The Land and the People*, 2nd ed. (New York: Oxford University Press, 1973); and Kempton E. Webb, *The Changing Face of the Northeast* (New York: Columbia University Press, 1974). For more general works providing a representative introduction to Brazil, see José Maria Bello, *A History of Modern Brazil, 1889–1964*, 2nd ed., tr. James Taylor, notes by Rollie E. Poppino (Stanford, Ca.: Stanford University Press, 1968); E. Bradford Burns, *A History of Brazil* (New York: Columbia University Press, 1970); José Honório Rodrigues, *The Brazilians: Their Character and Aspirations*, tr. Ralph Edward Dimmick, notes by E. Bradford Burns (Austin: University of Texas Press, 1967); T. Lynn Smith, *Brazil: People and Institutions*, 4th ed. (Baton Rouge: Louisiana State University Press, 1971); and Charles Wagley, *An Introduction to Brazil*, rev. ed. (New York: Columbia University Press, 1971). For an excellent guide to specialized reference works on various aspects of Brazilian history, see Poppino, *Brazil*, pp. 338–69. For further listings, see also *Nordeste brasileiro: Catálogo da Exposição* (Rio de Janeiro: Biblioteca Nacional, 1970).
37. Poppino, *Brazil*, p. 89.

The single most important population increase in what was to be *folheto* country occurred around 1822 when Brazil separated from Portugal to become an independent empire. This dramatic growth was largely a result of changes in imperial land policy. Between 1822 and 1850, the authorities granted no new *sesmarias*, allowing previously landless as well as new settlers to gain title to legally unoccupied land through homesteading. The new ruling intensified the already steady fragmentation of the great seventeenth- and eighteenth-century estates, creating a pattern of tiny landholdings throughout the interior of Paraíba, Ceará, Rio Grande do Norte, Piauí, and Pernambuco. While in the colonial era the all-powerful cattle industry had overshadowed farming, now small-scale independent agriculture became the mainstay of the region's economy. By the second half of the nineteenth century, the overwhelming majority of backlands inhabitants were subsistence farmers.[38]

Those landless ambulatory workers collectively known as *agregados* represented the largest as well as the poorest segment of the backlands population. The *cordel* would sing the virtues of the more privileged cowman, but both poet and public would come from this landless tenant class.

The increasing number of independent, productive units called for a more extensive network of markets than had previously existed. Cyclical, usually weekly exchanges offering goods and services were the logical response to this demand. Such markets (*feiras de consumo*), to which scattered references are made in nineteenth-century travel literature, could be found from an early date in the coastal region. Nevertheless, the backlands fair became a significant presence only around the middle of the century as farmers sought an arena in which to sell their excess produce and purchase needed goods.[39]

The rise of a series of markets held on succeeding days in different towns within a given radius was crucial to the success of the *folheto*. Pamphlets by Brazilian authors may have circulated before the turn of the century, and some form of popular poetry almost certainly existed in

38. See Manuel Diégues Júnior, *População e propriedade da terra no Brasil* (Washington, D.C.: Pan American Union, 1959), for documentation of changes in land tenure patterns. A more general discussion of nineteenth-century landholding and some of its problems is available in Warren Dean, "Latifundia and Land Policy in Nineteenth-Century Brazil," *Hispanic American Historical Review*, 51 (1971): 606–25.

39. For a discussion of the Northeastern fair as an institution, see Joyce F. Riegelhaupt and Shepard Forman, "Bodo Was Never Brazilian: Economic Integration and Rural Development Among a Contemporary Peasantry," *Journal of Economic History*, 30 (1970): 100–16; Joyce F. Riegelhaupt and Shepard Forman, "Market Place and Marketing System: Toward a Theory of Peasant Economic Integration," *Comparative Studies in Society and History*, 12 (1970): 188–212. See also Shepard Forman, *The Brazilian Peasantry* (New York: Columbia University Press, 1975), pp. 87–140.

manuscript form. The *cordel*, however, was not an economically viable enterprise before the latter part of the nineteenth century because there were not enough potential buyers and no effective system of distribution. Then, too, printing presses, which had been limited in Brazil before independence, took another sixty or seventy years to show up in the interior.

The introduction of printing presses was partly owing to new wealth from cotton, a key crop in the eighteenth century, whose importance had fallen off as a result of competition from the United States. The American Civil War, which forced British textile firms to seek new sources of raw fiber, brought both money and numbers to the backlands with the beginning of a second boom. After 1860, large numbers of individuals began moving from the coast across the interior in search of arable land. Although the demand had begun to taper off by 1875 and the region was hard hit by a series of disastrous droughts, some people made considerable profits. Increased revenue from cotton does much to explain the presence of secondhand printing presses in such relatively insignificant cities as Areia, Itabaiana, Guarabira, and Catolé da Rocha (Paraíba), or Novas Russas (Ceará) and Currais Novos (Rio Grande do Norte). The need to generate new sources of business in a limited environment made these presses, which became active several decades before the end of the century, an important stimulant to *folheto* production. Although these pamphlets had to be produced cheaply, they far exceeded erudite publications in number, making them profitable for printers as well as poets.[40]

The first half of the twentieth century saw a number of changes in the Northeastern interior: the gradual eradication of banditry, the sporadic institution of schools, the slow growth of cities, and the amenities of city life. Nevertheless, the political hegemony of coast over interior, confirmed by the revolution of 1930, which brought Getúlio Vargas and a new industrial elite to power, limited the degree of progress in the countryside. The structure of the backlands economy remained largely unchanged until 1950. The abysmal quality of roads, which had so hindered the nineteenth-century cotton trade, continued until after World War II. Railroad service, electricity, street lighting, and municipal water supplies were rare. The first banks did not appear in the interior until after 1920, and agricultural loans were almost unheard of. Industry remained virtually non-

40. The classic discussion of the Brazilian cotton industry remains Stanley Stein, *The Brazilian Cotton Manufacture: Textile Enterprise in an Underdeveloped Area, 1850–1950* (Cambridge, Mass.: Harvard University Press, 1957). For a discussion of the printing industry in one Northeastern state, see Luiz do Nascimento, *História da Imprensa de Pernambuco, 1821–1954* (Recife: Arquivo Público, Imprensa Oficial, 1962). For a more general consideration of the press in Brazil, see Nelson Werneck Sodré, *História da imprensa no Brasil* (Rio de Janeiro: Civilização Brasileira, 1966).

existent. In many rural districts, the literacy rate did not rise above 10 percent. "The majority of workers," asserts one historian, summing up the situation succinctly,

> were at the bottom of the barrel. The rural birthrate exceeded the urban rate nearly five to three whereas the death rate stood about the same. Nearly half the rural population suffered from malaria, schistosomiasis or Chagas disease, virtually all were afflicted by lesser (but equally debilitating) parasitic ailments, and many showed the effects of rickets as well. A 1937 survey found that 63 percent of all girls were either married or widowed by fifteen years of age and that 87 percent of the rural workers interviewed wore no protection on their feet in the fields.[41]

These conditions did not make backlands inhabitants happy or productive. They did, however, sustain the need for the *folheto*. Given the absence in most cases of alternate means of information and entertainment, *cordel* authors and poet-singers continued to play a necessary role in daily life. Only as new roads and the media began to reach into the interior in the 1950s did this situation begin to change. As coastal cities mushroomed, creating a need for more and cheaper food, which in turn placed new demands upon the market system of the interior, the backlands became both a potential national market and an important labor pool. All this was to make for notable changes in the life of the subsistence farmer as well as in the fortunes of the *literatura de cordel*.[42]

Production and Distribution of *Folheto* Stories

Poets have always varied not only in talent but in family background, place of residence, education, temperament, and degree of professionalism, among other characteristics. Nevertheless, the relative homogeneity in backgrounds of most *cordel* authors as well as their sense of themselves as spokesmen for a particular community make it possible, despite these sometimes considerable differences, to talk about them as a group.[43]

Cordel authors range anywhere from thirteen to ninety years of age. The great majority write their first *folheto* before they are thirty though it may take them a while to get a story into print. Women have traditionally helped their author-husbands and fathers in writing down and revising

41. Levine, *Pernambuco*, p. 53.
42. For an overview of these changes within the Northeast proper, see Manuel Correia de Andrade, *Cidade e campo no Brasil* (São Paulo: Editora Brasiliense, 1974).
43. See Appendix B for an overview of these persons. The bulk of the information in this section comes from interviews conducted in 1977–1978.

stories, and there have been some well-known female *repentistas*, but to-day, though one may find an occasional recent *folheto* by a woman, vir-tually all professional poets are men. This is partly because becoming a *cordel* author requires the ability to read and write, skills relatively rare among women, who, in the past, were even less apt than men to acquire even a rudimentary education. More important, *folheto* writing and selling is generally a full-time occupation, which conflicts with women's tradi-tional duties in the home and fields. The long trips, stays in rustic hotels, and obligatory participation in fairs make the *cordel* a man's domain.

A sizable percentage of poets come from families in which there is already one or more *cordel* authors or *cantadores*, but family ties are by no means a prerequisite for success. The encouragement of one or another relative seems more important than the actual presence of a poet in the family. *Folheto* writers often speak of an uncle who bought them stories as a child or a mother who recited these tales by heart. Although some indi-viduals become poets against their parents' wishes, it is more common for these persons to receive some sort of initial family backing. Sometimes, the death of his father at an early age prompts a boy to turn to the *cordel* as a source of income.

Some of the most successful poets come from relatively privileged households; the vast majority, however, trace their roots to the subsistence farmer class. Now, as in the past, the *cordel* represents one of a rural inhabitant's few alternatives to back-breaking, poorly paid work in the fields. Given their limited means, most authors have had little if any for-mal schooling, having taught themselves to read and write with the help of *folhetos* and an ABC card. Much of their knowledge comes from ex-perience, the oral tradition, and a few standard texts such as an atlas-geography, a Bible, an astrological almanac, a book of saints' lives, a dictionary, or elementary science texts. Schoolbooks brought home by a son or daughter, battered paperbacks, the little stories sometimes found inside soap wrappers—all that falls into the poet's hands becomes grist for the mill.

Today popular poets live in many of Brazil's major cities. They can be found not only in the Northeastern capitals but wherever emigrants cluster. There are *folheto* writers in Brasília, Belo Horizonte, São Paulo, and Rio de Janeiro, as well as in the states of Pará, Amazonas, and Rio Grande do Sul.[44] Although almost all of these authors were born in the Northeast, a few of the Rio-based poets were actually born in the South.

The accelerated movement of poets from the countryside toward major

44. The *folheto* has always accompanied Northeastern emigrants. During the periodic rubber booms before 1950, for instance, a *folheto* press began in Belém do Pará. For a discussion, see Vicente Salles, "Guajarina, folhetaria de Francisco Lopes," *Revista Brasi-leira de Cultura*, 3 (1971): 87–102.

urban centers corresponds to a similar movement in the population at large. Previously, a number of poets retained plots of land to which they returned between sales trips, but today only a handful are even part-time farmers. As *cantadores* find the radio increasingly indispensable to success, they too move toward urban centers.

Now, as in the past, some poets are more prolific than others. Leandro Gomes de Barros is said, rightly or not, to have authored well over a thousand *folhetos*. Rodolfo Coelho Cavalcante claims some fifteen hundred, mostly eight-page stories. Although some poets may write or find the means to publish a mere half-dozen stories, many authors have well over a hundred titles in print, with many unpublished manuscripts cluttering their drawers. Most *folhetos* go through a minimum of two thousand copies; some reappear at a later time in subsequent printings. Manuel d'Almeida Filho's *Vicente and the King of the Thieves* has sold some six hundred thousand copies; Rodolfo's *The Girl Who Beat Her Mother and Was Turned into a Dog* sold 432,000; and Manuel Camilo dos Santos' *The Valiant Sebastian* has topped the three hundred thousand mark.[45]

Most poets have always struggled to make ends meet. Some, admittedly, have been more successful than others. João Martins de Ataíde, for example, was able to buy up a series of houses in the center of Recife with the profits from his *folheto* sales. João José da Silva relied at one time on airplanes to deliver his poetic merchandise to major cities scattered throughout Brazil. Nevertheless, even the most successful poets have never been especially wealthy. Thus, although José Bernardo da Silva eventually became one of the largest *folheto* printers in the Northeast, with agents from Belém to Maceió, his wife Ana continued to slit the pages of his booklets with a scissors for almost twenty years before he finally invested in a *guillotine* ("paper cutter").

Before becoming successful, many poets supplemented their income from *cordel* sales with activities related to astrology and herbal medicine. They worked as farmers, *cantadores*, printers, and graphic artists in addition to writing and selling stories. As was done by poets in various parts of Europe, they devised almanacs, wrote prayers, charted horoscopes, and prepared remedies designed to relieve specific ills.[46] Today, some authors still continue this "moonlighting" tradition, though many of their present activities are considerably more mundane. Some poets sell commercially prepared potions, secondhand movie magazines, samba lyrics, school and office supplies, handkerchiefs, socks, and other sundries. Although most

45. Interviews Aracaju, Sergipe, June 7, 1978; Salvador, Bahia, June 5, 1978; and Campina Grande, Paraíba, March 6, 1978.
46. For a suggestive study of the French almanac and its relation to other forms of popular culture, see Geneviève Bollème, *Les almanachs populaires aux XVIIᵉ et XVIIIᵉ siècles: Essai d'histoire sociale* (La Hague: Mouton, 1964).

poets who live in the Northeast earn two or three times the abysmally low prevailing wages of farmers, their gross monthly income is usually still less than one hundred dollars. Rio-based writers may earn considerably more, although the cost of living in southern Brazil is also much higher. It is difficult to calculate just how many full-time poets there are in Brazil today. Estimates range from less than two hundred to as many as two thousand, if one includes those *cantadores* who also produce an occasional *folheto*.[47]

Turning out a finished story requires three major steps: writing, printing, and distribution. One man may take charge of all three activities, or the three stages may be divided between two or more persons. Most individuals begin their poetic careers as vendors. After mastering the tradition through steady reading and live performances, which acquaint them with the expectations of their audience, they then try their hand at writing. The poet-vendor next attempts to acquire enough money to become an agent for other writers and/or a *folheto* publisher. In the latter cases, he generally employs other persons to sell his stories in the marketplace. Although not all vendors are poets, most poets are vendors or publishers.

The ordinary poet customarily writes in his spare time on bumpy buses or at the kitchen table after his family has gone to sleep. Some authors compose pieces of, or even whole, stories in their heads, but most do the bulk of their creating on paper. The majority of manuscripts are written on lined notebook paper doubled or quadrupled to resemble a *folheto* page. The poet or a school-age son or daughter then recopies the original, correcting errors in spelling and grammar and checking to see that the verses and stanzas contain the requisite number of lines by metrically beating out the syllable count with either hand or foot.

Some poets put great store by titles, refusing to go on with the story proper until they are satisfied with its name. Many work out the beginning and end of the tale before starting to write. Although a poet may compose an eight-page story in a few hours, he often takes a month or more to complete a full-fledged *romance*, depending on his need for money, the time he can devote to writing, and, of course, the disposition of an often fickle muse.

Once his *folheto* is ready, the poet has three major options: he may sell his work to a printer or to an *editor* ("publisher") who may or may not also be a printer; he may pay for the edition himself; or he may acquire a printing press and begin publishing his own stories as well as works by other writers.

47. Átila de Almeida, co-author of an extensive dictionary of popular poets and singers, estimates that there are some five hundred *cordel* authors writing today. Not all of these, however, are necessarily full-time poets; interview, Campina Grande, Paraíba, March 4, 1978.

If the author sells his story outright, he generally is paid a portion of booklets (the payment is called a *conga*). Generally, this is about 10 percent of the first edition, or two hundred to five hundred copies. Theoretically, he will receive the same percentage of any subsequent printings as well. It is the printer's responsibility to cover all publication costs and to arrange for a cover illustration. Given most poets' precarious financial state, this sort of direct sale on terms established by verbal agreement has always been the most common if least desirable course of action. Poet Severino Borges, for example, has parted with all but some two dozen of his 110 originals in this manner.[48]

If the poet sells his *folheto*, he loses all legal right to the first as well as future editions. Therefore, most writers are understandably reluctant to adopt this course of action. Outright sale brings painfully little profit. It also means that the buyer may place his own name on the cover together with or instead of the author's. Carelessness as much as willful plagiarism often results in confusion regarding authorship. Although the poet often tacks on a final identifying acrostic as a precaution against literary pirates, it is not difficult for a fellow poet to rework the initial letters of the last stanza, thereby obliterating the original name. Many writers express dissatisfaction with the abuses of direct sale, but their dependence on the publisher, who provides loans, credit, and various favors, allows the system to continue.[49]

The author does not, however, always relinquish his rights to a story. If he can manage to scrape together the money for the edition (today, anywhere from twenty-five to fifty dollars for two thousand copies, depending on the length of the story), or if he can convince the publisher to do the work on credit, he remains the legal owner. The most advantageous option, however, is for the poet to acquire his own printing press.

In the past, individuals often made great sacrifices to acquire a rustic hand press. "I would have bought one instead of a house; I would have sold the shirt off my back in order to print my own stories!" exclaims one *cordel* author.[50] Once the poet has his own press, he can print his own as well as others' *folhetos* at will, eliminating the need for an onerous down payment. A poet-publisher can substantially reduce production costs, supplementing *cordel* publication if need be with calendars, announcements, and other types of work. He can corner the regional market, buying up the work of other poets until he emerges as a powerful middleman. In the case of journalistic *folhetos*, where salability is directly related to speed, he can

48. Interview, Timbaúba, Pernambuco, March 28, 1978.

49. See Sebastião Nunes Batista, "Restituição de autoria de folhetos de catálogo," in *Estudos*, pp. 333–419, for a discussion of some of the problems associated with determining authorship.

50. Interview, José Francisco Borges, Bezerros, Pernambuco, January 20, 1978.

count on getting out his booklet before the majority of his competitors. Because the press is almost always a family business, the poet can further reduce costs by calling on his wife and children to aid in collating, folding, and binding the booklets.

Over the past two decades, however, the rising cost of paper and type has eaten into potential profits. At the same time, the number of *folheto* buyers has fallen off. Unable to surmount these twin obstacles, many one-man presses have simply vanished, the machines themselves becoming museum pieces. Whereas poets such as Caetano Cosme da Silva, José Soares, and José de Souza Campos were once printers as well as authors, they are now simply poet-vendors. Furthermore, even a number of larger presses have folded. Twenty years ago, there were three major *cordel* publishers: João José da Silva (Luzeiro do Norte, Recife), Manuel Camilo dos Santos (Estrella da Poesia, Campina Grande), and José Bernardo da Silva (Tipografia São Francisco, Juazeiro do Norte). Today, only the São Francisco press continues to function, its production limited almost exclusively to a roster of *cordel* classics to which the press still holds the rights.

Then, too, whereas a number of small presses could once be found scattered throughout the interior and transitional zone known as the *agreste*, contemporary *folheto* production is increasingly restricted to major urban centers. At present, some three publishers account for approximately 40 percent of all *folhetos* printed each year. Only one of these three leaders, the São Francisco, is a traditional regional press. The other two, the Luzeiro and the Baiana, are commercial operations centered in São Paulo and Salvador and turn out spruced-up classics with comic book covers together with a small number of new stories. Though these booklets sell best in the Southern states and Bahia, the Luzeiro has begun to build a network of agents throughout the Northeast, where it has managed to corner a growing percentage of the market. It has also been successful in purchasing the rights to a number of classic stories from the São Francisco press.[51]

The increasing disappearance of a number of small *cordel* presses represents a serious problem for many authors. Although there are exceptions, most commercial printers are reluctant to accept *folheto* orders because the booklets, which must be handset, demand a variety of different types, which slows the normal flow of work.[52] Furthermore, even an order of five thousand booklets is small for an office accustomed to turning out

51. Arlindo Pinto de Souza, owner of the Luzeiro Publishing Company (interview São Paulo, December 13, 1977), estimates that he prints some four hundred thousand *folhetos* a year, which are distributed by an estimated six hundred agents throughout Brazil. I am grateful to Antonio Augusto Arantes Neto (interview, Campinas, São Paulo, December 11, 1977) for providing the 40 percent figure.

52. One such exception is Antônio Pimentel (interview, Campina Grande, Paraíba,

large quantities of tickets, labels, and calendars. These publishers not only charge higher rates than poet-printers but do not do the necessary folding and binding. In 1977–1978, the minimum cost of printing an eight-page *folheto* was around five hundred *cruzeiros* (one *cruzeiro* equaled just under six cents). Sixteen-page booklets cost around seven hundred *cruzeiros*, *romances* one thousand.

Assuming that he succeeds in getting his *folheto* printed one way or another, the poet must then look for customers. If he is a *cordel* salesman himself, he simply adds the new story to his stock, which normally includes works by a variety of authors. Generally, a poet's store or *sortimento* will include several hundred titles though some local peddlers may carry as few as a dozen.

Small vendors usually buy *folhetos* from middlemen who deal directly with the major presses. These individuals inevitably live in or near cities that funnel the outlying trade. Though the bulk of poets and buyers has traditionally come from the countryside, urban centers have been indispensable in the printing and distribution process. In fact, in some places *folhetos* are called *arrecifes*, eloquent testimony to Recife's role in the *cordel*'s evolution. Generally, those poets who are most successful gravitate toward cities where they can become even better known whereas rural poets are frequently forgotten.

The distribution system normally involves not just one but a number of middlemen. Suppose, for instance, that Maria de Jesus Diniz, present owner of Juazeiro do Norte's São Francisco press, prints two thousand copies of *The Mysterious Peacock*. In three or four days, Edson Pinto in Recife will receive the three hundred copies he has ordered by mail. Smaller distributors in Bezerros, Condado, and Caruaru will then buy up lots of fifty on their weekly trip to the city. They in turn will sell five or six at a time to small-time vendors who frequent local fairs. At each step along the way, the *folheto* increases in cost. Thus, while the customer who walks into the Juazeiro press will pay around four *cruzeiros* for the booklet, a fairgoer in Bezerros may pay as much as eight.

Traditionally, the poet made the rounds from fair to fair, traveling on foot or horseback. Today, however, most pay for a seat in a pickup truck or bus. Before 1950, most big cities had at least a half-dozen *folheto* vendors at their weekly fairs, and even hamlets might have two or three vendors. The makeshift stalls of the poets were routinely grouped together in that part of the fair dedicated to entertainment and the sale of medicines, crafts, and toys. Vendors normally took turns reading their stories aloud. From time to time, they might be accompanied by a rustic violin.

March 6, 1978), who, since he began work as an independent publisher in 1975, has actively sought out *folheto* authors and has printed some two hundred titles.

Today, the practice of reading *folhetos* aloud is less common. It still occurs, however, in the South and in smaller Northeastern fairs. Those poets who continue to rely on oral performance employ a special sort of singsong that allows the voice to carry and is therefore easier on the lungs than normal speech. This chant or *toada* also brings out the rhythm of the verses, making listening more pleasurable. There are special patterns for different kinds of stories, and *toadas* usually vary from singer to singer. Although people who have grown up outside the tradition have difficulty hearing differences among singers, *folheto* buyers can usually tell whether a particular story is going to be happy or sad after the first few lines.[53] The best-known singers have developed distinctly personal styles.

Although it is common for vendors to promote a new *folheto*, they always size up their audience before beginning to read. Most agree that some kinds of stories appeal more to certain groups than to others. Old women, for instance, are known to like prophecy and religious themes; young men favor adventure stories and plenty of humor; teenage girls prefer tales of love and suffering. Furthermore, some types of *folhetos* do consistently better than others. One popular poet explains that while sales of love stories have fallen drastically "because they are too innocent for today's buyer," adventure tales are doing better "because they include a little bit of everything—love, humor, a good message—and so appeal to everyone." According to him, most vendors' sales are presently 30–40 percent adventure stories, 20–25 percent humorous tales, 10–15 percent "sufferings" and martyrdom, and 10 percent love themes, the remainder being news stories. Therefore, most selections for live performance tend to fall into the first two categories, though a particularly sensational news account or brand-new story may sometimes steal the show.[54]

Reading the *folheto* he has chosen, the poet tends to follow the text before him. He may, however, skip whole passages or, less frequently, improvise new ones. He may consciously or unconsciously change certain words or phrases to fit his audience's needs. Then, too, he normally pauses between stanzas every so often to insert a prose aside. The exact location of these breaks depends on both the particular story and the immediate context. Usually, however, they occur about once every eight or twelve stanzas. The prose asides are called *trancas* or *chaves*, *trancar* meaning "to lock" and *chave* meaning "key." They are particularly interesting as evidence of individual creation within a set form. These intervals allow the singer to give rein to his own imagination, to provide a needed change

---

53. For a discussion of the musical aspects of Northeastern popular poetry, primarily related to poet-improvisers but revealing useful parallels to singers in fairs, see Luiz Heitor Correia de Azevedo, "A arte da cantoria," *Cultura Política*, 4 (1944): 183–87; and Dulce Martins Lamas, "A música na cantoria nordestina," in *Estudos*, pp. 235–70.

54. Interview, Manuel d'Almeida Filho, Aracaju, Sergipe, June 7, 1978.

of pace, to alert his public to facts which the original author may have taken for granted, and, consequently, to make the story more intimately theirs.

The poet also uses these opportunities to demand the public's wavering attention. He may summarize the story for those who have just joined the group or make a humorous comparison between the tale and an event from daily life. ("Well, this story of Padre Cícero's fight with the devil may have happened a long time ago, but you can be sure that Satan's hand is as strong as ever. . . . Just think of that boy who murdered his old mother right next door in Gravatá just two weeks ago!") He also uses the occasion to remind his listeners that he too works hard for a living, coaxing them to take home a booklet ("Come on friends, I can see that you're all enjoying the story. So why don't you make it worth my while to tell you what happened to the poor princess whom we left there shivering with her innocent baby in that gloomy cave? Will the duke find her in time or will she be eaten by some awful monster? Just five little *cruzeiros* to see!")

Though brief, this initial description should be enough to suggest why the *literatura de cordel* is such a special kind of literary creation. All of its components are known, but the particular, dynamic constellation that these borrowings form is necessarily unique. The work of known poets, the *folheto* is still community property. If its creator is a literary author, he is also an on-the-spot storyteller, who devotes considerable time and effort to perfecting his technique.[55]

55. Much recent folklore scholarship has been geared to the performer and to storytelling as a particular form of communication. Among those book-length studies I have found most helpful are Daniel J. Crowley, *I Could Talk Old-Story Good: Creativity in Bahamian Folklore* (Berkeley: University of California Press, 1966); *Explorations in the Ethnography of Speaking*, ed. Richard Bauman and Joel Sherzer (Cambridge: Cambridge University Press, 1974); *Folk Narrative Research: Some Papers Presented at the VI Congress of the International Society for Folk Narrative Research*, ed. Juha Pentikäinen and Tuula Tuurikka (Helsinki: Suomalainen Kirjallisuuden Seura, 1976); *Folklore: Performance and Communication*, ed. Dan Ben-Amos and Kenneth Goldstein (The Hague: Mouton, 1975); *Folklore Genres*, ed. Dan Ben-Amos, American Folklore Society No. 26 (Austin: University of Texas Press, 1976); *Frontiers in Folklore*, ed. William R. Bascom, A.A.A.S. Selected Symposia Series, No. 5 (Boulder, Co.: Westview Press, 1977); and Paredes and Bauman, *Towards New Perspectives in Folklore*. For a good, short overview of recent publications in the field, see Richard A. Bauman, "Verbal Art as Performance," *American Anthropologist*, 77 (1975): 290–311.

II. The Poet and His Public:
The *Cordel* in a National Context

The *Folheto*'s Traditional Audience

The persons who search their pockets for those "five little *cruzeiros*" to persuade the poet to finish his story vary from region to region and even from fair to fair. Nevertheless, like poets, they reveal common characteristics, which allow them to be seen as part of an extended community. Chapters 7 and 8 will deal in depth with the relationship between the *cordel* author and his traditional audience. It is useful, however, to have a general idea of that audience before considering the new market for the *folheto* within Brazil today.

The public to whom most poets appeal today is generally more heterogeneous than it was fifty or even twenty years ago. Though retaining close ties to the interior, even when making their homes in cities, buyers like writers vary in family background and education, revealing differences in age, occupation, income, degree of involvement with the mass media, and attitudes toward the *folheto* itself. They live in both urban centers and the country, primarily in the Northeast but also in the South.

The people who make up the *roda* or circle that surrounds a poet at a given fair range in age from nine to ninety years old. Younger children may be present, but they are usually left at home because they create difficulties in crowded fairs where their parents must devote their energies to bargaining; therefore, they are more apt to hear *folhetos* retold at home.

In rural marketplaces today, both men and women gather about the poet, much as they always have, and he may still sing his stories. Though men are more apt to make an actual purchase, wives often urge their husbands to buy one or another story. In urban marketplaces, however, today's ring of listeners is predominantly male partly because the seedy character of most of these locations makes them unattractive to women concerned about their reputations. Also, in urban areas, vendors tend to be appendages to established marketplaces rather than an attraction at a periodically recurring fair; there is no special incentive for shoppers, many of whom are women, to congregate about these vendors on any particular morning. As a result, there are usually not enough potential customers to warrant a taxing live performance, and the poet tends to simply sit or stand behind his wares.

Clearly, these differences between the rural and urban areas have a great deal to do with far-reaching changes in the regional market structure.[1] Just as the growth of a particular kind of exchange network favored the *folheto*'s rise in one and not another area of the Northeast during a particular epoch, so present changes in this network have struck hard at the *cordel*. The decreasing importance of the weekly fair has affected the popular poet every bit as much as rising production costs and competition from the mass media.

As previously suggested, many individual farmers used to sell their own crops in local markets. But as Brazil continues to industrialize and as urban centers grow, the increasing demand for food makes a series of small producers impractical. The tendency for previously independent sharecroppers to become wage laborers in the fields or to take factory jobs in the cities has made the rotating market less important and the fair itself a less crucial institution. In Recife, for example, where formerly a weekly Saturday fair attracted peasants from miles around, one major food-buying cooperative now controls the inflow of most produce into this city. As the growth of neighborhood supermarkets and refrigeration makes fresh food available to urban inhabitants throughout the week, they are less likely to wait until Saturday to make their purchases. Since the farmer, who formerly carted his wares to the city every weekend, now sells these to a wholesaler and can find most of the items he himself wants right at home, he has little reason to make a taxing and ever more expensive trip to the city. The area surrounding the Recife market, like the outskirts of most urban marketplaces, has become today a magnet for drifters, and the poet's most frequent customers are now itinerant peddlers, petty thieves, and dollar-a-shot prostitutes. "In this very plaza," one poet remarks with obvious sadness,

> there used to be eight or ten poets every Saturday morning fighting to see who would be next to sing. Today, look; there are never more than three of us, and no one even asks to hear a favorite story.[2]

At the same time that urban centers have become less effective distribution centers for the *folheto*, the system of rural fairs is also undergoing

1. See Shepard Forman, *The Brazilian Peasantry* (New York: Columbia University Press, 1975), especially Chapter 3, for a description of these changes. The book contains an extensive bibliography for further consultation.

2. José de Souza Campos, conversation, Recife, January 15, 1978. For a series of photographs of Recife's São José market, see Liêdo Maranhão de Souza, *O mercado, sua praça e a cultura popular do nordeste* (Recife: Prefeitura Municipal, Secretaria de Educação e Cultura, 1977).

crucial changes. Although these markets still attract a variety of people, more and more fairs take place not on successive weekdays but on Saturday or Sunday when sugar mills and factories are idle. Therefore, the rural poet can no longer plan on working six or seven days a week but must restrict his sales to weekends. This makes a "weak" fair or rain disastrous. Then, too, he must also cope with the increased price of travel, new "floor taxes" (fees for the use of a space in the marketplace levied by the city), harassment from local authorities who consider him a vagabond or a subversive, and, sometimes, competition from loudspeakers when he does not own one. The petty officials known as *rapas* have always made life difficult for popular poets and peddlers. Despite the attempts of some government agencies to combat this problem, it has, if anything, increased.[3] Given all these difficulties, it is no wonder that today one finds so few young vendors. Most are older poets who continue to write and sell *folhetos* as much out of a lack of alternatives as of a deep sense of loyalty to their profession.

To be sure, the poet's situation in Southern cities is somewhat different from his position in the Northeast. Interestingly enough, the biggest audience today is found not in the *folheto*'s traditional homeland but in Rio de Janeiro. Were such groups not prohibited by city ordinance from assembling in São Paulo, the crowds surrounding the poet would undoubtedly be even bigger there since the city has twice as many Northeastern emigrants, and *folheto* sales through newsstands are considerable. In present-day Northern fairs, audiences normally vary anywhere from ten to sixty persons, depending on the weather, time of day, season of the year, and, to be sure, the poet's talent. In Rio de Janeiro's weekly São Cristóvão market, crowds of two to three hundred persons are not uncommon. A small percentage of buyers are Southerners and foreign tourists, but the great majority are workers from the rural Northeast. Some have lived in Rio for decades; others are recent arrivals. The majority continue to travel back and forth between their jobs and their families, whom they have left behind.[4]

Folheto buyers in Rio de Janeiro tend to be construction workers, night watchmen, janitors, waiters, domestics or factory employees. Urban buyers in the Northeast may also engage in similar manual or service occu-

3. See Maria Luiza Rolim, "Cantadores são perseguidos nas feiras do nordeste," *Diário de Pernambuco*, May 20, 1979. Although there are rumors of roundups and imprisonment of *cordel* authors who had written stories on leftist candidates and causes after the military coup of 1964, this is not a popular topic of conversation and is therefore difficult to prove.

4. See Appendix C on *folheto* buyers for a statistical breakdown of two hundred *folheto* buyers in the Rio de Janeiro area. There is no study dealing specifically with the emigrant in Rio de Janeiro. However, for a suggestive overview of these individuals in the Brasília area, see Cláudia Menezes, *A mudança* (Rio de Janeiro: Editora Imago/MEC, 1976).

pations. One also finds a number of ambulant vendors, farmers in from the countryside for the day and drifters in Recife's São José market. I have, for instance, spoken to fortune tellers, forgers of paintings, and manufacturers of snake cures.

Urban audiences in both South and North also include a growing number of students and tourists. Although these buyers tend to purchase large numbers of *folhetos*, they are seldom habitual customers. In contrast, traditional buyers from the lower classes often buy one or two stories every week. Though not collectors per se, they tend to store the booklet carefully after reading it for future reference. In some cases, they may give it to a friend or relative.

Urban buyers tend to have more education than *folheto* buyers (usually subsistence farmers) in the countryside. Only one out of every four buyers interviewed at the weekly country fair of Bezerros said that he or she could read, for instance, but roughly half of all respondents in the Rio area had had at least three years of school.[5] Nevertheless, the average reading level of most *cordel* buyers, like poets, is low. Many individuals are illiterate; others have had a year or less of schooling. Those who can read have often taught themselves using the *folheto* as a guide. Old stories found in farmhouses often reveal writing in the margin where a succession of owners copied, then recopied words or phrases, poignant testimony to their hunger to learn.

In short, literacy, while desirable, is not necessary within the *cordel* tradition, and often the poet sings his stories not only to attract attention but to communicate their content to potential buyers who cannot read. If a person who cannot read likes the story, he will buy the booklet to take home to a friend or relative who will read it aloud to him. In the past, the landowner or his wife would often retell stories to their tenants.

. Although a rise in the national literacy rate means that more people can now read *folhetos*, many still prefer the oral experience. As we shall see later, a sizable percentage continues to read the story aloud even when they are alone. Many persons can memorize parts of or even whole *folhetos* after reading them or even after hearing them. Individuals who prefer a group reading situation also tend to prefer a live poet to recordings of *cordel* tales.

Traditionally, the poet was not only an entertainer and supplier of otherwise unavailable information but also a trusted interpreter. Thanks to his ability to read and his frequent travels, he experienced things which others did not. This knowledge made him a prime example of a "culture broker"

5. For a consideration of literacy and its effects on more traditional communities, see Robin Horton and Ruth Finnegan, eds., *Modes of Thought* (London: Faber, 1973); and John Rankine Goody, *Literacy in Traditional Societies* (New York: Cambridge University Press, 1968).

or person who mediates between community-oriented and nation-oriented groups by virtue of his position at crucial junctures connecting the local system to the larger whole.[6]

The poet's buyers, whose horizons were typically more limited than his, could count on him to relay these perceptions in an intelligible as well as enjoyable manner. The *cordel* author's skill at fitting new and often puzzling information into a familiar form tended to make it more acceptable and less threatening. The fact that it is still entirely possible for journalistic *folhetos* to exist alongside radio and television reports upon which they may be based indicates that the poet still serves this informational function for a number of buyers.

However, as advances in communication and transportation begin to permit individuals to develop a more direct relationship with the world around them, their need for a mediator may diminish or even disappear. As they begin to see other parts of their own state and country either in person or via films and television, they become more tolerant of differences and less "different" themselves. As their children go to school and the world of print seems less forbidding, the old boundaries between center and periphery fade or take on new dimensions.[7]

Furthermore, the general decline of the written word in favor of the spoken word has affected *folheto* production and sales. In the past, the ability to read was more precious than it is today because fewer persons had access to schools and because reading symbolized entrée into a larger world. In older *cordel* stories, the heroes and heroines are not only handsome and virtuous but also literate. "There are two things in this life for which I have always longed," says an elderly farmer at the Bezerros fair,

> health for myself and all my family and the ability to read. How wonderful it must be not to suffer the humiliation of having to sign a document that you do not understand with a thumbprint; what a thrill to look at a page and then hear the words written there singing in your own head!

Today, however, radio and television have begun to replace newspapers and books throughout Brazil, and the elderly farmer's children rush home from school to watch their favorite programs. In the realm of popular

6. For a general discussion of the culture broker, see Eric R. Wolf, "Aspects of Group Relations in a Complex Society: Mexico," *American Anthropologist*, 58 (1956): 1065–78. For one particularly interesting example, see Clifford Geertz, "The Javanese Kijaji: The Changing Role of a Culture Broker," *Comparative Studies in Society and History*, 2 (1960): 228–49.

7. For a helpful overview of modernization as a process, see S. N. Eisenstadt, *Tradition, Change, and Modernity* (New York: John Wiley & Sons, 1973); and *Communication and Change: The Last Ten Years—and the Next*, ed. Wilbur Schramm and Daniel Lerner (Honolulu: University of Hawaii Press, 1976).

poetry, the increasing importance of radio and television has meant a resurgence of the poet-improviser or *repentista*. "If a *cantador*'s show is canceled for even one day," the director of one of Campina Grande's two radio stations asserts, "the farmers have their bosses' wives call in from all over the countryside." *Cordel* writers, however, have not shared these singers' good fortune. "Thirty years ago," one popular poet remarks,

> the author was regarded as superior to the improviser because he could read and write. When someone wanted to say that a singer was really good, he compared him to "a genuine poet." Today, no, things are just the opposite. The *cantadores* draw crowds for miles around, and the poets are left alone in the streets with their stories. If it weren't for the tourists, plenty of them would go hungry.[8]

In cases where former readers have more or less abandoned the *folheto*, few can give clear reasons for their flagging interest. Many, in fact, remember one or another story with pleasure, eagerly sketching in the plot or singing a stanza or two from memory. "I don't know," says one middle-aged woman in Juazeiro do Norte,

> it's funny, in the old days everyone used to sit out on the sidewalk at night with one person reading and everyone else just listening. Today, no; I guess most people would rather be inside now that they have television and electric lights.

Buyers themselves may perceive the relative decline of the *folheto* as a result of the larger changes that have affected not only the community but themselves as individuals. "Twenty years ago," remarks an older woman in the Sant'Ana Hills some three hours from Juazeiro,

> we were still living at the very back of the world, but today there is a jeep that goes up and down the mountain two or three times a week. I myself go into town once every month to collect my pension, but I can remember when the only people who left here went in hammocks, that is, all but dead. And so, I like those old stories, but they are really meant for bumpkins, and there are hardly any bumpkins in the whole world anymore.

The poet, to be sure, still has enthusiastic supporters. The strength of the bonds still uniting *cordel* authors and traditional audiences will become more evident as this discussion progresses. It would be misleading

8. José Cutsino de Siqueira, superintendent of Campina Grande's Caturité radio, broadcasts a poet-singer program "Os Bambas da Viola" ("Rough and Ready Guitarists") six mornings a week. José Alves Sobrinho, interview, Campina Grande, Paraíba, March 3, 1978.

to imply that the *folheto* tradition is no longer vital, but it certainly does not exert the same hold it once did, especially in the Northeast. The reluctance of popular poets to advertise their problems as well as the appearance of new sources of funding may obscure this decline. Barring, however, truly radical reverses, this generation is almost certainly the last for old-style *romance*-writing poets and with them the *folheto* as we have known it. However, numerous jeremiads to the contrary, all *cordel* stories are not going to disappear overnight.[9] The old favorites will almost surely continue to appear in the familiar flimsy editions as well as in the new sleek ones, and perhaps some new breed of poet will emerge. Still, the *folheto* is no longer a regional phenomenon. Just as its readers and writers have been absorbed into a larger national context, so too it has ceased to function within its own quite special world.

The New Public for the *Cordel*

Interest in the *folheto* is part of a more widespread movement originally spearheaded by artists and writers but now involving the middle class at large. Not only the *cordel* but a variety of other art forms such as the dancelike form of combat known as the *capoeira*, the samba, and a host of local festivals now prompt considerable attention.

As initially suggested, the *cordel* was always part of a larger community that included members of the backlands aristocracy. Though many of these individuals wielded all but absolute power within a limited radius, few could be considered members of a national elite. As most were only relatively wealthy and a good number remained illiterate, residents of the richer, more progressive coastal zone often looked down on them as boorish. Thus, the *folheto* absorbed much from a larger regional context, but most persons who considered themselves intellectuals purposely ignored it.

Granted, a small number of educated Northeasterners did take an active interest in popular traditions. Societies formed by intellectuals for the exchange of ideas, such as the late nineteenth-century School of Recife and the "Spiritual Bakery" of Ceará, brought together thinkers and artists concerned with the social and linguistic aspects of the local culture. Responding largely to currents then fashionable in Europe (first romanticism, then

9. Brazilian newspapers have been predicting the imminent demise of the *folheto* for at least three decades. In 1950, folklorist Gustavo Barroso warned in a major Rio daily that the *cordel* was "at the gates of death because the radio will surely kill it," calling for the salvation of "the ultimate vestiges" of the tradition (*A Manhã*, February 10, 1950). I am grateful to Adriano da Gama Kury for allowing me access to the Casa de Rui Barbosa *cordel* clippings file.

realism), a number of members from these associations collected ballads and *folhetos* while others took to writing novels with a strong Northeastern flavor. Some of these, such as the tale of one outlaw, *O Cabeleira*, by Franklin Távora, actually utilized bits and pieces of the *literatura de cordel*. Nevertheless, not until the publication in 1902 of Euclides da Cunha's *Revolt in the Backlands*, an account of a federal military campaign against a particular messianic community in the interior of one Northeastern state, did intellectuals in other parts of the country begin to give serious thought to regional realities.[10]

Pioneer studies by poet-novelist Celso de Magalhães, novelist José de Alencar, and philologist Sílvio Romero appeared in the latter part of the nineteenth century. Twentieth-century authors such as Luís da Câmara Cascudo and Leonardo Mota not only documented a series of folk customs and beliefs but began recording the work of various poet-singers. Although the majority of these authors were Northeasterners, some Southerners also became interested in these manifestations. Mário de Andrade, leader of the São Paulo-based modernist movement of the 1920s, devoted a sensitive essay to the *literatura de cordel*. With its emphasis on national character or *brasileiridade*, modernism had a decided impact on the back-to-the-roots push known as regionalism in the Northeast.[11]

10. Franklin Távora, *O Cabeleira*, rev. ed. (Rio de Janeiro: Tecnoprint Gráfica, 1966; originally published in 1876); Euclides da Cunha, *Os sertões: Campanha de Canudos*, 15th ed. (Rio de Janeiro: Liv. Francisco P. de Azevedo, 1940). For an English version, see *Revolt in the Backlands*, 2nd ed., tr. Samuel Putnam (Chicago: University of Chicago Press, 1970). The first Brazilian edition appeared in 1902. For a good introduction to Brazilian writing, see Antônio Cândido, *Formação da literatura brasileira: Momentos decisivos*, 2 vols, 5th ed. (São Paulo: Editora da Universidade de São Paulo Editora Itatiaia Ltda., 1975); and Antônio Cândido, *Literatura e sociedade: Estudos de teoria e história literária*, 3rd ed. rev. (São Paulo: Editora Nacional, 1973). See also Wilson Martins, *História da inteligência brasileira,* 6 vols. (São Paulo: Editora Cultrix, 1977–1978). A helpful guide to works on individual authors is the *Pequeno dicionário de literatura brasileira*, 2nd ed., ed. José Paulo Paes and Massaud Moisés (São Paulo: Editora Cultrix, 1964). A good introduction to the school of Recife is Antônio Paim, *A filosofia da Escola do Recife* (Rio de Janeiro: Editora Saga, 1966).

11. Celso de Magalhães, *A poesia popular brasileira*, rev. ed. (Rio de Janeiro: Divisão de Publicaçoes, 1973); José de Alencar, *O nosso cancioneiro* (Rio de Janeiro: Livraria São José, 1962); Luis da Câmara Cascudo, *Cinco livros do povo* (Rio de Janeiro: José Olympio, 1953); Luís da Camâra Cascudo, *Vaqueiros e cantadores* (Porto Alegre: Liv. do Globo, 1939); Leonardo Mota, *Cantadores* (Fortaleza: Imprensa Universitária do Ceará, 1961); Leonardo Mota, *Sertão alegre* (Fortaleza: Imprensa Universitária do Ceará, 1963); Leonardo Mota, *Violeiros do norte* (Fortaleza: Imprensa Universitária do Ceará, 1962); and Sílvio Romero, *Estudos sobre a poesia popular do Brasil (1879–1880)* (Petrópolis: Vozes, 1977); Mário de Andrade, "O romanceiro de Lampeão," in *O baile das quatro artes* (São Paulo: Martins/MEC, 1963). For a good introduction to the extremely important modernist movement, see Mário da Silva Brito, *História do modernismo no Brasil*, 2nd ed. rev. (Rio de Janeiro: Civilização Brasileira, 1964); and Wilson Martins, *O modernismo* (São Paulo: Editora Cultrix, 1965). In English, see John Nist, *The Modernist Movement in Brazil* (Aus-

Although individual writers maintained an interest in the *folheto* throughout the 1930s and 1940s, educated Brazilians as a group still tended to equate popular culture with a "primitivism" embarrassing to those who continued to look to Europe for standards. Those writers who did write about folklore often chose a picturesque pen name. (Author Gustavo Barroso, for instance, signed himself "João do Norte" or "North Country John" in his initial studies of poet-singers.)[12]

Only after World War II when rapid technological advances began seriously to threaten a more traditional way of life did a growing number of persons begin to think more deeply about previously ignored traditions. In 1958, two years before the inauguration of the new capital of Brasília, the Kubitschek regime created the national Campaign for the Defense of Folklore. The first all-Brazil festival featuring poet-singers, held a year later in Rio de Janeiro, brought Northeastern popular poetry to a Southern public's attention. Judged by such outstanding members of the intelligentsia as author Manuel Bandeira, who wrote a poem in honor of these improvisers, the event drew support from organizations such as the city's Chamber of Deputies, Standard Brands of Brazil, and the Antarctica Company (which donated five hundred bottles of soda!).[13] A rousing success, the festival prompted a wave of new interest in all forms of regional culture.

The next important spur to the study of the *cordel* proper occurred in 1962 when the Casa de Rui Barbosa research center published an important catalogue of its *folheto* holdings.[14] The growing interest in these stories by Sorbonne professor Raymond Cantel assured dubious Brazilian intellectuals that this new concern had international support. As a result, the enthusiasm for popular traditions, which had surfaced sporadically ever since the nineteenth century, became a veritable boom.[15]

---

tin: University of Texas Press, 1967). Further listings are included in Xavier Placer, ed., *Modernismo brasileiro: Bibliografia* (Rio de Janeiro: Divisão de Publicações e Divulgação, 1972).

12. Gustavo Barroso (João do Norte), *Ao som da viola: Folk-lore* (Rio de Janeiro: Livraria Editora Leite Ribeiro, 1921).

13. For a copy of the poem, see Manuel Bandeira, "Saudação aos cantadores do nordeste," *Jornal do Brasil*, September 12, 1959. I am grateful to Sebastião Nunes Batista for providing a xerox copy of the clipping from his scrapbook. These sorts of festivals and public demonstrations actually began a decade earlier in Recife. In 1947, author Ariano Suassuna staged a presentation of poet-singers in the city's Santa Isabel theater. A year later, the Commission for the Defense of Folklore was created in Pernambuco.

14. *Literatura popular em verso: Catálogo* (Rio de Janeiro: Fundação Casa de Rui Barbosa/MEC, 1962).

15. The importance of Raymond Cantel to *folheto* research in Brazil cannot be underestimated. The author of various studies on the *cordel*, he periodically gives courses and lectures throughout the country, which are given ample coverage by the Brazilian press. See, for instance, the articles by Heloisa Castello Branco: "Cordel, a literatura mais rica do mundo para um especialista da Sorbonne," *Jornal do Brasil*, December 16, 1977; "Francês

During the past two decades, virtually every major Northeast Brazilian university has become involved in some way with *folheto* collecting and publishing. Hundreds of articles, books, and theses in Portuguese and other languages have appeared. Writers, graphic artists, actors, directors, filmmakers, musicians, dancers, and even comic strip designers have turned to the *literatura de cordel* for inspiration. Children who do not learn ballads at their mother's knee may learn them from a teacher, and high school as well as university students seek out various folk artists. In the same way that popular poets rewrite soap operas, television writers base new programs on *cordel* stories. Hundreds of articles appear each year in newspapers, house journals, the Brazilian newsmagazine *Veja*, and even true romance magazines.[16] Government and industry pour money into festivals, exhibits, lectures, and publicity campaigns. Despite the fact that this movement has its less serious aspects, it undoubtedly constitutes one of the most significant developments within twentieth-century Brazil. It is impossible to appreciate fully the recent, often radical changes in the country's social and economic structure without an understanding of shifting attitudes toward popular traditions.[17]

Though unique in certain aspects, this surge of interest is not unprecedented. A similar concern for popular culture occurred in many parts of Europe almost two centuries ago.[18] Originating at the end of the eighteenth

especialista de cordel ganha *folhetos* sobre Getúlio," *Jornal do Brasil*, March 10, 1972; "Francês dá curso de cordel no Rio," *Tribuna da Imprensa* (Rio de Janeiro), July 24, 1976; and "Para professor francês, subvenção matará o cordel," *O Estado de São Paulo*, July 29, 1976. I am grateful once again to Adriano da Gama Kury for access to the Casa de Rui Barbosa's file of clippings.

16. An example of a soap opera based on a *folheto* is Dias Gomes' *Saramandaia*, which looks to João Melquíades Ferreira's *The Mysterious Peacock*. One example of a *cordel* version of a soap opera is Joaquim de Sena's *História da Novela de Antonio Maria*, 2 vols. (Fortaleza, 1969). The true romance magazine article is Mário Souto Maior's "O sexo na literatura de cordel," *Ele e Ela* (Rio de Janeiro), 69 (1975): 59–62. There are well over a thousand newspaper articles dealing with the *cordel* on file in the libraries of the National Foundation for the Arts (FUNARTE, Rio de Janeiro), Casa de Rui Barbosa, *Jornal do Brasil*, and Instituto Joaquim Nabuco in Recife.

17. For a study of these shifts in attitude toward folk traditions in another context, see William A. Wilson, *Folklore and Nationalism in Modern Finland* (Bloomington: Indiana University Press, 1976). For a discussion of nationalism and its cultural implications within Brazil, see E. Bradford Burns, *Nationalism in Brazil: A Historical Survey* (New York: Frederick A. Praeger, 1968). An interesting example of the sort of changes presently taking place is evident in Ricardo Noblat, "Ganhando status: Um simpósio universitário estuda o cordel," *Veja*, no. 529, October 25, 1978, p. 152.

18. An excellent discussion of Europeans' relationship to popular culture can be found in Peter Burke, *Popular Culture in Early Modern Europe* (New York: New York University Press, 1978), which has an extensive bibliography. For a discussion of the new interest of American writers and artists in native traditions, see Gene Bluestein, *The Voice of the Folk:*

century in a divided Germany, enthusiasm for "spontaneous" and "communal" art forms became one of the keystones of a more universal Romantic movement whose impact was felt in the New World. In Brazil, toward the middle of the nineteenth century, intellectuals began indulging in a generally exotic Indianism exemplified by the regionalist novels of José de Alencar.[19] The fact that the world at large is presently undergoing an intense wave of neopastoralism has only emphasized Brazil's present concern for its own traditions.[20] In the same way that urban dwellers in other countries manifest enthusiasm for a variety of popular arts from batik to reggae music, Brazilians have discovered a still-living heritage within the borders of their own country, making their own search for roots particularly dramatic. As in other times and places, this new enthusiasm for regional expression reveals a variety of intellectual and aesthetic as well as political and economic motives and can be seen as an intensification of nationalist feeling.

The nature of individual Brazilians' interest in the *literatura de cordel* varies. For some who grew up in the Northeast, the *folheto* represents a now-distant way of life. A number of these persons see it as both a personal and communal document, "a fictionalized memory of the Northeast."[21] Many artists and writers who rely on popular poetry in their own work regard it as part of their own experience. Though it may become an object of study, it remains a special presence, which many are reluctant to treat like any other fact. "I was born in the interior of Ceará," a Rio-based journalist explains in typical fashion,

> and I passed my entire childhood there. My house was always full of *folhetos* that I read and reread swaying in a hammock, sleepy but bedazzled. Sometimes, at night, illiterate adults would group in the patio, and by moonlight I would read them story after story that we all knew by heart.[22]

Folklore and American Literary Theory (Amherst: University of Massachusetts Press, 1972). For an overview of cultural nationalism in a number of different contexts, see *The Cry of Home: Cultural Nationalism and the Modern Writer*, ed. H. Ernest Lewell (Knoxville: University of Tennessee Press, 1972).

19. For a complete collection of José de Alencar's writings, see his *Obra completa*, ed. M. Cavalcanti Proença, 4 vols. (Rio de Janeiro: J. Aguilar, 1960–1965). For an English translation of one of his best-known novels, see *Iracema: The Honey Lips*, tr. Isabel Burton (London: Bickers & Son, 1886).

20. For a general study of pastoralism as an intellectual current, see Renato Poggioli, *The Oaten Flute: Essays on Pastoral Poetry and the Pastoral Ideal* (Cambridge, Mass.: Harvard University Press, 1975). For a discussion of one contemporary manifestation of this phenomenon in Brazil, see Candace Slater, "Folklore and the Modern Artist: The Northeast Brazilian *Movimento Armorial*," *Luso-Brazilian Review*, 16 (1979): 160–90.

21. Manuel Diégues Júnior, interview, Rio de Janeiro, November 9, 1977.

22. Mário Pontes, interview, Rio de Janeiro, October 31, 1977.

Persons interested in the *cordel* are not, however, necessarily associated with the Northeast. Even those born in other regions of the country tend to see it as a national heritage "every bit as precious as an eighteenth-century Baroque church." Although various individuals have quite different visions of their country, most would agree that the *folheto* is quintessentially Brazilian. Persons with radically different viewpoints concur that the *cordel* represents an antidote to their Europeanized culture, pointing to the *cordel* poet as proof that "a truly national art and literature have always flourished." The fact that chapbook literature was originally an Iberian tradition does not bother those who claim that "what is truly popular becomes in turn Brazilian."[23]

The current interest in folk and popular traditions reflects an identity crisis that rapid postwar industrialization has accentuated. One noted critic sounds a common note when he observes that most things in the country only take on value when perceived as foreign. "I find the *cordel* important," he says, "precisely because it shows that we have native artists who have escaped this mania to destroy our own values in order to go searching for new ones somewhere else."[24]

In Brazil as in other developing countries, accelerated changes in both the physical and human landscape have created a diffuse sense of anxiety. ("The only people in the country to make more money than industrialists are their psychiatrists," one student tells another.) In this context, one artist finds the *cordel*'s resilience to be its most important feature. "We have become a people without a face, and these stories remind us of our former appearance," he explains.[25] Like many others, he suggests that the future of the *folheto* and the country are related, taking heart in the popular poets' continued struggle against seemingly impossible odds. Similarly, while expressing doubts about "the survival of mankind in general, let alone its poets," one young filmmaker insists that the destiny of the Brazilian people and the *cordel* are intertwined.[26]

Though persons interested in the *folheto* may single out one or another aspect for special attention, many point out that the tradition is distinctly multifaceted. The *cordel* may, for instance, serve as doorway to a community with which the individual would otherwise have little contact. It may also function as an artistic sourcebook. Thus, while one critic denies any special interest in popular culture in its own right, he emphasizes the impossibility of appreciating the work of a number of contemporary Brazilian painters and printmakers without an understanding of the *cordel*

23. Horácio de Almeida, interview, Rio de Janeiro, October 31, 1977.
24. Antônio Houaiss, interview, Rio de Janeiro, November 22, 1977.
25. Newton Cavalcanti, interview, Rio de Janeiro, October 24, 1977.
26. Tânia Quaresma, interview, Rio de Janeiro, November 3, 1977.

tradition.[27] At least one psychologist sees *folhetos* as a kind of photograph of the unconscious, revealing "terrifying monsters who turn out to be reflections of our deepest selves."[28]

Interest in the *cordel* often transcends the *folheto* proper. For instance, filmmaker Nelson Pereira dos Santos first became involved with the tradition after getting to know a group of Northeastern slum dwellers in Rio de Janeiro. Internationally known novelist Antônio Callado wrote a play based on the *cordel* tradition after preparing a series of reports about the Peasant Leagues for a Rio-based newspaper. "I stayed a little while in a sugar mill called Galiléia where Francisco Julião first began organizing fieldworkers in the early 1960s, and I saw the possibility of using popular poetry in order to create a panoramic vision of the Northeast," he explains.[29]

The interest of many younger persons in the *cordel* represents a conscious political statement. Asserting that a concern for popular culture is inextricably connected to wider ideological issues, they argue that one cannot study the *folheto* apart from its problem-ridden context. According to one documentary maker who adheres to this position, anyone who works in the field of art and who has some sensitivity to the political destiny of the country "has no other choice but to become a voice of the Brazilian people, that is, of the great mass of the oppressed."[30]

In this vein, insights gleaned from study of the *cordel* may help shape a particular program of action. An anthropologist in his early thirties explains that during the pro-change Goulart years, the Left made the mistake of attempting grassroots shifts without sufficient knowledge of the persons these would affect. "We tried," he affirms, "to serve as the vanguard of the people without bothering to learn enough about them."[31] Although the military coup in 1964 put an end to these attempts, such individuals are determined to profit from experience.

Concern for popular culture may indicate dissatisfaction with the status quo, but not all persons interested in the *cordel* share the same political stance. While some view such art forms as vehicles for change, others see them as a repository of values, which they would forcibly preserve. Such individuals often emphasize the poet's "purity" and "ingenuity," express-

27. Roberto Pontual, interview, Rio de Janeiro, November 14, 1977.

28. Roberto Bello, interview, Rio de Janeiro, November 13, 1977.

29. Antônio Callado, interview, Rio de Janeiro, November 17, 1977. The play is *Forró no Engenho Cananéia* (Rio de Janeiro: Civilização Brasileira, 1964). For more information on the Peasant Leagues, see Francisco Julião, *Que são as Ligas Camponesas?* (Rio de Janeiro: Civilização Brasileira, 1962).

30. Geraldo Sarno, interview, Rio de Janeiro, November 24, 1977.

31. Antonio Augusto Arantes Neto, interview, Campinas, São Paulo, December 11, 1977.

ing a romantic admiration for the *cordel* as "the work of humble people with their hearts in their hands."[32]

Before the military coup, a number of educated authors and song writers began using art forms like the *folheto* to make political as well as artistic statements about the need for reform. The Goulart government itself took an active interest in popular culture, encouraging its study and supporting the efforts of various traditional as well as folk-inspired artists. In the state of Pernambuco, for instance, the progressive Arraes regime, which fell in 1964, backed a popular culture movement to "revitalize popular traditions as an instrument of social integration and formal education designed to serve the people."[33] The funds destined for regional manifestations did not dry up after Goulart fell in 1964. Although rechanneled toward quite different objectives, official support of popular traditions not only continued but actually intensified. Particularly after 1968, a period of extreme repression, the new military government sought to prove its nationalistic spirit through a massive folklore program.

Today, federal universities, state and city agencies, and publicly funded tourist and development bureaus seek to document and disseminate Brazilian traditions. The celebration for National Folklore Week is held every August in a different part of the country. Contests, festivals, and conferences seek to acquaint a varied public with the national heritage. The rechristening of the original Campaign for the Defense of Folklore as the National Folklore Institute in 1979 symbolizes the increasingly permanent character of government support.

Although individual programs sponsored by state and federal agencies have benefited participants from all social classes, it would be a mistake to overlook political goals. In a country racked by inflation and an astronomical national debt, such measures are clearly politically astute. It is not simply chance that a whole gamut of popular artists should provide the entertainment for graduation exercises at the National College of War or that tourist bureaus should carefully stage various popular festivals on the anniversary of the 1964 coup. "Popular Poets to Be Prophets of Progress" reads one newspaper headline, going on to explain how Recife's Center for Social Communication (CECOSNE) is training singers and writers "to preach the benefits of economic development."[34]

32. Stella Leonardos, interview, Rio de Janeiro, November 17, 1977.

33. Part of the Arraes' regime's General Plan of Action, first printed in *Última Hora* (Recife), February 3, 1963, is reprinted in Ivan Maurício, Marcos Cirano, and Ricardo de Almeida, *Arte popular e dominação*, 2nd ed. (Recife: Editora Alternativa, 1978), p. 97. For a discussion of protest music allied to various popular art forms, see José Ramos Tinhorão, *Música popular: Um tema em debate* (Rio de Janeiro: JEM Editores, 1969).

34. See "Militares festejam revolução," *Diário de Pernambuco* (Recife), March 31, 1978, Section A, p. 5; and "Violeiros nordestinos serão profetas do desenvolvimento," on

Not surprisingly, multinationals, who play a leading role in the Brazilian economy, are among the current folklore movement's most enthusiastic supporters. Shell Oil, for instance, has sponsored a handsome anthology of Northeastern popular poetry.[35] The huge calendar with dazzling scenes from one Afro-Brazilian festival distributed by government agencies is a gift of the Phillips Corporation. Xerox continues to place arresting ads in magazines with national circulation. "Take good care of your country's folklore," they warn, "because it has no copy."

To be sure, commercial interest in popular culture is not limited to industrial giants. São Paulo music stores stock not only samba and the latest American rock records but also offer an extensive selection of Northeastern hillbilly albums. The oversize clay figure of a backlands cowman stands vigil before a series of specialty shops in Rio's fashionable Leblon district. Recife alone has a half-dozen folk art galleries that cater above all to tourists from the South and abroad.[36] Due to the expanding hotel and travel industry, cruises down the São Francisco River, a traditional highway into the Northeastern interior, now vie with guided tours of the Amazon as a vacation scheme. Folk-based artists and musicians sell scores of paintings and records, playing to sell-out audiences in every corner of Brazil.

The question of the relationship of educated Brazilians to the *folheto* becomes a heated issue in this setting. Some individuals claim that change within the *cordel* and other art forms is natural; others respond to transformations with extreme distaste. Despite the fact that this debate is not peculiar to Brazil, its participants frequently have a personal involvement in its outcome, which makes it far more than a merely academic question.

Persons unhappy about present changes in the *folheto* often pin the blame for its supposed demise or adulteration on the intervention of fellow intellectuals. Novelist Rachel de Queiroz, for instance, observes that

the same page. I am grateful to Mário Pontes for making a number of clippings from the *Jornal do Brasil* available to me.

35. The anthology is Sebastião Nunes Batista, *Antologia da literatura de cordel* (Natal: Fundação José Augusto, 1977), published in collaboration with Shell, Brasil. Actually, both Shell and Esso have published studies of the *cordel* from time to time in their respective magazines. See, for instance, Orígines Lessa, "Literatura de feira," *Revista Esso*, 27 (n.d.): 13–16; and Orígenes Lessa, "Poesia de cordel: Ingénua ou mágica?" *Revista Shell*, 1970, pp. 17–20.

36. For a study of this sort of music, see Waldenyr Caldas, *Acorde na aurora: Música sertaneja e indústria cultural* (São Paulo: Nacional, 1977); and José de Souza Martins, "Viola quebrada," *Debate e Crítica*, 14 (1974): 23–49. A revised and enlarged version of the latter is available as "Música sertaneja: A dissimulação na linguagem dos humilhados," in *Capitalismo e tradicionalismo* (São Paulo: Editora Pioneira, 1975). For an overview involving a variety of art forms including the *cordel*, see Murilo Carvalho et al., *Artistas e festas populares* (São Paulo: Editorial Brasiliense, 1977).

popular art forms are only valuable when spontaneous, and "once people begin to encourage, to program, to cultivate something like the *folheto*, it loses its authentic character and begins to die."[37]

Other individuals are more apt to regard present transformations in the *cordel* as part of a larger and inevitable historical process. Thus, according to the director of the National Folklore Institute, what we are seeing "not only in the *literatura de cordel* but in all forms of popular culture is an increasing cultural homogenization imposed by the mass media."[38] Poet Ferreira Gullar expresses yet another viewpoint when he finds capitalism itself to be the *folheto*'s greatest enemy. He insists that "the poison that the system bears within it" kills all such popular art forms because "they are not efficient from a material standpoint."[39]

The practical question of what if any role more privileged Brazilians ought to play in the *folheto*'s future is also particularly sensitive. Many individuals feel that popular poets ought to be left to their own devices since "although the *cordel* itself has no defenses, the people who read and write it do."[40] Others insist that intellectuals have not only a right but an obligation to protect both this and similar art forms.

People who feel that popular poets need help have acted on their beliefs. Individuals as well as universities and federal agencies have sought in many cases to encourage *folheto* authors. General Umberto Peregrino, for instance, has begun to turn his own house into a center for *cordel* production and distribution designed to serve those poets who are not succeeding in finding publishers for their work. "I am going to print up *folhetos* on a rustic hand press," he explains, "without any thought of profit so that any author who wants to can see his work in print."[41]

Individuals who conceive of the *cordel* as a process more than as a largely autonomous object are generally more hesitant to provide such direct aid. Some are not against the idea of preserving the *folheto* by helping individual writers but feel that only the poet's customary public can determine whether or not the tradition should continue. One young poet dismisses attacks on his practice of publishing his own (nonpopular) work in *folheto* form and stresses the need for grassroots support. "What little faith my critics have in the *cordel*'s vitality!" he says. "Really, if *I* could kill the *folheto* singlehanded, it would be far better off ten feet below the earth."[42]

Help for *cordel* authors in the form of subsidies for needed supplies,

37. Rachel de Queiroz, interview, Rio de Janeiro, December 4, 1977.
38. Braulio do Nascimento, interview, Rio de Janeiro, November 16, 1977.
39. Ferreira Gullar, interview, Rio de Janeiro, November 24, 1977.
40. Gilberto Galvão, interview, Campinas, São Paulo, December 11, 1977.
41. Umberto Peregrino, interview, Rio de Janeiro, November 16, 1977.
42. Xico Chaves, interview, Rio de Janeiro, November 18, 1977.

documents to avert police harassment, and loans for publication expenses and new equipment is not the real issue, according to individuals who express support for such measures in theory but who balk at the manner in which they may be administered. Many insist that would-be benefactors have an obligation to ask the poet whether he wants or needs assistance before rushing in with aid. Thus, the head of Rio de Janeiro's State Department of Culture asks if the best manner of preserving the *cordel* may not be to insure that its creators get enough to eat. "If the price of guaranteeing the survival of such popular art forms is to insure a certain picturesque poverty," he says, "well then, I say good riddance!"[43]

Some Effects of Widespread Interest on the Popular Poet

This new attention from persons whom they perceive as powerful and important has naturally affected *folheto* writers. Today visitors from Stuttgart to São Paulo snap pictures of vendors and buyers in local marketplaces. School buses packed with children pull up beside their doors to watch "a typical poet" at work. Film crews zoom into urban slums or dusty hamlets to interview one or another author about a recent story.

The rapid growth of national interest in previously marginal art forms has had a number of quite varied results. Burgeoning concern has created a new awareness and sense of self-worth among many popular poets. It has opened up new sources of funding and provided an alternate if frequently problem-ridden new publishing route. The growth of a middle-class market for *folhetos* has given the poet new customers while fostering the creation of an informal official circuit. In some cases, this circuit has benefited poets by providing new financial opportunities. In others it has divided authors from one another as they find themselves competing for a limited number of favors.

This interest is also responsible for certain changes in the *cordel*'s physical appearance as well as its subject matter. The emergence of new themes and a new vocabulary owes as much to the growth of a quite different public as to changes within the traditional audience. Today's most successful *cordel* authors have adapted to these changing conditions by assuming nontraditional roles while a growing contingent of nonpopular poets geared toward a more sophisticated audience has begun to join their ranks.

---

43. Paulo Affonso Grisolli, interview, Rio de Janeiro, November 17, 1977. For another, particularly eloquent statement of this position, see Hermilo Borba Filho, "Cultura popular ou barriga cheia," in Maurício et al., *Arte popular e dominação*, pp. 34–36.

If sometimes overwhelmed by this new attention, popular poets are also flattered to find themselves in vogue. "Who would have guessed," one vendor says,

> that the *folheto*, once so humble, would ever come to this? I've sold *cordel* for over thirty years now, and I never gave it a second thought. Today, no, it's not just country people who come around to buy *folhetos*, there are doctors, lawyers, professors all lined up before my stall.[44]

Poets themselves have begun to assign a new value to their work. "When I think of all those stories I tossed off without setting aside a single copy," asserts a *folheto* author,

> I want to kick myself. Why today if I want to take a look at something that I wrote twenty years ago, I have to ask one of those collectors to make a copy for me.[45]

Individual authors often reveal a new awareness of the *cordel* as a tradition. "Did you know," one poet asks a customer in a marketplace far in the interior, "that the *folhete* came here all the way from Portugal hundreds of years ago?"[46] *Cordel* authors cite the interest of educated persons in these stories as yet another reason why their usual customers ought to buy their wares. An announcement printed on the flipside of a set of stories emphasizes the new respectability of "the *Literatura de Cordel*, formerly known as Popular Poetry." "The *cordel* today offers an enriched vocabulary," writes the author, "and is the best possible pastime because it has not only been improved but is supported by the authorities to the point of becoming the subject of study in the university!"[47]

The growth of an increasingly diverse market for popular art forms has fostered the establishment of a sort of official circuit. Those poets who are successful in allying themselves with it not only tend to earn more money but normally undergo a series of new experiences. Particularly if they are also *repentistas*, they may be invited on national tours, asked to make recordings or give lecture-demonstrations in concert halls and schools. Recently, for example, the Society for the Protection of the Environment in Fortaleza hired a group of poets to perform for an "ecological picnic" designed to save a forest.[48]

44. Edson Pinto da Silva, interview, Recife, Pernambuco, January 18, 1978.
45. José Soares, interview, Recife, Pernambuco, January 17, 1978.
46. I overheard this in a fair in Crató, Ceará, on April 4, 1978.
47. João José da Silva, "A Literatura de Cordel em Foco," 1978. This advertisement appears on the back page of all of the poet's *folhetos* published during 1978.
48. See "Cearenses fazem hoje o primeiro 'piquenique ecológico' do país," *Jornal do Commércio* (Recife), April 2, 1978, Section 3, p. 1.

Even though some *cordel* authors were always better connected than others, the growth of official interest has intensified these differences so that today there is a greater than ever gulf between an urban poet accustomed to chatting with journalists and professors and the rural vendor who continues to hawk his booklets in dusty country fairs. Those poets who recently visited the national minister of education and culture with a petition demanding "a place in Brazilian culture" clearly have little in common with their often illiterate cousins who still roam the interior, battered suitcase in hand.[49]

Not surprisingly, today's most successful *cordel* authors are individuals who have managed to ally themselves with modernizing forces. Those who have the fewest problems have invariably found some way to appeal to a larger public, and none, except perhaps Manuel d'Almeida Filho, advisor to São Paulo's Luzeiro press, is a traditional poet devoted to writing those thirty-two-page *romances*, once the backbone of the *folheto* trade.

Some enterprising *cordel* authors, for instance, rely heavily upon their skills as graphic artists. José Francisco Borges, Dila Soares, and José Costa Leite supplement their incomes considerably through designing blockprints. Their work not only appears on a sizable number of ordinary *folheto* covers but in the living rooms of well-to-do Brazilians, and all three have had their prints exhibited throughout Brazil as well as in foreign museums such as the Louvre and the Smithsonian Institution.

Some of today's most successful poets utilize their skills as singers. Azulão, for instance, is not only the sole poet to sing his verses in Rio's weekly São Cristóvão fair but is also a now familiar presence at officially sponsored gatherings. He has visited a number of states on government-organized tours and cut a record for the National Folklore Institute.[50] In the Northeast, Pedro Bandeira, the most visible member of an enterprising family of poet-singers, both emcees a particularly successful radio program and turns out a steady stream of eight-page stories. Probably the wealthiest popular poet in Brazil today, Bandeira lives in a new house in the best part of Juazeiro do Norte, a small city known for its religious fervor and resistance to many sorts of change. The poet, however, attends the university with his wife in nearby Crato and talks about making a world tour "or at least of the U.S."[51]

Still other poets have cultivated a number of special talents. A few years

49. "Euro Brandão recebe poetas e manifesto," *Diário de Pernambuco* (Recife), January 30, 1979, Section B, p. 8.

50. José João dos Santos (Azulão), "Literatura de Cordel" (record) MEC/DAC/CDFB, July 1975.

51. For a book-length study of the poet, see Joaryvar Macêdo, *Pedro Bandeira: Príncipe dos poetas populares* (Fortaleza: Imprensa Oficial do Ceará, 1976).

ago, for instance, the Brazilian magazine *Manchete* ran an article on José Francisco Soares of Recife, dubbing him "poet-reporter of the Northeast." Since that time, television crews have periodically created traffic jams around his stall near the São José market. Soares, who claims to have scooped major dailies on more than one occasion, displays a special fondness for stories based on urban rumors and major sports events. Frequently sought after by politicians bent on gaining popular support, he has written *folhetos* for a long string of the most diverse candidates.[52]

Finally, yet another type of writer who has adapted to a changing market is Rodolfo Coelho Cavalcante, whose version of the best-selling novel *Tereza Batista* is discussed in Chapter 6. Consciously appealing to middle-class collectors through ads on the backs of his *folhetos* and in his poets' journal, he has written a series of biographies of outstanding Brazilians such as Oswaldo Cruz and Rui Barbosa, which have sold well among educated buyers. As head of an influential poets' association with members in various states, Cavalcante has had a hand in organizing over ninety festivals and *cordel* fairs, which appeal now more than ever to a varied audience.

While the growth of official support has been a boon to individual poets, it has not been without its drawbacks. The publication of *folhetos* free of charge by certain university presses has created some problems. It is not always clear, for instance, who will decide what is to be published or on what basis choices will be made. Where does editing leave off and censorship begin? Will literary merit be the primary criterion for publication, or should each poet be assured the opportunity of printing a certain number of stories? And how does one define merit anyway? In the case of cash awards, must the recipient use the money to publish the winning *folheto*? Who should design the cover?

An example of the problems that can arise when educated individuals set out to help popular poets is the city of Recife's monthly prize. Theoretically, awards are made on the basis of aesthetic merit to those three poets who submit the best eight-, sixteen-, and thirty-two-page *folhetos*. Many authors suggest, however, that the prize has little or nothing to do with literary achievement but represents instead a kind of dole. What often happens is that a poet who has already had his turn will write a new story that an individual who may or may not be a *cordel* author submits as his own; when the tale wins, the two divide the money. "It's ridiculous!" one writer says. "How would you like to enter a story you had worked hard

52. See Maria Edileuza Baptista, "A história do poeta-repórter que não foi agricultor, não deu para pedreiro e vive feliz escrevendo cordel," *Jornal do Commércio*, February 1, 1978, Section C, p. 8.

on in that contest only to see it lose to one full of mismatched verses or another 'written' by an ordinary peddler?"[53]

Regardless of their good or devious intentions, would-be benefactors often find themselves the target of attacks. For example, the Casa da Criança (Children's House Foundation) in Olinda is reported to have bought up and then not published a large number of manuscripts from poets eager to see their work in print. Some writers argue that organizations such as the Olinda Poets' Association, which has strong ties to the foundation, are not well-disposed to serve as forums for their members' needs. "No matter how hard he tries, if a person is not a popular poet, he cannot really understand our way of life, our problems," one *folheto* author asserts.[54]

One particularly thorny question that has arisen in the past few decades concerns the use by educated artists of stories by living *cordel* poets as a basis for their own creative work. Since educated and popular artists hold different concepts of "property," "originality," and "artistic license," it is difficult to reach agreement on the sort of borrowing both parties consider ethical as well as what if any financial responsibilities the borrower incurs. Various journalists have printed denunciations by popular authors whose work has allegedly been used without payment or consent. These charges have triggered countercharges, retractions, new accusations, denials, and angry words on each side.[55] Given the present appeal of *cordel*-inspired plays, music, and painting, the problems raised by "folk-based" art are likely to intensify.

Changes associated with the emergence of a new market for popular art forms affect not only the poet's way of life but the *cordel* itself. New developments in *folheto* covers are a good case in point. At a time when mass-produced comic book-like pamphlets are increasingly popular among traditional buyers, more educated persons favor other, apparently more rustic, covers. Although the designers of such blockprints may be the sons and grandsons of popular poets (for example, Stênio Diniz in Juazeiro do Norte, Jerónimo and Marcelo Soares in Recife), there is also a new class of professional artists who design these covers primarily for pleasure. Ciro Fernandes in Rio de Janeiro is perhaps the best example of these. From a rural Northeastern background himself, he now provides popular poets such as Azulão with a series of stylized prints in the traditional manner.

53. José Francisco Borges, interview, Bezerros, Pernambuco, July 17, 1978.
54. Rodolfo Coelho Cavalcante, interview, Salvador, Bahia, June 5, 1978.
55. The accusations, printed in Maurício et al., *Arte popular e dominação*, pp. 67–94, have, for instance, triggered a continuing exchange.

Folheto texts themselves reveal new influences. In some cases, a heavily regional vocabulary has been enlarged to include a variety of new terms including urban slang. Introductions aimed at students and collectors explain the history of the *cordel*. New themes and actors, such as singer Roberto Carlos, television personality Chacrinha, and soccer star Pelé, appear alongside familiar *folheto* presences such as the famous Northeastern bandit Lampião or one of various backlands prophets.

Although such stories may appeal to the poet's traditional public, other *folhetos* geared primarily to the middle classes have begun appearing within the past ten years. Some, for instance, explain for the uninitiated what a *cordel* author does. Others deal with subjects that the popular writer thinks will interest this new public: descriptions of a well-placed individual or humorous treatments of urban problems. In the past the popular poet always offered his services to persons from all social classes; today the number of *folhetos de encomenda*, stories written at the request of a customer with specific guidelines, has dramatically increased. One finds not only the usual pamphlets commissioned by political candidates but others paid for by church organizations (about the need for land reform, for instance), public health programs (*Vaccinate Your Child!*), tourist bureaus (*My Trip to Amazonas*), city councils (*Get to Know Goiana*), and various commercial operations such as banks (*The Money Tree, or Why It Is Smart to Save*).

Significantly, despite the obvious multifaceted impact of this new market on popular poets, the majority still continue to cater primarily to their traditional public. In a clearly transitional position, those men who began writing twenty and thirty years ago have continued to incorporate new influences into a form long familiar to a particular community. Thus, even though changes in today's *cordel* cannot be underrated, the tradition on which these stories draw is still much the same.

This commitment to a larger group distinguishes such traditional authors from the growing number of newer poets. Almost never from the rural lower classes, the latter tend to write above all for an educated audience while making use of traditional presses and marketplaces. There is, for instance, Teo, owner of a small electric press in São Paulo, who is also a samba writer and nightclub performer; Abraão Batista, a pharmacist and former university professor; and Francisco Zénio and Edgley Ribeiro, two students from Juazeiro do Norte. Such writers should not be confused with artists, such as Rio-based poet Xico Chaves, who use the *folheto* form for economic as well as aesthetic motives but who would not call themselves popular poets or attempt to place their work in fairs, which cater primarily to a lower-class audience.

Cordel vendors often stock booklets by one or another of these nonpopular writers. Most assert that this is for the benefit of educated collectors who can be counted on to buy any story no matter how bad. In general, these tales tend to sell poorly among more traditional buyers. "This *folheto* is lousy, and I've always been a good customer," complains one young man in the Recife market. "Take it back and give me that old story of John Cricket—at least I know that it is good!"[56]

It is usually not difficult to distinguish the work of these new authors from stories by authentic (by which I mean community-oriented) *cordel* poets. The meter, which seasoned writers dismiss as "done by eye, not ear," is often faulty. The language is either too literary or else overly "folksy," lacking the *folheto*'s everyday, colloquial tone. In addition, the subject matter is often unrelated to most buyers' lives. Stories about the death of a prominent socialite, a new bridge in Rio de Janeiro, an international drug ring, or the death of singer Elvis Presley generally fail to interest traditional readers. Furthermore, the moral perspective and kind of humor revealed by most authors not born into the tradition are different from those found in the majority of *folhetos*. In the new stories, an evil-doer may get away unpunished or the poet may poke fun at a monster, which an experienced *cordel* writer would feel obliged to treat at least half seriously. Finally, the telltale six-step pattern outlined in the next chapter is usually absent or distorted. This factor, more than any other, makes the particular story, according to one poet, "something else, don't ask me what, but certainly not *cordel*."[57]

56. Complaint addressed to me as vendor at José de Souza Campos' stall, São José market, Recife, June 27, 1978. The customer seemed right, so I took back the *folheto* called *Conversation Between an Asslicker and His Guardian Angel* and gave him *John Cricket* instead.

57. José de Souza Campos, interview, Recife, July 4, 1978.

III. Theoretical Approaches to the *Literatura de Cordel*

s the preceding chapter has suggested, the *folheto* has interested a scattered group of educated persons for almost a century. These individuals have tended to be artists, scholars, journalists, and those all-purpose men (and sometimes women) of letters so characteristic of Brazilian intellectual life. However, owing largely to a long history of ambivalence toward popular traditions within a nation accustomed to looking abroad for cultural models, the *cordel* has only recently become an acceptable subject for public lectures, exhibitions, and university courses.

To date, the bulk of writing on these stories in verse in both scholarly and less specialized publications has been primarily descriptive. The classic studies of poets and singers are essentially transcriptions of texts held together with a variety of personal observation, biographical material, and, in some cases, considerable scholarship. Thanks in part to the efforts of the *cordel* division within the Casa de Rui Barbosa research center in Rio de Janeiro, now allied to a new *folheto* library within the Federal University of Paraíba, a stream of books and articles continues to appear. Some of these newer studies are discussions of a general nature. Others are treatments of more specialized topics such as urban *folhetos*, the "ideology" of the popular poet, or the role of Catholics and Protestants or even *cachaça* ("sugar rum") in Northeastern popular poetry.[1]

Most authors of general studies have sought to create some order in their subject by proposing one or another classification scheme. Their major objective has been to provide a thematic definition of the *cordel* tradition. In addition, since *folhetos* so often give incomplete or incorrect in-

1. For urban *folhetos*, see Manuel Diégues Júnior, "Cidade e vida urbana em folhetos populares," *Cultura* (Brasília), 3 (1973): 59–67. For ideology, see Renato Carneiro Campos, *Ideologia dos poetas populares do nordeste*, 2nd ed. (Recife: Instituto Joaquim Nabuco de Pesquisas Sociais/MEC, 1977); Antônio Fausto Neto, *A ideologia da punição* (Petrópolis: Vozes, 1979); and Ivan Cavalcanti Proença, *A ideologia do cordel* (Rio de Janeiro: Imago Editora, 1976). For Catholics and Protestants, see Raymond Cantel, "Les querelles entre protestants et catholiques dans la littérature populaire du nordeste brésilien," in *Mélanges à la mémoire de Jean Sarrailh* (Paris: Centre de Recherches de l'Institut d'Etudes Hispaniques, 1966), pp. 176–89. For *cachaça*, see João Farias, "A cachaça na literatura de cordel," *Boletim da Comissão Fluminense de Folclore*, 1 (1970): 23–25.

formation regarding author, publisher, and date of publication, many studies have designed systems to serve as coherent cataloguing models as well.

These critics have had to deal with volumes of material. There are at least a dozen major *cordel* collections within Brazil, each numbering close to five thousand not necessarily identical titles, as well as a host of smaller public and private library collections both within and outside the country. Furthermore, thanks in no small part to the new role of numerous university and foundation-related presses in *folheto* publication, new works continue to swell already crowded shelves.[2]

Various authors have proposed somewhat different classification systems. Orígenes Lessa, for instance, makes a distinction between (1) perennial themes such as *pelejas* ("poetic contests"), tales of bandits and cowmen, and prophecies; and (2) other subjects of more immediate interest (crimes, wars, elections, etc.). Ariano Suassuna breaks down *cordel* stories according to form (*romances*, ABCs, *pelejas*, and songs) then suggests a series of cycles including the heroic, the marvelous, the humorous, the historical and journalistic, and the romantic. Manuel Cavalcanti Proença proposes divisions based on four types of hero, nature themes, moral and religious subjects, verse debates, and specific historical figures. Manuel Diégues Júnior offers a basic tripartite division of traditional subjects, current events, and verse debates. Carlos Alberto Azevêdo singles out ten major topics: utopias, cuckolds, the devil, talking animals, exempla, historical and current events, as well as love, adventure, and satiric tales. Liêdo Maranhão de Souza claims to follow the lead of popular poets in separating *folhetos* (counsel, historical cycles, saints' tales, etc.) from *romances* (love, suffering struggle, and enchanted kingdoms). Roberto Câmara Benjamin divides *folhetos* according to one of three functions: information, entertainment, and social criticism.[3]

2. The major public *cordel* collections in Brazil are in the Casa de Rui Barbosa, in the FUNARTE libraries in Rio de Janeiro, in the Mário de Andrade Library within the University of São Paulo, in the State Department of Education and Culture in Recife, and in the *cordel* library of the Federal University of Paraíba in João Pessoa. Individuals with extensive *folheto* collections include Horácio de Almeida, Sebastião Nunes Batista, Roberto Bello, Orígenes Lessa, Umberto Peregrino, and Ivan Cavalcanti Proença in Rio de Janeiro; Liêdo Maranhão de Souza in Olinda, Pernambuco; and Raymond Cantel in Paris.

3. For further information on individual classification schemes, see Carlos Alberto Azevêdo, *O heróico e o messiânico na literatura de cordel* (Recife: Edicordel, 1972); Roberto Câmara Benjamin, "A religião nos folhetos populares," *Revista de Cultura Vozes*, 64 (1970): 609; Manuel Diégues Júnior, "Ciclos temáticos na literatura de cordel," in *Literatura popular em verso: Estudos* (Rio de Janeiro: Fundação Casa de Rui Barbosa/MEC, 1973), p. 29; *Literatura popular em verso: Catálogo* (Rio de Janeiro: Fundação Casa de Rui Barbosa/MEC, 1962), p. 394 (Manuel Cavalcanti Proença scheme); Liêdo Maranhão de Souza, *Classificação popular de literatura de cordel* (Petrópolis: Vozes, 1976); and Ariano Suassuna, "Notas sobre o romanceiro popular do nordeste," in *Ariano Suassuna:*

Taken as a whole, these systems have various advantages. First, they give even a reader unfamiliar with the *cordel* a sense of its range and nature. A mere glance at their groupings reveals that *folhetos* embrace both traditional (largely medieval) and contemporary themes and that stories have both a religious (otherworldly) and mundane, satiric side. Second, many of these schemas underline the presence of a wealth of regional and national themes. Finally, each individual system serves to highlight a different aspect of the tradition. Suassuna, for instance, singles out the role of oral poetry within the *folheto*. Roberto Câmara Benjamin underlines the *cordel*'s social significance. Souza calls attention to the popular poet's view of his own craft.

Nevertheless, both singly and together these systems reveal a number of serious drawbacks. The fact that seven authors have produced seven separate models should be ample proof that thematic schemes are largely subjective. Although many schemes reveal at least some common features, there is no ultimate consensus. This means that the individual interested in classifying the *cordel* in accord with subject-oriented categories must either decide among a number of existing systems or invent yet another of his own.

Moreover, as some of these critics themselves point out, a number of their models look a good deal like others proposed for the French *littérature de colportage*, the English pamphlet story, and the Spanish *pliego suelto*. To be sure, the *folheto* is an heir to these European chapbooks, and it is therefore natural that they should have much in common. Nevertheless, the *cordel* has distinguishing national characteristics. Some writers have attempted to stress these by devoting whole cycles to the thoroughly Brazilian bandit Lampião or the politician Getúlio Vargas. The moment, however, that one expands such unique-sounding categories to include more than one figure, thereby suggesting more general headings such as "bandit" or "political leader," they lose their specifically national flavor.

The basic problem with these categories is that they are amorphous. Although they can be pinned down somewhat through subdivision, this process often raises more problems than it solves. Is "satire," for instance, a sufficiently inclusive category, or is it necessary to specify "satire dealing with women," "satire directed at political figures," "satire in which the protagonist becomes the object of criticism"? Or in the case of the hero

---

Seleta em prosa e verso (Rio de Janeiro: José Olympio/INL/MEC, 1974), pp. 162–90. For a general discussion of thematic cycles, see Diégues, "Ciclos temáticos," pp. 26–30. For a discussion of some of the problems associated with content-oriented classificatory schemes, see Roger Abrahams, "The Complex Relations of Simple Forms," *Folklore Genres*, ed. Dan Ben-Amos (Austin: University of Texas Press, 1976), pp. 193–214; and Dan Ben-Amos, "Analytical Categories and Ethnic Genres," *Folklore Genres*, pp. 215–42.

cycle, must one break down the heading into animal, human, and supernatural or male and female heroes? How must one make these cuts and
how often?

In the long run, the drawbacks of this content-oriented approach out-
weigh its virtues because it cannot do justice to either the inherent unity
or genuine diversity of the *cordel* tradition. Dividing up *folhetos* into six,
seventeen, or twenty-three different categories suggests that each of these
groupings has its own, quite separate character. Conversely, grouping together all *pelejas* or all news accounts or all *folhetos* about one particular
bandit implies that such stories are related whereas in fact two *folhetos*
about the same outlaw may present him in quite distinct roles, and two
pelejas between the same contestants may serve very different ends. Also,
because most *cordel* tales present a multiplicity of themes, the problem of
overlapping is inevitable. The reader is regularly compelled either to
single out one dominant strand in an arbitrary manner or to cross-classify
the material under a plethora of headings. In short, the divisions designed
to bring order to this sprawling corpus may actually compound its apparent fragmentation.

The more structural approach outlined in the following pages eliminates
a number of these difficulties. I am not the first to suggest this type of
analysis in relation to the *folheto*, nor do I see it as the ideal or only way
of looking at the *cordel*. The structural approach, like the more traditional,
theme-oriented approach, says nothing about the performance context so
integral to the *folheto* or about the larger cultural framework within which
it functions, ignoring a number of important linguistic features as well.
And yet, while there is no need to limit oneself exclusively to a structural
approach, this method has a number of advantages, which in the case of
the *folheto* make it an all but indispensable tool.[4]

4. For a structural analysis of thirty-two-page *romances*, see Ruth Brito Lêmos Terra
and Mauro W. B. de Almeida, "A análise morfológica da literatura popular em verso: Uma
hipótese de trabalho," *Revista do Instituto de Estudos Brasileiros*, 16 (1975): 1–28. I have
also seen works in progress by Professors Antonio Augusto Arantes Neto (Universidade
Federal de Campinas), Claude Hulet (University of California, Los Angeles), and Idelette
Musart Fonseca dos Santos (Universidade Federal da Paraíba). A succinct overview of the
concepts underlying structural and semiotic approaches is provided by Terence Hawkes,
Structuralism and Semiotics (Berkeley: University of California Press, 1977). For an exten-
sive bibliography related to structuralism, see Bengt Hølbek, *Formal and Structural Studies
of Oral Narrative: A Bibliography* (Copenhagen: Institut for Folkemindevidenskab,
Kobenshavns Universitet, 1978). I have made particular use in this section of Claude Bremond, *Logique du récit* (Paris: Editions du Seuil, 1973); Alan Dundes, *The Morphology of
North American Indian Folktales*, Folklore Fellows Communications, No. 195 (Helsinki:
Suomalainen Tiedakatemia, 1964); Alan Dundes, *Analytic Essays in Folklore* (The Hague:
Mouton, 1975); A. J. Greimas, *Sémantique structurale* (Paris: Larousse, 1966); *Sign, Lan-
guage, Culture*, ed. A. J. Greimas (The Hague: Mouton, 1970); Claude Lévi-Strauss, *An-
thropologie structurale* (Paris: Plon, 1958)—English ed.: *Structural Anthropology*, 2nd

First and foremost, this approach cuts across the rigid lines established by thematic cycles to reveal the essential unity of *cordel* stories. At the same time, it allows for considerable variation, emphasizing unsuspected relationships among apparently separate *folhetos* as well as crucial differences among supposedly similar tales. Finally, it stresses that the *cordel* is not only a collection of stories but an underlying, quite particular vision of human life. In proposing the six-step sequence outlined below, I am not suggesting that all *cordel* tales are reducible to a single pattern but rather that there is within the tradition a basic structure capable of generating a wide variety of narratives. Less a preestablished mold than a set of guidelines demanding constant reelaboration, this sequence is something which each poet intuits, then manipulates at will.

There are a small number of exceptions worth mentioning before launching into a more detailed explanation of the six-step pattern that represents the rule. Certain compositions of a religious nature routinely printed in *cordel* form, for instance, are less apt to reveal this underlying sequence essentially because they are not true narratives. It is worth noting in this case that poets themselves often refer to these booklets by more specific names, such as *oração* ("prayer") or *bendito* ("hallelujah"), leaving the more general term *folheto* for reference to actual stories. Though a thirty-two-page booklet is technically a *romance*, vendors are more apt to refer to these as *folhetos* than they are to use this broader heading in reference to a prayer or hallelujah.

The pattern also works less well for a limited group of *folhetos*, which includes works by nonpopular authors, stories written expressly for a particular client who may impose his own wishes in the process, and tales based on raw material that does not obey or actually conflicts with this pattern. In the last case, the source may be a text or a movie with which many persons are familiar (for example, Romeo and Juliet), an actual occurrence (a local crime, the death of a national hero) or part of well-

---

ed., tr. Claire Jacobson and Brooke Grundfest Schoepf (New York: Basic Books, 1963); Elli Köngas Maranda and Pierre Maranda, eds., *Structural Analysis of Oral Tradition* (Philadelphia: University of Pennsylvania Press, 1971). See also *Structural Models in Folklore and Transformational Essays* (The Hague: Mouton, 1971); Ladislav Matejka and Krystyna Pomorska, eds., *Readings in Russian Poetics: Formalist and Structuralist Views* (Cambridge, Mass.: MIT Press, 1971); Vladimir Propp, *Morphology of the Folktale*, rev. ed., tr. Laurence Scott (Austin: University of Texas Press, 1969); Tzvetan Todorov, *Grammaire du Décaméron* (Paris: Editions du Seuil, 1969); Tzvetan Todorov, *Poétique* (Paris: Editions du Seuil, 1968); and Tzvetan Todorov, *Théories du Symbole* (Paris: Editions du Seuil, 1977). See also Guido Ferrari, *Per una semiotica del folklore* (Torino: G. Giappichelli Editore, 1978). There are also a number of "applied" studies which I have found interesting. See, for instance, Paul Bouissac, *Circus and Culture: A Semiotic Approach* (Bloomington: Indiana University Press, 1976); and Will Wright, *Sixguns and Society: A Structural Study of the Western* (Berkeley: University of California Press, 1968).

known traditions, especially certain African or South American Indian oral traditions, which may not fit the normal scheme.

One can discern a tendency within the *cordel* tradition to "correct" certain stories which do not fit the customary pattern. Thus, it is likely that José Bernardo da Silva rewrote Leandro Gomes de Barros' *The Mysterious Bull* as *The Story of the Sorcerer Bull and the Mysterious Horse* not only because the former, which contains a number of pieces of indigenous legends, sold well but also because its uncharacteristic ambiguity bothered the poet. Unlike Leandro who tells a strange tale of an unearthly being who is neither good nor bad in the usual *cordel* sense, Zé Bernardo relegates the bull to a supporting role in a far more typical story of a brave cowman who succeeds in marrying the lovely daughter of a powerful rancher.[5]

Zé Bernardo's reworking, like the great majority of *folhetos*, reveals six clearly discernible steps. Within this framework, certain sequences or "narrative chains" may be repeated, and one or more steps may be implicit.[6] All six steps, however, are necessary to an understanding of most *cordel* stories, and each supports the underlying notion of a two-way, two-member pact.

In broadest terms, the *folheto* begins by depicting a state of (1) *harmony*, which reflects the fulfillment of moral and material obligations implied by this agreement. In most cases, the pact is between social unequals, though there is one group of stories in which the two partners are evenly matched. Inevitably, this initial harmony is threatened when one member of the pact (who may be a community as well as an individual) faces a (2) *test*, which represents not only a trial of his own character but of the power and legitimacy of the pact itself. His (3) *response*, be it right or wrong, triggers a (4) *counterresponse* by the other member, and the body of the text normally reveals a series of these back-and-forth actions, which reach a climax in the moment of (5) *judgment* when right is rewarded and wrong punished. The story then closes with a (6) *reaffirmation* of the initial pact. Although different kinds of stories obey slightly different rhythms of development, almost all progress from equilibrium through imbalance back to equilibrium in accord with the following scheme:

5. Leandro Gomes de Barros, *O Boi Misterioso* (Juazeiro do Norte: Tipografia São Francisco, 1976), and José Bernardo da Silva, *História do Boi Mandingueiro e o Cavalo Misterioso*, 2 vols. (Juazeiro do Norte: Tipógrafia São Francisco, 1951). Both works are available in *Literatura Popular em Verso: Antologia*, I (Rio de Janeiro: Fundação Casa de Rui Barbosa/MEC, 1973) (hereafter cited as *Antologia*). For a comparative discussion of these two *folhetos*, see Braulio do Nascimento, "O ciclo do boi," in *Literatura Popular em Verso: Estudos* (Rio de Janeiro: Fundação Casa de Rui Barbosa/MEC, 1973), pp. 184–232.

6. The term *narrative chain* is Bremond's. It refers to two or more steps which are normally associated, one necessarily implying the presence of the other(s). See his discussion of the work of Propp in his *Logique du récit*, pp. 11–47.

1	2	3	4	5	6

pact⟶ test ⟶ response ⟩ counterresponse ⟩judgment ⟩pact reasserted

The meaning of each of the six steps within a given story varies somewhat depending on the nature of the pact to be tested, making it useful to
introduce four variations that are based on the identity of the participants
in the pact.[7] The first two variations group themselves according to
whether or not the central two-member pact involves a divine agent. These
two groups are then divided according to whether or not the partner being
tested (always a human being) gives the right or wrong response. For the
sake of convenience, I will abbreviate these four categories as *HR* (two
human participants, both give right response), *HW* (two human participants, one gives wrong response), *DR* (one divine and one human participant, human gives right response), and *DW* (one divine and one human
participant, human gives wrong response). It is important to note that not
all the participants in these crucial pacts are necessarily actors in the story.
Though the underlying agreement always includes a human (or animal)
protagonist, the other partner to the contract may be a divine force who
usually does not function as an actual character. (God is never portrayed;

Figure 1: Participants in Pact

Human/Human	Divine/Human
HR	*DR*
HW	*DW*

7. I first became aware that a fairly rigid underlying structure must exist within *cordel*
stories when I was talking with popular poet Apolônio Alves dos Santos (Rio de Janeiro,
October 18, 1977). When I asked him why he had included a stanza about the high cost of
living in a *folheto* about the march of progress, he replied, "You know, you're right! Those
verses don't belong there. But I'll move them around to the beginning and that way the end
will come out right."

Jesus, Mary, and the saints are often actors.) Thus, the pact underlying one story may involve two poet-singers or two men (one rich, one poor), who are also its protagonists; whereas the *actors* in another story may be a poor young man, his mother, an evil king, a lovely princess, and a magic horse while the *members of the pact to be tested* are the young man and God. (See Figure 1.) A more specific breakdown of the six-step pattern, which will be discussed point by point, is outlined in Figure 2.

These four variations are not entirely objective since while the strong dualistic vision characterizing the *folheto* makes it fairly easy to distinguish between "right" and "wrong" responses, it is somewhat harder to determine the severity of individual errors. Then, too, the hierarchy in which "human" and "divine" actors function forms a continuum rather than a true divide. This means that it is not always clear when, say, a particular king is acting as an individual mortal and when he must be seen as a divine representative. (Naturally, there are instances in which he may be both.) Finally, these categories are not necessarily exclusive. One can, for example, on occasion find a *DR* tale within a *HW* frame. Nevertheless, if not entirely airtight, these categories make the basic six-step pattern both clearer and easier to apply to specific cases.

Before discussing each of these categories, I want to touch briefly on the question of the *cordel*'s originality. Clearly, the *folheto*'s language and many of its themes and actors are thoroughly Brazilian. The origin of its underlying structure is, however, less clear. Is the six-step scheme apparent in the *cordel*'s chapbook forebears, or is it particular to these Northeastern stories on a string?

A glance over a wide range of pamphlet literature from various times and countries confirms the presence of a general trial-response pattern, which may or may not reveal exactly six steps. This structure is apparent in various stories from not only the Iberian peninsula but also from France, Germany, and Great Britain. As in the case of Brazil, narratives more than prayers, horoscopes, or lyric poems are apt to reveal this pattern, which is pronounced enough to set the *cordel* firmly within a European chapbook tradition.

And yet while the seeds of the Brazilian six-step sequence are clearly present in the *folheto*'s literary forebears, the design of these European stories tends to be less uniform. Many tales contain a series of elements that lend themselves better to a kind of multifunction-oriented analysis than a more streamlined sequence composed of a half-dozen quite specific steps. Even in those Portuguese stories in verse that reappear in the Brazilian *folheto* (*The Gambler Soldier*, *John of Calais*, etc.) the critical notion of a two-partner pact is definitely less distinct. Unlike the Brazilian *folheto* where the spotlight tends to remain on a single individual who undergoes a set of trials, these stories are more apt to shift focus. For

Figure 2: Variations on the Six-Step Pattern

	HR	HW	DR	DW
1 Pact	A and B where both are equals—initial harmony (A and B are protagonists *and* principal members of pact)	A and B where A is socially inferior to B—implicit harmony (A and B are protagonists *and* principal members of pact)	A and B where A is a human being with obligations to God, which B (usually human) will test—initial harmony reflecting fulfillment of obligations (A and B are protagonists but pact is between A and God)	Implicit harmony—A is a human being with obligations to God, which will be tested by a person (B) or difficult situation (A is protagonist, pact is between him and God)
2 Test	A tests B	A tests B after B provokes A	A faced with death: (1) of a friend or relative or (2) threat of death to himself	A faced with temptation to break terms of pact
3 Response	B responds correctly, thereby testing A	B shows lack of judgment, unsuitable behavior in response to test	A displays *firmeza* (right response)	A succumbs to temptation, displays *falsidade* (wrong response)
4 Counter-response	A responds correctly, thereby testing B	A "punishes" B, usually through ridicule	Divine intervention, which may be (1) direct or (2) indirect, in either case including help from the community either (a) en masse or (b) through representative(s)	Warning by divine and human agents followed by further infractions on terms of initial pact
5 Judgment	Contest results in draw, implying mutual satisfaction	B's attempt to strike back triggers material loss and/or humiliation	(1) Good rewarded in moral and material terms (hero and community together) and (2) evil punished	Punishment according to gravity of error: (1) material loss/humiliation or (2) death
6 Pact Reasserted	A and B go their respective ways as equals, making community content—harmony	B reduced in status, harmony restored	Harmony restored, A and community emerge better off than before thanks to fulfilled obligations	Harmony restored when A is (1) reinstated into social order in chastened state or (2) removed from social order (banishment or death)

instance, the Brazilian version of *The Princess Magalona* presents the story primarily from the viewpoint of the hero, but the Portuguese original jumps from Magalona to her husband Pierre and back.[8]

Historical reasons account in part for the European chapbooks' more diffuse nature. Particularly in the sixteenth and seventeenth centuries, these pamphlets were above all a physical form, a convenient and novel catchall for miscellaneous material. As already mentioned, chapbook printers in sixteenth-century Spain and Portugal turned out not only a mixture of new and traditional ballads but also dabbled in a wide variety of other literary genres. As a number of writers in various countries have demonstrated, it is possible to extract a more or less comprehensive worldview from this heterogeneous material. Nevertheless, it is hard to think of these early chapbooks as representatives of an autonomous tradition.

It is also difficult if not impossible to find a single structural pattern that will account for all chapbooks in any given country let alone Europe as a whole. Thus, although the six-step pattern is not unique to the Northeast, its clarity and consistent application within the Brazilian *folheto* set apart this form of chapbook literature from all others. The *cordel*'s identity as poetry, its obvious debt to a particular group of readily identifiable popular poets, its relatively late appearance, and its specific geographic context help explain in part this distinguishing consistency.

From the start, the *folheto*'s all but exclusive dependence upon one particular verse form disposed it toward a tighter, more concentrated framework than most nonverse narratives. If one looks, for example, at European chapbooks in prose, it is easy to find cases in which the writer, much like the medieval preacher, has simply adapted a preexisting story through minimal additions and subtractions, tacking on a final moral. Since, however, the *cordel* writer is obligated to "translate" his material into poetry, he is disposed from the beginning to do a great deal more rewriting, with the result that his stories are more apt to have an all-of-one-piece air. There is no source which will escape this filtering process because there is nothing, except for an existing Brazilian *folheto*, which the author can copy word for word. If the *cordel* resembles Portuguese chapbooks more than other European chapbooks, this is not only because of similarities in language but, in many cases, similarities in form since a number of these booklets—though not all of them—are in verse.

Also, as already suggested, Brazilian *folhetos* were most probably "invented" by an already existing group of semiprofessional singer-poets thoroughly steeped in a particular verse tradition. These individuals could

---

8. For one Portuguese and one Brazilian version of the Princess Magalona story (both in verse), see Luís da Câmara Cascudo, *Vaqueiros e cantadores* (Porto Alegre: Livraria do Globo, 1939), pp. 35–53.

apply elements from their own poet-singer background to a mature chapbook form that had been evolving for four centuries. The underlying presence of the Northeastern *peleja* in these Brazilian stories gives them a distinctive back-and-forth, test-contest motion, which is not as marked in similar European tales. The Brazilian version of the Donzela Teodora story is, for instance, a far more balanced exchange than the Portuguese original, which is essentially a monologue interspersed with questions.[9]

Finally, the circumscribed and relatively static context in which the *folheto* developed did much to assure its coherent character. Whereas in Europe the chapbook could be found in countries with different languages, literary traditions, and historical circumstances, for most of its short life the Brazilian *cordel* has been associated with a specific geographical and social setting. In addition, European chapbooks were not a strictly urban phenomenon. Nevertheless, their printers and writers, as well as many of their customers, lived in major cities. Limited by a lack of money and education, these individuals were still affected by the diverse influences that these centers attracted.

The situation of the Brazilian *cordel* is different. Even though the *folheto* has always been dependent on regional capitals as centers of production and distribution, these cities could not be considered true centers of national, let alone international, culture when the *folheto* emerged around the turn of this century. Though it incorporated outside influences, the wider context upon which its writers could draw was still severely limited. Furthermore, the popular poet's primary support has always come from the countryside, which, until after World War II, remained largely impervious to change. Only now in the latter part of the twentieth century, as the *folheto*'s public undergoes profound changes, is a truly urban *cordel* beginning to emerge within Brazil.

HR Tales (two human participants, both give right response)

The first group of *folhetos* within the six-step framework features two nondivine participants, who may be either human beings or animals with human characteristics. Virtually all *HR* tales may be plotted as shown in Figure 2 on page 62. The overwhelming majority of stories in this *HR* category involve a poetic contest or *peleja*. Intimately associated with the Northeast, where each singer typically sang the glories of the community

9. Compare the Brazilian with the Iberian versions of the Donzela Teodora story in Luís da Câmara Cascudo, *Cinco livros do povo* (Rio de Janeiro: José Olympio, 1953), pp. 35–143.

that he represented, the *peleja* form has also found success within the new Southern *cordel*.

Cordel pelejas draw heavily upon the oral tradition. Despite the impression created by early folklorists such as Leonardo Mota, however, these *folhetos* are literary compositions rather than transcriptions of actual oral performances. In them, two more or less evenly matched competitors seek to outdo each other in questions of objective knowledge and verbal skill. Examples of *HR* tales include the classic encounters between Leandro Gomes de Barros and Francisco das Chagas Batista, Bernardo Walnut Tree and Black Lemon, João Martins de Ataíde and the Southerner called Bald Raimundo, and Windstorm and Blue Stone.[10]

Folhetos, like live, on-the-spot exchanges, begin when one partner poses a question or makes an assertion that the other must counter in a similar manner. Form and content are all but indistinguishable in these contests since the "rightness" of the response depends in large part on how it is expressed.[11] If both participants live up to their reputations (and the audience's expectations), the bout will end in a draw. If this draw is not explicitly declared, the exchange tends to terminate rather abruptly on the bottom of the final (usually eighth) page. If, however, the draw is explicit, the two contestants will acknowledge each other's worth, as in the following passages.

10. Those stories which are asterisked may be found in the Casa de Rui Barbosa anthology (*Antologia*, I), from which I have taken many of my examples in this and the following chapters. I have done this in order to provide the reader with a number of well-known examples as useful comparison with the less-known, contemporary *folhetos* I discuss in Chapters 4, 5, and 6. I have also chosen this approach because the anthology is readily available, making these stories more accessible than other *folhetos* found only in their own editions. The Portuguese titles of works cited in English in the text will be given in footnotes, which will include the author (which refers to the edition at hand) and, where available, the date and place of publication as well as the relevant pages in the Casa de Rui Barbosa anthology, when the story appears there. In all cases I have given the edition of the *folheto* which I myself have used, and the reader should bear in mind that there may be dozens of other editions in which the text may or may not be identical. Unless otherwise specified, the publisher of a *folheto* printed in Recife is João Martins de Ataíde, and in Juazeiro do Norte, José Bernardo da Silva. It is important to note that there may be many versions as well as prints of a given text. ("Author" refers to the version at hand.) For the *HR* tales just cited, see Leandro Gomes de Barros: **O Encontro de Leandro Gomes com Chagas Batista* (Recife, n.d.), *Antologia*, pp. 279–81; João Martins de Ataíde: *Peleja de Bernardo Nogueira e o Preto Limão* (Juazeiro do Norte, 1976), and *Peleja de João Athayde e Raimundo Pelado do Sul* (Juazeiro do Norte, 1974); and José Bernardo da Silva: *Peleja de Ventania com Pedra Azul* (Juazeiro do Norte, n.d.).

11. See Manuel Diégues Júnior, "A poesia dos cantadores do nordeste," in *Estudos e ensaios folclóricos em homenagem a Renato Almeida* (Rio de Janeiro: Ministério das Relações Exteriores, 1960), pp. 621–37; and Manuel Diégues Júnior, "Poetas que nascem feitos," *Américas*, 10 (1958): 29–32.

C. *Eu também não quero mais*	C. "I too want no more.
que a hora está chegada	The hour to stop has arrived.
pois cantei a noite toda	My throat is tired.
minha guela está cansada	I have sung all night
nem dei e nem apanhei	without striking or being struck,
está ou não consolada.	and now I want to know if you
	are satisfied."
L. *Estou muito satisfeita*	L. "I am very satisfied,"
respondeu a Lavandeira	responded Lavandeira.
nunca pensei que você	"I never thought that you
cantasse dessa maneira	would sing as well as you did,
mas agora conheci	but now I see that you
que sua volta é madeira.	are very skilled indeed."[12]

It may seem somewhat odd to speak of the poetic contest as a pact. Nevertheless, even though the obligations involved here are of a more limited linguistic nature rather than of a moral or social one, these exchanges stand apart from normal everyday activities. As will become still clearer in the concluding chapter, this contest represents a covenant or recognized agreement between two persons to perform (as well as to refrain from performing) in a certain manner. If one thinks about the rationale for verse dueling in general—the channeling of aggression into play and art—the implications of such behavior for the wider community become more obvious.[13] Each participant is bound by mutually accepted rules that constitute a definition of the tradition proper. Since such contests demand the presence of an audience, who serves as judge, these terms are socially sanctioned and collectively enforced. Both fictional and flesh-and-blood singers respect conventions involving not only style but content. Despite the frequent assertion that "anything goes" in these contests, certain subjects such as history, geography, current events, the exploits of well-known individuals, and various forms of lore definitely prevail.[14] Furthermore, both partners rely on formulaic questions and answers.

---

12. Caetano Cosme da Silva, *Peleja Entre Caetano Cosme da Silva e Maria Lavandeira* (Recife: João José da Silva, n.d.).

13. The sparring origins of the poetic contest are explained in J. Wickersham Crawford, "*Echarse Pullas*: A Popular Form of *Tenzone*," *Romanic Review*, 6 (1915): 150–64. For a discussion of two quite different sorts of contemporary verbal dueling, see Alan Dundes, Jerry W. Leach, and Bora Ozkök, "The Strategy of Turkish Boys' Verbal Dueling Rhymes," *Journal of American Folklore*, 83 (1970): 325–49; and Roger D. Abrahams, "Playing the Dozens," *Journal of American Folklore*, 75 (1962): 209–20.

14. A look over the standard collections (Chagas Batista, Câmara Cascudo, Coutinho Filho, Mota) reveals a certain sameness. As in the *cordel*, the idea is not so much invention but perfection of an existing form. See Dell Hymes, "Breakthrough into Performance," in *Folklore: Performance and Communication*, ed. Dan Ben-Amos and Kenneth S. Goldstein (The Hague: Mouton, 1975), pp. 11–74.

These are not only verses that the singer has prepared beforehand and then slips in as though spontaneously (this trick is called "stringing one's hammock"—*armar a rede*) but responses which he shapes under pressure in accord with familiar rules.

Furthermore, while insults are the very stuff of poetic contests, they are carefully ritualized. Thus, the singer may refer to his opponent as "ignorant" and "ugly" so long as the words rhyme. He may make jibes about his race or supposed lack of sexual prowess ("He has no beard.") if these are sufficiently humorous. He is not, however, going to question his partner's integrity or call his wife or mother a whore if he does not want the verbal parry to turn into a fist fight. The fact that a number of on-the-spot poetic contests do indeed turn violent reaffirms the existence of bounds that some contestants may forget or overstep. This sort of overstepping is, to be sure, unlikely in a *cordel peleja* where a single author controls each step of the exchange by putting his own words into each contestant's mouth.

HR cordel stories seldom reveal story lines, typically skipping like live contests from one topic to another. For this reason, this category is the least diverse of the four variations. And yet despite the structural monotony of these stories (the response-counterresponse, response-counterresponse in terms of the six-step pattern) and their topical and local nature, which often make them of scant interest to a reader not born within the tradition, these *HR* stories are important, for the *HR* scheme's pendulum-like test-response, test-response motion characterizes the *cordel* as a whole.

The back-and-forth motion most apparent in *HR* tales, for instance, is readily visible in those adventure stories that today account for over a third of *cordel* sales. Although a more natural form of dialogue replaces direct back-and-forth exchanges in these stories that may feature a variety of actors, many of these tales are nothing less than a two-way contest. In fact, many titles involving two names (for example, *The Perverse Colonel Sparrowhawk and the Suffering Slave*) could actually be prefaced with *Peleja Between.* . . . Alternating stanzas could be labeled with the competitors' initials, thus producing the question-answer format.

HW Tales (two human participants, one gives wrong response)

As any *cordel* reader knows, fictional *pelejas*, like real ones, do not always end in a draw. If one competitor clearly outshines the other, the *folheto* becomes a human, wrong response (*HW*) tale. This *HW* category includes most stories that have traditionally been labeled "social satire":

accounts of bumpkins, rogue or trickster tales, animal fables, and battles between peddlers and tax collectors or rum guzzlers and Protestants. Most "obscene" or "pornographic" *folhetos* also fit this *HW* framework. Examples of *HW cordel* stories include *The Exploits of Peter Evil-Arts*, *The Life and Legacy of the Rogue Cancão de Fogo*, *The Goings-On Between the Dog and the Cat*, *The Wedding of Chico Tingolé and Maria Puff-of-Smoke*, *The Poor Man and the Ambitious Rich Man*, *Dr. Root and the Miraculous Herbs*, *Dr. Diarrhea*, and *The Encounter Between the Bumpkin Selling Roll Tobacco and the Old Woman Selling Leaf Tobacco*.[15] These *HW* stories can be summarized as in Figure 2 on page 62.

Stories of the *HW* variety focus the reader's attention on the social order, highlighting abuses of power with an eye toward punishment and reform. In such tales, the socially inferior member of an implicit pact tests his social superior. *A* may either be the community or, more frequently, one of its representatives whereas *B* is a member of a somewhat higher social class. In the course of the story, *A* typically puts *B* in a situation in which he (*B*) displays greed, inattention, pride, or one or more other petty sins, for which the inevitable penalty is humiliation and/or material loss.

Significantly, in those poetic contests that fall into this category, the winner is normally the underdog. The loser, who has initially lorded it over him, is forced to hide his head in shame in typical "world-upside-down" fashion. Thus, in the well-known *peleja* between Laurindo Cat and Marcolino Green Snake, Laurindo initially gobbles down a whole chicken while Marcolino nibbles at a crust of bread. However, the lowly challenger emerges as the community's new favorite, forcing the once-arrogant incumbent to throw away his guitar forever in disgrace.[16]

Poet and public clearly enjoy these reversals, chortling in delight at the outrages committed, for example, by a Dr. Diarrhea. These stories, however, carefully temper their explicit criticism of the status quo. Those per-

15. Francisco Sales Areda, *As Prezepadas de Pedro Malazarte* (Recife: João José da Silva, n.d.); Leandro Gomes de Barros, *A Vida de Cancão de Fogo e o seu Testamento*, 2 vols. (Juazeiro do Norte, 1975), *Antologia*, pp. 420–56; José Pacheco, *Intriga do Cachorro e o Gato* (n.p., n.d.), *Antologia*, pp. 205–09; João Ferreira Lima, *O Casamento de Chico Tingolé com Maria Fumaça* (Juazeiro do Norte, 1976); Apolônio Alves dos Santos, *O Compadre Pobre e o Rico Ambicioso* (Guarabira: José Alves Pontes, 1973); Delarme Monteiro, *Dr. Raiz e suas Ervas Milagrosas* (Recife, Universidade Federal de Pernambuco, n.d.); *Dr. Caganeira* (n.p., n.d.); and João Parafuso (José Costa Leite), *O Encontro da Velha que Vendia Tabaco com o Matuto que Vendia Fumo* (n.p., n.d.).

16. João Martins de Ataide, *Peleja entre Laurindo Gato e Marcolino Cobra Verde* (Juazeiro do Norte, 1975). For a series of discussions of reversals in literature and other symbolic manifestations, see *The Reversible World: Symbolic Inversion in Art and Society*, ed. Barbara A. Babcock (Ithaca: Cornell University Press, 1978). Of particular interest to this study is David Kunzle, "World Upside Down: The Iconography of a European Broadsheet Type," in Babcock, *The Reversible World*, pp. 39–94.

sons singled out for punishment are never the most powerful members of society but rather merchants, petty officials, and simple priests. Thus, the terrible "doctor" only makes a mess before the doors of shameless sweet-hearts, corrupt policemen, and lazy clerics, ignoring plantation owners, bank presidents, and local politicians.

Because these *folhetos* deal with relatively minor transgressions of the social order, death is seldom present. This means that these, like *HR* tales, reveal considerable repetition on a structural level, seldom building up to that climactic ending found in *DR* and *DW* stories. The typical *HW* sequence is, however, somewhat more complex than the simple pendular movement that characterizes the evenly matched *peleja*. Tales belonging to this category generally display four steps: test, response, counterresponse, and judgment—which may be repeated anywhere from three to a dozen times. Below is outlined a representative *HW* story. The numbers correspond to those in the six-step pattern.

The Exploits of John Cricket by João Martins de Ataíde

2. Priest asks for water, trickster offers wine.   Test.

3. Priest accepts wine and gets drunk.   (Wrong) response.

4. Trickster informs priest that "water" is urine.   Counterresponse.

5. Priest is furious but can do nothing.   Judgment (humiliation).

then:

2. Priest is hearing confession; trickster arrives to confess.   Test.

3. Priest recognizes him and orders him to stand.   (Wrong) response.

4. Trickster sets a lizard on priest's side of the box.   Counterresponse.

5. Lizard crawls up priest's leg.   Judgment (humiliation, physical discomfort).

An apparent exception to this pattern of inferior-tests-superior occurs in contemporary *folhetos* about bumpkins (*matutos*). According to the six-step scheme, these countrymen should win, but they almost always lose. Nevertheless, these tales do not represent an exception so much as a new development related to changing socioeconomic conditions. Thus, an examination of the earliest *folhetos*, such as Leandro Gomes de Barros' *Discussion Between a Bumpkin and a City Dweller*, reveals that originally the bumpkin won. Only as time goes on does the city dweller emerge victorious. Furthermore, many of those stories written two or three decades later permit quite separate readings. In *Joe Bumpkin in the Big City*, most probably by Francisco Firmino de Paula, for instance, the countryman is ostensibly defeated even though it is possible to see him as an affirmation of a saner way of life.[17] Thus, a breakdown of the two *folhetos'* narrative structure reveals a change in roles rather than the basic drama.

Discussion Between a Bumpkin and a City Dweller
by Leandro Gomes de Barros

1. (Implied harmony).	Pact.
2. Countryman and city dweller bid on a cheese at holiday fair.	Test.
3. City dweller insults countryman; demands cheese as recognition of superior status.	(Wrong) response.
4. Countryman outbids him; takes cheese.	Counterresponse.
5. City dweller protests; protest is turned against him.	Judgment (humiliation).
6. Countryman exits victorious, much acclaimed and admired.	Pact reasserted.

Joe Bumpkin in the Big City
by Francisco Firmino de Paula

1. (Implied harmony) countryman in country, city dweller in city.	Pact.
2. Joe buys second-class ticket for city; sits in first-class section.	Test.
3. Conductor orders Joe to move.	Response.
4. Joe refuses in great anger.	Counterresponse.
5. Conductor makes Joe pay the difference: other passengers laugh.	Judgment (material loss, humiliation).
6. (Joe finally returns to countryside).	Pact reasserted.

17. Francisco Firmino de Paula(?), *Zé Matuto na Praça* (n.p., n.d.). For a fuller discus-

DR Tales (one divine, one human participant, human gives right response)

Despite the fact that traditional classification schemes routinely treat *pelejas* as an autonomous cycle, these contests may be not only *HR* or *HW* but also *DR* tales. As we have seen, if the competitors are flesh-and-blood singers debating a series of facts or simply asserting their personal superiority ("I'm smarter and stronger than you are, and I come from a much better part of the country"), the contest will end in either (a) a draw, in which each participant successfully tests and is tested, in which case the story is an *HR* tale; or (b) a victory for the contender, who proves himself more knowledgeable or articulate, in which case the *folheto* belongs to the *HW* group (two humans, one gives wrong response).

If, however, the debate hinges on a moral or theological problem, it leaves the human arena to become a *DR* tale. As there can only be one correct response to spiritual questions in the world of the *folheto*, the human protagonist becomes a representative of right (*firmeza*); any opponent(s) are representatives of wrong (*falsidade*).

Firmeza, the noun form of the adjective meaning "firm" or "enduring," has a variety of dictionary definitions: fortitude, stability, constancy, steadfastness. It may be translated loosely as "character." *Falsidade*, its opposite, suggests hypocrisy, deceit, slander, and double-dealing. A person who embodies *firmeza* will be solid and centered; one characterized by *falsidade* will be hollow, light, unbalanced, and subject to change. Not only the protagonist but all actors in a given story represent either one side or the other, and the poet is obliged to account for all participants, whether human, superhuman, or animal, in the final stanza. In tales of virtue triumphant, the representative of *firmeza* will necessarily triumph in accord with the *DR* scheme in Figure 2 on page 62.

In some *DR* poetic contests, both singers are human beings. One, however, may be a Catholic ("right"), the other a Protestant ("wrong"). One may insist that all pleasures are fleeting ("right"), the other that the only way to live is to eat, drink, and be merry ("wrong"). In other contests, the human protagonist's opponent may be a supernatural force such as a representative of the devil or the devil himself, as in the classic exchanges between *Francisco Sales Areda and the Black Man Known as "Vision"* and *Manuel River and the Devil*.[18] In either case, the ever-present audi-

---

sion of this and other "hillbilly" *folhetos*, see Candace Slater, "Joe Bumpkin in the Wilds of Rio de Janeiro," *Journal of Latin American Lore* 6 (1980): 5–53.

18. Francisco Sales Areda, *A Malassombrada Peleja de Francisco Sales Areda com o "Negro Visão"* (n.p., n.d.), *Antologia*, pp. 283–92; Leandro Gomes de Barros, *Peleja de Manuel Riachão com o Diabo* (Juazeiro do Norte, 1955), *Antologia*, pp. 293–302.

ence serves both as the "right" singer's ally and the contest's final judge.

While there are classic stories in each of the four categories or variations of the six-step pattern, the greatest number of perennial favorites comes from this *DR* group. Such all-time favorites as *The Mysterious Peacock*, *The Story of the Empress Porcina*, *The Story of Mariquinha and José de Souza Leão*, *Green Coconut and Watermelon*, *The Sufferings of Genoveva*, *The Assassin of Honor or the Madwoman in the Garden*, and *A Night of Love* are only a few of the best known.[19] Most *folhetos* involving trials known as "sufferings" or "martyrdoms," love stories, and adventure tales fall into the *DR* category. So do segments of some trickster tales and a number of news stories. Strange as it may seem, the *folheto* version of the trial of Sacco and Vanzetti is a *DR* story because of the poet's insistence that the men he sees as innocent victims find justice in heaven.[20]

It is important to note that in *DR* stories, unlike *HR* and *HW* tales, the parties to the underlying pact are no longer the tale's principal characters. While the immediate contest or drama is between the virtuous man or woman and his opponents, the pact or principle that the story seeks to illustrate is between the human actor and God. Thus, in *DR* tales, the human member of the human-divine partnership is invariably the one to stand trial. Often these *folhetos* will include a *DW* subplot centering about a tester or tempter who makes the protagonist suffer unjustly, thereby giving him the chance to prove his mettle. The hero is then rewarded and the culprit punished.

The initial harmony often merely implied in *HR* and *HW* stories tends to be actively depicted in *DR folhetos*. Tales often begin with verbal portraits of a beautiful young princess aiding the sick and crippled, a king counseling his ministers, a humble but kindhearted fisherman sharing a single loaf of bread with an animal in distress. This initial balance is then threatened by a test or series of tests. Unlike *HR* and *HW* tales in which this test endangers the individual's social or economic status, *DR* stories almost always involve the threat of death. Generally either (1) a person or persons related to the protagonist die, or (2) the protagonist finds himself in mortal danger when, say, the king threatens to chop off his head if he does not answer a series of riddles correctly.

19. João Melquíades Ferreira, *Romance do Pavão Misterioso* (Juazeiro do Norte, 1951), *Antologia*, pp. 57–74; Francisco das Chagas Batista, *História da Imperatriz Porcina* (Recife, 1946), *Antologia*, pp. 101–36; João Ferreira de Lima, *História de Mariquinha e José de Souza Leão* (Juazeiro do Norte, 1949), *Antologia*, pp. 160–76; José Camelo de Melo Resende, *Coco Verde e Melancia* (Juazeiro do Norte, 1976); Leandro Gomes de Barros, *Os Martírios de Genoveva* (Recife, 1943), *Antologia*, pp. 29–56; Caetano Cosme da Silva, *O Assassino da Honra ou a Louca do Jardim* (Recife: João José da Silva, n.d.); João Martins de Ataíde, *Uma Noite de Amor* (Juazeiro do Norte, 1974).

20. João Martins de Ataíde, *Sacco e Vanzetti aos Olhos do Mundo* (Recife, n.d.), *Antologia*, pp. 177–185.

The imminence of death in these stories underscores the seriousness of the pact being tested. The threats uttered by *folheto* kings ("Bring me a hair of Genie X's head or I'll throw you into a man-sized kettle.") are purposely exaggerated in order to emphasize the gravity of the principles on trial. Since the *cordel* places great stress on the question of whether or not an individual keeps his end of the bargain, these symbolic earthly tests become a matter of life and death.[21]

The protagonist meets these challenges correctly by displaying loyalty and good character (*firmeza*) in one of various ways. He or she may, for instance, protect a social inferior or animal threatened with physical harm. A hero may stand up to a powerful but unreasonable father who refuses to part with his lovely daughter. A heroine may endure all manner of physical hardship and exile rather than give in to the demands of a would-be seducer.

This correct response (or responses, since such tests are often multiple) eventually triggers divine intervention. This action may be direct (a voice from the sky, a celestial chariot, a flurry of bells) or indirect (help in the form of a talisman, talking horse, or other magic being or device; for example, the deer who protects a martyred queen and her child, the stalwart mare who directs the hero to pluck a radiant feather from a bird of fire). In either case, the protagonist almost always also receives additional help from the populace at large. If divine intervention is to be direct, the entire community prays for this help. If it is to be indirect, a representative of the group aids the protagonist by, for example, feeding or hiding him from pursuers, risking his own life by smuggling a letter past hostile guards, or hiding the hero instead of putting him to death as ordered.

As a result of this divine and to a lesser degree human assistance, the protagonist emerges triumphant. If there is a wrongdoer who has caused him to suffer, he or she is punished in a way determined by three primary factors. These are the protagonist's relationship to the culprit, the culprit's social identity, and, above all, the nature of the error.

Wrongs perpetrated in *folhetos* can be divided by and large into instances of pride (*orgulho*) and of deceit or betrayal (*falsidade*). These divisions correspond more or less to the Roman Catholic concepts of venial and mortal sins. The former is a transgression against the law of God that does not deprive the soul of divine grace either because it is a minor offense or because it was committed without full understanding of its gravity, the latter a grave and conscious offense that threatens the well-being of others and that may result in the sinner's spiritual as well as physical

---

21. The threat of death serves much the same function in a number of fairy tales, upon which, as already suggested, the *cordel* heavily relies. For a consideration of various psychological implications of such devices, see Bruno Bettelheim, *The Uses of Enchantment*, 2nd ed. (New York: Vintage Books, 1977).

death.[22] As already suggested, it is sometimes difficult to distinguish the gravity of wrongs in *cordel* stories in absolute terms. It is usually possible however, to determine the individual author's judgment of the offense by looking at its consequences. Whereas those displays of pride so common in *HW* tales are typically met with humiliation and/or material loss (for example, the miserly priest is forced to hand over his money to the rogue), *DR* and *DW* stories customarily portray offenses that merit punishment by death.

As lenience is not popular in the world of the *folheto*, those culprits who do get a second chance are either small-time sinners or persons related by blood or marriage to the protagonist, such as his father-in-law. Normally, these persons are of higher social status than the hero: kings, landlords, etc. They may also be the hero's mother or father. If a socially superior individual or a parent has committed a grave offense, he or she generally takes his or her own life, thereby sparing the protagonist the unpleasant (and socially dangerous) task of taking justice into his own hands. Every once in a while an exasperated princess will push a particularly detestable old king into a cauldron of boiling oil, but these actions represent exceptions rather than the norm.[23]

The reform or elimination of the hero's opponent(s) is part of his reward for living up to the terms of a spiritual agreement, whose terms, if not directly stated, are implicitly understood. He also receives other, material signs of favor that he shares not only with all deserving members of his family, whom he quickly summons, but with the community at large. If the populace helped the protagonist by calling for divine intervention, its members join him in celebrating his victory. If a particular representative of the community helped him, he or she is singled out for a handsome reward. Thus, the little old lady who risked punishment to carry a message from the hero to the imprisoned heroine in *Mariana and the Sea Captain* receives not only fourteen silk dresses but a large sum of money for her efforts.[24] Faithful horses trot in for praise, compassionate fishermen inherit palaces, and loyal servants are taken into their masters' family by marriage.

22. The *folhetos* are clearly imbued with a particular kind of Roman Catholicism. For two particularly interesting discussions, see Riolando Azzi, *O catolicismo popular no Brasil: Aspectos históricos* (Petrópolis: Vozes, 1978); and José Comblin, *Teologia da enxada: Uma experiência da Igreja no nordeste* (Petrópolis: Vozes, 1977). See also J. B. Libânio, *O problema da salvação no catolicismo do povo* (Petrópolis: Vozes, 1976); and for a historical background, Eduardo Hoornaert, *Formação do catolicismo brasileiro, 1550–1800: Ensaio de interpretação a partir dos oprimidos* (Petrópolis: Vozes, 1974).

23. See, for instance, Severino Borges Silva, *A Princesa Maricruz e o Cavaleiro do Ar* (Recife: João da Silva, n.d.).

24. See José Bernardo da Silva, *Mariana e o Capitão do Navio* (Juazeiro do Norte, 1951), *Antologia*, pp. 137–59.

Not all *folhetos* of the *DR* variety have a well-developed story line. *A Trip to São Saruê*, for instance, is essentially a cataloguing of rewards for good behavior (step 5, judgment, in terms of the six-step pattern) in an imaginary kingdom by a narrator who points out the inhabitants' various virtues (thereby implying steps 2, 3, and 4—test, response, counterresponse).[25] Most *DR* stories, however, have a definite plot. Though they may involve considerable repetition, each step tends to be distinct. Furthermore, these tales characteristically reach a climax, which occurs with the intrusion of death.

DW Tales (one divine, one human participant, human gives wrong response)

DW tales represent the mirror image of *DR folhetos*. Like them, they rely on an underlying pact whose members are no longer the story's principal actors but the protagonist (a human being) and God. In the case of *DW* tales, which may be either the subplots of *DR* tales or independent stories, the human being does not live up to his or her obligations, and punishment ensues. As in the judgment section of various *DR* tales, this punishment will vary according to the nature of the wrong response as well as to the quality and timing of the protagonist's repentance. The basic pattern in these stories is diagrammed as shown in Figure 2 on page 62. The pattern may be further broken down to reflect differences in the wrong response (pride or deceit) and in the wrongdoer's ensuing repentance, as shown in Figure 3.

Because these stories present the greatest number of options, the *DW* group is potentially the most complex variation of the six-step pattern. Most *folhetos* involving vengeance, disasters, and explicitly labeled moral examples (*exemplos*) are *DW* tales. So are various news accounts, *oh tempora! oh mores!* ("alas! alack!") stories, tales of hard times (*caréstia*), and prophecies. As with other types of stories, it is not necessary that every step be explicit although all six must be implied. Prophecies, for instance, tend to rely on a simple back-and-forth motion involving a warning (potential punishment, step 5), followed by an exhortation to reform (step 2) and definition of the right response (step 3). Specific examples of *DW* tales include *Ah! If the Past Could Return!*, *Padre Cícero's Dream*, *The Terrible Train Disaster of October 31, 1949—Seven Deaths and Nine Injuries*, *The Woman Who Asked the Devil for a Child*, and *The Plague of Grasshoppers in the Paraiban Interior*.[26]

25. Manuel Camilo dos Santos, *Viagem a São Saruê* (Campina Grande: Estrella da Poesia, 1956), *Antologia*, pp. 555–59.
26. Laurindo Gomes Maciel, *Ah! Se o Passado Voltasse!* (Juazeiro do Norte, 1948),

Figure 3: Options for the *DW* Variant

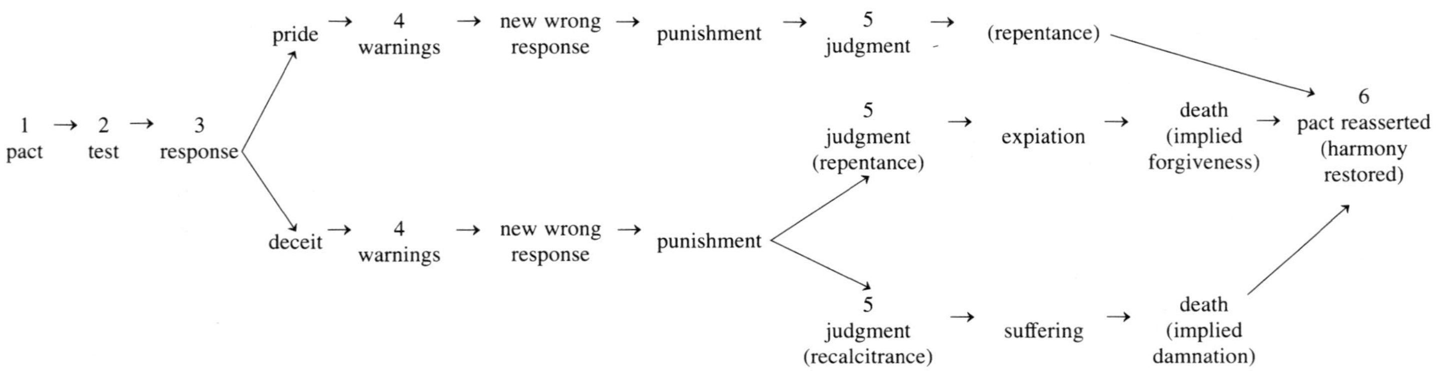

NOTE: The steps will vary somewhat depending on whether the human protagonist is guilty of pride or the more serious offense of deceit.

Though each tale depends on an initial state of equilibrium, this harmony may be implicit so that the *folheto* may start with an improper action on the part of the human protagonist. Generally, this first transgression will not be irremediable. The individual may talk back to a superior, think about taking a lover, doubt God's power aloud, or run about in tight pants or short skirts. The divine partner then warns the protagonist of the consequences of his or her actions through a community member or a divine messenger. For instance, in the story of *The Girl Who Turned into a Snake*, both a pilgrim and a parent chide the young woman for speaking irreverently of the saintly Padre Cícero.[27] She fails to heed these warnings, however, committing new and more serious misdeeds, each demanding a sterner response.

In retaliation for continued misbehavior, the divine partner normally prompts a reduction in the protagonist's status from rich to poor, human to animal, or normal to handicapped. In the snake story, for instance, the blasphemous girl declares that she will only believe in the backlands patriarch "when he punishes me, / makes my legs fall off, / my arms too, / gives me a pointed head and fangs / so that I run about as a snake / biting everyone I meet." She wakes up one morning to find herself transformed into a serpent. The divine partner may also cause the erring protagonist to suffer a terrible fright through the sudden appearance of a devil, witch, or monster. Terrible creatures drawn from oral tradition, such as werewolves and headless mules as well as new creations such as the hairy leg, a single limb that jumps about scaring the godless, are familiar figures in the pages of the *cordel*.[28]

Confronted with this more emphatic divine response, the human offender may either repent or continue in his or her mistaken ways. When the initial misdeed involves pride, repentance is the norm. Divine mercy is shown through (1) reversal of the transformation and restoration of a chastened actor to his or her rightful state and/or (2) removal of the fearful, extrahuman presence. If the protagonist has been reduced to an animal

---

Antologia, pp. 543–45; Antônio Batista, *O Sonho do Pe. Cícero Romão Batista* (Juazeiro do Norte, n.d.), *Antologia*, pp. 353–55; Moisés Matias de Moura, *Pavoroso Desastre de Trem no Dia 31 de Outubro de 1949—7 Mortos e 9 Feridos* (n.p., n.d.), *Antologia*, pp. 187–93; Galdino Silva, *A Mulher que Pediu um Filho ao Diabo* (Salvador: n.p., n.d.), *Antologia*, pp. 251–56; and Caetano Cosme da Silva, *A Praga de Gafanhoto no Sertão Paraibano* (n.p., n.d.), *Antologia*, pp. 243–49.

27. Severino Gonçalves, *A Moça que Virou Cobra* (n.p., n.d.), *Antologia*, pp. 232–38.

28. For three different authors' views of the hairy leg rumored to be hopping about Recife and its surrounding area, see José Costa Leite, *A Véia Debaixo da Cama e a Perna Cabeluda* (n.p., n.d.); Olegário Fernandes da Silva, *Exemplo da Perna Cabiluda: Os Cinais do Fim da Era* (Caruaru: Jardim da Poesia, n.d.); José Francisco Soares, *A Perna Cabeluda de Olinda* (Recife; n.p., 1976); and José Francisco Soares, *A Perna Cabeluda de Tiuma e São Lourenço* (Recife: n.p., n.d.).

state, he or she will be restored to human form. The repentant girl-snake will find herself once more a woman. The hairy leg will hop off into the depths from which it emerged. The individual or collective protagonist then expresses gratitude, relief, and the intention to live up to obligations implied by the pact. The poet as spokesman for the community abstracts and articulates the lesson, giving thanks to God for the restoration of order.

In cases involving sins of pride, the *folheto* may reveal a humorous vein. Thus, in *The Example of the Life of Caroline*, the repulsive if not exactly solemn "heroine" makes a terrified young man promise never to fritter away his time in dancing the samba again.[29] The fact that it is hard to regard the baby devil born to an overly eager mother or a single hairy leg jumping up and down the railroad tracks in an entirely serious manner emphasizes the propensity of these tales to teach through laughter.

Stories in which the protagonist displays deceit are not, however, funny. Should the individual offender endanger the community by ignoring his obligations, the consequences are sure to be serious. The punishment for foolish errors is always reversible, but the effects of breaking one's word, murder, adultery, or premarital sex are more drastic and enduring. Divine wrath takes the form of permanent transformation or a reduction in social status involving ostracism by the community. In *The Knight Roland*, for instance, Charlemagne banishes his beloved sister Berthe and orders her killed because she is pregnant and unwed.[30] Like most such protagonists, Berthe suffers physical and material loss as her health, wealth, and beauty vanish overnight.

After this initial rejection, the individual can either repent or continue to err. In the first case, he or she pleads for mercy, which is granted when God spares his or her life and offers forgiveness in return for protracted penance. The persons whom the individual has wronged typically become instruments of earthly justice as in *The Death of Alonso and the Vengeance of Marina*, where the wronged wife continues to hound her husband's murderer, or in *Evil in Exchange for Good*, where the aggrieved Rosa pretends that she has forgiven the once-dastardly Lino only to leave him in the lurch.[31]

Although the repentant protagonist suffers, he does not flinch before such treatment, which, after all, represents a second chance. Instead, he

29. João do Cristo Rei, *O Exemplo Interessante da Vida de Carolina (Juazeiro do Norte, n.d.), Antologia, pp. 267–71.

30. Antônio Eugénio da Silva, *O Cavaleiro Roldão (Campina Grande: Estrella da Poesia, 1958), Antologia, pp. 313–21.

31. Leandro Gomes de Barros, A Morte de Alonso e a Vingança de Marina (Juazeiro do Norte, 1976); and Barros' O Mal em Paga do Bem, ou Rosa e Lino de Alencar (Juazeiro do Norte, 1950).

continues to atone for past sins until the hour of his death. Typically, this death is seen as a release and is thus unlike other demises in which the individual proves recalcitrant. Prostitutes, for instance, whom the poet often portrays as hardened sinners, generally meet a truly gruesome end. Sick, penniless, and forced to accept alms from happily remarried husbands who do not recognize them, these figures repent too late.[32]

Regardless of whether the divine member of the pact plays an active role in *DW* as in *DR* stories, right triumphs because both parties to the underlying bargain keep their word. Thus, the real question around which these narratives develop is not the simple "Is good or evil stronger?" but "Will God honor his obligation to help the man who lives up to His expectations by being good?" and thus by extension "Is it worth it (to me, the reader) to continue to play by the rules when faced by overwhelming odds?" Needless to say, the answer implicit in the six-step pattern is, "Yes, God keeps his side of the bargain, so you be sure to keep yours." *DW* tales provide a built-in "or else" by demonstrating what happens when the human member fails to keep his side of the bargain. Thus, these stories speak not just to a metaphysical problem involving the properties of good and evil but to everyday situations demanding practical choices. The implications of this pattern will become clearer as we move on now to some specific examples. The next three chapters deal with three *folhetos*, which appear very different on the surface but which all reveal the same underlying *DR* scheme.

32. For a discussion of how folk and popular traditions serve to reinforce "correct" behavior, see Roger Abrahams, "Personal Power and Social Restraint, the Definition of Folklore" in *Towards New Perspectives in Folklore*, ed. Américo Paredes and Richard Bauman (Austin: University of Texas Press, 1971), pp. 16–30.

IV. *The King, the Dove, and the Sparrowhawk* by José de Souza Campos

Before discussing this *folheto* version of a nearly two-thousand-year-old Buddhist parable, it is worth saying a few words about the scope of this chapter and the next two chapters as a whole. Each analyzes a single tale by one of three unrelated authors, which is then reproduced with its English translation at the end of the discussion. Although the stories may appear very different on the surface, all three actually reveal the same basic (*DR*) plot.

I have purposely chosen representatives of this *DR* category because it has played such a central role in the history of the *folheto*. Furthermore, these stories, like many *DR* tales, imply a *DW* subplot, thereby permitting consideration of both variants within a single work. Since the *HR* category includes a relatively limited number of stories that are largely self-explanatory, and the HW scheme has been discussed elsewhere, these chapters will focus exclusively on the *DR/DW* scheme.[1]

The following case studies have three principal objectives: (1) to demonstrate how the six-step pattern outlined in the last chapter cuts across content-oriented cycles to unite seemingly disparate stories, (2) to provide specific instances of the creative process at work in the *folheto*, and (3) to suggest the range and nature of contemporary *literatura de cordel*. The stories selected for analysis are *The King, the Dove, and the Sparrowhawk* by José de Souza Campos, *The Monstrous Kidnapping of Serginho in Bom Jesus de Itabapoana* by Apolônio Alves dos Santos, and *Tereza Batista* by Rodolfo Coelho Cavalcante.[2] These choices, which are by and large representative not only of contemporary *cordel* but of the tradition in general, were based on a number of factors. All three *folhetos* are by living authors with whom it was possible to conduct lengthy, and, in two cases, multiple, interviews including specific questions about each text. All three authors are originally from the Northeast, and two are from the countryside; each

---

1. For a discussion of a *HW folheto*, see Candace Slater, "Joe Bumpkin in the Wilds of Rio de Janeiro, " *Journal of Latin American Lore* 6 (1980): 5–53.

2. José de Souza Campos, *O Rei, a Pomba e o Gavião* (Recife, 1978); Apolônio Alves dos Santos, *O Monstruoso Crime de Serginho em Bom Jesus de Itabapoana, Estado de Rio de Janeiro* (Guarabira: José Alves, 1977); Rodolfo Coelho Cavalcante, *Tereza Batista* (Salvador, 1973).

now lives in a major urban center in a different part of the country: Recife, Rio de Janeiro, and Salvador, respectively. Because the authors do not know each other personally and function in quite separate contexts, similarities in their works must reflect internal dictates of the *cordel* tradition.

As for the texts themselves, each of the three *folhetos* was written in the last decade. As one story has sixteen pages and the other two have eight pages, they reflect the present trend toward relative brevity. All rely on contemporary, written source material: a parable from a widely circulated almanac, a newspaper account, and a best-selling novel, respectively, all three of which I have summarized or reproduced. The availability of these sources makes it possible for the reader to pinpoint specific transformations in the passage from prose to a special kind of narrative poetry. The *folhetos* are apparently very different, one dealing with a Buddhist king, the second a recent local murder, the third a prostitute. Each, however, reveals the same *DR* variation of the basic six-step sequence.

In their reliance on the mass media and, in two cases, on essentially urban themes, the stories are typical of the majority of *folhetos* written today. However, the poets and their settings are quite different, and the range revealed here is representative of the *literatura de cordel*. Respectively, one writer works within a fairly traditional context, one is a Southern transplant, and one has long been an active organizer of his fellow poets and enjoys a personal relationship with various internationally known writers and artists. Nevertheless, despite disparities, which will become more obvious as the discussion progresses, all of these individuals can be considered genuinely popular writers who come from and continue to write for a quite specific segment of the population.

To be sure, in some ways these *folhetos* also stand out from the tradition as a whole. First, although popular poets have always drawn on written sources, whether chapbooks imported from Lisbon, the Bible, or novels by erudite authors, direct re-creation of a single text is not the norm. It is more usual for a poet to mingle a number of oral and written sources, pruning and padding as he goes along. Then, too, although the following three examples are representative of much contemporary *cordel*, they are not classics. Interesting and often beautiful or moving, they do not have the sustained poetic force or the same universal quality of those stories, usually *romances*, which have topped the one hundred thousand mark. Finally, none of these poets is one of those rural, highly religious writers, like contemporary *cordel* author Natanael de Lima or the recently deceased Manuel Tomás de Assis, an increasingly rare type today but one who still represents an important aspect of the tradition. Though each of the three men considered here is both poet and vendor, none travels extensively, and only one still reads his verses aloud to would-be buyers.

Each of the following analyses begins with a brief biographical sketch of the particular poet. An identification of the *folheto*'s source follows. Then comes a breakdown of the story into the usual six-step pattern together with a discussion of any significant differences which this pattern implies between the *folheto* version and the source. A look at the *folheto* within the larger *cordel* tradition concludes each chapter.

The Poet

José de Souza Campos has been a poet for nearly half a century. He wrote his first story, about Noah's ark, at the age of fourteen. Shortly after its publication, he left the then-distant fields of Timbaúba, now only two hours by bus, for Recife, where he sought to enter the *folheto* trade. He is presently almost sixty, and the straw hat that shades his eyes hides all but a thin fringe of white hair.

Every weekday morning when the sun shines and even some days in the winter months of May and June when dawn is ominously cloudy, he locks up his house in the muddy outskirts of Recife and takes the bus to town. When it stops not far from the São José market, he gets off, then pushes his way through one of the narrow streets crowded with peddlers perched behind piles of coat hangers and carrots, tins of Johnson's baby powder, notebooks, pins, and long slabs of meat. He stops briefly at a warehouse just before the plaza to pick up the beach umbrella and backless chair he leaves there every night.

Once in the plaza proper, he opens a large wooden suitcase full of *folhetos*, sets it on a makeshift platform, then begins to arrange the booklets in a multicolored fan. The umbrella will protect both the poet and his wares from the ever-hotter sun.

José's stand is sandwiched in between two on-the-spot shoemakers and a watch repairman. Barbers and photographers line the sidewalk to his left. Across the plaza a peddler wielding a boa constrictor proclaims the glories of a patent medicine. A young *folheto* vendor named Miné strews his booklets across a table, then hooks up a loudspeaker several yards away. Aging prostitutes in short bright skirts linger beneath the trees and listen as the record stalls play samba after samba. Because of the complaints against the women by the priest in the big church that overlooks the plaza, the police are everywhere. A few peasants in from the country haggle over the price of beans as the soldiers yawn.

From an early age, José wanted to be a poet. Like most children of subsistence farmers, he learned more from the *cordel* than from the makeshift school in which he studied for several months. While his first *folheto* was "all full of errors," he soon learned "how to rhyme, how to end one section and begin another" from the older poets whom he met in Recife.[3] After three years of informal apprenticeship in the big city, he went back to Timbaúba to bring his brothers Francisco and Manuel to the city. Once installed in Recife, the younger men began writing their own stories under José's direction. All three sold *folhetos* at various points throughout the city, branching out into the countryside on frequent trips.

At one time, José traveled regularly throughout the Northeast, especially Pernambuco and Paraíba. He can still rattle off the names of towns too small to show up on most maps. Today, however, he remains in the Recife market, venturing out to nearby Limoeiro every Sunday for the fair in which he often earns more than he will during the whole week. Traveling, he says, holds no more interest for him. Not only are his lungs not what they used to be back in that time when he sang "like a mermaid," but the effort does not pay. Instead, he simply stands behind the table with its careful display. Besides *folhetos*, José sells songs, samba lyrics, and copies of *The Cross of Calaveira*, a book of "mysteries" dating back to the Middle Ages sold today in a glossy edition sealed in a plastic sack.

In Limoeiro, most of José's customers are farmers. In Recife, however, most work around or in the plaza or are unemployed. Every once in a while a grizzled farmer, often a long-time acquaintance, appears. Some buyers ask specifically for one or another title, a classic like *The Exploits of John Cricket* or *The Mysterious Peacock*. Others leaf through the booklets on the table at random, ask the price of one or another, and then generally wander off. Still others simply drop by the stand to talk. The conversation may touch on a new way of restoring a dead battery with steel wool, rumors of injections given in hospitals that turn people into monkeys, and the ornery and shameless nature of women.

Given Recife's important role in the *cordel* trade, poets from the outlying towns of Caruaru, Bezerros, Condado, and Bom Jardim frequently appear. They often buy *folhetos* from wholesaler Edson Pinto, whose stand is around the corner, and from João José da Silva, once an important publisher, who still controls the rights to many stories and who now works for the São Paulo-based Luzeiro press. The poets exchange information about the profession: Manuel d'Almeida in Aracaju has put off his trip north because of ill health; there was a match between two poet-singers in Bezerros last week that lasted well past dawn; Maria de Jesus, owner of the São Francisco press in Juazeiro is going to see her sister in Brasília and may well raise her prices, etc.

Despite the obvious pleasure he takes in such exchanges, José is not

3. José de Souza Campos, March 3, 1978. All quotes in this chapter are from a recorded interview with the poet and his brother Francisco in São Lourenço da Mata, Pernambuco, and from numerous conversations with the poet between January 12, and July 26, 1978.

happy about the present state of the plaza. He prefers to recall the days thirty years ago when the press owned by João Martins de Ataíde turned out a steady stream of new stories, and a dozen poets lined the sidewalk for the weekly fair to which farmers as well as city dwellers flocked.

Today, José complains, the plaza, which is given over to games of chance, "riffraff," and the most down-and-out prostitutes, is no longer a suitable place for poetry. He blames the city for not banning the use of loudspeakers and alcohol and is bitter about the poet's need to pay a daily five-*cruzeiro* tax "as if the *folheto* were just like shoelaces or cakes." José would like to see a pavilion just for poetry erected in the middle of the plaza. "If this were a good place again, I mean one really worthy of poetry," he says, "more buyers would appear." Though he watches the fist-fights that break out several times a day with a gleam of interest, he still shakes his head to emphasize his disapproval of the status quo.

Declining sales and rising costs have not led José to stop writing. He admits that there is nothing else that he can do to earn a living. Even if there were, however, he insists that he would continue to be a poet "because that is what I was born to be and have always been." Author of some thirty *folhetos*, he has managed to publish slightly over a third of these. Though fondest of thirty-two-page *romances* such as *Angelita's Passion and Lino's Prowess*, and *The Brave Deeds of Joe Numbskull and the Love of Risomar*, he has also written a story about Padre Cícero and the devil, two laments in the *oh tempora! oh mores!* vein, and a *folheto* ordered by the government-sponsored literacy campaign aimed at adults known as MOBRAL.[4] He is presently in the middle of a story about a sparrowhawk and an eagle, which he is already worried about publishing. The approximately 1,500 *cruzeiros* (one hundred dollars) he makes a month are barely enough to pay for his bus fare, the daily "floor tax," and a lunch of bread-fruit and milky coffee, let alone the cost of publishing a new *folheto* that may or may not sell.

Nevertheless, José refuses to despair. When he is not writing, he is often arguing about what it means to be a poet with his brother Francisco, who lives nearby in São Lourenço da Mata. Although José asserts that he writes above all "to instruct the buyer" and his brother maintains that the poet must say what his public wants to hear, both men take a similar pride in

---

4. Aside from *A Paixão de Angelita e a Competência de Lino* (Recife, n.d.) and *As Bravuras de Zé Bobo e o Amor de Risomar* (Guarabira, n.d.), José is the author of *A Luta de Padre Cícero com o Diabo* (Recife, 1962), *A Mocidade Hoje em Dia no Sistema do Quadrão* (n.p., n.d.), *Uma Peinha de Nada no Sistema do Quadrão* (Olinda, n.d.), *O Caminho para o Mobral* (Recife, 1978), *Peleja de José de Souza Campos com João Antônio de Barros* (Olinda, n.d.), and *A Voz de Noé* (Olinda, n.d.). MOBRAL (Movimento Brasileiro de Alfabetização) is a literacy campaign sponsored by the federal government, which provides local, usually evening, classes for adults. It has been active since 1970.

their craft. According to José, "the poet wants not only to write the best rhyme possible but to improve his awareness at the same time." Agreeing that all poets write for money, he nevertheless makes a distinction between those who are "authors by vocation" and those who see poetry merely as a source of income. He asserts that one can tell a false from a true poet because the former writes "in a forced way that has no life of its own." Also, such a writer has "no interest in perfecting what he writes" but is rather "like any peddler who only thinks of money, money, money."

Given his strong opinions on this and other matters, it is not surprising that José's personal life has been somewhat stormy. He is separated from his wife, and his relations with his five grown children remain strained. The eldest son sells belts near the entrance to the plaza, but the two men seldom speak. Once the owner of a handpress, José gave up his idea of printing *folhetos* when his family insisted that the *cordel* was no way to make a living. "Not everyone understands what it means to be a poet," he explains.

Difficulties on many fronts have led José de Souza Campos to think a good deal about not only poetry but life. Like many popular poets, he considers himself a Catholic but does not go to church. Instead, he regularly visits a spiritualist center and has come to believe in reincarnation as "a continuation of the lives which make up life." He points out, however, that although good routinely conquers evil in the pages of his *folhetos*, everyday experience creates many doubts. "The real problem," José says, "is not that evil is stronger than good but that the two can look just like each other. So sometimes you get confused and end up making a mistake."

The King, the Dove, and the Sparrowhawk is the poet's most recent *folheto*. After reading the prose version of the story in a popular almanac, he decided to "translate" it into verse. Asked why he chose this story rather than another, he says that it was "clearer" to him than the others in the almanac. "When I read about that dove, it was almost as if I heard a voice inside my own head," he explains, "and that is always a sign to the poet that it is time to begin writing."

The Source

José de Souza Campos took his story *The King, the Dove, and the Sparrowhawk* from a parable of the same name in *O Almanaque do Pensamento*. This almanac, which is published yearly by the São Paulo-based Pensamento Publishing Company, is nothing less than an updated, mass-produced version of the centuries-old *Lunário Perpétuo*, an astrological guide first translated into Portuguese from Spanish in 1703. The Pensamento almanac offers a series of horoscopes, advice on agricultural matters, charts of the moon and planets, information on the tides, "curiosities" in the manner of Ripley's *Believe It or Not*, crossword puzzles, riddles and "enigmas," various anecdotes and "inspirational" poems, and stories on the order of the parable (reproduced at the end of this chapter). Although the format of the almanac remains unchanged from year to year, the contents vary from edition to edition. The book, which sells for a little over a dollar, is available in bookstores around the first of each year. José de Souza Campos looks forward to buying a new almanac every year because he finds it interesting and informative, "not just junk like comic books."[5]

José's tale, *The King, the Dove, and the Sparrowhawk*, originally comes from a Buddhist scripture, the Sûtralâmkâra or Sutra-Ornament, which most scholars date back to the first century A.D. The text, part of a collection of pious legends after the model of the Buddhist birth stories or Jatakas, was apparently written by Ashvaghosha, one of the leaders if not the founder of the Mahayana ("Great Way") school. It was incorporated into the Hindu tradition some centuries later, and it is this later Hindu version upon which the Brazilian almanac draws. The almanac's compilers relied on a Spanish translation of a French rendition of the Sanskrit source.[6]

The Brazilian version of the story appears on the same page of the almanac as a description of the advantages of fluoride in the treatment of

5. "O Rei, a Pomba e o Gavião" in *Almanaque do Pensamento* (São Paulo: Editora Pensamento Ltda., 1978), pp. 104–05. The almanac, which has appeared since 1912, is an annual supplement to the magazine *Revista do Pensamento*. "Astrological and literary" in character, it is an heir to the *Lunário Perpétuo*, the first Portuguese edition of which was published by Miguel Menescal in 1703 under the full title *O non plus ultra do lunário e prognóstico perpétuo, geral e particular para todos os reinos e províncias, composto por Jerónimo Cortez, valenciano, emendado conforme o expurgatório da Santa Inquisição e traduzido em português*. For a very interesting overview of the almanac in general terms within Brazil, see Luis Beltrão, "Os Almanaques," in *Folk-communicação: Um estudo dos agentes e dos meios populares de informação de fatos e expressão de idéias*, 2nd ed. (São Paulo: Melhoramentos, 1971), pp. 87–110. The version of the story which appears in the almanac was translated by Nair Lacerda from Vicente García de Diego, *Antología de leyendas de la literatura universal* (Barcelona: Editorial Labor, 1955). I am grateful to Diaulas Riedel of the Pensamento Publishing Company for this information (letter, São Paulo, July 6, 1979). The Spanish version was taken in turn from Edouard Huber's *Sûtrâlamkâra: Traduit en français sur la version chinoise de Kumârajîva* (Paris: Ernest Leroux Editeur, 1908), II, 329–41.

6. See "King Shibi and the Bird" in *Buddhist Parables: Translated from the Original Pâli*, tr. Eugene Watson Burlingame (New Haven: Yale University Press, 1922), pp. 314–24. For a brief but helpful introduction to the sutra-ornament and to its author, Ashvaghosha, see J. K. Nariman, *Literary History of Sanskrit Buddhism*, 2nd ed. rev. (Delhi: Motilal Banarsidass, 1972), pp. 28–40.

arterial disorders. The two small drawings accompanying the text picture a Viking-like king beside two small birds, and a scale with a dove on one side, a hand in mudra position on the other, and a question mark in the middle. José makes no attempt to hide his debt to the parable and is surprised at the suggestion that some persons might regard his work as plagiarism. "The best *folhetos*," he asserts, "come directly from the poet's imagination, but there are other stories like this one that deserve to be translated into verse."

The Six-Step Pattern

Similarities in the almanac version of the story and the *folheto* are obvious. Both describe a good king who successfully passes a difficult test, going on to reap significant rewards for his courage and loyalty to his word. Because not only the basic story line but whole phrases are nearly identical, it would be easy to dismiss the *folheto* as simply a poetic rendering of the parable with a few "Brazilian" touches here and there.

Both parable and *folheto* versions of *The King, the Dove, and the Sparrowhawk* reveal the basic six-step *DR* sequence. Though the prose account lacks an explicit statement of the first and last steps, these are more or less implied. Below is a prose elaboration of how the pattern works in both the parable and the *folheto*, the numbers referring (as before) to the six steps. (See Figure 2 on p. 62.)

PARABLE	FOLHETO
1. *Pact*: Implied fulfillment of kingly duties ("The king was known throughout the country for the help that he always gave to those in need").	1. *Pact*: King keeps vigil over country: looks out for the poor, cultivates his lands, oversees his wealth, counsels all social classes, allies self with nobles, etc.
2. *Test*: Dove asks protection from cruel pursuer.	2. *Test*: Dove asks protection from cruel pursuer.
3. *Response*: King guarantees her protection ("I will give my very life for yours").	3. *Response*: King guarantees her protection ("I will give my entire kingdom for your salvation").
2. *Test*: Sparrowhawk demands either dove or equivalent weight in king's flesh.	2. *Test*: Sparrowhawk demands either dove or equivalent weight in king's flesh.

3. *Response*: King agrees to give his own flesh ("You show a conciliatory spirit in making this proposal").

4. *Counterresponse*: Jeweled chariot arrives; heavenly nectar bathes king.

5. *Judgment*: King restored to original state; disappears into sky as chariot ascends.

6. *Pact reasserted*: Narrator promises reward of virtue ("He who protects others will undoubtedly have a similar end").

3. *Response*: King agrees to give his own flesh and proceeds to cut self to the bone despite expressions of horror by subjects.

4. *Counterresponse*: Community en masse prays for help ("Oh God, have mercy on us!"); direct divine intervention as celestial harp sounds and fragrant mist envelops king.

5. *Judgment*: Sparrowhawk dies; king restored to better than original state; subjects rejoice.

6. *Pact reasserted*: King and community live happily ever after; poet (and thus community) expressly rejects sparrowhawk.

A comparison of these two stories shows that while there are differences in details, the basic structure remains unchanged.

Divergences

Although the parable and the *folheto* are unmistakably related, there are, nevertheless, important details that distinguish the two texts. The changes summarized below are attributable in no small part to both the requirements of the *folheto* as a particular literary tradition and the poet's socioeconomic background with its deeply internalized values.

PARABLE	FOLHETO
DR plot, no subplot.	*DR* plot plus subordinate, complementary *DW* tale.
Main characters are king, dove, sparrowhawk.	Main characters are king, dove, sparrowhawk, *and* community (*povo*).
Prose form.	Verse form.
Third-person narrative; omniscient, anonymous author who presents the text as fact.	Third-person narrative within first-person framework; truth of text often "guaranteed" by eyewitness author.

Erudite, "literary" language.	Colloquial language, mixture of styles.
Buddhist parable.	Christian homily illustrating the nature of *firmeza* and *falsidade*.
Eastern trappings (court), in which hunger is literary device.	Brazilian setting (countryside), in which hunger is practical problem.

The single most important difference between the two stories is structural in nature. Although both parable and *folheto* fall into the same six-step *DR* sequence, the prose version lacks the complementary *DW* plot apparent in the poem. Thus, we have in one a single-strand narrative, in the other a double-strand narrative. In addition, despite the fact that the king is the unmistakable protagonist of both stories, it is also possible to read the *folheto* as the sparrowhawk's story. The bird's unreasonable demand for human flesh is decidedly a wrong response to the test of hunger. Having sought the death of a good king, he must pay with his own life. Below is the six-step pattern outlined with its back-and-forth variations when the sparrowhawk is the protagonist, that is, in the *DW* scheme. (See Figure 2 on page 62.)

DW Plot

1. *Pact*: Sparrowhawk, granted certain rights by "the gods who rule the air," spends his time pursuing doves.
2. *Test*: Humane king denies the hawk a particular dove.
3. *(Wrong) response*: Sparrowhawk defies king, asserting that the question of the dove is beyond his lawful sphere of concern.
2. *Test*: King offers sparrowhawk any other type of food.
3. *(Wrong) response*: Sparrowhawk refuses offer, demanding either the dove or the king's flesh.
4. *Counterresponse*: Sparrowhawk's insistence causes king and dove to look to heaven.
5. *Judgment*: Divine intervention results in sparrowhawk's death.
6. *Pact reasserted*: King and community live happily ever after; poet expressly repudiates hawk.

Like the overwhelming majority of *cordel* stories, *The King, the Dove, and the Sparrowhawk* reveals a series of oppositions that may be found in various other Brazilian as well as non-Brazilian popular traditions. Characters are either good or bad, actions either right or wrong, making ambiguous behavior atypical.[7] This binary division is present in the parable

7. Binary oppositions appear to be all but universal in folklore. See, for instance, Alan Dundes, "The Binary Structure of 'Unsuccessful Repetition' in Lithuanian Folktales," *West-*

as well as the *folheto*. However, although the hawk plays a major role in the almanac version of the story, he disappears after the king agrees to his demands. This means that the author does not develop the potential *DW* subplot, thereby revealing a quite different vision of wrong and its consequences from that evident in the *folheto*. The fact that this is one of the very few places in which the *cordel* story diverges from the original confirms the poet's loyalty to the concepts of good and evil, defined more precisely in the *folheto* as *firmeza* and *falsidade*.

The good/evil split underlying the *cordel* tradition in general compels this particular *folheto* to include not only a *DR* sequence similar to that in the story but also a complementary *DW* plot. The bird, whom the parable describes as "precious," "little," and "heaven-borne" (*pomba celeste*), appears from the start in the *folheto* as "heavenly," "sublime," and "divine." The fact that the poet explicitly equates the sparrowhawk with Satan and the dove with Jehovah guarantees the hawk's future punishment. José's version thus reveals a visible split between human (in this case good) and animal (in this case bad) behavior epitomized by the king and the bird.

GOOD (*firmeza*)	EVIL (*falsidade*)
King (human)	Hawk (animal)
Compassionate, looks out for others, especially those less fortunate.	Cruel.
Just, treats all persons well regardless of rank.	Tyrannical.
Steadfast, true ("The King of Benares keeps his word").	Deceitful (dove becomes heavier as king places more of his own flesh on the scale).
Authoritative (the king's word is law), but reverent (king identifies self as "undeserving creature" before God).	Presumptuous (challenges king's right to interfere).
Courageous (does not flinch at the prospect of doing injury to self).	Cowardly (does battle with a creature weaker than himself).

It is also possible to see this good/evil split in the figures of the dove and the sparrowhawk. While the former represents those positive qualities associated in the *cordel* with femininity, the latter stands for "bad" masculine behavior as opposed to those "good" masculine traits summed up

---

ern Folklore, 12 (1962): 165–74. See also the work of Elli Köngas Maranda and Pierre Maranda, and Claude Lévi-Strauss.

in the king. It is therefore possible to break down these actors into the following sets of contrasting characteristics.

Dove: (feminine, positive)	King: (masculine, positive)	Hawk: (masculine, negative)
Innocent.	Well-intentioned although knowledgeable in the ways of the world.	Ill-intentioned.
Beautiful.	Handsome.	Unattractive ("cruel eyes").
Chaste, withdrawing.	Pure in heart, stands firm.	Aggressive, harms others without motive.
Representative of love and peace.	Conciliatory though fearless.	Warlike.

Not surprisingly, the poet attributes many of the same qualities to both the king and God, making the "resistant arm" of the monarch an extension of the "untiring arm" of the divinity. The epitaphs for Jehovah, *semente do sumo bem* ("seed of greatest good"), *ordenador, bom e justo* ("wise and good ruler"), and *unificador* ("unifier"), are attributes that might also be applied to the king. God, like the sovereign who represents Him on earth, is like all masculine embodiments of *firmeza*, kind, just, true, and strong. Above all, he is capable of guaranteeing the harmonious existence of his dependents by quashing any threat to the stability of the system in which they participate. In reference to the sparrowhawk of the *folheto*, José explains that

> he had to be punished because he was unreasonable; he had everything he could have wanted, and still he demanded the king's flesh. Not only that, the sparrowhawk knew just how many people were going to suffer—how much turmoil there was going to be without that good king. And so, I don't feel even a little bit sorry for him. I think that he deserved to die, and I am glad that he did. Imagine not being able to go hungry even one day when so many people don't have a crust of bread for two or three!

Although the preceding list applies specifically to *The King, the Dove, and the Sparrowhawk*, those oppositions singled out there permeate the *cordel*. The larger framework into which they fit is clearly a hierarchical pyramid in which each person occupies a specific place. Individuals higher up on the social scale, and God himself, owe those lower down protection and justice whereas their inferiors owe them respect, service, and unquestioning loyalty. Though the parable only deals with the pinnacle of this social order, limiting its focus to kings, queens, and heavenly dancers, the *folheto* presents a community that includes poor persons as well as nobles. Thus, while the king allies himself with the nobles, keeping close watch over the ministers who "follow his every order," he also "counsels every social class."

The author of the parable offers no motive for the king's suffering; it simply happens. The poet, however, refers almost immediately to the *bendita sina* or "blessed fate" of the king, going on to hint at those "cruel moments" the future will bring. The notion of *sina*, generally translated as "destiny," seldom crucial in *DW*, *HR*, and *HW* tales, is a necessary part of all *DR* stories that include a *DW* subplot. It provides an explanation of why the just individual, who is fulfilling all his obligations, should suffer. In fact, the term *sina* is often used interchangeably with the particular test situation, for example, "The dragon was waiting for him. It was his *sina*."

The word *sina* has several related meanings. Aside from "lot," "fate," or "fortune," *sina* also means "ensign," "flag," "banner," and, significantly, "portion" or "share." The verb *assinar* means "to mark out," "to assign," "to designate." A person's *sina* is therefore that share which has been allotted him, that mark or standard which an omnipotent hand (God, the fates) has obligated him or her to bear. Since an individual's destiny has little to do with his actions, he or she must make the best of what befalls, regarding misfortune as a trial demanding courage and faith. Thus, in the *folheto* version of *The King, the Dove, and the Sparrowhawk*, the king immediately sees that he is to be tested, greeting the dove as a full-fledged divine messenger:

> Your eyes show
> that you were sent from Heaven
> to this abyss of Earth
> to speak with this undeserving creature
> who regards you with naked eye,
> unaided by veil or curtain.

Although the king stands trial as an individual, he never ceases to represent the nation at large. Given that the *cordel* has always been community property, this is not surprising. The hero, if he is good, embodies the group and its aspirations, serving as its idealized representative. If he is evil, he becomes a symbol of shared oppressors, thereby inviting violent punishment.

To the extent that the hero's fate is inseparable from that of the group, *The King, the Dove, and the Sparrowhawk* is a typical *DR* tale. While the almanac version presents a series of dialogues between the king and each of the two birds, the *folheto* introduces a fourth actor, who is none other than the group. In this case, as elsewhere, the community is both intercessor and beneficiary. The story begins in typical fashion by portraying the king amidst his people, watching over the harvest and ensuring harmony among his charges. "He was beloved by everyone / in his beautiful nation," says the poet. "Poor men respected him, / rich men listened to him / because of his just nature / and good heart." When he makes his terrible sacrifice, not just the queen(s) of the parable but the masses respond with "tears, protests, and shouts of alarm."

A collective plea for divine intervention follows this wave of discontent. "Oh God," the people shout, "have mercy upon us . . . / and don't let our country / be needlessly orphaned!"

The group's continued need for its wise leader explains the *folheto*'s earthly ending. There is nothing to keep the Buddhist sovereign from riding off into nirvana, but the Christian king must continue to guide his fellow men.

To be sure, both texts present a moment of supernatural intervention.

PARABLE	FOLHETO
They say that heavenly music was then heard and a shower of nectar began to descend over the king, restoring his body intact. Magnificent flowers of an unknown variety fell from the heavens and the gandaras and apsaras sang and danced.	Suddenly a fragrant mist enveloped the scale where the good king had cut off his own flesh. The wind carried the sound of a divine harp to those below.

The parable continues in this exalted vein by whisking the sovereign off beyond an eternal horizon whereas the *folheto* leaves him to renew his vigil over his herds and fields.

PARABLE	FOLHETO
Finally, a magnificent carriage appeared, which, as it drew nearer, shone brighter and brighter, covered as it was by precious stones. As the carriage entered the presence of the dancers, they escorted the king to the marvelous carriage and ascended with him into the sky.	From that day on, the good king kept increasing vigil over his people, saw to his animals, revered innocence, and watched over the fields.

Not only the king but his kingdom prospers in the *cordel* story. The community proceeds to emulate its ruler's actions, sharing in his good fortune.

> His subjects
> followed his example.
> The king's drama was recounted
> throughout the world,
> and authors wrote books about the king,
> the dove, and the sparrowhawk.

Passing now from questions of content to others linked more closely to style, we see clearly that the parable is prose, the *folheto* poetry. The particular demands of the verse form on the poet may be somewhat less obvious. The *folheto*'s customary eight-, sixteen-, or thirty-two-page format demands that the story include a set number of stanzas. This means that the author's raw material must be either cut or, in most cases, expanded. In this instance, José has followed the original quite faithfully, but he has clearly added a stanza here and there to bring the total to sixteen pages. Thus, at the same time that the sequence regarding food is an important addition in its own right, its length is explained in part by the author's need to meet a poetic quota.

Then, too, the necessity of rhyme clearly affects the course of the story. The poet claims to have eliminated elements such as the axoka tree or the celestial dancers (apsaras) because of their foreign nature ("What do the people I write for know about such things?"). The fact that they are difficult to rhyme is yet another reason for their absence in the *folheto*.

Both versions of *The King, the Dove, and the Sparrowhawk* are third-person narratives, but the body of the *folheto* is set within a first-person frame. The poet speaks directly to the reader in the first four and last six of the story's sixty-four stanzas. The use of the "I" in both introductory and concluding segments of the story is standard procedure in the *cordel*. The initial invocation, a conventional device in classical literature, is used by *folheto* writers to call on God or the muse for inspiration to explain how they came to write the tale ("an old man I once knew told me this story.") and/or to orient the reader either by outlining the plot or its underlying message. Plot summaries are particularly common in cases where the story represents a continuation of a previous volume that the customer may not have read. At the end of the *folheto*, the poet often recapitulates the moral, both urging his audience not to forget the example he has just provided and exhorting them to help him and/or show support for the moral posture he has taken by buying a booklet to take home. In the case of *The King, the Dove, and the Sparrowhawk*, José begins his story by calling for divine aid. He ends the tale by reasserting the story's basic message, which, in turn, reaffirms his own faith in God.

These concluding stanzas also introduce an "eyewitness," who supposedly provides the poet with the information for his tale:

> Still today in Benares
> where this event occurred,
> there is an eyewitness
> who wrote to me about it.
> Thanks to his ample studies,
> he is the author of distinguished books.

Such witnesses are a stock device in the *cordel*. They serve both as "proof" of the story's truth (in this case, the poet refers to his supposed informant's superior learning) as well as a regulatory device allowing the reader to accept as much of the tale as he finds believable, dismissing the rest without discrediting either the poet or the story as a whole.

Because in the parable the story is presented as fact by an omniscient, anonymous author, such a warning device is unnecessary. The *folheto*, however, is clearly the work of one man. The "I" in the frame is identified within the text itself in the final acrostic where the beginning letters of each of the six concluding lines spell out "J. SOUZA."

As previously mentioned, acrostics are common throughout the *literatura de cordel* because of constant problems with property rights. Although they can be easily dismantled by a poet intent on claiming the story as his own, a good percentage of *folhetos* bearing only the publisher's name on the cover reveal unaltered concluding stanzas. In the case of *The King, the Dove, and the Sparrowhawk*, one finds not only this common identifying feature but an extended internal acrostic. The initial letters of the first line of the first twenty-two stanzas actually spell out "AUTOR JOZE DE SOUZA CAMPOS." This atypical identifying scheme is a result of José's original plan to allow an acquaintance to enter his story in the Recife competitions. Despite the fact that José backed out of the deal ("I just wouldn't feel right about it, and besides, that's *my* story."), he did not change the embedded acrostic, which he had devised to prove to future generations that the story was his own.

The interplay between first and third person, private and public concerns, gives this *folheto* a certain heterogeneous flavor not found in the parable. Clearly "literary," the prose text's carefully chosen images create a harmonious effect quite different from the *folheto*'s often somewhat haphazard mixture of styles. José's language, like that of most *cordel* authors, is uneven, causing the story to alternate between highly colloquial sections and other, consciously elevated passages.[8]

The *cordel* version draws on a Brazilian, and, more specifically, lower-class, rural, Northeastern vocabulary. Because it deviates from standard

---

8. For a discussion of the popular poet's language, see Marlene de Castro Correia, "O saber poético da literatura de cordel," *Cultura*, 3 (1971): 49–54.

written usage (the spoken language of even the best educated Brazilians is not that found in grammar books), some critics dismiss it as "bad" Portuguese. In reality, those mistakes in spelling and grammar, which are not owing to typographical errors, reflect the author's sensitivity to everyday pronunciation as much as his lack of formal schooling. The fact that the poet writes *sorria em vê* for *sorria em ver*, *crués* for *cruéis* indicates that he writes primarily by ear in utilizing a verse form few university graduates would find easy to sustain.

In translating the *folheto* so that its meaning will be clear to an English-speaking reader, I have sometimes eliminated what, from an official viewpoint, might be considered grammatical errors. In the second stanza of the original, for instance, the poet allows "a little disheartened" to modify "sickness" rather than the "I" which I have inserted for clarity. The colloquial flavor of the story is apparent in expressions such as *em prol de sua gente* ("on behalf of his people"), *dar um chute na pobreza* ("give poverty a swift kick"), *acabar com a moleza* ("put an end to hesitation"), *moleza* (implying "spinelessness"), and the diminutive and thus familiar *pombinha* ("little dove").

The *folheto* author tends to eliminate unfamiliar or high-sounding elements present in the parable or else replaces these with homely details, such as the lovely "nest woven from dry leaves and nettles," when not eliminating them entirely. This tendency is particularly obvious in the following comparison.

PARABLE	FOLHETO
"Be calm, little bird. How can you be so terrified, almost dying of fright, you who are so lovely, of the same color as the newly opened lotus flower, who have eyes the same color as the flowers of the axoka tree?	You, who are as lovely as a half-open flower, ask my protection, and it will surely be granted. Calm your fears, heavenly bird, and do not be alarmed.

In between these phrases, however, the poet includes a number of his own verbal flourishes. He may, for instance, speak of "the sylphs who rule the air" or "the fauna of the beguiling birds." The dove becomes *sublimada* (dictionary definition "subliminated" but by which José means to say "sublime"). While these sections do not always make strict sense, buyers find them "elegant," "poetic," and proof of the poet's superior knowledge. Furthermore, they have a meaning for the writer and his readers. Although "sylphs," for instance, may not be much different in function from the Indian *gandaras*, they are part of a familiar cosmogony. José subscribes to the medieval theory that the world is divided into four elements: water, earth, fire, and air, each with its own elemental spirit. Like the other spirits, the sylphs, which are the spirits of the air, form a link between material and nonmaterial beings. The poet interprets the sylphs as real, immortal beings who know more of the present and future than does man. Extremely powerful, they show displeasure by creating lightning.[9]

Even though both the parable and the *folheto* speak of the need for loyalty, endurance, and repayment of reciprocal favors, the first is a Buddhist tale, the second a Christian homily in which the more "exotic" aspects of the parable take on a familiar cast. The *cordel* story takes place in a conveniently distant Benares, but the king is an eminently Christian ruler. The parable is a clear-cut object lesson in which the king shows no hesitation in performing his duties. The hero of the *folheto*, however, undergoes a true test of character. Unlike the original monarch, he experiences "complete despair" before taking consolation in a sudden vision of "hammer, cross, and wood." The same salvation awaits both, but it is interesting to note that in the parable the earth shakes *while* the king makes his sacrifice, but in the *folheto* signs of a divine presence only *follow* his successful response.

The shift from Buddhism to Christianity parallels a similar shift from East to West in which the multiple, gold-bedecked wives of the parable yield to a single, unadorned queen. The "heavenly dancers" (apsaras and gandaras) disappear; the nectar becomes "a fragrant mist" much like the baths associated with Afro-Brazilian religious cults; and references to lotus flowers are replaced by those to guinea pigs.

The single best example of the *folheto*'s peculiarly Northeastern flavor is undoubtedly that passage devoted to food. In the parable, the king offers the hawk three more or less equivalent choices: bull, wild boar, or stag. In the *folheto*, he lists no less than thirty-two alternatives. Some of these choices are clearly not Brazilian, and few if any of the poet's readers will have ever seen a zebra, flamingo, or gazelle. However, the majority are closely associated with the Northeastern backlands, and it is not easy to find translations for *cutiá, furão, prea, tiú, mocó,* or *paca,* most, by the

9. Webster's Third International Dictionary defines a sylph as "an elemental being inhabiting the air." The term, coined by the Swiss physician and chemist Paracelsus (1493–1541), most probably comes from the New Latin *sylphus,* a contraction of the Latin *sylvestris nympha,* meaning "nymph of the woods." The sylphs, like other elemental spirits—the salamanders or spirits of fire, the gnomes or spirits of earth, and the undines or spirits of water—form the link between immaterial and material beings because though, like men, they eat, drink, speak, travel, sicken, and beget children, they resemble the more elevated spirits in the litheness and transparency of their bodies and their rapidity of movement; they also know more of the present and future than man does. According to José, although they are immortal, they are unhappy because they do not know God.

way, edible rodents, which few non-Northeasterners would find appetizing.

This kind of rambling catalogue, so common in the *cordel*, suggests the *folheto*'s poet-singer heritage. *Repentistas* routinely demonstrate their superior learning by producing long lists of examples: names of plants, rivers, countries, etc. Thus, while in the parable the sparrowhawk simply dismisses the king's one-sentence offer with an equally terse "I do not eat the meat of boars or bulls or stags," in the *folheto* he matches the king's two stanzas with two of his own.[10]

The hawk refuses the monarch's proposal because the flesh of all animals except doves "gives him a fever," an assertion which the educated reader is apt to find anticlimactic if not downright amusing. Nevertheless, most *folheto* buyers regard the hawk's objection a quite logical extension of their own very definite attitudes toward certain foods.

In reality, eating is often a near obsession in the *folheto* owing largely to the poet's and the public's difficulty in filling their own stomachs. In the classic **Journey to São Saruê*, for example, the poet describes his ramblings through a distant utopia in overwhelmingly gustatory terms, envisioning mountains of *cuscuz* (a sort of regional corn bread) whereas more privileged writers might imagine rubies or emeralds. A mother consoles a worried daughter in *The Story of Rose White or the Fisherman's Daughter* by rushing off to fry two eggs. In *The Story of the Soldier Robert and the Princess of the Kingdom of Canan*, the hero is aided by three old ladies, each of whom cooks him a delicious dinner before presenting him with a magic dog. Here, in *The King, the Dove, and the Sparrowhawk*, hunger is not just a narrative device but a real and profound problem with which the average reader is sure to identify.[11]

The *Folheto* and the *Cordel* Tradition

In sum, although the two versions reveal obvious similarities, there are also significant differences stemming from the *folheto*'s loyalty to a particular tradition with its own rules as well as the specific context in which

10. For an interesting discussion of the language of poet-singers, which clearly has bearing on the *folheto* author, see Clóvis Monteiro, *A linguagem dos cantadores: Segundo textos coligidos e publicados por Leonardo Mota* (Rio de Janeiro: n.p., 1933).

11. Manuel Camilo dos Santos, **Viagem a São Saruê* (Campina Grande, 1956), *Literatura popular em verso: Antologia*, I (Rio de Janeiro: Fundação Casa de Rui Barbosa/ MEC, 1964), pp. 555–59 (hereafter cited as *Antologia*). Luís da Costa Pinheiro, *História de Rosa Branca ou a Filha do Pescador* (Juazeiro do Norte, 1956); and Luís da Costa Pinheiro, *História do Soldado Roberto e a Princeza do Reino de Canan*, 2 vols. (Juazeiro do Norte, 1951).

this tradition functions. Although some formal (the internal acrostic) and stylistic features (the very personal nature of the poet's initial appeal to God) distinguish this story from others, there are many ways in which it may be considered representative of not only contemporary *folhetos* but these stories in general. Briefly, the salient features of most *cordel* tales are:

> Necessary six-step structure; decided back-and-forth motion reflecting *repentista* heritage.
> Inclusion of the community as a full-fledged actor.
> Poetic form.
> Third-person narrative within first-person framework, individual authorship emphasized by devices such as final identifying acrostic; reliance on "eyewitness" or other corroborating source.
> Regional, colloquial language; errors in spelling and grammar; archaisms; mixture of styles (elevated/everyday often in same stanza).
> Christian overtones evident in *firmeza/falsidade* division, reliance on *sina* in *DR folhetos*.
> Unmistakably Brazilian setting; lower-class concerns, e.g., hunger, sickness, lack of money and education.

Although *The King, the Dove, and the Sparrowhawk* clearly fits this standard framework, it is difficult to provide direct comparisons with other *folhetos*. There are plenty of kings in the *literatura de cordel*, but these tend to play the role of tester rather than of testee, posing a series of trials and obstacles, which the (generally plebeian) hero must overcome before attaining the hand of the princess, thereby gaining admission to the charmed circle of plenty. When the protagonist is of royal blood, he is almost never a king. The figure may be a young prince in danger of losing his throne because of the machinations of a nefarious relative (*The Prisoner of Black Rock Castle*) or a gracious queen unjustly accused of infidelity (*The Sufferings of Genoveva* or *The Empress Porcina*). Most often, the aristocratic protagonist is a beautiful young princess, who defies her father's orders in order to marry the poor man of sterling character whom she loves, proving her fidelity by waiting for him to rescue her from a dungeon or parental castle (*The Mysterious Peacock*).[12]

There is a reason for the dearth of protagonist kings in *folhetos*. Because *DR* stories are by definition trials of the inferior member of a pact involving a divine participant, it is far more dramatic to make this individual a

---

12. João Martins de Ataíde, *O Prisioneiro do Castelo da Rocha Negra* (Juazeiro do Norte, 1976); Leandro Gomes de Barros, *Os Martírios de Genoveva* (Recife, n.d.), *Antologia*, pp. 29–56; Francisco das Chagas Batista, *História da Imperatriz Porcina* (Recife, 1946), *Antologia*, pp. 101–36; João Melquíades Ferreira, *O Pavão Misterioso* (Juazeiro do Norte, 1951), *Antologia*, pp. 57–74.

penniless youth or pious fisherman than a king. Such a choice is also more believable since most *folheto* buyers would assert that rich people have fewer problems than poor people, no matter what the poet may say about the leveling powers of destiny. Finally, kings are symbols of the state and, as such, supposed to be good. It is more than a little dangerous to question their authority not only because of overt censorship but because of the troubling doubts such questioning awakes in both the poet's and reader's minds. The fact that a king is the protagonist in the story, not a prince or faithful peasant, attests to the emotional force of the parable. Because the tale corresponds so closely in structure and in worldview to the poet's own framework, he could versify this material with only minor alterations, making the king a representative *folheto* hero and an unmistakably Northeastern figure. "Where is Benares?" asks the poet, and then he answers:

> Well now, I'm not all that sure. I think that it is a foreign country like Japan or Turkey but since good kings are pretty much the same anywhere you find them, I never thought that much about it. . . . Someday, when I have a chance, I'll have to look it up.

Parable and *Folheto*[13]

Parable: The King, the Dove, and the Sparrowhawk

They say that a precious dove fell from the sky to the garden where King Vrixadarba of Benares was sitting. Breathing with difficulty because she arrived exhausted, the dove asked the monarch to protect her from a sparrowhawk that pursued her. The king was known throughout the country for the help that he always gave those in need. Seeing the terror that had overcome the bird, he said to her,

"Be calm, little bird. How can you be so terrified, almost dying of fright, you who are so lovely, of the same color as the newly opened lotus flower, who have eyes the same color as the flowers of the axoka tree? Do not fear because no one ought to be afraid when they seek protection in this palace. I am capable of marshaling my entire kingdom in your defense, and, if necessary, I will give my very life for yours. Be calm, dove of the heavens, because the king of Benares does what he promises."

The cruel sparrowhawk, who had heard everything, now alighted near the king and said,

13. This is my English translation of the parable that appears in the *Almanaque do Pensamento*, pp. 104–05. A bilingual version of José de Souza Campos' *folheto* follows. The reader should note that the *cordel* author's spelling and capitalization have been preserved in this, as in all, *folheto* transcriptions.

"This bird is my food. She was destined as such by the gods. You ought not to protect what is rightly mine because I worked hard for this prisoner. Oh, king! My life is threatened by hunger. The dove is mine because her body bears the mark of my claws. You know very well that you have the right to intervene in conflicts between human beings. But what lawful power do you have over the birds who fly freely across the sky? If you want to obtain holy merit by helping this dove, think also of me who may die of hunger."

The king then said to him,

"Very well, let my servants prepare you a bull, a wild boar, or a stag. You will eat all that you want, but you will not eat this bird."

The sparrowhawk, regarding him with cruel eyes, responded,

"I do not eat the meat of boars nor bulls nor stags. Doves are the food that was destined for me. But, oh humane sovereign, if you have so much love for this bird, then there is a solution. You will give me the equivalent of this dove's weight in your own flesh. Then I will be satisfied."

The king said,

"You show a conciliatory spirit in making this proposal. What you suggest will be done."

The king immediately began to cut pieces of his own flesh, which he placed in one of the balance pans of the scale while the dove lay in the other. The queens, adorned from head to toe with gold, arrived and began to shout so loudly that the noise rose heavenward like a terrible storm. The earth shook on seeing that the king of Benares not only did all that he promised but that he was capable of a sacrifice that the most valiant warriors of his kingdom would never make even for love of their own children.

The monarch went on cutting flesh from his legs, his thighs, his arms and setting it on the balance. The more flesh he set in the balance pan, the more the dove appeared to weigh. Finally, reduced almost to bone now, the king threw himself upon the scale.

They say that heavenly music was then heard, and a shower of nectar began to descend over the king, completely restoring his body. Magnificent flowers of an unknown variety fell from the heavens and the celestial dancers called gandaras and apsaras sang and danced. Finally, a magnificent carriage appeared, which, as it drew nearer, shone brighter and brighter, covered as it was by precious stones. As the carriage entered the presence of the dancers, they escorted the king to the marvelous carriage and ascended with him into the sky.

He who protects others will assuredly have a similar end. And whosoever recounts this story will be purified of all sin as will whosoever hears it with love.

Folheto: *O Rei a Pomba e O Gavião* / *The King, the Dove, and the Sparrowhawk* by José de Souza Campos

A Deus farei um pedido
Não sei se será pecado
Para Ele conceder-me
Um viver mais liberado
Sinto a luta e o desgaste
Já me deixando cansado

I will make a request to God
(I don't know if it is a sin)
that He grant me
an easier existence
because I am beginning to weary
of the constant struggle.

Um pouco desanimado
A doença me atrofia
A familia me impurtuna
A era me desafia
A pobresa me desgosta
A verdade me vigia

I am a little disheartened.
Sickness wears at me,
my family importunes me,
the epoch itself defies me,
and my poverty weighs on me,
even though the Truth protects me.

Tenho vontade de um dia
Dar um chute na pobreza
Unir-me com a coragem
Acabar com a moleza
Abraçar-me a elegância
E segurar-me a riqueza

I have a desire to one day
give poverty a swift kick,
take on new courage,
put an end to hesitation,
embrace elegance
and assure myself wealth.

Ouvi uma voz falar-me
Pra que você imagina
Clarei o seu pensamento
E descreva a bendita sina
Do grande Rei Vrixadarba
E uma ave divina

I heard a voice within me say,
"Clear your mind
so that you can imagine
and describe the blessed fate
of the great King Vrixadarba
and a heavenly bird."

Residiu em Benares
Uma nação estrangeira
O bondoso Vrixadarba
E era de tal maneira
Que em prol de sua gente
Ocupou-se a vida inteira

The good Vrixadarba
lived in Benares,
a foreign country.
He was the kind of person
who dedicated his life
to helping his people.

Junto com os seus ministros
Percorria as suas terras
Por baixadas e colinas
Por vale montanha e serras
Pra tudo era previnido
Menos pra esporte e guerras

When he and his ministers
toured the kingdom's
hills and dales,
valleys and mountain ranges,
he was prepared for everything
except idle pleasure and war.

O que mais lhe interessava
era cuidar da pobreza
Cultivar as suas terras
Conservar sua riqueza

His chief interests were
looking out for the poor,
cultivating his lands,
keeping an eye on his wealth,

aconselhar toda classe
Unir-se com a nobreza

counseling members of every social
  class,
and getting along well with the
  nobles.

Zelava seus animais
Admirava as lavouras
Agradecia a fortuna
Vinda das mãos protetoras
Sorria em vê a fauna
Das aves encantadoras

He cared for his animals,
and admired the crops in the fields,
expressing gratitude for the good fortune
bestowed on him by protective hands.
He smiled to see the fauna of
the beguiling birds.

Era querido por todos
Da sua bela nação
Pobrezinho lhe estimava
Rico lhe tinha atenção
Por ele ser justiceiro
E ter um bom coração

He was beloved by everyone
in his beautiful nation.
Poor men respected him,
rich men listened to him
because of his just nature
and good heart.

Dos reis de outras nações
Ele era visitado
Pra receber quem chegava
Nunca mostrou-se enfadado
Seu ministério seguia
Tudo por ele ditado

The kings of other nations
came to visit him,
and he never tired
of receiving whoever arrived.
His ministers followed
his every order.

Esse monarca era o dono
Do Reino de Benares
Desempenhava com gosto
Seus concientes papéis
Sem pensar de no futuro
Lhe vir momentos crués.

This monarch was the ruler
of the kingdom of Benares.
He fulfilled his obligations
with pleasure,
never thinking that
difficult days lay ahead.

Senhor rei um dia estava
No lindo jardim sentado
Ouvindo o cântico das aves
Num olor abençoado
Sintiu que por algo estranho
Estava sendo visitado

The king was seated one day
in his lovely garden
listening to the birds caroling
and enjoying the heavenly fragrance
when he sensed that
he had a visitor.

Ouviu um leve sussurro
Pequena asa soprou
Em redor de sua aura
Num arvoredo pousou
Uma sublimada pomba
Que muito lhe admirou

He heard the low murmur
of a small wing
fanning the air.
A sublime dove
whose beauty astounded him
alighted in the grove.

Um gesto aterrorizado
O lindo pássaro mostrou

The lovely bird
made a terrified gesture,

Nisso um cruel gavião	and at that moment a cruel sparrow-
Junto ao rei tambem pousou	hawk
Pedindo ao rei proteção	also alighted near the king.
A pombinha se expressou	Asking the sovereign's protection,
	the little dove said,
Zelai pela a inocência	"Look out for the innocent,
Dai-me vossa proteção	and grant me your protection,
Livrai-me das tristes garras	by freeing me from the grievous
Deste cruel gavião	clutches
Que vive a me perseguir	of this cruel sparrowhawk
Sem a menor compaixão	who pursues me
	without compassion."
Assim falou a pombinha	Thus the little dove
Para o grande suberano	addressed the lofty monarch.
Sua expressão comovia	Her words would have moved
A qualquer cristão humano	any living Christian,
E a causa do seu terror	and the cause of her terror
Era o gavião tirano	was the tyrannous sparrowhawk.
Com um ligeiro ar de riso	The great king said to her
Lhe falou o grande rei	with a little smile,
Não temas pássaro divino	"Do not be afraid, divine bird,
Pois eu te ajudarei	because I will help you.
Por ti minha própria vida	If possible, I will give my own life for
Se for possível eu darei	yours.
A tu que és tão bonita	You, who are as lovely
Como uma flor entre-aberta	as a half-open flower,
Pedes minha proteção	ask my protection,
És atendida na certa	and it will surely be granted.
Tranqüilisa-te ave santa	So calm your fears, heavenly bird,
E não fiques inquieta	and do not be alarmed.
Milhares de seres vivos	Finding themselves in difficulty,
Se achando em embaraço	thousands of creatures call on me
Vindo a mim, tem o auxílio	and encounter help
Do meu resistente braço	in my strong arm.
Pra salvar uma existência	I would give my fortune
Da riqueza eu me desfaço	to save a life.
Pois darei o reino inteiro	And I will give my entire kingdom
Pela a tua salvação	for your salvation
Contanto que livrarei-te	so that I will free you
Das garras do gavião	from the sparrowhawk's claws.
Falo-te com as palavras	I give you the word
De verdadeiro cristão	of a true Christian.
Os teus olhos mostram que	Your eyes show

Foste enviada do Céu	that you were sent from Heaven
Pra no abismo da terra	to this abyss called Earth
Falares com este réu	to speak with this undeserving crea-
Que te vê a olhos nus	ture
Sem cortinado nem véu	who regards you with naked eye,
	unaided by veil or curtain.
Sussega pássaro divino	Be calm, divine bird—
Contra a ti ninguém se mete	no one will rise against you,
Livrar-te de qualquer mal	I have promised to free you
Isso agora me compete	from all evil
Pois o rei de Benares	and the king of Benares
Cumpre tudo que promete	keeps his word."
O gavião que estava	The sparrowhawk, who was
Toda a cena observando	observing the whole scene,
Chegou pra perto do rei	then approached the king
E foi assim lhe falando	and started talking to him.
Encima dos meus direitos	"I am within my rights," he said,
A muitos tempos que ando	"I have been pursuing this dove a long
	time,
Essa pomba me pertence	and she belongs to me.
Com trabalho ganhei ela	It took effort to win her,
Pois se ela é minha presa	and now she is my prisoner.
Apesar de ser tão bela	Despite her beauty,
A marca das minhas garras	the mark of my claws
Já estão no corpo dela	is on her flesh.
Foi doada pelos silfos	She was given to me by the sylphs,
Deuses que dominam o ar	those gods who rule the air,
Pois ela é minha comida	because she is my food,
Tenho que a devorar	and I must eat her.
É impossível que deixes	Surely you cannot allow me
Eu de fome me acabar	to die of hunger.
Se és protetor das aves	If you are the protector of the birds,
Então proteges a mim	then protect me
Sou mais livre do que ela	because I am freer than she
Sinto uma fome sem fim	and feel a boundless hunger.
Entrega o que não é teu	Surrender what is not yours;
A lei do justo é assim	this is the law of the just.
Se essa pomba escapar	If this dove escapes,
Esse gavião não come	this sparrowhawk will not eat.
Como podes desse geito	How will you enhance
Engrandeceres teu nome,	your reputation
Dando vida a uma escrava	by giving life to a slave
E matando o dono de fome	and starving its owner?

Sendo com lei e justiça	Since the law is on my side,
Quem tem direito sou eu	I ought to win.
Os ares não te pertencem	The heavens do not belong to you;
Este céu é dela e meu	this sky is hers and mine.
Se com trabalho achei ela	If I struggled to find her,
A natureza me deu	then this dove is Nature's gift.
Portanto caro monarca	So, dear monarch,
Já expuz minha razão	I have explained my position.
O rei deveria opor-se	A king ought to take sides
Entre luta de cristão	in a fight between Christians
Não poderia intervir	but has no right to intervene
Entre pomba e gavião	in a struggle between hawk and dove."
Então; replicou o rei	"So then," the king replied,
E só tu queres falar?	"do you alone have the right to speak?
Pois estás na minha terra	Here you are in my country,
No meu reino, em meu pomar	my kingdom, my orchard.
Se uma fala e outro cala	How can there be any exchange
Pode assim dialogar?	if one speaks and the other is silent?"
Respondeu-lhe o gavião	The sparrowhawk responded,
Deixarei teu reino agora	"I will leave your kingdom now
A questão é ordenares	if you order
Que a pomba vá embora	the dove to leave too.
Ela no teu reino é minha	If she is lawfully mine within your
Quanto mais se sair fora	borders,
	how much more so outside them!"
O monarca respondeu-lhe	The king answered him,
Aqui não sofre ninguém	"Here no one suffers.
Eu não só protejo a pomba	I protect not only the dove but you.
Como a você também	Tell me what you want to eat
Diga-me o que comer	and put an end
E mate a fome que tem	to your hunger.
Sendo pra matar a fome	You may eat whatever you want
Você come o que quizer	to satisfy your hunger.
Tudo eu tenho com fartura	I have everything in abundance:
Mate outro bicho qualquer	kill whatever other animal you
Sendo doméstico ou selvagem	choose,
Escolha e diga o que quer	be it wild or tame.
	Choose, you have only to say what
	you wish.
Do camondongo ao cobaia	There is mouse, two kinds of guinea
Tiú, mocó, jararaca,	pig,
Porco burrego ou cabrito	lizard, and viper,
Cutia veado ou paca	pig, lamb, or kid,

Onça capivara ou zebra
Lobo javalí ou vaca

agouti, lamb, or paca,
mountain lion, capybara, or zebra,
wolf, wild boar, or cow,

Préa, punaré, coelho
Raposa ou maracajá
Timbú, preguiça ou tatu
Gato, guaxinim, guará
Garrote bode ou carneiro
Gasela ou tamanduá

cavy, rat, rabbit,
fox, or ocelot,
timbú, sloth, or armadillo,
cat, guaxinim, flamingo,
calf, goat, or sheep,
gazelle, or anteater."

Disse o gavião: não como
Tiu, nem camaleão
Não como porco nem cobra
Nem cutia nem furão
Não como cabra nem vaca
Nem veado nem leão

The sparrowhawk said, "I don't eat
lizard or chameleon,
snake or pig,
agouti or grison.
I don't eat goat or cow,
deer or lion.

Eu não como javalí
Nem que meu bico se quebre
Carneiro, mocó, nem onça
Tudo isso me dar febre
Nem paca nem capivara
Nem zebra, rato nem lebre!

I don't eat wild boar;
even if my beak breaks I don't eat
sheep, guinea pig, or mountain lion.
All this gives me a fever.
I don't eat paca or capybara,
zebra, rat, or hare.

Portanto meu alimento
São essas pombinhas belas
Por isto, eu reviro o mundo
Voando em procura delas
A não ser carne humana
Só me alimento com elas

My only food is
these beautiful little doves,
and so I scour the world
for them.
The only other thing I eat
is human flesh.

Ainda faço um negócio
Se quiseres aceitar
Dá-me carne do teu corpo
Para eu me alimentar
Que pese igualmente a pomba
E podes com ela ficar

I will still make you a proposition:
if you want to, give me
an equal portion of your own flesh,
which I will eat,
and you can
have the dove."

O Rei ficou satisfeito
E a proposta aceitou
Uma faca uma balança
Logo providenciou
Numa das conchas a pomba
Ligeiramente pousou

The king was satisfied
with his proposal.
He immediately arranged
for a knife and scale
and quickly set the dove
on one side of the balance.

E o rei sem ter demora
Cuidou logo em se cortar
E carne na outra concha
Começou ele a botar

And without delay, the king
set about cutting
his own flesh, setting it upon
his side of the scales,

Quanto mais botava carne	but the more he set there,
Mais via a pomba pesar	the more the dove appeared to weigh.
Cortava carne das coxas	He cut flesh from his thighs
Igualmente um açougueiro	just like a butcher,
E sacudia na concha	shaking the scales
Em completo desespeiro	in complete despair
Logo mentalmente viu	when he had a sudden vision
Martelo, cruz e madeiro	of hammer, cross, and wood.
Concentrou-se em Jesus Cristo	He concentrated upon Jesus Christ
Pensando, pediu perdão	and asked forgiveness,
Sentiu-se pessoalmente	feeling himself ready and willing
Com toda desposição	to die for the dove
Com o peso do seu corpo	as the scale kissed the ground
A concha beijou o chão	with the weight of his body.
Ali chegaram a rainha	Then the queen arrived,
A princesa e um marquesão	the princess and a grand marquis.
Enfim pra seu ministério	All his ministers
Não houve conformação	were opposed to the idea of a king
Em um rei ter se cortado	cutting his own flesh
Para um simples gavião	for a mere sparrowhawk.
Choro, protesto e alarma	There were tears, protests, and shouts
E o povo em desespeiro	of alarm.
Gritava não faça isso	His despairing subjects shouted,
Por nosso Deus verdadeiro	"Stop this in the name
Viva pra sua nação	of our true God!
E o povo do mundo inteiro	Live for the sake of our nation
	and the people of the whole world.
Nosso rei enlouqueceu!	Our king has gone mad!
Oh! Deus tende piedade	Oh God, have mercy upon us," they
Nosso país ficar orfão	shouted,
Sem haver necessidade	"and don't let our country
Quanto protesto do povo	needlessly be orphaned!"
E quanta intranquilidade	How many protests
	and how much agitation!
O rei bastante estragado	Much the worse for wear
Mas estava vivo e falou	but still alive, the king spoke.
Gritou para o povo: calma!	"Silence!" he shouted to the people
O povo silenciou	and they grew quiet.
Subiu a concha da pomba	Then the dove's side of the balance
E a concha do rei baixou	rose and the king's sank.
O rei levantou a vista	The king raised his eyes
Olhou para a amplidão	and looked at the multitude.

Ao longe viu a pombinha	From afar he saw the little dove
Voando sem direção	flying at will across
Transpondo este manto azul	that blue cloak of the sky
Para a Celeste Mansão	in the direction of the Celestial Mansion.

Nisso um intervalo opaco	With that,
Deixou o sol escondido	the sun momentarily dimmed.
Por traz de uma nuvem grossa	From behind a dense cloud,
O povo que tinha ouvido	the people who had heard
A voz do bondoso rei	the voice of the good king
Parou mais o alarido	grew yet stiller.

Passou a nuvem e o sol	The cloud passed, and the sun
A sua luz forneceu	shone again
Aos habitantes da terra	upon the earth's inhabitants,
Porém, ninguém percebeu	but no one noticed
Como a pombinha do céu	how the little dove way up there
Dali desapareceu	in the sky had disappeared.

De repente uma neblina	Suddenly a fragrant mist
De essência projetou-se	enveloped the scale
Por sobre a balança aonde	where the good king
O bondoso rei cortou-se	had cut his own flesh.
Um som de harpa divina	The wind carried the sound
Para o povo o vento trouxe	of a divine harp to those below.

E o som harmonioso	And its music grew
Foi tomando todo espaço	until it filled the skies
Da terra ao firmamento	without the slightest difficulty.
Sem o menor embaraço	It was God
Era Deus mostrando a força	displaying the might
Do seu incansável braço	of His tireless arm.

E enquanto o som estava	And while the people were overcome
A o povo dominando	by that heavenly sound,
A neblina de essência	the fragrant mist
Estava a o rei molhando	was descending over the king,
E toda carne cortada	restoring the flesh
Pro local ia voltando	he had cut.

Cinco minutos depois	Five minutes later,
O rei estava perfeito	the king was just as he had always been.
Seu corpo não demonstrava	His body revealed
Nenhum sinal de defeito	no defect whatsoever.
O justo sofre na terra	The just suffer on earth,
Porém por Deus é aceito	but God stands by them.

O rei tornou-se mais jovem	The king became younger,
Mais elegante e simpático	more elegant and appealing,
Graças ao nosso bom Deus	thanks to our gracious God,
E ao chuvisco aromático	the fragrant drizzle,
E seu viver de equilíbrio	and, to be sure,
Por no assunto ser prático	the king's own exemplary life.
O rei fez tudo pra dar	The king did everything he could
Ao gavião, alimento	to feed the sparrowhawk
Esse morreu por querer	who died as a result of his insistence
Muito alto o pagamento	on an overly high payment,
E a pombinha sumiu-se	and the little dove vanished
No azul do firmamento	into the blue of the firmament.
Desse dia por diante	From that day on,
O bom rei cada vez mais	the good king
Protegia a sua gente	kept increasing vigil
Zelava seus animais	over his people,
Adorava a inocência	saw to his animals, revered innocence
E conservava os vegetais	and watched over the fields.
Todo povo do reinado	His subjects
Seguia a mesma instrução	followed his example.
O drama foi divulgado	The king's drama was recounted
Por quase toda nação	throughout the world,
Fizeram livros do rei	and authors wrote books about the
Da pomba e do gavião	king,
	the dove, and the sparrowhawk.
Ainda hoje em Benares	Still today in Benares
Aonde o caso se deu	where this event occurred,
Tem testemunha ocular	there is an eyewitness
Quem para mim escreveu	who wrote to me about it.
É autor de grande livros	Thanks to his ample studies,
Pelo o nobre estudo seu	he is the author of distinguished
	books.
Quem ler esta narrativa	Whoever reads this story
Medite e preste atenção	should reflect well upon it;
Diga se hoje tem homem	then tell me if there is a man today
Com esta desposição	who would cut his own flesh
De se cortar pelo um pássaro	for a bird who appeared
Que desceu da amplidão	from the heavens.
Mais o rei tinha a idéia	The king was of the opinion
Que aquele passarinho	that that little bird
Vinha de outras esferas	came from another world
E não foi criado em ninho	and did not grow up in a nest
Ticido em nosso vergel	woven from dry leaves and nettles
Com folha seca e espinho	within our garden.

Quem achar que isto é lenda
E não merece atenção
Pense lá como quizer
Porque tem sua razão
Eu mesmo sou que não quero
Pensar como o gavião

The person who thinks that this is just
  a story
that doesn't deserve attention
has the right to his opinion,
but for my part, I would not want
to be like the sparrowhawk.

Aquele gavião era
Um anjo do satanaz
E a pombinha divina
Era a pombinha da paz
Que veio a terra mostrar
Como é que o justo faz

That sparrowhawk was one
of Satan's angels,
and the divine little dove
was the dove of peace
who came to earth to demonstrate
the ways of the just.

Jeová, o santo nome
Semente do sumo bem
Ordenador, bom e justo
Unificador também
Zelai pela a minha vida
Amo a vós e mais ninguém.

Jehovah, holy name,
seed of greatest good,
just and gracious ruler
and unifier,
watch over my life!
I love you and no one else.

FIM
27 – 4 – 1978
Recife   Pe.

END
27 – 4 – 1978
Recife   Pe.

V. *The Monstrous Kidnapping of Serginho* by Apolônio Alves dos Santos[1]

The Poet

On the first day of a sweltering new year, Apolônio Alves dos Santos is one of the few men in his neighborhood who does not appear the worse for wear. Dressed in an old undershirt and rumpled pants but carefully shaved and clear-eyed, he grins at a friend, who has clearly had his share of rum the night before. Apolônio's wife hands him a bottle of carbonated apple juice, the Christmas gift of her employer, and he takes a penknife out of his pocket, opening the "champagne" with a pop. Dogs and children rush about the room as the friend collapses into the only chair. Apolônio smoothes his mustache with a certain glee. "Any food around here?" the friend mumbles, rubbing the sides of his head. "Beans, leftover beans, take all you want," the poet tells him, laughing when the man groans.

Apolônio has lived for twelve years now in a part of Rio de Janeiro called Benfica. Like him, most of his neighbors are originally from the Northeast. "Street" is not quite the right word for the two rows of makeshift houses behind the Sixteenth Division Police Headquarters where the numbers run from one to thirty-seven, then skip to sixty-two. When it rains, the mud engulfs mounds of garbage, bottle caps, and dead rats. When the sun beats down, as it usually does from December to April, it bakes the refuse into the ground, where it stays until it rains again. Ducks, pigs, and roosters wander through the houses or stretch out in the scant shade, leaving a lone goat to defy the heat. Trains shriek by overhead every ten or fifteen minutes.

Presently fifty-eight years old, Apolônio was born in the countryside surrounding the small city of Guarabira between the Paraiban backlands

1. A preliminary version of this chapter was presented as a paper at the American Folklore Society meetings in Salt Lake City, October 18, 1978. I am grateful to Edigar de Alencar, author of various literary works and studies of popular culture, as well as a long-time writer for *O Dia*, for providing me with a series of clippings from the newspaper's files dating from between June 11 and 19, 1977. These are the reports on which Apolônio claims to have based his own *folheto*. I would also like to thank Mário Pontes for sending me corresponding reports from *O Jornal do Brasil*.

and the coast. He left the Northeast for Rio de Janeiro almost thirty years ago. The last time he returned home was for five days in 1970. "I could write a whole geography lesson about this city," he says, "you name it and I've lived there: Caxias, Tijuca, Rio Comprido, São Cristóvão, Iguaçu."[2] Though he first worked as a bricklayer and night watchman, Apolônio now limits himself to selling *folhetos* to other vendors as well as to buyers in fairs. He would like to get a license, which would permit him to set up a full-time stand.

Although no one in his family had ever been a poet, Apolônio was attracted to *cordel* stories from an early age. His father, who "had a little vein of poetry inside him," used to bring home *folhetos* from the fair for his son to read to his mother and sisters. Apolônio wrote his first story at the age of eighteen; it was about a girl who hid behind a wooden mask in order to escape an unwelcome suitor. The well-known popular poet Manuel Camilo dos Santos corrected the *folheto*'s errors for him, encouraging him to persevere. His second tale was published by Manuel Camilo's assistant, José Alves Pontes, who continues to print the stories which Apolônio periodically sends north. "Of course this makes for problems," says the poet. "I keep doing business with him because he gives me credit, but it took him so long to get *Serginho* back to me that people had lost interest in the story, and I only sold a thousand copies. Now if I had a printer here, ah, I would have sold at least ten times that!"

Although the poet studied for less than a year in a country school, he succeeded in teaching himself to read and write. Today his library includes a history of Brazil, two dictionaries, the Bible, a book of German fairy tales, a pulp novel, the text of a soap opera ("The Vanquished Goddess"), a catechism, and José Américo de Almeida's classic novel *Cane Trash*. He also owns a copy of the Casa de Rui Barbosa study of the *literatura de cordel*, which he hopes to "get around to reading since, after all, I write *folhetos*."

Apolônio has always enjoyed writing journalistic stories whether they are "true events," like the kidnapping of Serginho, or stories like that of a man in Minas Gerais rumored to have given birth to a child. "I don't say that such a thing could never happen," Apolônio says with a wink; "I just think that it would be, well, difficult."

The poet is also fond of *pelejas*, and though not a *repentista*, he has written himself into a number of poetic contests, in which he naturally emerges as the winner. Tales about now-legendary cowmen and roundups also appeal to him. Although he has trouble picking out the *folhetos* he

2. Apolônio Alves dos Santos, Rio de Janeiro, January 1, 1978. Quotations in this chapter are taken from a recorded interview in Apolônio's home in the Benfica section of Rio de Janeiro on December 22, 1977, and from conversations with him between September 24, 1977, and January 4, 1978, and again on July 28 and August 1, 1978.

likes best from among the dozens he has written, some of his favorites are *The Hero Napoleon in the Kingdom of Doors*, *The Woman Who Had a Passion for Priests*, and *The Man from Minas Who Bought a Trolley Car in Rio de Janeiro*. He also has a number of unpublished stories, including one attacking Afro-Brazilian cult religions called *The Mysteries of Macumba*, and a *folheto* version of Monteiro Lobato's novel *Jeca Tatú*.[3] "If I were to publish all the books I have ever written, I would spend every penny I own, and my house would be so full of paper that I would have to move," he says.

Apolônio's Northeastern identity provides a recurrent theme in his poetry. He and his fellow poet Cícero Vieira da Silva (Mocó), also from Paraíba, often talk about their early days there. Aside from Mocó, who now works as a bus driver, Apolônio knows at least seven or eight other Rio-based *cordel* authors. Five are Northeasterners, who settled in the big city around the same time he did. The others are Southerners, who took a liking to the *folhetos* brought to Rio by emigrants and decided to enter the trade. Even though Apolônio considers the latter's stories "a little strange," he maintains friendly relations with them. "Poets have to count on one another and especially here, where things are different," he explains.[4]

Apolônio believes that it is easier to earn a living as a poet in Rio de Janeiro than in the Northeast. He himself normally sells fifty to a hundred booklets on weekend nights in the Largo do Machado and almost double that number on Sundays in the São Cristóvão fair. Though Northeasterners frequent both sites, the two are really very different. Though both were originally depots for transports arriving from Pernambuco and Paraíba, one has the flavor of an amusement park whereas the other resembles a weekly produce market in at least some aspects.[5]

At the time I was there, the Largo, located between the districts of

3. *O Herói Napoleão no Reino das Portas* (Guarabira: José Alves Pontes, n.d.), *A Mulher que gostou dos Padres* (Guarabira: José Alves Pontes, 1977), *O Mineiro que comprou um Bonde no Rio de Janeiro* (Guarabira: José Alves Pontes, n.d.). To the best of my knowledge, *Os Mistérios da Macumba* and *Jeca Tatú* are still in manuscript.

4. As of 1978, there were some nine *folheto* writers in the greater Rio area. Six of these were Northeasterners: Apolônio Alves dos Santos, João Lopes Freire, José João dos Santos (Azulão), Expedito da Silva, Sebastião Palmeira da Silva (Palmeirinha), and Cícero Vieira da Silva (Mocó). While not in residence at the time of my interviews, Joaquim de Sena, from Fortaleza, tends to divide his time between the South and the North. The other three *cordel* authors, Flávio Moreira, Cosme Damião Vieira de Oliveira (Catapora), and Paulo Teixeira, are from either the city or state of Rio de Janeiro and became interested in the *folheto* as a result of their contact with Northeastern emigrants. Although Azulão and Moreira are financially better off than their fellow poets, all these individuals live in the working-class outskirts of the city known as the Baixada Fluminense. The State Ministry of Education and Culture has published a collection of twenty-five *folhetos* by five of these authors.

5. For an overview of buyers at the two sites, see Appendix C.

Flamengo and Catete in the center of the city, was temporarily torn up to accommodate a future subway. Ringed by restaurants, bars, and movie theaters, it attracts a number of curious passersby, and on Saturday and Sunday nights from around 7 to 10 is crammed with small groups who mill about talking before moving on for a night on the town. One can find *capoeira* dancers, accordion players, fire eaters, *repentistas*, and a number of vendors selling coffee, roasted corn, and ice cream. Couples sit together on stone benches surrounding a stagnant pond. During periodic blackouts caused by power overloads, the crowd lets out a whoop.

Apolônio's customers in the Largo do Machado tend to be younger than most buyers in the São Cristóvão fair. They wear T-shirts with sayings in French or English, blue jeans, denim jackets, and stylishly long hair. Most work but many also study at night. Some come to the Largo with a girlfriend; others arrive alone or with a group of friends.

The Northeasterners who buy *folhetos* stand around the poet, reading aloud to themselves or to a friend. Other would-be buyers from Rio or São Paulo leaf through the booklets curiously. "This is the weirdest comic book I've ever seen!" exclaims one in a neon-colored shirt. From time to time Apolônio picks up a story from among those which he has spread out before him on a plastic cloth. Singing to himself in a low voice, he barely notices as people gather round. When somebody asks for a particular title that he cannot find among his booklets, he sends him over to the black man called Jair, who specializes in the shiny-covered variety. "He doesn't hurt business," Apolônio explains with typical good humor. "Those who like the glossy covers buy from him. Those who like the blockprints buy from me, and in the end we come out even."

The buyers in São Cristóvão, where Apolônio works on Sunday morning, are older and more apt to be from Pernambuco, Paraíba, or Ceará. Although his stand is up against the wall of the large concrete building that serves as a market on weekdays and thus is "not a good location," he prefers the fair to the Largo not only because it is both bigger and nearer to home but also because "there is more to see." Individual stalls extend for three whole city blocks. Shoppers can choose between glittering belts, freshly pressed cane juice, enormous petticoats for use in Afro-Brazilian rituals, coconut candy, plastic madonnas, and live crabs on a string. Around the table, which Apolônio rents for fifty *cruzeiros* every Sunday, there are on-the-spot tailors, heaps of bananas, envelopes, and keyrings that say "Souvenir of the Northeast." Long strings of peek-in photos dangle from a nearby pole.

Although Apolônio does a healthy business, there is no question that it is José João dos Santos, better known as Azulão, who dominates the fair. A *repentista* as well as a writer, he has managed to find favor with various government agencies devoted to the preservation and dissemination of popular traditions and is regularly invited to make records and give talks in universities. He is also the only *cordel* author to sing his verses in the fair. With the money that he earns every Sunday from the sale of his own and others' stories, he has built a house with a real bathroom on a hillside two hours out of town, which is the envy of his friends. Apolônio does not begrudge Azulão his success, nor is he particularly concerned about the forces behind it. Though unwilling to predict the *cordel*'s future, he nevertheless regards the present with hope. "Things aren't easy here," he says, "but at least in Rio the poet has a fighting chance. In the North, there is no security and many writers go hungry. I'd like to return home as soon as I retire, but just now I don't want to. No, no, for the moment I am going to stay right here."

The Source

On the afternoon of June 8, 1977, eleven-year-old Sérgio Dutra de Almeida, better known by the diminutive "Serginho," was kidnapped on his way home from school, then murdered. His murderer, a forty-nine-year-old television repairman baptized José Pereira Borges and nicknamed "Radio Joe," had long been an inhabitant of the small city of Bom Jesus de Itabapoana in the extreme north of the state of Rio de Janeiro. Dominated by the Borges family, whose head served as deputy for a time to the state assembly, the town was once the center of a thriving coffee industry. Today Bom Jesus depends largely on sugar cane and dairy products.

Radio Joe, a second cousin of the victim, had known the boy's father, Messias Borges de Almeida, since childhood. At the time of the crime, Radio Joe had been experiencing emotional and financial problems. Largely as the result of a series of ill-fated love affairs with local prostitutes, he found himself faced with a debt of well over a thousand dollars, which he saw no way of paying off. When Messias, a relatively well-to-do farmer who had helped him with loans in the past, refused this time to lend him the money, Joe lost his head, resolving to kidnap and hold for ransom "the first rich man's son I see." Probably not by coincidence, the first such child to cross his path turned out to be Messias's eleven-year-old son, who had a habit after school of stopping by the television repair shop where Joe worked.

Joe later insisted that he had no plans to murder his hostage. When Serginho, however, began to struggle and shout, he became frightened and hit him over the head with a metal bar. Wrapping the corpse in a sack, which he secured with electric cable, he put it in his car, then drove to the river where he weighted it with a stone and watched it sink. He next wrote an anonymous letter to the boy's parents as if the child were still alive, demanding six thousand dollars in cash as ransom. The money was to be left beside an isolated highway marker some eight miles from town.

Before paying the ransom, the boy's parents had alerted the authorities to Serginho's disappearance, and numerous friends and relatives had joined in the search. The whole town was therefore stunned when two fishermen discovered Serginho's corpse. The police intensified their search for a pair of photographers who had recently taken a series of pictures of the boy, which his father had refused to buy. When questioning confirmed the men's innocence, the authorities sent out another false alarm for two strangers recently sighted giving sweets to children.

Radio Joe had joined in the search from the beginning. His exaggerated eagerness to help gradually aroused the investigators' suspicions. When detectives sent to Bom Jesus from the city of Rio de Janeiro learned of Joe's debts, they brought him in for questioning. On June 16, a little more than a week after the murder, he confessed to the crime, exhibiting great remorse and begging to be hanged. What Joe had not spent of the ransom money and more of the wire with which he had bound the body were discovered in his little shop. Given the intense emotion generated by the boy's funeral a week earlier, the prisoner was transferred under heavy guard to another prison just before celebration of a Seventh Day Mass for the Dead. As may be imagined, the crime caused a great furor in the usually sleepy city and surrounding countryside. Newspapers throughout the state published scores of tearful letters and editorials denouncing the murder, along with detailed accounts of the murdered boy and his family. The reports on which Apolônio claims to have relied for his story come from the Rio tabloid, *O Dia (The Day)*, which published daily accounts of new developments as well as a number of articles describing the town of Bom Jesus, the murderer, and his victim.

The Six-Step Pattern

As the news reports upon which Apolônio based his story span some two weeks, it is impossible to duplicate all of these here. I have therefore reproduced a summary, published on June 18, at the end of this chapter, drawing on bits and pieces of other reports to support my major points.[6]

6. The summary, *Seven Days That Shook Bom Jesus (7 Dias que Abalaram Bom Jesus)*, which is translated at the end of this chapter, appeared as part of an article entitled "Killer of Serginho Says, 'I want to hang!'" ("Matador de Serginho: QUERO SER LINCHADO!") in Rio de Janeiro's largest daily, *O Dia*, on June 19, 1977. Because most readers would have been familiar with the events from over a week of reports, the summary does not attempt to provide a truly comprehensive overview. It is interesting because of what it indicates of the tone and outlook of these accounts.

Although Apolônio claims to have followed the *O Dia* account to the letter ("What I have said in my *folheto* is all true; I didn't change a single word"), a comparison of the summary with his story reveals a number of differences, the most important of which are outlined below:

NEWSPAPER REPORTS	FOLHETO
Elements not unlike others found in *DW folhetos* but no six-step structure. Articles answer questions "Who?" "What?" "Where?" "When?" and "Why?"	Usual six-step pattern (*DR/DW* in this case)
Spotlight upon murderer and victim.	Spotlight upon parents and community.
Human interest stems from individualizing details.	Human interest stems from generalizing and allegory.
Overall fidelity to facts:	Changes in several apparently minor facts:
Serginho and Radio Joe are second cousins.	Radio Joe identified as Serginho's uncle and Messias' brother.
Investigators take Joe in for questioning.	Messias denounces Radio Joe as result of sudden inspiration.
Joe repents of his crime and asks for death.	Radio Joe does not repent, prompting poet to call for divine punishment.

Because the newspaper coverage of the Serginho kidnapping was an ongoing story with many installments, it differs from the *folheto*, a one-shot effort written after all the facts were in. Each additional "chapter" in the real-life "whodunit" focuses on a new development: the delivery of the ransom note, the discovery of the body, Radio Joe's electrifying confession, and the townspeople's cry for vengeance. Because the reporter does not have all the facts at his disposal until quite late, early versions of the story in particular are necessarily hard to fit into a given mold.

In terms of *cordel* patterns, the newspaper reports come closest to a *DW* frame. The summary entitled "Seven Days That Shook Bom Jesus" tells of a criminal brought to justice, a tragic mystery solved. The moral of the story is that crime does not pay. Nevertheless, even this after-the-fact overview cannot be considered a true *DW* story, and the report does not fit the *cordel*'s six-step pattern because it lacks the necessary element of divine intervention (step 4, counterresponse, in the six-step sequence). Furthermore, while the reporter clearly slants his story to achieve the maximum degree of human interest, he does not treat his subject in the same way as a *cordel* author. Radio Joe is definitely the culprit, but the reporter introduces humanizing details that make him less than a representative *folheto* villain.

In Apolônio's story, the murderer becomes a prime example of *falsidade*. Although the boy's parents and the community are the protagonists, the author guarantees a strong *DW* subplot in his treatment of Radio Joe. I have outlined first the *DR* and then the *DW* story line within the *Monstrous Kidnapping of Serginho folheto* in order to make the structure clearer. (See Figure 2 on page 62 for the *DW* and *DR* patterns.)

DR Plot

1. *Pact*: Father "of pure and good heart" and devoted mother lavish love and affection on their "beloved little boy."
2. *Test*: Boy does not return home.
3. *(Right) response*: Parents go looking for boy and ask help of neighbors and then police in all-out effort to find son.
2. *Test*: Kidnapper demands considerable sum of money.
3. *(Right) response*: Money no object; parents ask authorities to do nothing because they want their son back "safe and sound."
2. *Test*: Fisherman discovers body.
3. *(Right) response*: Parents overcome by grief. Mourning community asks justice of God.
4. *Counterresponse*: Church bells toll, "an unmistakable sign" that the murderer is nearby. Serginho's father suddenly remembers a loan he had denied one of his brothers a few days back.
5. *Judgment*: Brother brought in for questioning, confesses guilt. Police apprehend half the ransom-money.
6. *Pact reasserted*: Poet calls on group to join him in asking justice of God, resulting in severe punishment of "that murderous monster" and therefore in renewed calm.

The *folheto*'s complementary *DW* plot may be outlined as follows. Notice that the newspaper account may be broken down into more or less the same steps except for step 4, in which investigators, acting on a hunch, bring Radio Joe in for questioning.

DW Plot

1. *Pact*: Tranquil town of Bom Jesus goes about its business. Radio Joe is accepted member of the community. ("He was liked though regarded as a little 'folkloric,'" one newspaper account explains.)
2. *Test*: Radio Joe confronts severe financial and emotional difficulties.
3. *(Wrong) response*: Radio Joe murders an innocent child.

4. *Counterresponse*: Divine justice inspires the boy's father to denounce Radio Joe.
5. *Judgment*: Repudiation by community, loss of ill-gotten gains, generalized cry for punishment.
6. *Pact reasserted*: Punishment guaranteed, criminal removed from community's midst.

In order to impose this *DR/DW* structure on his material, the poet had to introduce some changes. His first move was to establish the customary division between *firmeza* and *falsidade*, or good and evil. To facilitate this split, he first reduced the number of characters, eliminating figures unessential to his purpose, such as the unjustly accused photographers, the chief of police, the second fisherman, and, of course, the eager reporter, who plays such an active role in the newspaper accounts. This left the poet with a more manageable cast composed of the boy's father and mother, a single fisherman who discovered the body, a series of nameless officials, the extended community, and, to be sure, Serginho and Radio Joe.

In order to sustain the reader's interest particularly on those days in which there were few new developments, the newspaper reports included a little bit of everything. There are articles, for instance, on the boy's family, on the history of Bom Jesus, on Radio Joe's sex life, and on other celebrated kidnappings within and outside Brazil. Nevertheless, the bulk of the reportage concerned the victim and the murderer. Approximately three-quarters of these items were devoted to the details of the crime and to the two principals. The summary proper emphasized each new step in the drama starring Radio Joe and the unfortunate child.

Apolônio, however, devotes little attention to the murderer or his victim. Although he refers to Serginho on a half-dozen occasions, the boy is always offstage. Likewise, Radio Joe, who appears for the first time toward the bottom of the sixth page (the *folheto* has eight pages) is referred to by name only once. Thereafter, Apolônio refers to him by a series of epithets, including "the villain," "that monster," "the cruel assassin," and "that monstrous beast."

Instead, the poet lavishes attention on the boy's grief-stricken mother and, above all, father, whom he mentions by name over twenty times. The central relationship in the *folheto* is not between Radio Joe and his victim Serginho but between the child's parents, whose faith is tested by this bitter loss, and God. It is not Serginho who suffers in the *cordel* story but the father and mother who remain behind on earth. Unlike the reporter who stresses the gruesome details of the crime itself, the poet dwells on its effects on other people.

In the *folheto*, the community becomes an extension of the boy's family. The fisherman (two of them in the newspaper story) is a convenient symbol of this larger group. Although Apolônio is casual about the man's name, referring to him as "Antonio Solange" instead of "Antonio Salvador" Silva, the actual name, he describes his grief upon finding the body in great detail. After the fisherman walks "almost ten miles" to the police station to report his find, the entire population attends the funeral in an expression of solidarity with the victim's parents.

It is true that the community is also important in the newspaper stories. Nevertheless, it is not seen as a specific instrument of divine justice. These reports end with the authorities' carting off the wrongdoer, but the poet implies that justice remains to be done. Calling on his readers to join his call for heavenly retribution, he deliberately overlooks Radio Joe's tearful confession. To be sure, Apolônio does more than simply shift his focus. Although as intent as the reporter on mustering human interest, his approach is somewhat different. If the former individualizes in order to make the people and setting more easy to visualize, the latter generalizes, stressing the underlying patterns.

Some students of journalistic *folhetos* have stressed the popular poet's ability to play on his audience's feelings, suggesting that *cordel* stories are more sensational than newspaper accounts. "Newspaper items transmitted by *folhetos*," says Luiz Beltrão, in representative fashion, "always include impassioned commentary, given that the mass of readers is not sensitive to cold journalistic objectivity."[7] But the newspaper accounts are clearly neither "cold" nor particularly "objective." In fact, most observers would find them more sensational than the *folheto* version.

An insistence on particulars runs through the reports on the Serginho murder. Thus, Radio Joe is carefully described as "wearing a green shirt, a mustard-colored pullover, gray cotton pants and brown boots, with trembling, handcuffed hands." The reporter also provides numerous points of interest about the killer, not all of which are negative. For instance:

He was born in the Barra de Pirapitinga, some eight miles from Bom Jesus.
He completed only grade school.
He took first place in a course given by the Phillips Company in São Paulo.
He was a Mason who was expelled from the Lodge.
He was once a member of the Baptist church.
He was a talented television technician who did much to improve the area's once faulty reception, installing the television set in the town's central square as well as the town's PA system.

7. Luiz Beltrão, "Os folhetos" in *Folk-comunicação: Um estudo dos agentes e dos meios populares de informação de fatos e expressão de idéias*, 2nd ed. (São Paulo: Melhoramentos, 1971), p. 71.

He was a pioneer in ham radio operation.
He had various lovers, one of whom, "Baby Mary," he lived with for a
    year and a half. When he discovered that she had been cheating on
    him, he broke everything in the house and "even part of the iron
    railing around it."

The same approach is used with the murdered child in one of many
accounts of the fateful day. In this case, the journalist restricts himself to
details which will highlight the child's innocence, making the crime seem
yet more heinous.

June 8, 6:30 A.M. Dona Valma wakes her son Sérgio. He kneels by his bed,
prays just as he does every morning, dresses, and then asks his mother to
make him manioc cakes. Blond hair, around four feet tall, sixty pounds,
Serginho was a frank, happy little boy, a good student accustomed to getting 100 in everything. . . .
11 A.M. He puts on his navy blue trousers and white shirt, the uniform of
the Pereira Passos public school, which has the school emblem embroi-
dered on the pocket. After his father arrives home from tending his cattle,
the family eats lunch. Sérgio tucks his homework into his bookbag along
with several manioc cakes.[8]

The specific flavor of this passage stands in direct contrast to the *folheto*,
where it is impossible to find more than the most general descriptions of
individuals. These references are inevitably to roles rather than idiosyn-
cratic traits. Thus, Dona Valma is "an affectionate mother" and her husband Messias "a devoted father," but there is nothing to distinguish them
from a hundred other paragons of parental virtue. The *folheto* purposely
overlooks such tempting raw material as the little boy's poignant last
words to a playmate or the murderer's tearful, self-deprecating confession.
If one strips away the adjectives "good," "bad," and their synonyms, few
descriptive terms remain, underscoring the *cordel*'s interest in moral over
physical realities.

There is no question that Apolônio had all the material he needed at his
disposal. The newspaper accounts include numerous photographs of the
murderer, the boy, and his family. The articles are full of all sorts of details: names, places, dates, and appealingly personal anecdotes. Since the
poet readily admits to basing his account upon the newspaper stories, there
must be a reason for these omissions. The reader must conclude that
Apolônio made his characters allegorical figures rather than flesh-and-
blood people because that is the way he wanted them to be.

Like other forms of Northeast Brazilian popular art (and much folk art

8. *O Dia*, June 17, 1977, Section A, p. 6.

in general), the *folheto* stylizes, keeping individual peculiarities to a mini-mum when not eliminating them entirely. Circus acts, Carnival celebra-tions, and puppet plays all strive toward an interchangeable ideal. Because no element should detract attention from the underlying message, the artist must refrain from arousing interest in any one character. Nothing is more surprising than an *ex voto* (a replica of the whole or one part of the body offered to a saint or God in exchange for help in healing the injured mem-ber), which in some way recalls a particular person. *Cordel* personages who do stand out in some way are therefore memorable. For example, although Aunt Dina is a very minor character in *A Night of Love*, a sur-prising number of buyers remember her sad plight. "Oh yes, wasn't she the one who had the unhappy marriage?" persons who cannot remember the name of the protagonist, her niece, may ask.[9]

Because the *cordel* tradition does not permit too much attention to the individual, the writers tend to reserve the use of details for descriptions of places or things. This is obvious in Apolônio's story, where he says noth-ing about the color of Serginho's hair or about the cakes his mother always baked for his snack at school, but he does name the road marker where the parents were to leave the ransom, gives the number of days between each new event, and describes the state of the corpse. Thus, while the *cordel* author generalizes his treatment of human beings to the point of making them walking virtues or vices, he provides a specific orbit for them by sketching in a number of concrete objects (cables, stones, a letter) and by being quite precise in measurements of time, space, weight, and money.

And yet in transcribing these details more or less as they appear in the newspaper stories, Apolônio introduces a number of minor changes. Some, such as the identification of Serginho's mother as "Walda" not "Valma," the assertion that the boy was strangled rather than bludgeoned, and the telescoping of the two fishermen into a single person, have little effect upon the story. Some, however, are slight shifts that are crucial. These include Apolônio's identification of Radio Joe as the brother of the

9. João Martins de Ataíde, *Uma Noite de Amor* (Juazeiro do Norte: Tipografia São Fran-cisco, 1974). It is certain that the passage in question (p. 23) is a particularly poignant and therefore memorable statement.

Um dia a tia Diná	One day her Aunt Dina said,
Disse: querida sobrinha	"My dear niece, I know that you
Sei que não amas ao duque	do not love the duke.
Tua sorte é igual à minha	Your fate is the same as mine
Uni-me a quem não amava	because I entered into a union
E vivo sempre sozinha.	with someone whom I didn't love
	and for this reason, I live alone."

victim's father and thus Serginho's uncle rather than his second cousin, his insistence upon divine intervention in the culprit's apprehension, and his deliberate exclusion of Radio Joe's heartfelt confession.

It is quite true that Radio Joe was a relative of the boy he murdered. As one newspaper report points out, the little city of Bom Jesus was founded less than a century ago by Antonio José Borges, "patriarch of a family of more than three hundred members and for all practical purposes patriarch of the city itself, which erected a statue in his honor in the central square." Like so many small towns dominated by a single extended family, Bom Jesus reveals a high degree of intermarriage. Thus, the fact that Radio Joe, the son of one of Antonio José Borges' sisters, was the second cousin of the victim is not surprising. Furthermore, as one can see from the following confusing quotation from the newspaper, this relationship was hardly direct. Radio Joe

> grew up in Barra do Pirapitinga, in the golden era of King Coffee, playing with his cousins Messias Borges de Almeida (son of Pedro José de Almeida, married to Jovita Borges, daughter of Messias Borges Ribeiro, who, for his part, was the brother of Francisco Borges Sobrinho, father of Zezé Borges and son of the first Borges patriarch, Antonio José Borges; and Walma Dutra Borges, daughter of Walter Pereira Borges, brother of Joaquim Pereira Borges who, for his part, is the father of Radio Joe.[10]

Apolônio, however, posits much closer ties between murderer and victim. Since, as suggested, his real interest is the relationship between Radio Joe and the boy's father, the key word here is "brother." One may dismiss this substitution as a slip, but the fact that the term is used not once but four times is significant. The close relationship that the poet attributes to Radio Joe and Messias has a dual effect. On the one hand, it heightens the barbarous quality of the crime by presenting the murderer as a man who would raise his hand against his own brother by seeking revenge upon his defenseless son for an imagined wrong. On the other, it makes the crime paradoxically more understandable by fitting it into a whole group of *folhetos* involving violence among immediate family members. The *cordel*, like many of the traditional ballads and stories brought to Brazil from Spain and Portugal, is full of such themes. Daughter murders mother and is turned into vampire; father threatens daughter with death after she refuses to sleep with him; blackhearted brother betrays youngest member of family; mother murders child; or son beats mother and is whisked away to hell by a two-headed monster.

By creating parallels between the *Serginho* story and others similar to it, ostensibly true *folhetos* such as José Francisco Borges' *The Daughter*

10. *O Dia*, June 17, 1977, Section A, p. 6.

Who Murdered Her Mother in Order to Flee with a No-Good or Antônio Patrício de Souza's *Poem of the Son Who Killed His Father on the Araçá Farm Between Arara and Serraria*, Apolônio reduces an erratic action that has threatening overtones to a safe pattern with which his readers are familiar.[11] The fact that Radio Joe decides to seek vengeance for a mere refusal of a loan does not weaken the poet's case in his audience's eyes. Rather, the thought that someone would murder his brother's child for such an apparently flimsy motive makes the incident a more emphatic case of *falsidade*. Since family members routinely commit such atrocities in *folhetos*, the action does not trouble the reader in the same way that an apparently gratuitous attack would.

To be sure, not every *cordel* murderer is related to his victim. Every such crime must, however, have a motive, and the fact that a number of killers are disgruntled relatives creates a tendency for poets to create such blood relationships. The knowledge that Radio Joe was a distant cousin of Messias is enough to make him an actual brother in Apolônio's mind. When I asked him why he had chosen to refer to the two men as "brothers," he insisted that they were described as such in the newspaper accounts, to which he had referred me. When I then appeared with a series of photocopies, asking him to point out where he had found this information, he shrugged, pulled at his mustache, and waved his hands impatiently. Well, if the fact wasn't there, it had to be somewhere. He was "sure he had read it," and there was "no doubt that it was true." Similarly, asked if Radio Joe and Serginho's father were really brothers, one young Rio buyer looked surprised and said, "Well, I'm not really sure, but look, what does it matter? If they weren't brothers, then they might as well have been."[12]

As to the question of divine intervention in the *folheto*, we see that it is dealt with here by the poet's omission of Radio Joe's tearful confession. Apolônio not only carefully attributes the solution of "the tragic mystery" to divine intervention but sees punishment as coming from an outside force, not an internal conscience. Because both the *DR* pact and the com-

11. José Francisco Borges, *A Filha que Matou a Mãe pra Fugir com um Maloqueiro* (Olinda, n.d.); Antônio Patrício de Souza (Antônio da Mulatinha), *O Poema do Filho que Matou o Pai no Sítio Araçá entre Arara e Serraria* (Campina Grande, 1977). Actually, physical violence may substitute for death. There are many *folhetos* like Alípio Bispo dos Santos' *The Son Who Kicked His Mother and Ended up with a Rounded Foot* (*O Filho que Chutou na Mãe e o Pé Ficou Redondo*, Salvador, 1978). While there are also parents who wrong children, these cases are less common. The willful son or daughter provides a clear example of the inferior who challenges legitimate authority by overstepping his or her bounds.

12. The buyer is a hotel doorman, age 24, from São Luís, Maranhão, who has been in Rio de Janeiro since 1971. The conversation occurred in Rio's Largo do Machado on December 10, 1977.

plementary *DW* pact call for divine intervention, the poet simply invents
his own version of how the murderer is brought to justice. Newspaper
reports leave no doubt that officials came to suspect Radio Joe after he
began anticipating future investigations and suggesting new measures.
When the ransom note revealed the use of the regional "watchman" (*vigia*)
for the standard "policeman" (*polícia*), the detectives began screening the
townspeople. Upon discovering Radio Joe's sizable debts, they brought
him in for questioning. Although he first denied any involvement, his
confession was not long in coming. Once he had admitted his guilt, he
was overcome by remorse. The newspaper quotes Radio Joe as exclaim-
ing, "I am a monster! Take me out of here, and let the people hit me, spit
upon me, kill me! I am filth, I am a devil! I want to hang! I want to be
punished!"[13]

Apolônio, however, says nothing about the detectives' growing suspicions. According to him, the boy's father has a sudden inspiration as the
bells toll for Serginho and the townspeople at his funeral call on God for
justice. A sudden vision of "one of his brothers to whom he had recently
denied a loan" prompts him to rush off after Radio Joe.

> Without delay, the landowner
> had his brother arrested
> and brought in for questioning,
> and during the punishment
> he revealed all of his ingratitude.

Although Radio Joe then confesses, the *folheto* version skips over the
confession, which the newspaper records in intimate detail. According to
Apolônio, the killer shows no trace of repentance. He admits his guilt only
when forced to during "the punishment," an unfortunately apt synonym
for many such official interrogations. Moreover, the culprit remains un-
moved by the consequences of his actions, triggering the poet's concluding cry for heavenly vengeance.

> I beg Divine Justice
> of the Omnipotent Judge.
> May he severely punish
> that murderous monster
> who bathed his evil hands
> in the blood of an innocent child.

In reality, given the *folheto*'s *DR* identity, it is hard to imagine any other
end. The story cannot end like most fictional *DR* tales with a restoration

13. *O Dia*, June 17, 1977, Section A, p. 1.

of losses since this would contradict the facts, which readers would already know from newspaper, radio, and television accounts.

Were the *folheto* fiction, the course of events would be different. The faithful fisherman who walked ten miles to make his report would be rewarded with not just praise but a tidy sum of money. Radio Joe would most probably have left Serginho, still alive, to die beside the river where a passerby would have discovered him, returning him intact to his parents' arms after various adventures. Given the realities of the crime recorded in his sources, however, Apolônio's options are severely limited. As there is no way he can resurrect Serginho from the dead, he must attempt to soften the parents' grief by making the murderer's punishment particularly emphatic. The poet's insistence upon Radio Joe's recalcitrance is thus calculated to make him a consummate villain on whom the reader can safely vent his own anger, frustration, and fear. The "ingratitude" that Apolônio condemns is not only directed at the killer's brother but ultimately at God, making Radio Joe a prime example of the most blatant sort of *falsidade*.

Although these changes may seem small, they reflect a particular vision of the way things ought to be. José de Souza Campos strives in *The King, the Dove, and the Sparrowhawk* to make the tone of his story more recognizably Brazilian. Just so, Apolônio reworks details in *Serginho* to make the real-life crime conform to the way his readers think a murder ought to be.

The *Folheto* Within the *Cordel* Tradition

Apolônio's account of the Serginho kidnapping is one of many journalistic *folhetos*. These news stories in verse are usually called *folhetos de acontecimento* (*acontecimento* means "happening" or "event") or *folhetos de época* (stories which "have their epoch") and are therefore of passing interest.[14]

Although the Serginho story is clearly of the *DR/DW* variety, news *folhetos* may also be *HR* or *HW* stories, depending on the poet's treatment of the facts. Clearly, some raw material lends itself better to one purpose

14. For a discussion of journalistic *folhetos*, see Beltrão, "Os folhetos," pp. 67–87; Roberto Câmara Benjamin, "Os folhetos populares e os meios de comunicação social," *Symposium* (Recife), 11 (1969): 47–54; Theo Brandão, "As cheias de Alagoas e a literatura de cordel," in *Folclore de Alagoas* (Maceió: Oficina Gráfica da Casa Ramalho, 1949), pp. 158–72; Raymond Cantel, *Temas da atualidade na literatura de cordel*, tr. Alice Mitika Koshiyama et al. (São Paulo: Universidade de São Paulo, Escola de Comunicações e Artes, 1972); and José Ossian Lima, "Cordel e jornalismo," *Revista de Comunicação Social* (Universidade Federal do Ceará), 5 (1975): 22–40.

than another. The great majority of *cordel* news stories are *DW* accounts of disasters: *The Terrible Fire in Copacabana* and *The Damage Done by the 1975 Floods* are cases in point.[15]

If it is difficult to give exact figures in speaking of *folheto* production in general, it is particularly hard to gauge the number of *cordel* news stories published each year. Journalistic accounts, which, more than love or adventure stories, tend to be limited to a specific region, often go through only limited editions. Since the subject itself is usually of passing interest, they are usually the first booklets to be discarded. Though the most famous may become classics in their own right, the great majority of these accounts simply disappear.

Some *folhetos de época* are written in anticipation of a particular occurrence. A poet may, for instance, describe the competing teams in an important soccer match well before the game, simply leaving a space for the final score. He may write the entire biography of an aged religious leader or well-loved public figure, waiting to tack on a final stanza giving the date and place of his death.[16] Normally, however, the journalistic *folheto* is written in a hurry since it is precisely the element of surprise that makes the story sell. Because the poet often simply expands on information transmitted by the media and thus assumed to be common knowledge and also because he has little time to correct errors or polish his work, these accounts are often rough or incomplete.

Articles by educated observers about the current state of the *cordel* often imply that the poet finds himself defenseless before growing competition from television and radio. Most *cordel* authors, however, do not share this view. Quick to admit that the now omnipresent transistor radio has hurt business, they themselves are still usually avid media consumers. Even those who see the most direct link between the *folheto*'s declining popularity among traditional buyers and the growth of the communications industry often insist that the media helps in their work as poets. Most *cordel* authors read magazines, newspapers, and paperback books and either watch or listen to news reports. In many homes, the radio remains on all day long. "You almost missed me!" exclaimed the old poet in the hinter-

15. Apolônio Alves dos Santos, *O Grande Incêndio em Copacabana* (Guarabira: José Alves Pontes, 1955); José Francisco Soares, *Os Estragos da Cheia 75* (Recife, 1975). A transcription of the former appears in Sebastião Nunes Batista, *Antologia da literatura de cordel* (Natal: Fundação José Augusto, 1977), pp. 35–39.

16. A number of poets have, for instance, already written *folhetos* about the death of the still-living but old and frequently ill religious leader Frei Damião. Regarded by many persons as the successor to the much-loved Padre Cícero, Frei Damião's death will no doubt result in considerable *cordel* sales. For a discussion of the man and his importance for the Northeastern populace, see Abdalaziz de Moura, *Frei Damião e os impasses da religião popular* (Petrópolis: Vozes, 1978).

lands of Paraíba as I arrived toward sunset. "Next time you want to see me, just say so on the radio. The whole village listens, even in the fields!"[17]

Apolônio himself shrugs off the suggestion that the mass media are his rivals. "Brazil grows every day," he says,

> so there are always more and more people to buy my stories. It doesn't matter if some stay home watching television or listening to the radio. I don't care if some people buy newspapers or magazines because there are always others who will want to read *folhetos*. The newspaper and the radio help the poet by giving him all the facts he needs. The television gives him ideas for new stories. So I think that poets who say that things are bad because of the radio or television are only looking for an excuse. Poets grow old and die, but poetry? Ah, never!

Educated writers, struck by the continued success of news *folhetos* in the face of widespread industrialization, have attributed their vitality to the desire of readers to hear about current events in their own regional, poetic language. They have also cited the group's tendency to trust an individual poet with whom its members can identify more than an "impersonal" radio or television announcer. Finally, they have claimed that the "objective" nature of journalistic *folhetos* makes them better in tune than other *cordel* stories with the spirit of the times.

Certainly the poet does not write about just any occurrence but chooses events that he thinks are important to his readers. Rather than lament the death of a famous author whose books are unfamiliar to *folheto* buyers, he will single out a figure who in some way touched their lives. Always on the lookout for new victims of injustice, he may also focus on subjects such as an astronaut's trip to the moon, a local miracle, or a particularly intriguing rumor.

It is also true that the *cordel* author uses a special, distinctly regional poetic language. This does not mean, however, that his readers are necessarily uncomfortable with the standard Portuguese they normally hear on the radio and, especially, on television. Individuals may, of course, gravitate toward the familiar, colloquial flavor of the *folheto*, finding the poetic form with which they have grown up both easier and more enjoyable to read. Nevertheless, the great majority of persons who can get through a *folheto* are quite capable of understanding an article in a mass circulation newspaper and in fact may well read both. Also, the fact that journalistic *folhetos* continue to sell at the same time that the number of *cordel* vendors who read aloud in the marketplace is decreasing suggests

17. Manuel Tomás de Assis, Olivedos, Paraíba, March 7, 1978.

that it is not the individual poet whom readers trust but rather those time-honored patterns upon which all *cordel* authors rely.

The notion that news accounts have managed to hold their own because they are somehow more objective than other sorts of *cordel* stories is, finally, largely unfounded. Facts, to be sure, provide necessary parameters in *cordel* news stories. Apolônio is not going to claim that Radio Joe did not really murder Serginho, that the event took place in Pernambuco instead of Rio de Janeiro, or that Radio Joe was struck down by lightning for his wicked ways. Nevertheless, despite the fact that the poet must respect this raw material to a certain extent, he may also modify it to suit his own ends.

Although the popular poet has considerable freedom in the way he chooses to interpret the six-step pattern, this pattern must remain more or less intact. "A rich man can win over a poor man in very special circumstances," explains Apolônio, "but evil can never win. In a contest between good and evil, good must always be victorious. That is because that is the nature of the world."

At heart, these accounts represent a quite special kind of fiction since although they do rely to at least some extent on facts, they have other goals. Despite a certain interest in transmitting "what really happened," the poet's primary allegiance is to a special vision of the world. Although all news stories of any sort reveal a particular viewpoint, the *cordel* author's commitment to time-honored values is generally more explicit than the professional reporter's.

The Monstrous Kidnapping of Serginho is typical of most news *folhetos* in its insistence on at least a just if not also happy ending. In this story as elsewhere, the "poet-reporter" begins by finding universal significance in an event in which he also manifests a hyperbolic personal concern.

> Overcome by
> sadness and emotion,
> I am going to recount
> a heartrending tragedy,
> the blackest crime
> which has ever occurred in our nation.

He then proceeds to mix moral reflection with description in a way that lifts the *folheto* beyond the here-and-now to become an illustration of some larger truth. Like so many accounts of murders, atrocities, and other man-made and natural disasters, the *Serginho* story serves to caution the reader about the dire consequences of *falsidade* at the same time that it promises protection for the long-suffering, just people of the world. Like other types of *folhetos*, news stories often serve as both check and escape valve for pent-up emotions since culprits such as Radio Joe are not only negative examples but convenient scapegoats. Since the desperate financial situation of most *cordel* readers may lead them to consider, even if fleetingly, one crime or another, Radio Joe is a prime candidate for their own feelings of guilt.

A look over the titles of contemporary journalistic *folhetos* reveals a wide range of subjects written in a variety of styles, which may be either humorous or solemn. The work of the Recife-based writer José Francisco Soares, probably the best-known *cordel* journalist today, includes such diverse topics as *The Gasoline: It Gave Out? or Did the Gasoline Give Out?*, *Divorce in Brazil*, *The Weeping of the Lion and the Jokes of Fu Manchu* (two soccer teams), and *The Two-Foot-Long Snake and the Pig That Raised a Dog*. Regardless of subject matter or tone, however, the great majority of journalistic *folhetos* end with the reiteration of a moral coupled with a cry for justice.[18]

This appeal for justice may be fairly general. The poet may simply ask for divine guidance as Soares does in the concluding stanzas of his *Marvel of Marvels—the São Francisco River Goes Dry*.[19]

O santo Deus incriado	Oh, holy God ever-present,
Não deixe esse rio secar	don't let this river go dry.
Do teu poder sacrossanto	I cannot rebel against
Não posso recalcitar	your sacred power
Nem da tua onisciência	and ought not to question
Não devo mesclatisar.	your omniscience.

Such appeals may also be specific cries for vengeance. The poet may seek to take justice into his own hands, as in *Arlindo, the Murderous Beast*, where author Manoel Pereira Sobrinho complains that the failure to punish injustice makes it continue.[20]

Se eu fosse autoridade	If I were an authority
Que pudesse dominar	who had power,
A sentença deste monstro	I would sentence
Era mandar enforcar	this monster to hang
Porque como este são três	because there have already been
Que há em nosso lugar.	three brutes just like him.

18. *Acabou a Gasolina? Ou a Gasolina Acabou?* (Recife, 1977), *O Divórcio no Brasil* (Recife, 1977), *O Choro de Leão e as Piadas de Fumanchú* (Recife, 1978), *A Cobra de 2 Pés e a Porca que Deu Cria a um Cachorro* (n.p., n.d.).

19. José Francisco Soares, *O Fenômeno dos Fenômenos: O Rio de São Francisco Secando* (Recife, n.d.), p. 8.

20. Manoel Pereira Sobrinho, *Arlindo, a Fera Homicida e os Mortos de Gravatá* (n.p., n.d.).

The poet may also go beyond the particular instance to comment upon the injustice of life in general. In his moving *Sacco and Vanzetti in the Eyes of the World*, for example, João Martins de Ataíde opposes the "justice of this world" to "the justice of the sky."[21]

Sair da Pátria natal	To leave one's own country,
Seguir para a terra alheia	to set out for a foreign land,
Sonhando com liberdade	dreaming of freedom
Morrer dentro da cadeia	only to die in a prison.
É engraçada esta vida	This life is strange—
Quanta esperança perdida	so much lost hope, so many castles in
Quanto castelo na areia.	the sand.
É como o filho sem mãe	It is like the child without mother,
É como a ave sem ninho	it is like the bird without nest,
É como a planta que nasce	it is like the plant which is born,
Desprezada no caminho,	despised, in the road.
A ave não tem parada,	The bird has no shelter,
A planta não é tratada	the plant is not cared for,
O filho não tem carinho.	the child receives no affection.

To see this cry for justice as an after-the-fact, largely mechanical ending would be to miss the point about *cordel* news stories. The journalistic *folheto* is not simply a news account with a bow here and there to tradition but a full-fledged incorporation of a wide range of facts within a given frame. The most objectively accurate news *folhetos* are therefore fundamentally different from newspaper accounts, upon which the popular poet draws. This is not, however, because the newspaper is somehow more "scientific" but because the reporter's goals are different.[22]

Attention-getting leads characterize both newspaper and popular verse accounts of local or international events. Nevertheless, despite a host of common features, journalistic *folhetos* differ from other kinds of news stories in at least one significant respect. Although newspaper, radio, and television presentations invariably include subjective elements, their raison d'être remains the supposedly impartial transmission of what most people would call facts. Clearly, the reporter slants, withholds, and heightens his material to suit the publication's needs. Consciously or unconsciously, he embeds a viewpoint of his own. Still, no self-respecting re-

21. João Martins de Ataíde, *Sacco e Vanzetti aos Olhos do Mundo* (Recife: n.p., n.d.). The *folheto* is reproduced in *Literatura popular em verso: Antologia*, I (Rio de Janeiro: Fundação Casa de Rui Barbosa/MEC, 1964), pp. 177–85 (hereafter cited as *Antologia*).

22. For in interesting contrast to the *folheto* see Américo Paredes, *"With His Pistol in His Hand": A Border Ballad and Its Hero* (Austin: University of Texas Press, 1958), and Alan Soons, "Spanish Ballad and News-Relation in Chapbook Form: The Index of a Mentality," *Kentucky Romance Quarterly*, 20 (1973): 3–17.

porter is going to get his facts wrong. If he wants to make the crime look more barbarous, he may identify Radio Joe and Messias as "blood relations" or "just like brothers," but he is not likely to say that the two were brothers if they were distant cousins.

Thanks to the eagerness of many poets to see things for themselves, *cordel* news stories may actually contain more detailed and immediate information than news relayed by the media. "I was there, and I can tell you how it was," Caetano Cosme da Silva asserts in his **Plague of Locusts in the Paraiban Interior.*[23] Nevertheless, the ultimate concern of these authors is not the news event as such but the confirmation of a preestablished vision.

The *cordel* poet himself generally perceives no tension between his role as reporter and his role as moral spokesman/literary craftsman. At heart, however, he is less committed to informing his readers than to conforming his material to literary rules that are related to the group's concept of how things ought to be.[24] Thus, no matter how accurate his account, he is at any given moment an artist interested in a qualitatively different sort of truth. Were he forced to choose between loyalty to the details or to deeply ingrained patterns, there is no doubt which would win. If *The Monstrous Kidnapping of Serginho* is by and large an accurate recasting of its newspaper sources, it is also a particularly graphic illustration of familiar rules. "When you hear about something like the murder of that little boy," says Apolônio, "you really have to stop and ask yourself, 'What is this? How can something like this be?' It really bothers you. You read the headline, and then you have to read it over because it makes no sense, I mean no sense at all."

Newspaper Summary and *Folheto*

Newspaper Summary: *Seven Days That Shook Bom Jesus*

Wednesday, June 8: Around 5 o'clock in the afternoon, Dona Valma and her husband Messias Borges de Almeida notice that their son is missing. Bom Jesus, normally calm and tranquil, begins to live apprehensive mo-

23. Caetano Cosme da Silva, **A Praga de Gafanhoto no Sertão Paraibano* (n.p., n.d.), *Antologia*, pp. 245–49.

24. This sort of reworking is certainly not restricted to the *folheto*. See, for instance, Gregory Gizelis, "Historical Event into Song: The Use of Cultural Perceptual Style," *Folklore*, 83 (1972): 302–20; Edward de Bono, *Lateral Thinking: A Textbook of Creativity* (New York: Harper & Row, 1970); and Barre Toelken, "Folklore: Worldview and Communication," in *Folklore: Performance and Communication*, ed. Dan Ben-Amos and Kenneth Goldstein (The Hague: Mouton, 1975), pp. 265–86.

ments. It is a day of questions, of searching, of uncertainty, of tears. Friends and relatives all look for Serginho. Neighbors join the search.

Thursday, June 9: The city extremely agitated, everyone taking part in the search. *O Dia* is the first newspaper to publish information about the kidnapping. Radio Joe writes a letter demanding some six thousand dollars for the safe return of the already dead child.

Friday, June 10: The boy's parents ask their friends and police to do nothing because they want their son back safe and sound, asserting that the money will be delivered no matter what.

Saturday, June 11: Police chief Heráclito Arcoverde returns to the city with a news team from *O Dia*, the first newspaper to arrive at the site of the events after conferring with chief investigator José Mendes about reinforcements to aid in the search. The first witnesses are heard. All remain on the alert.

Sunday, June 12: Unmistakable air of expectation. More than fifty cars participate in the search. Announcement that the ransom has been paid. Radio Joe, who takes an active part in the search and who seeks to arouse suspicions about two photographers, is called to testify at 2:30 in the afternoon. The authorities release numerous verbal descriptions of the suspects.

Monday, June 13: The search intensifies with various precincts now participating. The city is in an uproar. A rumor that the child's body has been found begins to circulate.

Tuesday, June 14: Two men sighted giving candies and ballpoint pens to children are arrested as suspects in the neighboring state of Espírito Santo, but the authorities soon free them. At exactly 12:45, Serginho's body is discovered on the banks of the Itabapoana River by two fishermen. Widespread feelings of dismay and revulsion. Members of the community swear to take justice into their own hands.

Wednesday, June 15: Police action. All-out search.

Thursday, June 16: Radio Joe confesses his crime to the police.

Friday, June 17: The murderer meets with newspapermen and is then taken from Laje de Muriaé by helicopter to either the Fortress of Água Santa or investigative headquarters in Niteroi to await preliminary sentencing. That night at 7 o'clock a Seventh Day Mass in honor of Serginho is celebrated. Place: the Church of São Geraldo, Bom Jesus do Norte.

Folheto: *O Monstruoso Crime de Serginho em Bom Jesus de Itabapoana / The Monstrous Kidnapping of Serginho in Bom Jesus de Itabapoana* by Apolônio Alves dos Santos

Com a alma transpassada	Overcome by
de tristeza e emoção	sadness and emotion,

vou descrever a tragédia	I am going to recount
que fez cortar coração	a heartrending tragedy,
o crime mais tenebroso	the blackest crime
que houve em nossa nação.	which has ever occurred in our nation.
Aconteceu no Estado	This heinous crime,
do grande Rio de Janeiro	which has shaken the whole world,
esse hediondo crime	took place in the state
que abala o mundo inteiro	of Rio de Janeiro,
com Serginho, um estudante	and its victim was Serginho,
filho de um fazendeiro.	a schoolboy, son of a landowner.
Foi na cidade de Bom	This landowner
Jesus de Itabapoana	of pure heart,
que reside o fazendeiro	father of the youth who became
de alma pura e humana	the victim of this cruel tragedy,
pai do menor que foi vítima	lived in the city of
dessa tragédia tirana.	Bom Jesus de Itabapoana.
Chama-se Messias Borges	The name of Serginho's father
o dito pai de Serginho	was Messias Borges.
e dona Walda, a mãe dele	His mother, Dona Walda,
a quem com tanto carinho	lavished all her love
dispensava amor imenso	and affection
ao querido filhinho.	on her beloved little boy.
A caminho da escola	He disappeared
ele desapareceu	on the way home from school
no dia 8 de junho	on June 8
assim que escureceu	just as twilight was falling.
não vendo o filho chegar	When she did not see her son arrive,
dona Walda entristeceu.	Dona Walda became distraught.
Assim passaram a noite	His worried parents
os seus pais em desatino	then spent the night
bateram por toda parte	looking everywhere
a procura do menino	for the boy
sem saberem para onde	without knowing where
ele tomara destino.	he might have gone.
Bateram em todas as casas	They asked in all the houses
daquele povo visinho	in the neighborhood.
então seu pai muito aflito	Then his anguished father
seguiu em outro caminho	tried another tack
comunicou no Distrito	and reported his son's disappearance
o sumisso do filhinho.	to the local police.
Já com dois dias depois	Then two days after
que isto aconteceu	all this happened,
quando menos esperavam	when he least expected,

o pai dele recebeu
uma carta anónima, dando
notícia do filho seu.

the boy's father received
an anonymous letter
with news of his son.

A carta dizia, que
Serginho foi sequestrado
e se o pai não quisesse
vê-lo morto ou maltratado
levasse 100 mil cruzeiros
em um lugar indicado.

The letter said that
Serginho had been kidnapped,
and if his father did not want
to see him injured or dead,
he should leave 100,000 *cruzeiros*
in a specific location.

O pai lendo a dita carta
tomou logo providência
a tal quantia exigida
logo arranjou com urgência
e foi a depositar
no lugar da exigência.

After reading the letter,
his father immediately took steps
to put together the sum demanded
by the writer, which he then
went to deposit
in the place mentioned in the letter.

Em uma placa de trânsito
pra ele não se enganar
no quilômetro 35
seria o dito lugar
conforme o sequestrador
pediu pra ele deixar.

The kidnapper had chosen a road
    marker
called "Kilometer 35,"
so that there would be
no mix-up
in following
his instructions.

Esperaram 5 dias
os pais em grande aflição
sua mãe chorava tanto
sem haver consolação
até visinhos também
choravam de compaixão.

The boy's parents waited five days
in great anguish.
His mother wept
so inconsolably
that even the neighbors
cried in sympathy.

Quando já desenganado
uma notícia chegou
na cidade Bom Jesus
que todo povo chorou
com essa triste notícia
toda cidade parou.

All hope faded
when a report reached
Bom Jesus.
Everybody cried
and the city came to a halt
with the sad news.

Dizia a notícia que
um pescador tinha achado
o cadáver dum garoto
num saco plástico amarrado
no rio Itabapoana
com o rosto amordaçado.

The report said that
a fisherman had found
the body of a boy
in the Itabapoana River.
He had been bound in a plastic bag
and was blue from strangulation.

Também uma enorme pedra
no seu pescoço amarrada
com fios de telefones

There was also an enormous stone
weighing almost 80 pounds
which had been fastened

a dita estava laçada
e com 35 quilos
de peso, sem faltar nada.

Juntou-se as autoridades
e todo povo apressado
rumaram para o local
já bem perto do Estado
de Vitória, Espírito Santo
foi o cadáver encontrado.

Antonio Solange Silva
o nome do pescador
que encontrou o cadáver
naquele estado de horror
pensou tratar-se de crime
ficou partido de dor.

E bastante acometido
de trauma emocional
caminhou cinco quilômetros
ao Distrito local
comunicou a tragédia
no Posto Policial.

Logo as autoridades
seguiram para o local
trouxeram o corpo do jovem
para o médico legal
os rádios e os jornais
anunciaram em geral

Logo o médico legal
chamou o pai de Serginho
e ele reconheceu
o corpo do seu filhinho
prantiou angustiado
o fruto do seu carinho.

Logo dali conduziram
aqueles restos mortais
pra cidade onde viveu
com os seus queridos pais
todo mundo mergulhou
em prantos sentimentais.

Serginho ia fazer
12 anos de idade
juntou-se no seu enterro

around his neck
with telephone wire.

The authorities assembled,
and the whole town
hurried to the site
near Vitória in the state
of Espírito Santo
where the body had been found.

Antonio Solange Silva,
the fisherman
who discovered the corpse
in that terrible state,
surmised that there must have been a
    crime
and was suffused with grief.

Wracked with sorrow,
he walked
almost ten miles
to the local police station
where he proceeded
to report the tragedy.

The authorities immediately
set out for the site.
They brought back the boy's body
for a medical report
while the newspapers and radio
spread the news of his death.

The coroner immediately
summoned Serginho's father,
who identified the body
of his small son.
He wept in anguish
for the fruit of his love.

They brought back
the boy's remains
to his hometown.
Everyone drowned in tears
along with the beloved parents
of the victim.

Serginho was going to be
twelve years old.
The entire population attended

todo povo da cidade
todo mundo lamentava
aquela barbaridade.

Somente os pais de Serginho
pelo grande sentimento
não suportaram assistir
do filho, o sepultamento
ficaram em casa chorando
as dores do sofrimento.

Quando retiram o corpo
de dentro do necrotério
levaram pra tumba fria
lá no chão do cemitério
os sinos dobraram tristes
que parecia um mistério.

Era a Justiça Divina
dando um aviso certo
que o tal monstro assassino
estava ali muito perto
sem saber que brevemente
iria ser descoberto.

Todo povo revoltou-se
com a monstruosidade
toda multidão gritava
pedindo a Divindade
justiça para o monstro
daquela barbaridade

O pai de Serginho teve
seu pensamento voltado
para um de seus irmãos
que lhe falou emprestado
há dias, 100 mil cruzeiros
e pelo qual foi negado.

Chamava-se Zé do Rádio
aquela fera assassina
porque ele possuia
alí uma oficina
e lá consertava rádio
porém sendo clandestina.

Sem demora o fazendeiro
mandou prender seu irmão
o qual foi submetido

his funeral,
where everyone bewailed
that barbarous crime.

Only Serginho's parents,
overcome by grief,
did not attend the burial
but remained at home,
weeping for their loss,
prostrated with sorrow.

When they brought out the body
from the morgue
and carried it to the cold tomb
within the graveyard,
the bells tolled so sadly
that they seemed to indicate a mystery.

It was Divine Justice
giving an unmistakable sign
that the monstrous assassin
was nearby,
unaware that he would soon
be discovered.

The entire community
was revolted
by the monstrous crime
and asked God
that the barbarous perpetrator
be punished.

Then Serginho's father suddenly
    thought
about one of his brothers
to whom he had denied
a loan
of 100,000 *cruzeiros*
several days ago.

That murderous beast
was known as Radio Joe
because he had a shop
where he illegally
serviced radios.

Without delay, the landowner
had his brother arrested
and brought in for questioning.

a uma enterrogação
no castigo descobriu
toda sua ingratidão.

E confessou que estava
em completo desespero
para sanar suas dívidas
precisava de dinheiro
o qual falou emprestado
ao irmão fazendeiro.

Como ele se negou
a emprestar para ele
aqueles 100 mil cruzeiros
pois não confiava nele
pensou logo de tomar
vingança no filho dele.

O garoto todo dia
entrava em sua oficina
quando vinha da escola
então a fera assassina
aproveitou o ensejo
e fez a carnificina.

Depois com fios elétricos
deixou todo enquerido
diminuindo o volume
fez o cadáver encolhido
para quando escurecesse
ser no carro conduzido.

Quando correu a notícia
da ausência do menino
ele ajudou procurá-lo
com seu instinto ferino
pra ninguém saber que foi
o seu cruel assassino.

Porém já tarde da noite
com a maior precaução
colocou-o dentro de uma
caixa de televisão
e foi sacudir no rio
sem a menor compaixão.

Voltando logo escreveu
para o pai de Serginho
dizendo:—Meu caro amigo

During the punishment [interrogation]
he revealed
all of his ingratitude.

And he confessed that
he had been in despair
as to how to pay off
his many debts,
having counted on the loan which his brother,
the landowner, had denied him.

Because the landowner,
who lacked faith in Joe,
had refused to give him money,
Joe decided
to take revenge
on his brother's son.

The boy entered the shop
every day on his way home
from school.
The murderous beast
therefore took the opportunity
to kill him in cold blood.

He then went on to bind the corpse
with electrical wiring,
thereby diminishing its size,
and waited for night to fall
so that he could
drive off with it in his car.

In accord with his brutal instincts
Joe joined in the search
when the boy's absence was noted
so that no one would suspect
that he was
the cruel assassin.

Later that night, however,
he placed the corpse
in a television carton
with great caution
and dumped it in the river
without the slightest compassion.

Upon returning home,
he immediately wrote a letter
to Serginho's father saying,

eu tenho o seu gurizinho
mas só por cem mil cruzeiros
devolverei seu filhinho.

"My dear friend, I have your
little boy, but I will only
give him back
if you pay me 100,000 *cruzeiros*."

Finalmente contou tudo
agora prisioneiro
a polícia arrecadou
a metade do dinheiro
que tomou do seu irmão
como ladrão desordeiro.

Finally, the murderer
confessed everything in prison,
and the police were able to get back
half the money
that he had stolen from his brother
like a common thief.

Peço a Justiça Divina
do Juiz Onipotente
que ao monstro assassino
castigue severamente
que banhou as mãos malignas
com sangue dum inocente.

I beg Divine Justice
of the Omnipotent Judge.
May He severely punish
the murderous monster
who bathed his evil hands
in the blood of an innocent child.

Apolônio Alves dos Santos
Aconselha aos bons leitores
Levar um livrinho deste
Vejam meus caros senhores
Espero que meus ouvintes
Sejam meus bons protetores.

Apolônio Alves dos Santos
counsels his faithful readers
to buy one of these little booklets.
My friends,
I hope that you listeners
will also be my loyal protectors!

Facing page: The King, the Dove, and the Sparrowhawk *by José de Souza
Campos (Recife: 1978). Note the similarities between the cover illustration by Marcelo Soares, son of well-known* cordel *poet José Francisco
Soares, and the picture of the king that appears in the* Almanaque do
pensamento *(from which the tale was taken).*

AUTOR   José   de   Souza   Campos

O Rei a Pomba e o Gavião

MARCELO

o rei
a pomba
e o gavião

ALMANAQUE DO PENSAMENTO

horóscopo do ano ● horóscopo
para todos ● dias favoráveis e
desfavoráveis em 1978 ● guia
prático astrológico ● agricultura e
pecuária ● influência da lua nova ●
tábua lunar e planetária ●
calendário ● fenómenos do ano ●
tábua das marés, etc.

ASTROLÓGICO
LITERÁRIO

ciência popular ● contos ● poesia ●
curiosidades ● palavras cruzadas ●
enigmas ● charadas ● anedotas, etc.

o mais completo guia astrológico

*The cover of the "literary and astrological" almanac offered annually by
the Pensamento Publishing Company. The book, which sells for slightly
over a dollar, contains horoscopes, agricultural advice, lunar charts, information about the tides, popular science articles, poems, short stories,
crossword puzzles, and various "curiosities." The almanac is a mass-produced descendent of the seventeenth-century* Lunário perpétuo. *The parable about the king, the dove, and the sparrowhawk appears on the same
page as a description of the benefits of fluoride in relieving arterial disorders.*

Mas o rei tinha a ideia
que aquele passarinho.
Vinha de outras esferas
e não foi criado em ninho.
ticido em nosso vergel
com folha seca e espinho.

quem achar que isto é lenda
e não merece atenção.
pense lá como quiser
porque tem sua razão
eu mesmo sei que não quero
pensar como o gavião.

Aquele gavião era
um anjo do satanaz.
e a pombinha da divina
era a pombinha da paz
que Deus a terra mostrar
como é que o justo faz.

e ó Deus, o Santo nome
Sementes do sumo bem.
Ordenador, bom e justo
nificador tambem.
Elai pela a minha Vida
amo a vós, e mais ninguem..   fim

The last page of the original of The King, the Dove, and the Sparrow-hawk. *José de Souza Campos recorded his story in a schoolboy's notebook with a picture of a ship on the cover. The unsteady handwriting and various spelling errors (e.g.,* ticido *for* tecido*) are not surprising, given the poet's three months of formal schooling.*

Autor: APOLONIO ALVES DOS SANTOS

O Monstruoso Crime de SERGINHO, Em Bom Jesus de Itabapoana, Estado do Rio de Janeiro

The Monstrous Kidnapping of Serginho in Bom Jesus de Itabapoana, State of Rio de Janeiro *by Apolônio Alves dos Santos. The facing page shows a newspaper report entitled "Serginho's Murderer Says 'I Want to Be Lynched!'" taken from the June 18 edition of* O Dia. *Note the resemblance between the photograph of the kidnapped boy and the* folheto *cover illustration, a blockprint by José Costa Leite.*

Matador de Serginho:
QUERO SER LINCHADO!

B OM JESUS DE ITABAPOANA (De Mário Dias e Alberto Dirma) — «Eu sou um monstro! Me tirem daqui e me levem para Bom Jesus para que o povo possa me bater, me linchar, acabar comigo!» — Foram palavras ditas por Zé do Rádio, matador do menino Serginho, acometido de uma violenta crise no xadrez de Laje de Muriaé, minutos depois de ser apresentado aos repórteres, perante os quais contou a maneira como assassinou friamente a criança, respondendo em seguida a várias perguntas, num encontro que durou 50 minutos cravados. Durante a entrevista Zé do Rádio fez uma revelação estarrecedora: espalhou na cidade que os fotógrafos Silvio Alves Emiliano e José Carlos Alves, que haviam fotografado Serginho, seriam os autores do crime, para se vingar do pai do menino, que se negava a comprar as fotos. Pretendia encontrá-los, baleá-los nas pernas e entregá-los ao povo, a fim de que fossem linchados.

— «Aí eu ficaria livre de qualquer acusação, já que tudo morreria com eles». Ontem, mesmo, por determinação superior, Zé do Rádio foi transportado de helicóptero de Laje de Muriaé para outro lugar — Presídio de Água Santa ou DPJ, de Niterói — onde permanecerá até segunda-feira próxima, quando será pedida a sua prisão preventiva.

ENCONTRO FOI ANTECIPADO

A apresentação de Zé do Rádio aos repórteres estava marcada para ontem, às 13 horas, mas os policiais que trabalham na ocorrência, temendo reação popular, resolveram antecipar o encontro, promovendo a entrevista na madrugada de anteontem mesmo, o que ocorreu precisamente às 2h30min, tendo a duração de 50 minutos.

Ficou combinado, então, que, tão logo a cidade estivesse recolhida, os repórteres seguiriam para a Delegacia às 3 horas.

Assim foi feito. Quando tudo era silêncio, o Delegado Heráclio Arcoverde deixou a Delegacia, mas deu ordem para que o carro a ser seguido fosse uma Veraneio, placa RJ MZ 19-96, de cor azul, que partiria meia hora depois.

O Delegado saiu sozinho e às 3 horas em ponto, e às 3 horas a Veraneio seguiu o mesmo caminho, desta vez sendo seguida por todos os representantes dos jornais.

Trafegaram no rumo de Itaperu-

Serginho, em foto bem recente

— Pioneiro do radioamadorismo na região.

7 DIAS QUE ABALARAM BOM JESUS

Quarta-feira, dia 8 — A partir das 17 horas, dona Vaiana e seu marido Messias Borges de Almeida notaram a falta do filho. Bom Jesus, normalmente tranquila e calma, passou a viver momentos de apreensão. Foi um dia de procura, de buscas, de incerteza, de lágrimas. Parentes e amigos à procura de Serginho. Vizinhos colaborando.

Quinta-feira, 9 — A cidade toda abaladíssima, já participava das diligências e O DIA era o primeiro jornal que publicava a matéria do sequestro. Zé do Rádio encontrava o bilhete exigindo 100 mil pela libertação do menino que já estava morto.

Sexta-feira, 10 — Os pais pediam aos amigos e à Polícia que não fizessem nada, pois queriam o filho de volta são e salvo. O dinheiro seria entregue de qualquer maneira.

Sábado, 11 — O delegado Heráclio Arcoverde, depois de manter contato com o diretor do DPJ, José Mendes, pedindo reforços para as buscas, retornava à cidade com a reportagem de O DIA, primeiro jornal a chegar ao local dos acontecimentos. Iniciava-se a tomada de depoimentos. Tudo em sigilo.

Domingo, 12 — A expectativa era grande. Mais de 50 carros tomavam parte nas diligências. Já se sabia que o resgate havia sido pago a Zé do Rádio, que colaborava ativamente e fazia carga contra os dois fotógrafos, era chamado a depor às 2h30min. As autoridades distribuem muitos retratos falados dos possíveis criminosos.

Segunda-feira, 13 — Intensificam-se as diligências com a participação de vários delegados. A cidade está em polvorosa. Corre o boato de que o corpo da criança fora encontrado.

Terça-feira, 14 — Dois homens são presos no Espírito Santo e apontados como os sequestradores. Motivo: num colégio, distribuíam balas e canetas às crianças. Mas, são logo inocentados pelas autoridades. Às 12h50min, precisamente, o corpo de Serginho é encontrado às margens do Rio Itabapoana, por dois pescadores. A revolta é geral. O povo jura vingança. Quer fazer justiça aos criminosos.

Quarta-feira, 15 — Ação policial. Verdadeira caçada.

Quinta-feira, 16 — Zé do Rádio

EXEMPLO do Filho que matou os Pais para Ficar com A Aposentadoria

AUTOR: J. BORGES

Four news folhetos *displaying a variety of styles of illustration. Like the* Serginho *story, each features a family member who turns murderer. Above:* The Example of the Son Who Murdered His Parents in Order to Get His Hands on Their Retirement Benefits, *written and illustrated by José Francisco Borges. Right:* The Poem of the Son Who Murdered His Father on the Araçá Farm Between Arara and Serraria, *written by Antônio da Mulatinha, illustrator unknown.*

Autor: ANTONIO DA MULATINHA

O Poema do Filho que Matou o Pai no Sitio Araçá entre Arara e Serraria

O RAPAZ QUE MATOU A FAMILIA ACONSELHADO PELO DIABO

AUTOR:- Manoel D'Almeida Filho

1ª. Edição . . . . . janeiro de 1974 - Preço Cr$ 1,00

Editor autorizado Rodolfo Coelho Cavalcante - Rua Alvarenga Peixoto, 158 - Liberdade - 40.00
SALVADOR-BAHIA

Above: The Young Man Who Murdered His Family on the Advice of the Devil, *author Manuel d'Almeida Filho, illustrator unknown. Right:* The Daughter Who Murdered Her Mother in Order to Run Off with a No-Good, *written and illustrated by José Francisco Borges.*

Autor: José Francisco Borges

A FILHA QUE MATOU A MÃE PRA FUGIR COM UM MALOQUEIRO

CASA DAS CRIANÇAS DE OLINDA

TEREZA BATISTA
CANSADA DE GUERRA

AUTOR: Rodolfo Coelho Cavalcante
Trovador Popular Brasileiro

Folheto Autorisado pelo Escritor Jorge Amado — 1a. Edição: Setembro de 1973
PREÇO . . . . CR$ 1,00

Tereza Batista *by Rodolfo Coelho Cavalcante, illustrator unknown.*
Note the striking difference between the popular artist's conception
of the heroine and the image of her that appears on the cover of the
English-language translation (shown on the facing page) of Jorge
Amado's novel Tereza Batista, Home from the Wars, *from which the*
folheto *was taken.*

TEREZA BATISTA
Home From The Wars

"SHE'S FIRE AND ROSES, STEEL AND HONEY. A LEGEND
TO BE SUNG IN HER OWN TIME." *THE WASHINGTON POST*

JORGE AMADO
Author of GABRIELA, CLOVE AND CINNAMON

BARD
34645
$2.95

One of the illustrations by the Salvador-based artist Carybé from the first Brazilian edition of Jorge Amado's Tereza Batista. *The novel is divided into sections meant to recall* folhetos. *This "ABC of Tereza Batista's War Against the Black Smallpox" follows the* cordel *model in its subdivision into parts beginning with succeeding letters of the alphabet. The stylized blockprint is reminiscent of* folheto *covers. The illustration appears on page 96 of Jorge Amado's* Tereza Batista cansada de guerra *(São Paulo: Martins, 1972).*

Autor: João Martins de Atayde

A Triste Sorte da Meretriz

A version of João Martins de Ataíde's The Sad Fate of the Prostitute, *origin of photograph unknown. The story itself dates back at least forty years. This and the following three illustrations show* folhetos *dealing with prostitutes and prostitution. Note again the variety of styles.*

JOÃO MARTINS DE ATAYDE

A SORTE D'UMA MERETRIZ

Another version of The Fate of the Prostitute, *illustrator unknown.*

LITERATURA DE CORDEL N, 1412
O VIVER DA MERETRIZ

1ª. Edição - outubro de 1976

Preço : Cr$3,00 ☆ Em outro Estado: Cr$4,00

The Life of the Prostitute, *written by Rodolfo Coelho Cavalcante and illustrated, with obvious irony, by Luiz Sales. This story and the following one were written within the last ten years.*

The Person Who Likes Corruption Wants to Live in Campina,
written and illustrated by José Costa Leite.

VI. *Tereza Batista*
by Rodolfo Coelho Cavalcante[1]

The Poet

Shortly after noon on an unusually breezy Sunday, Rodolfo Coelho Cavalcante returns to his small stucco house in Liberdade, a particularly hilly section of Salvador, capital of Bahia and once of all of Brazil. He lays the suitcase stuffed with *folhetos* entitled *The New Dance Called the Gute-Gute* and seven shades of handkerchiefs on a nearby table, then wipes his forehead with his hand. Dressed in a purple suit too big for him and a matching fleur-de-lys necktie, the poet paces restlessly about the room. "I'm going to take a bath," he announces to his family but instead picks up the suitcase and walks out to the adjoining office where he keeps his printing press. The room is stacked from floor to ceiling with bundles of *cordel*. "Did you sell a lot, Dad?" asks his daughter, bouncing a baby on her lap as he goes by. Rodolfo nods. "Not bad," he says, "almost a hundred *folhetos* and some two dozen handkerchiefs just this morning up near São Joaquim."

Sixty-two years old, Rodolfo is not only a poet, publisher, and vendor but an inveterate leader of what he calls "the poet class." At one time a circus clown, fruit vendor, grade school teacher, magician, and messenger boy, he turned to the *folheto* almost forty years ago. Author of some fifteen hundred titles, he continues to turn out stories at the rate of two a month. "Poetry built this house," he claims. "Its foundations are the booklets that I sold one by one in country fairs. And for that very reason, I will only stop being a poet when there is no one left to read the stories that I write."[2]

Unlike the majority of *cordel* authors, who were born in the Northeastern countryside, Rodolfo grew up in a small coastal city in the state of Alagoas. The son of a poverty-stricken house painter, he began working in the streets at an early age. Although he had no time for school, he

1. Separate sections of this chapter were presented as papers at the Modern Language Association meetings in New York City on December 27, 1978, and at the Second Symposium for Portuguese Traditions at the University of California, Los Angeles, on May 11, 1979.

2. Rodolfo Coelho Cavalcante, Salvador, Bahia, June 5, 1978. All quotations in this chapter come from this recorded interview unless otherwise noted.

taught himself to read. His brothers laughed at him when he scrimped to buy *folhetos*, but he soon learned enough from them to write love letters in verse.

Initially an author of circus plays in which he himself performed, Rodolfo stopped his travels temporarily when he married and decided to settle in Piauí.[3] His first *folheto* appeared in 1942 when he decided to write about the fires that broke out so often in the straw huts of one of the poorest sections of town. After learning the names of the victims from relatives, he was able to write an eyewitness account. "The residents said that it was the police who were setting the fires, and I knew it must be," says Rodolfo, "because there was a campaign to get rid of those houses at just that time. Of course I didn't say that. I just praised the mayor, the police, and the firemen and wrote about the victims' valiant struggle against the flames." After the success of this first *folheto*, he wrote about the country's entry into World War II on the Allies' side. When he sold every copy of *Brazil Has Entered the War, Germany Has Lost It*, he decided to become a poet in earnest. "I bought myself a typewriter and just started writing."[4]

Rodolfo was once accustomed to vending his wares throughout the interior. "I walked up, down, and across this old Northeast with two big suitcases crammed with stories," he explains. Now, however, he does not visit even nearby fairs unless he has a particularly sensational new *folheto* that he feels will repay his efforts. He has also given up selling *cordel* in the Terreiro de Jesus, a kind of amusement plaza in the heart of split-level Salvador's Upper City because today "it is a place for pickpockets, whores, and tin-pan peddlers, not self-respecting poets." Instead, he hawks his verses in the winding streets.

Although there is usually no place to form a ring of listeners in these narrow and crowded thoroughfares, Rodolfo generates business by chanting his verses as he walks up and down the hills. Generally, he carries copies of only a single story, which he has chosen to read that day, together

3. The circus actor phase of Rodolfo's life is particularly interesting, especially since his comments on circus plays, which he wrote from time to time both when he worked in Bahia and elsewhere, emphasize similarities between these and the *folheto*. It is also evident that the itinerant circus serves as a fundamental link in the evolution of a Northeastern popular theater. I am grateful to Nélson de Araújo for supplying me with a copy of part of an interview with Rodolfo, which is part of a study of popular theater in the Salvador area, *Duas formas de teatro popular do recôncavo baiano* (Salvador: Edições o Vice Rey, 1979).

4. *Brasil Entrou, Alemanha Perdeu a Guerra* (Terezinha, 1942). Brazil was the only South American nation to declare war on Germany (October 23, 1917) during World War I. The nation declared war again on August 22, 1942, making air and naval bases available to the United States in the Northeast and sending a small air force contingent and expeditionary force to Italy, where 451 Brazilian soldiers died. For documentation, see E. Bradford Burns, *A History of Brazil* (New York: Columbia University Press, 1970), pp. 298–99.

with a small bundle of handkerchiefs. "I go out every day, each day a different place," he says. "Some days are bound to be better than others, but I am a family man, and family men cannot afford to rest." There are some eight other *cordel* authors in Salvador, but Rodolfo clearly dominates the local trade. Though he asserts that Bahia is "not a mecca of popular poetry like, say, Paraíba," he manages to do a healthy business, usually earning close to five hundred dollars a month.

Even though this sum represents two or three times what most authors earn, Rodolfo's way of life is still precarious because of his deep commitment to promoting the *literatura de cordel*. Organizer of three different poets' associations over the past two decades, current president of the Brazilian Minstrels' Guild, founder of a series of journals dealing with popular poetry and poets, and member of a dozen cultural organizations ranging from the Castro Alves Academy of Letters to the Portugal-Brazil Friendship League, he has been "an active idealist" for well over two decades.

Half of his income presently goes into the current 109-member organization, which is not much different in either goals or structure from the original National Association of Minstrels and Poet-Singers (ANTV), which he founded in 1955 "for the moralization of popular poetry and the defense of authors' rights." Like its forebears, today's association strives for official aid and recognition while attempting to unite writers and singers through periodic congresses, a national journal, and various mutual assistance measures. Instrumental in organizing over ninety festivals from one end of Brazil to the other, Rodolfo himself spends a good part of each day answering letters from fellow poets and leaders of various cultural groups, preparing articles for his newsletter, and working on new *cordel* stories.[5]

Versatile and quick but less interested in developing a plot than in reflecting on its outcome, the writer has authored *folhetos* on everything from a long-awaited comet to a vampire rumored to have appeared in the nearby Santana fair.[6] He turns out biographies, adventure stories, denunciations of the black market dealing in the blood used for transfusions, and reports of local miracles with equal ease. The majority of his stories are short, eight-page accounts.

Frequently invited to official receptions, Rodolfo is proud of tributes such as the letter from Jacqueline Kennedy thanking him for his *folheto*

5. For further information about the original association, see "Estatutos da Associação Nacional de Trovadores e Violeiros," 1955. A mimeographed copy is on file at the Casa de Rui Barbosa *cordel* library. For information on the activities of the present-day association, see its monthly newsletter, *Brasil Poético*, published by Rodolfo in Salvador, Bahia.
6. *E a Terra Brilhará Outra Vez: A Vinda do "Cometa Kohoutek"* (Salvador, 1973) and *O Vampiro na Feira de Santana* (Salvador, 1972).

lamenting her husband's death. Clearly one of the most articulate, best-read popular poets alive today, he continues to write for "the little guy because I understand him." Furthermore, while best known for his well-developed journalistic sense and characteristic biting humor, Rodolfo considers himself above all "a moral and spiritual poet." His own life has been touched by tragedies, which have caused him to reflect upon a number of fundamental questions.

Admitting that he often feels disheartened, he guarantees that he will keep on fighting for the cause of popular poetry. "Look," he says, "I know very well that I am not a good writer. My stories are full of misplaced pronouns and misspelled words, and I have no time to make them better. The one thing that saves them is the fact that I have lots of inspiration, and my inspiration comes from all that I have lived. The world has been my professor and a strict one, but it has taught me plenty, and, really, if you think about it, what more could a person ask?"

The Source

First published in 1972, Jorge Amado's *Tereza Batista, Home from the Wars* recalls his other twenty novels in its slapdash use of local color and colloquial language as well as its debt to various Brazilian folk themes. Like most of his work, the book has been dismissed by some critics as facile and long-winded, and praised by others for its memorable characters and lively dialogue.[7] In *Tereza Batista*, the protagonist is a prostitute with the proverbial heart of gold, distinguished by her courage and perennial zest for life.[8]

English-speaking readers know Amado from at least a half-dozen books such as *Gabriela, Clove, and Cinnamon*, *Shepherds of the Night*, *Dona Flor and Her Two Husbands*, *Tent of Miracles*, and *Tereza Batista, Home*

7. Amado published *Tereza Batista cansada de guerra* (São Paulo: Martins) in 1972. For a critical introduction to Amado, see the collection by the author and other writers in his work entitled *Jorge Amado: Povo e terra* (São Paulo: Martins, 1972). Also of particular interest to this discussion is Nancy T. Baden, "Popular Poetry in the Novels of Jorge Amado," *Journal of Latin American Lore*, 2 (1976): 3–22; and Jorge Amado, "Biblioteca do povo e coleção moderna," in Gilberto Freyre et al., *Novos estudos afro-brasileiros* (Rio de Janeiro: Civilização Brasileira, 1937), II, 262–324.

8. The prostitute with a heart of gold is a common theme in the literature of many countries. For a general discussion, see Harold Greenwald, *The Prostitute in Literature* (New York: Ballantine Books, 1960). There are at least a half-dozen studies of the prostitute and prostitution within Brazil. The most helpful in terms of this discussion of *Tereza Batista* is probably Armando Pereira et al., *A prostituição é necessária?* (Rio de Janeiro: Civilização Brasileira, 1966), which includes a short but evocative portrait of prostitution in Bahia by filmmaker Glauber Rocha, "Um bom destino, entre outras misérias," pp. 89–94.

from the Wars, all of which have appeared in paperback editions within the past few years. Some of these novels have inspired film versions in both Brazil and abroad, and one, *Dona Flor*, is also responsible for a Broadway play.[9]

Amado's novels reveal a highly personalized kind of literary populism, which has generated considerable international debate.[10] The author is not alone, however, in his reliance on Northeastern traditions. Poet João Cabral de Melo Neto, playwright Ariano Suassuna, and novelist João Guimarães Rosa are the most obvious examples of twentieth-century Brazilian writers who have reworked popular art forms which have played a role in their personal development.[11] Within Salvador itself, Brazil's oldest and one of its most heterogeneous and colorful cities, a large number of artists look to popular culture as a foundation for their creative work. Not only writers but painters, sculptors, and musicians take pride in exploring the

9. All of these titles are available in paperback editions published by Avon. Amado first published *Tereza Batista cansada de guerra* (São Paulo: Martins) in 1972. It has been translated by Barbara Shelby as *Tereza Batista, Home from the Wars* (New York: Knopf, 1975, reprinted by Avon/Bard, 1977). The film, *Dona Flor and Her Two Husbands*, based on Amado's novel, has had extensive showings in the United States. *Dona Flor* has also been used as a basis for a Broadway play, *Saravá*. The translations from Amado's *Tereza Batista* that are employed in this chapter are from the Avon/Bard edition.

10. In most general terms, the debate centers on the social truth, or lack thereof, of Amado's protagonists. In the case of *Tereza Batista*, these positions are exemplified by Walnice Galvão, who argues that "Jorge Amado's prostitute is an outstanding imaginary product of Latin American machismo" (Walnice Galvão, "Amado: respeitoso, respeitável," in *Saco de gatos* [São Paulo: Duas Cidades, 1976], pp. 13–22); and Jon S. Vincent, who counters, "I don't know whether Amado expected his readers to believe Tereza Batista in a literal sense . . . , but it does strike me as useful to remember that these are characters in novels and therefore necessarily included in the suspension of disbelief required for all the other lies" (Jon S. Vincent, "Jorge Amado, Jorge Desprezado," *Luso-Brazilian Review*, 15 [1978]: 11–18).

11. Part of the writing of João Cabral de Melo Neto, most of that by João Guimarães Rosa, and virtually all of the work of Ariano Suassuna draw heavily on Northeastern folk and popular traditions. Examples of works which have been translated into English are the following by João Cabral de Melo Neto: *Morte e vida severina e outros poemas em voz alta*, 2nd ed. (Rio de Janeiro: Editora Sabiá, 1967), tr. Elizabeth Bishop, Sections 1, 2, and 14, in *An Anthology of Twentieth-Century Brazilian Poetry*, ed. Elizabeth Bishop and Emanuel Brasil (Middletown, Conn.: Wesleyan University Press, 1973), pp. 126–39. The following are the translated works of João Guimarães Rosa: *Grande sertão: Veredas*, 10th ed. (Rio de Janeiro: José Olympio, 1976), tr. James L. Taylor and Harriet de Onís as *The Devil to Pay in the Backlands* (New York: Knopf, 1963); *Primeiras estórias*, 8th ed. (Rio de Janeiro: José Olympio, 1975), tr. Barbara Shelby as *The Third Bank of the River and Other Stories* (New York: Knopf, 1968); *Sagarana*, 18th ed. (Rio de Janeiro: José Olympio, 1976), tr. Harriet de Onís as *Sagarana, A Cycle of Stories* (New York: Knopf, 1966). And those works of Ariano Suassuna that have been translated: *Auto da Compadecida*, 10th ed. (Rio de Janeiro: Livraria Agir/INL, 1973), tr. Dillwyn F. Ratcliff as *The Rogues' Trial* (Berkeley: University of California Press, 1963).

town's many nooks and crannies, participating in Afro-Brazilian religious services, and talking with people like Rodolfo. "We're just friends," the painter Carybé explains, "nothing more and nothing less."[12]

Rodolfo met Jorge Amado years ago in the Terreiro de Jesus and still sees him at official functions such as the annual *cordel* fair. He carefully sets aside the autographed copies, which the novelist continues to send him, and expresses appreciation for his periodic aid. "My life is a constant struggle that doesn't leave me time to hang around with intellectuals, but Jorge Amado helps me more than most, and I am grateful for that," he says. "He sent a film crew here to ask me to work on the movie versions of *Tent of Miracles* and *Shepherds of the Night*, and you know very well that something like that would not happen otherwise."

As for the novel proper, Amado's *Tereza Batista* mingles two quite separate strands of popular culture. One, the African thread, surfaces as a preoccupation with the rites and customs associated with the Afro-Brazilian religious practices known in Recife as *xangô*, in Rio de Janeiro as *macumba*, and in Salvador as *candomblé*.[13] The other, which might be loosely termed the ballad strain, is particularly apparent in other novels such as *Jubiabá* and *Tietá do Agreste*. As the subtitle *Home from the Wars* suggests, the figure of Tereza draws heavily upon the folk heroine called the *Donzela Guerreira*, the "Warrior Maiden." Amado is not the first educated artist to recast this martial figure. The Donzela also plays a leading role in João Guimarães Rosa's *The Devil to Pay in the Backlands* and Domingos Olímpio's *The Man Luzia*. Tereza is simply the maiden warrior's most recent and least maidenly incarnation.[14]

12. The conversation with Carybé (Héctor Bernabo) took place in Salvador on June 8, 1978.

13. See Roger Bastide, *O candomblé da Bahia: Rito nagô*, tr. Maria Isaura Pereira de Queiroz (São Paulo: Companhia Editora Nacional, 1961); and Edson Carneiro, *Candomblés da Bahia*, 2nd ed. rev. (Rio de Janeiro: Editora Andes, 1954). See also Bastide's more general *Les réligions africaines au Brésil: Vers une sociologie des interpénétration des civilisations* (Paris: Presses Universitaires de France, 1960), which has an extensive bibliography. For a consideration of *candomblé* and other Afro-Brazilian influences in Amado's work, see Russell G. Hamilton, "Afro-Brazilian Cults in the Novels of Jorge Amado," *Hispania*, 50 (1967): 242–52; Maria Luisa Nunes, "The Preservation of African Culture in Brazilian Literature: The Novels of Jorge Amado," *Luso-Brazilian Review*, 10 (1973): 86–101; and Clarivaldo Prado Valladeres, "As raizes da cultura baiana na obra de Jorge Amado," *Jornal de Letras*, 13 (1961): 13.

14. João Guimarães Rosa, *Grande sertão: Veredas*; Domingos Olímpio, *Luzia Homem*, 5th ed. (São Paulo: Melhoramentos, 1964). According to Menéndez-Pidal, the ballad of the Warrior Maiden, which was well known in the sixteenth century, is still sung today in Spain, Portugal, the Azores, Brazil, and Spanish America. It is also familiar among Sephardic Jews in Morocco, the Balkan Peninsula, and various parts of Asia Minor; see Ramon Menéndez-Pidal, *Flor nueva de romances velhos*, 19th ed. (Madrid: Espasa-Calpe, 1973).

Each of the five sections of Amado's novel presents a new trial, which the heroine overcomes with characteristic verve. The first section, "Tereza Batista's Debut at the Aracaju Cabaret, or Tereza Batista's Gold Tooth, or Tereza Batista and How She Gave the Usurer His Due," introduces the protagonist. "The Girl Who Bled the Captain with a Jerky Knife" focuses upon her courage. "The ABC of Tereza Batista's War Against the Black Smallpox" portrays her as the guardian angel of a particular community. "The Night Tereza Slept with Death" recounts her fall into prostitution. The last section, "Tereza Batista's Wedding Feast, or the Closed-Basket Strike in Bahia, or Tereza Batista Dumps Death into the Ocean," provides a romantic finale.

As may be evident from these titles and the fact that Amado calls these sections *folhetos*, his novel relies directly upon the *literatura de cordel*. "Plague, famine, war; love and death" reads the introductory epigraph, "Tereza Batista's life is a ballad to sing in the streets." Rodolfo himself makes a brief appearance in the last section, where Amado imagines him "immortalizing that convivial and truly unforgettable occasion of Tereza's marriage in a ballad." The interchange apparent here thus goes beyond the rather routine cross-over found in so many literary works. In *Tereza Batista*, an educated writer draws on a tradition which will actually reincorporate the resulting novel. Himself a supporting actor in a book which looks to folk and popular themes for inspiration, Rodolfo rewrites the work from his own viewpoint, thereby making it a triple and therefore particularly intriguing exchange.

The Six-Step Pattern

Rodolfo's copy of Jorge Amado's *Tereza Batista* sits between a Portuguese translation of Dickens' *Pickwick Papers* and an atlas, all three on one of the many bookshelves lining the long narrow room that he uses as his office. Rodolfo himself asserts that he has read Amado's book from one end to the other. Given the ease, however, with which *folheto* authors appropriate appealing titles just as they borrow unrelated cover photographs, the fact that his *cordel* story is called *Tereza Batista* means little in its own right. Furthermore, his tendency to get an increasing number of facts wrong about the novel as it progresses makes it less than certain that he has read all of its four hundred pages. Nevertheless, the many allusions to events in the book's initial section indicate a more than casual relationship between the two texts.

Rodolfo's decision to versify the novel is not unusual. Popular poets have periodically rewritten works by erudite authors. The best-known Brazilian examples are undoubtedly the *cordel* stories based on Shakespeare's

Romeo and Juliet, on José de Alencar's *Iracema*, on Bernardo Guimarães' *The Slave Isaura*, and on Jorge Amado's *Gabriela, Clove, and Cinnamon*.[15] Whereas the poet may consult the original or an abridged version of the particular text, his audience is familiar with the stories almost exclusively through movie or television adaptations. Without this "advance notice," it is doubtful that such *cordel* versions would attract most readers' interest. The fact that *Tereza Batista* was not made into a film or television soap opera explains in part the *folheto*'s only moderate sales. Though many of Rodolfo's stories have gone through multiple printings, this one sold only slightly over six thousand copies. (The poet generally prints five thousand copies at a time.) "I wrote about Tereza because I liked her," explains Rodolfo in conversation,

> but I knew from the beginning that the story wouldn't sell. Now, however, I am writing an *ABC of Jorge Amado*, and because it talks about lots of books with which ordinary people are more familiar, you can be sure that it will do a good deal better.

There are, to be sure, many differences between the long novel and the eight-page narrative poem, most of which have less to do with what Rodolfo excluded than with how he changed what he chose to use. The following list summarizes the most important differences between the *folheto* and its source:

NOVEL	FOLHETO
Prostitute with heart-of-gold theme does not fit any of the four variations of the *cordel*'s six-step pattern.	Vision of prostitute as both victim and sinner results in *DR/DW* mix within primary story line, allowing the *folheto* to be read from either point of view.
Action-oriented plot, Tereza as prime mover (use of present tense).	Story is a reflection on Tereza as a symbol of the poet's and his readers' sufferings (use of past tense).
Happy ending (marriage), confirms view of prostitution as not necessarily demeaning.	Unhappy ending (death) mitigated by "canonization" reveals somewhat ambiguous view of prostitution as both offense against society and form of martyrdom.

15. João Martins de Ataíde, *Romance de Romeu e Julieta* (Juazeiro do Norte, 1975), and his *Iracema, a Virgem dos Lábios de Mel* (Juazeiro do Norte, 1978); Severino Borges, *A Escrava Isaura* (Recife, n.d.); Manuel d'Almeida Filho, *Gabriela* (São Paulo: 1976). Caetano Cosme da Silva also has a *folheto* entitled *A Escrava Isaura* (n.p., n.d.), but the story is unrelated to the nineteenth-century novel *A Escrava Isaura* by Bernardo Guimarães

The underlying structure of the novel is relatively straightforward. Although Amado embellishes the standard goodhearted prostitute scheme with a wealth of detail, the plot itself may be diagrammed as a repetition of simple tests triggering right responses and then a final reward. The author includes a number of Afro-Brazilian saints to give his story a consciously regional flavor, but these do not function as divine forces from a structural point of view. A certain picaresque quality recalls elements of *HW* folhetos, and yet the novel does not fit this scheme both because death is omnipresent and because Tereza's social superiors are not uniformly foolish.

Although the *folheto* follows the *cordel*'s customary six-step pattern, it is an uneasy blend of what would normally be two variations. Tereza's identity as a prostitute forces the author to wedge both *DR* and *DW* into one uneasy whole, making it possible to read the *folheto* as either a *DR* or a *DW* story. In either case, it is necessary to emphasize certain elements while suppressing others with the result that the meaning of the story depends largely on the reader's point of view. Below is an outline of both *DR* and *DW* readings of the *folheto*. (See Figure 2 on page 62 for the *DR* and *DW* patterns.) Note that Tereza is the protagonist in both readings and that the *folheto* is thus unlike José de Souza Campos' *The King, the Dove, and the Sparrowhawk* or Apolônio Alves dos Santos' *Serginho*, in which the *DR* and *DW* schemes require different protagonists: good king and evil hawk, good father and evil brother. Note also that steps 1 and 2 are identical for both readings.

Tereza Batista (folheto, DR reading)

1. *Pact*: Tereza born in countryside under sign of the lion; poor but part of apparently harmonious community and family.
2. *Test*: Tereza loses parents at an early age.
3. *(Right) response*: Tereza pushes onward "without the least sign of cowardice," refusing to succumb to "the gale of misfortune."
2. *Test*: Tereza seduced while still an adolescent by the most Bohemian notable of the city.
3. *(Right) response*: Tereza lives her martyrdom with courage, faces a "thousand troublemakers," endures beatings by drunks, stands up to knives and daggers, all the while remaining "virtue itself, / sweetness and kindness personified."
4. *Counterresponse* (divine intervention): Tereza finds the "inner force" to go on; she "suffered, struggled, and triumphed" because "she never sold her honor."

(Rio de Janeiro: Briquiet, 1941). The Rui Barbosa *Antologia* also mentions a version of the novel by Francisco das Chagas Batista (p. 507), but I have not had the opportunity to consult this one.

5. *Judgment*: "A sanctuary of courage / in her valiant struggle," Tereza dies alone in accord with her sad destiny. Even no-goods weep on the day of her death (intercession of community), and she becomes "more like a saint" in the afterlife.

6. *Pact reasserted*: Tereza gone, her "familiar name / and grievous drama / live on" in the hearts of poet and populace as an example of "the deepest truth."

Tereza Batista (*folheto*, DW reading)

1. *Pact*: Tereza born in countryside under sign of the lion; poor but part of apparently harmonious community and family.

2. *Test*: Tereza loses parents at an early age.

3. *(Wrong) response*: Tereza sheds "few tears" and leaves the countryside for the big city "where life is a constant struggle / for the despised class of have-nothings."

2. *Test*: Tereza seduced while still an adolescent by the most Bohemian notable of the city.

3. *(Wrong) response*: Tereza persists in a life of sin, becoming the lover of sugar mill owners, mistress of a judge, a priest's concubine, etc., leading the poet to describe her as an unfortunate being "poised / upon the rim of an abyss."

4. *Counterresponse* (divine intervention): Tereza meets the fate of every woman who turns to prostitution, lost amidst a "sea of corruption."

5. *Judgment*: Tereza dies alone, "a battle-weary woman."

6. *Pact reasserted*: Tereza disappears from the community's midst, having met the "fate of every woman / who turns to prostitution" by ending up in her work like "vermin in the mud."

Because the single most important difference between the novel and the *folheto* lies in the authors' treatment of the protagonist, let us concentrate upon this aspect. In order to show how Rodolfo altered Amado's *Tereza*, it is necessary to refer back to the folk source from which the novelist took his story.

In the centuries-old anonymous Iberian ballad of the Warrior Maiden, the heroine, usually the youngest of seven daughters, sets out to battle in order to assuage her father's anguish upon finding himself the ailing head of a family without sons. The old man is responsible for the defense of his reputation according to the Mediterranean honor code, but age and ill health will not allow him to defend his country, as required.[16] The elderly gentleman tries to dissuade the young woman, whose name changes from

16. For an excellent, multifaceted analysis of the honor code's socioeconomic bases and psychological implications, see *Honour and Shame: The Values of Mediterranean Society*, ed. J. B. Péristiany, The Nature of Human Society Series (Chicago: University of Chicago Press. 1966).

version to version, from leaving home with a series of questions emphasizing her unsuitability to the role she is assuming ("What will you do to hide your long hair, your small hands, your breasts?"). The daughter, however, has a ready answer to each of his objections and finally sallies forth in soldier's garb.[17] Her commander turns out to be a handsome young bachelor, who suspects from the look in her eyes that she must be a woman. He is, however, strangely incapable of discovering the truth for himself and must turn to his mother for aid in ascertaining the new conscript's true identity. The older woman devises a number of tests aimed at tricking the would-be man into revealing "his" identity by selecting ribbons instead of a sword in the marketplace or by sniffing a rose instead of stripping the petals from it. The maiden succeeds in passing all these trials until the captain finally forces her into a situation—usually a bath in a river—in which she must remove her clothes. At this point she conveniently receives word of her father's imminent death and goes hurrying home with the young man in amorous, though properly marriage-minded, pursuit.

Looking back over the story as a whole, one sees that it is concerned on at least one level with a dual cross-over in traditional Iberian sex roles—feminine shame, masculine honor—in which equilibrium is restored only at the end. It is essential that the woman go off to war not because she enjoys fighting but because of the absence or inability of males to play the necessary aggressive role. Since her father is no longer able to defend his own honor and has no sons to take on this responsibility for him, she must abandon her habitual shyness and restraint to defend the family's good name. The young captain adopts just the opposite tack by abdicating a suitably vigorous role in dealing with his doubts about the young soldier, relying on his mother to resolve them in this case. The older female is, however, unsuccessful, and the young woman effectively sidesteps her

17. The story of a woman who dresses in men's clothing, thereby evading discovery of her sex until a dramatic moment, has both Russian and Italian antecedents; See Stith Thompson, *Motif-Index of Folk Literature: A Classification of Narrative Elements in Folktales, Ballads, Myths, Fables, Medieval Romances, Exempla, Fabliaux, Jest-books, and Local Legends*, rev. ed., 6 vols. (Helsinki: Suomalainen Tiedakatemia, 1955–1958), in which the tale is classified as 884B. The single most comprehensive study of the theme in a Luso-Brazilian context is Fernando de Castro Pires de Lima, *A mulher vestida de homem* (Coimbra: Fundação Nacional para a Alegria no Trabalho, 1958). Versions have been collected in Espírito Santo, Minas Gerais, Pernambuco, Santa Catarina, São Paulo, and Sergipe. Of particular interest to this study are the seven specifically Bahian variants included in Hildegardes Vianna, "A mulher vestida de homem," *Revista Brasileira de Folclore*, 6 (1963): 177–93. For further references and a discussion of the dual cross-over on which the ballad hinges, see Candace Slater, "The Romance of the Warrior Maiden: A Tale of Honor and Shame," in *El romancero hoy: Historia, comparatismo, bibliografía crítica*, ed. Antonio Sánchez-Romeralo et al. (Madrid: Gráficas Condor, 1979), pp. 167–82.

schemes. Consistently choosing the "wrong" (read "male") response, the maiden paradoxically affirms her femininity by showing that she knows how things ought not (and therefore also ought) to be. She is thus a suitable candidate for marriage once her father's real or imaginary death provides the cue for an upside-down world to right itself. The old man's impending exit obviates the daughter's need to take his place, thereby freeing her to assume a feminine—that is, suitably yielding—role vis-à-vis her future husband, who, significantly, reveals no inclination to consult with his mother before galloping off after the girl.

The ballad's underlying purpose is therefore unmistakable. By outlining a series of incorrect behavior patterns in such a thoroughly engaging manner, the Donzela's story reinforces time-honored mores. The tale also stresses the importance of marriage in assuming a fully adult role in society since both son and daughter emerge as autonomous individuals only after transferring the emotional energy previously focused on a parent to a spouse.

Turning now to Amado's novel, one sees the same basic theme of inverted sex roles in his story of Tereza Batista. The protagonist is, by no coincidence, an orphan entrusted to the care of an uncle, who soon develops sexual designs upon his young niece. True to form, this individual proves incapable of preventing his shrewish wife from selling the girl to a man known for his brutality. Forced by her weak uncle to assume an atypically aggressive role, Tereza struggles against her tormentor, who, temporarily, succeeds in breaking her will. Later, when a young, would-be liberator proves himself a coward, Tereza saves both their lives by stabbing the captain to death. She next meets up with an arrogant doctor, who runs off when a smallpox epidemic breaks out, leaving her to nurse the afflicted community back to health. After a brief interlude with a wealthy landowner, who is, unfortunately, too short-sighted to provide for her future, she is forced into prostitution. However, it is not long before Tereza organizes a general strike in response to the inability of the local administrators to deal with serious problems in the brothel district.

Although brief, this description should suffice to emphasize essential similarities between Tereza and the Warrior Maiden. Neither Tereza nor the Donzela participates in active combat, and each adopts the "male" role because no man is willing or able to play the part. Thus, Amado's novel begins when a local ruffian abuses a woman. While numerous male onlookers stare, Tereza jumps into the fray. Like her Iberian counterpart, the protagonist has the courage to do battle but then renounces her warrior ways when conditions permit. Not surprisingly, Tereza eventually meets a man who is a genuine fighter and whose promise of a child symbolizes a restoration of traditional male/female roles.

Naturally, there are many differences between the medieval maiden and

Amado's woman "home from the wars." The most outstanding of these is clearly his heroine's identity as a prostitute. While the Donzela spends seven years in the most virginal circumstances imaginable, from the time she reaches adolescence, Tereza goes to bed with all sorts of men. By making Tereza a "fallen" and yet admirable woman, Amado suggests that persons routinely excluded from polite society may be morally superior to their supposed betters and thus actually freer than they are. He also appears to be saying that since Tereza sleeps only with those customers for whom she has some feeling, sex-for-a-price is somehow not necessarily degrading in itself.

Rodolfo, however, is having none of this view of prostitution.[18] While continuing to emphasize Tereza's remarkable, genuinely Donzela-like courage, he rejects the idea that working in a brothel could be anything but shameful and humiliating. Amado portrays Tereza as an essentially joyous individual whose sensuality represents a slap in the face of a still relatively rigid middle class. "All copper and gold, a glorious woman in the full flower of her years," writes Amado, Tereza was "born to laugh and have a good time." Rodolfo, on the other hand, insists from the beginning of the *folheto* that Tereza's experiences as the "goddess of the brothel" are in no way enviable. Amado playfully nicknames his protagonist "Tereza Knifecut," "Tereza Wiggle Hips," "Tereza Seven Sighs," "Tereza Tread Softly," and "Tereza Honeycomb," but the only labels that interest the poet are "tired of battle" and "home from the wars," which he includes in the last stanza of his *folheto*. "If Tereza had not been born / under the sign of the lion," he declares earlier, "she would not have triumphed / because I firmly believe / that the prostitute is the same / as the drug addict or thief."

Furthermore, while in Amado's novel Tereza is, for all her larger-than-life qualities, an individual, in the *folheto* she is clearly a symbol. An embodiment of the "many prostitutes / in this world that God created," she is first and foremost "an example among harlots" in her suffering. Although the poet singles out his heroine as "that most sublime blossom [that] ever appeared," his chief interest is never the unique personality. "I wanted to write about Tereza," Rodolfo explains in conversation, "because she is like so many other women who suffer. You can see them in the

18. The conservatism in relationship to proper sexual behavior apparent in this and other *folhetos* does not mean that the *cordel* excludes sex altogether. On the contrary, there are a number of usually anonymous pornographic *folhetos* such as *A História do Velhinho que Lutava 72 Horas com um Cabaço sem Tocar Fundo ou Rebentá-lo* (*The Story of an Oldster Who Struggled 72 Hours with a Gourd Without Getting to the Bottom or Splitting It*), in which the poet throws his habitual reticence to the wind. *Folheto* heroines, however, are traditionally virginal, and it is common to find the most impassioned exchange of words followed by a handshake.

center of the city any day you walk by, poor things, selling their love in order to feed their families."

The poet's final identification with Tereza as a representative of all those who struggle against enormous odds is thus the *folheto*'s primary goal. "Tereza was able to withstand all those reverses, all those humiliations," claims Rodolfo. "Everybody has to fight in this life, but it isn't everybody who comes out ahead like her." The heroine is ultimately a pretext for a moral statement and a meditation upon the poet's experience and thus upon every *folheto* reader's experience. "If there is a hell, / this hell is here on earth," the poet asserts in the last stanzas, and "the drama of Tereza / is the drama of my own sorrows."

The *Folheto* Within the *Cordel* Tradition

The *folheto*'s underlying vision is thus far more "traditional" than the novel's. Nevertheless, when compared with other *cordel* stories on the same subject, it reveals elements that may be considered nontraditional, even radical. If this *folheto*'s structure is somewhat different from our other two case studies, it is precisely because of the poet's less than conventional moral stance in comparison with that of other popular authors.

As already mentioned in the section on *DW* stories in Chapter 3, prostitutes abound in the *cordel* tradition. Prime examples of *falsidade*, they are typically happily engaged or married women who deceive the men who love them, turning by choice to a life of sin. After enjoying the pleasures of the flesh, which the poet hints at in great and perversely satisfying detail, they suddenly find themselves alone and ill. Since it is too late to repent, they have no other recourse but to utter their own condemnation at the story's end. In João Martins de Ataíde's *The Life of a Prostitute*, the protagonist declares,

Estas dores que hoje sofro	These pains which I suffer today
É justo que sofra elas	are just,
Estas lágrimas que derramo	these tears which I shed
Serão em paga daquelas	are in payment for others
Que fiz gotejar dos olhos	that I made flow from the eyes
Das casadas e das donzelas.	of married women and virgins.

The poet himself frequently tacks on an additional warning, urging the reader to take heed of the fearsome example.

Não se engane com o mundo	Do not be misled by the world
Que o mundo não tem que dar	because the world has nothing to
Quem com ele se iludir	give

Iludido há de ficar	him who confides in it;
Pois temos visto exemplos	he will be deceived
Que é feliz quem os tomar.	because we have seen examples
	that the wise person will heed.[19]

Rodolfo, however, refuses to condemn Tereza in the usual all-out manner. Another poet might find a way around tradition either by (1) insisting that ill-intentioned persons had slandered an authentic virgin, or (2) admitting that Tereza was a prostitute but allowing her to undergo a suitably arduous penance. Rodolfo, however, does not resort to such tactics not only because of his loyalty to the novelist and the novel but also because of a new permissiveness toward sex, particularly apparent in urban centers such as Salvador. As the *folheto*'s dig at "the Bahian woman / given over to pleasure" suggests, Salvador displays a degree of sophistication not found in other Northeastern capitals of comparable size, such as traditionally more parochial Recife.

Prostitution itself is regarded somewhat differently in the big city than in the countryside. In small towns of the interior, the brothel district is a specific part of town reserved for women who have often been seduced and abandoned. Since everybody knows of their misfortune, these individuals have no hope of a normal life. Often scorned by their families, most see no choice but to earn their living through the sale of their affections.

In the city, on the other hand, respectable single or widowed women, who would normally be supported by an extended family in the countryside, may turn to prostitution as their only means of survival. Their peers, who are also often far from home, are likely to be somewhat more charitable toward them in these circumstances. Thrown together in urban slums, they may find that familiarity breeds less contempt than compassion.

Though confident that his readers are more or less ready to accept a less traditional view of prostitution, Rodolfo proceeds with caution. Significantly, he never actually condones sex-for-a-price itself, insisting that the "fate of every woman / who turns to prostitution / is to end up in her work / like vermin in the mud." Nevertheless, at the same time he describes the fallen woman as "a being marked out from others / like the unfortunate individual poised / upon the rim of an abyss," he portrays her as a victim rather than as a villain.

The poet also does some tinkering with the definition of prostitution. He admits that Tereza sleeps with everyone from judge to sailor yet also

19. João Martins de Ataíde, *A Vida de uma Meretriz* (Recife, n.d.). The *folheto* is only one of a number of stories with the same title and theme. "Prostitution punished" is a standard folktale motif. See Q243.1 in Thompson, *Motif-Index of Folk Literature*.

suggests that "she never sold / her honor." Dwelling upon Tereza's sterling personal qualities ("she was virtue itself / sweetness and kindness person-ified"), he sees her courage as her salvation. If Tereza sees sex as "her means of livelihood," she still remains in inviolable "sanctuary of cour-age," fighting back at her oppressors like "a fierce hyena." This means that although she takes many lovers, some of whom give her money, the poet can still proclaim her "pure of heart" and thus worthy not only of earthly admiration but also of divine salvation.

Throughout his *Tereza Batista*, Rodolfo alternates between passages that might appear in any traditional *folheto* as condemnation of sexual misconduct and other passages in which he insists that the prostitute is someone to be pitied. He generally voices these contradictory sentiments at different points in the story, but occasionally they actually appear within the same stanza. For example, after beginning the following passage in a typically disapproving manner, he switches course in midstream, going on to affirm that Tereza is not so much an example of *falsidade* as a potential model of *firmeza*:

> Poor unhappy woman
> who enters the brothel thinking
> that the goal of life
> is only carnal pleasure.
> In this unstable existence,
> Tereza, owing to her (unhappy) sexual
> experience, was a shrineless saint!

The uneasy balance between these two positions is especially evident in the *folheto*'s final stanzas. Unlike Jorge Amado, who ends his novel with an enormous wedding, Rodolfo has Tereza stage an exit worthy of any traditional *cordel* prostitute. Forgetting all about the husband he has given her at one point, he insists that her destiny (*signo* here is equivalent to *sina*) has "marked her to die single one day." Nevertheless, he then goes on to speak, atypically, of the community's sorrow ("on the day she died, / even no-goods wept"), resurrecting and actually canonizing her when he asserts that "today / Tereza is more like a saint."

In looking back over the *folheto* as a whole, one sees that the poet has astutely hedged his bets at every turn. If Tereza is "this century's / sinner saint," she is also its "saintly sinner," leaving the reader free either to accept both epithets or to select the judgment with which he feels more comfortable. Although such hedging is not common in *cordel* stories, it is necessary in this case because readers, many of whom have grown up with very specific ideas of right and wrong in regard to sexual behavior, may be unable to accept the notion that the prostitute is free of blame. Despite the fact that Rodolfo declares in private conversation that prostitutes are "created by a society that does not give people enough to eat," he is enough of a popular poet to say only what he thinks people are ready (and will pay) to hear. This *folheto*'s relative success indicates that he was essentially on target. If the story's underlying message is somewhat contradictory, it is true to the way many of his readers presently think.

The same kind of ambiguity pervades another *folheto* called *The Life of the Prostitute*, which Rodolfo wrote and published some three years later in 1976.[20] The story, which is an overview of prostitution in general rather than the portrait of a single individual, speaks of the prostitute as both "a sore" or blemish upon society and "a brutal victim." Although the prostitute leads the traditional wish-fulfilling high life, in which she "sleeps until noon, then gets up to eat / and dress for a night of dancing and drinking," she is ultimately not a sinner but—once again—a martyr.

Not surprisingly, Rodolfo is careful to back his still unconventional assertions with a wealth of biblical material. Citing the story of Christ and Mary Magdalene, which most *cordel* authors either dismiss or distort, he ends with a call to God to send his son once more to earth "because this place is presently a real mess." His radical (in *cordel* terms) suggestion that the prostitute be reintegrated into society as a wife and mother is cast as a favor to the Virgin Mary.

Meretriz também é Gente,	The prostitute is a human being
Por isso sendo amparada,	like any other.
Amanhã naturalmente,	Therefore, if treated with respect
Pode ser melhor honrada,	she can tomorrow lead
Tendo esposo e tendo filho	a more honorable life as wife
Não manchando o santo brilho	and mother, no longer dimming
Da Mãe-Virgem Imaculada!	the radiance of the Immaculate
	Virgin-Mother of Christ.[21]

Because this *folheto* reveals so many of the ideas first expressed in *Tereza Batista*, it is tempting to see the *cordel* version of Amado's novel as a trial balloon. If readers had not liked the Tereza story, Rodolfo could have claimed that he was simply versifying what a well-known novelist, not he, had said. Since, however, *Tereza Batista* had a relatively favorable acceptance, the poet wrote his second, more direct account of prostitution.

In sum, then, Rodolfo's treatment of the novel *Tereza Batista, Home from the Wars* provides a particularly interesting example of both the *cordel*'s conservatism and its flexibility.[22] Far closer to the traditional concept

20. Rodolfo Coelho Cavalcante, *A Vida da Meretriz* (Salvador: 1976).

21. Ibid., p. 8.

22. This pull between tradition and change is fundamental to virtually all forms of folk and popular art. See, for example, Richard Bauman, "Differential Identity and the Social

of "correct" feminine behavior exemplified by the medieval ballad of the Warrior Maiden than to Amado's fictional reworking, the *cordel* poet's account nonetheless reveals a number of new elements. If the *DR/DW* mix within the primary story line is decidedly uneasy, the poet's *Tereza* still relies on the familiar six-step pattern. Though different in a number of respects from José de Souza Campos' *The King, The Dove, and the Sparrowhawk* and Apolônio Alves dos Santos' *The Monstrous Kidnapping of Serginho*, this *folheto* still remains within the same tradition and can be read with a modicum of pinching and poking as a *DR* tale. Our three examples can be seen as composing a sort of continuum in which the first *folheto* adheres very closely to its raw material; the second makes a small number of far-reaching changes; and the third undertakes a more massive reworking of its source.

Naturally, each *folheto*'s relationship to its raw material is determined by a number of factors. These include the community's moral outlook and its receptivity to change, as well as any problems inherent in the raw material, that is, Apolônio is unable to deny the fact that the kidnapped boy was murdered; and Rodolfo cannot pretend that Tereza Batista was not a prostitute. Then too, much depends on the author's own vision of the world and his talent as a writer.

The tensions apparent on a structural level in the *folheto* version of *Tereza Batista* reflect profound changes within the poet's way of thinking as well as his public's shifting attitudes toward love and sex. The fact that the traditional six-step framework creaks and groans rather than cracks is ample proof of both its resiliency and Rodolfo Coelho Cavalcante's powers of invention.

Folheto: *Tereza Batista, Cansada de Guerra / Tereza Batista, Tired of Battle* by Rodolfo Coelho Cavalcante

Inspirado no Romance	Inspired by the novel
Do Escritor Jorge Amado	by writer Jorge Amado,
Dei o título do seu livro	I chose the title of his book
E no mesmo baseado	for my own *folheto*, and basing my
Vou descrever com lhaneza	story on it, I am going to describe
A história de Tereza	very simply the story of Tereza,
Cujo drama foi narrado.	whose drama it recounts.
Nasceu Tereza Batista	Tereza was born
Na cidade Barracão	in the city of Barracão
Que hoje é Rio Real	known today as Rio Real,
Situada no sertão	located in the interior

Base of Folklore," in *Towards New Perspectives in Folklore*, ed. Américo Paredes and Richard Bauman (Austin: University of Texas Press, 1971), pp. 31–41.

Entre Sergipe e Bahia,	between Sergipe and Bahia.
Nasceu ela em pleno dia	She was born in the summer time
De agosto, no verão,	in the middle of an August day.
Trazendo signo de Léo	Born under the sign of Leo
Tereza com precisão	in needy circumstances,
Tinha coragem e destreza	Tereza was courageous and able,
Da bravura do leão,	brave as a lion.
Foi a mulher pecadora,	She was a fallen woman, attractive
Atraente e sedutora	and seductive
Porém de bom coração.	but still pure of heart.
Sua infância de pobreza	Her childhood was marked by poverty.
Suportou a tirania	She endured the tyranny of misfor-
Da desventura da sorte.	tune.
Perdendo seus pais um dia	Losing her parents one day,
Pouca lágrima jorrou	she shed few tears
Para frente caminhou	but pushed onward
Sem a menor covardia.	without the least sign of cowardice.
O sertanejo, já disse	The inhabitant of the interior,
Euclides, que é ente forte,	as Euclides da Cunha once said,
Tereza não sucumbiu-se	is a valiant creature.
Com o vendaval da sorte,	Tereza did not succumb
Com 15 anos de idade	to the gale of misfortune.
Deixou a sua cidade	At the age of 15,
Pegando rude transporte.	she left home on a ramshackle trans-
	port.
Conseguindo uma passagem	Getting hold of a ticket,
Viajou no trem do "Leste"	she set out
Com destino a Aracaju	on the "East" train
A Capital do Nordeste	bound for Aracaju,
Onde a vida é agitada	capital of the Northeast,
Pela classe desprezada	where life is a constant struggle
Do homem "cabra-da-peste."	for the despised class of have-
	nothings.
Era Tereza uma Ninfa	Tereza was a nymph
De um porte magestoso,	of regal bearing
Com ar de menina-pobre	with the air of a waif.
Tinha o coração bondoso	She had a kind heart,
Mas seguindo a triste sina	but her sad destiny
Veio sofrer esta menina	led her to suffer
Um viver mais inditoso.	a most unfortunate existence.
Um certo dia um Doutor	One day a certain notable,
Mais boêmio da cidade	the most Bohemian of the city,
Vestiu-lhe como Rainha	dressed her like a queen,

E na sua puberdade
Conheceu o meretrício
Caindo no precipício
Da negra fatalidade!

and while still an adolescent,
she became a prostitute,
falling into the abyss
of black misfortune!

Todas as noites se via
No "EDIFÍCIO VATICANO":
A mulher moça mais linda
Do Cabaré Sergipano,
Era o ídolo dos boêmios
Os quais lhe ofertavam prêmios
Em troca do amor profano.

Every night
this loveliest young woman
of the Sergipe Cabaret
could be seen in "The Vatican."
She was the idol of Bohemians
who offered her various rewards
in exchange for worldly love.

Era Tereza Batista
O ídolo da juventude,
O anelo dos artistas,
Do Vate em decrepitude,
Porém Tereza vivia
Naquele mar de orgia
Vendendo carne e saúde.

Tereza Batista was the idol
of the city's youth,
desired by artists
as well as the failing poet,
but she lived
in that sea of orgy
selling health and flesh.

Foi amante de Doutores,
De ébrios, de taverneiros,
De poetas mais notáveis,
Dos humildes jangadeiros,
Não se sentia infeliz,
Era a doce meretriz
Dos ricos, dos carroceiros!

As the mistress of important men,
of drunks, of tavern owners,
of the most celebrated poets,
of humble fishermen.
She was not unhappy.
She was the sweet harlot
of rich men, of cart drivers!

Jamais queria Tereza
Vender sua Liberdade,
Como qualquer meretriz
Via na sexualidade
Seu Signo, sua profissão,
Na Natureza—um Leão,
No Coração—a bondade.

Tereza never sought
To sell her liberty.
Like any prostitute, she saw sex
as her destiny, her means of liveli-
    hood.
By nature, she was a lion,
but her heart was sheer goodness.

No "PARIS ALEGRE," as noites
Sábado a Segunda-Feira
Tereza Batista era
A Deusa da Gafieira,
Enfrentou mil desordeiros,
Apanhou de cachaceiros,
Enfrentou punhal, peixeira.

In the gay Paris every night
Saturday through Monday,
Tereza Batista was the goddess
of the brothel.
She faced a thousand troublemakers,
was beaten up by drunks,
and stood up to knives and daggers.

Quando surgia um valente
Que com ela desejava
Ter relações amorosas
E ela a ele não aceitava
Tereza enfrentava a briga,

When a fighting type wanted
to go to bed with her
and she wasn't willing,
Tereza was equal to the struggle
about whose tragic outcome

Que a própria polícia diga *Como a tragédia findava.*	you can ask the police.
Jamais Tereza entregou-se *A qualquer autoridade,* *Era uma hiena feroz* *Conhecida na cidade,* *Quem a ela não bolisse* *Era virtude em meiguice,* *O retrato da bondade.*	Tereza never yielded to any authority whatsoever. She was a fierce hyena known throughout the city, but for people who didn't antagonize her, she was virtue itself, sweetness and kindness personified.
De escrever toda a odisséia *Da vida desta mulher* *Só o Escritor Jorge Amado.* *Cuja descrição requer* *Um romance volumoso* *Do seu viver inditoso* *Que nem o Diabo quer.*	Only Jorge Amado, the writer, is capable of describing the entire odyssey of that woman's life. Her tale requires a hefty novel to tell about all these misfortunes that would cow the very devil.
Depois de muito gozar, *Depois de muito sofrer,* *Tereza deixou Sergipe* *Veio a Salvador viver,* *Sua vida de mundana* *Foi ela a mulher bahiana* *Que gozou todo o prazer.*	After a great deal of pleasure and a great deal of suffering, Tereza left Sergipe and went to lead her worldly life in Salvador. She became the epitome of the Bahian woman given over to pleasure.
Os mais notáveis artistas *Da Bahia apaixonados* *Conviveram com Tereza* *Deveras enamorados,* *Mesmo triste e maltratada* *Era a mulher cobiçada* *Dos mais ricos potentados.*	Impassioned, Bahia's most celebrated artists lived alongside Tereza, truly crazy for her. Even though sad and mistreated, she was the woman whom the richest potentates desired.
Foi amante de uzineiros, *Foi mulher de magistrado,* *Foi concubina de Padre,* *Foi meretriz de soldado,* *Foi prazer de marinheiro;* *Foi Deuza de jangadeiro,* *Teve um esposo ao seu lado.*	She was the lover of sugar mill owners, the mistress of a judge, a priest's concubine, a soldier's whore, a sailor's pleasure, a fisherman's goddess. She also had a husband at her side.
Pobre Tereza Batista *O teu romance contemplo.* *Foste dentre as meretrizes* *No sofrimento—um exemplo:* *Por seres mulher-perdida* *Na tua luta aguerrida*	Poor Tereza Batista, I reflect upon your story. You were an example among harlots in your suffering. A fallen woman, you remained a sanctuary of courage

Na coragem foste um templo.

Infeliz da pobre moça
Que se entrega ao lupanar,
Pensando que esta vida
Só tem um fim—é gozar!
E neste viver sem nexo
Tereza devido ao sexo
Foi Santa sem ter altar!

.Se Tereza não tivesse
O seu Signo de Leão
Não venceria na vida,
Pois a prostituição
Acredito, plenamente,
Ser a mesma equivalente
De maconheiros ou ladrão.

O fim de toda mulher
Que se entrega ao meretrício
É arrastar-se na lama
Como verme em seu ofício,
É a criatura marcada
Como uma desventurada
À beira de um precipício.

Porém Tereza Batista
Pelo um poder oriundo
Se o mundo fez a sofrer
Ela fez sofrer o mundo
Amou, gozou e sofreu
E no dia que ela morreu
Chorou até vagabundo!

Tereza no nosso século
Foi a Pecadora-Santa,
Foi a Santa-Pecadora
De tanta beleza, tanta,
Que o Nordeste a consagrou,
Outra flor não se gerou
Como a mais sublime planta!

Tereza foi um exemplo
Da mais pura realidade,
Distribuiu seu amor
Como exige a Sociedade,
O seu verdadeiro crime
Por sua vida se exprime
Não vender sua Liberdade!

in your valiant struggle.

Poor unhappy young woman
who enters the brothel thinking
that the goal of life
is only carnal pleasure.
In this unstable existence,
Tereza, owing to her (unhappy) sexual
experience, was a shrineless saint!

If Tereza had not been born
under the sign of the lion,
she would not have triumphed
because I firmly believe
that the prostitute is the same
as the drug addict or thief.

The fate of every woman
who turns to prostitution
is to end up in her work
like vermin in the mud.
She is a being marked out from others
like the unfortunate individual poised
upon the rim of an abyss.

Nevertheless, Tereza Batista,
thanks to an inner force,
made the world
suffer as much
as it inflicted suffering on her,
and on the day she died,
even no-goods wept.

Tereza was this century's
sinner saint
and saintly sinner,
so very beautiful
that the Northeast consecrated her.
No other flower equal to that
most sublime blossom ever appeared!

Tereza was an example
of the deepest truth.
She doled out her love
as society demanded
but her conception of genuine wrong
is apparent from her own life:
One should not sell one's freedom!

Quando ela na verdade	When she truly felt love for someone,
Por alguém amor sentia	she became a slave to her passion,
Logo era escravizada	and for this reason
Por isto muito sofria,	she suffered a great deal.
Cujo amor pouco durava	Her love was transient
Pois o seu signo marcava	because her destiny had marked her
De morrer solteira um dia.	to die single one day.
Tereza nasceu mulher,	Tereza was born a woman
Mulher sempre ela viveu,	and remained a real woman.
Consagrou-se ao amor-livre,	She gave herself to free love,
Sofreu, lutou e venceu,	suffered, struggled, and triumphed.
Jamais foi uma caftina,	She was never a procuress
Mesmo como libertina	and even as a libertine,
Nenhuma honra vendeu.	she never sold her honor.
Assim Tereza Batista	Thus Tereza Batista
Que viveu na podridão	who lived amidst corruption
Foi uma CANÇADA DE GUERRA	was her generation's
Dentro a sua geração,	battle-weary woman.
Hoje o seu nome famoso	Today her familiar name
Cujo drama doloroso	and grievous drama
Vive em nosso coração!	live on in our hearts!
Vê-se muitas meretrizes	There are many prostitutes
Neste mundo de meu Deus	in this world that God created
Como Tereza Batista	much like Tereza Batista
com todos os dramas seus,	with all her problems,
Outra igual nunca haverá	but there will never be another
Pois Tereza hoje está	exactly like her, readers, because to-
Mais Santa, leitores meus.	day
	Tereza is more like a saint.
Se é que existe um inferno	If there is a hell,
Este Inferno está na Terra,	this hell is here on earth.
Quem sofreu como Tereza	The person who suffers like Tereza
Na verdade um mártir encerra,	is indeed a martyr,
Tem razão o romancista	and the author is right
Chamar: Tereza Batista	to call Tereza Batista a woman
Mulher—CANÇADA DE GUERRA.	"tired of battle."
Me desculpe Jorge Amado	May Jorge Amado forgive me
Seu eu fui fraco trovado.	if I appear to be a bad poet,
Mas o drama de Tereza	but the drama of Tereza
É o drama da minha dor,	is the drama of my own sorrows.
Hoje Cançado de Guerra	Today, tired of battle, I continue
Sofro aqui na sua terra	to suffer here in her home,
CIDADE DO SALVADOR.	the city of Salvador.
FIM	END

José de Souza Campos, author of The King, the Dove, and the Sparrowhawk, *behind his distinctive fan-shaped display of* folhetos *in Recife's São José market. Courtesy Ricardo Noblat,* Manchete.

Apolônio Alves dos Santos, author of The Monstrous Kidnapping of Serginho, *in his home in Benfica, Rio de Janeiro. Courtesy Mário Pontes,* O Jornal do Brasil.

Edson Pinto da Silva at his folheto *stand in Recife's São José market. The sign "Literatura de Cordel" is approximately five years old. Before 1970 these booklets were known as* folhetos. *Today the vendor, who has been in the business for some four decades, also sells samba lyrics and second-hand paperbacks and movie magazines. Photograph by Arlindo Marinho,* Diário de Pernambuco.

Rodolfo Coelho Cavalcante.

José Francisco Borges at work in his home in the small town of Bezerros, Pernambuco, some two hours from Recife. Borges, whose blockprints have been exhibited in the Smithsonian and the Louvre, continues to write and print folhetos *on his own rustic press. In this photograph, his hair is somewhat longer than that of most popular poets, who tend to be conservative in such matters. Courtesy Tânia Quaresma.*

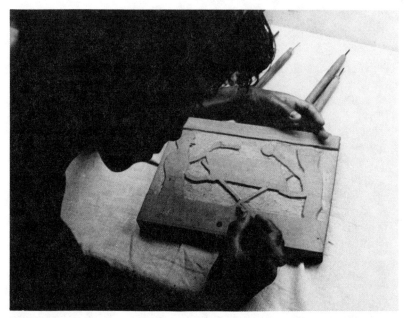

Borges' son at work on a blockprint. The design is first drawn on a piece of paper, then transferred to the block and the surrounding wood scooped out. Courtesy Tânia Quaresma.

João José da Silva (Azulão) singing on a Sunday morning in Rio de Janeiro's São Cristóvão fair. Note the microphone and the comic book cover on the folheto. *Azulão routinely draws crowds of up to several hundred persons. Courtesy Mário Pontes,* O Jornal do Brasil.

Cosme Damião Vieira de Oliveira, better known as Catapora, in his home in Jardim Gramacho outside the city of Rio de Janeiro. Catapora, who has never been in the Northeast, began composing verses as a clown in the festival known as the Folia dos Reis. He began writing folhetos *only recently. Here he composes verses on his guitar. Courtesy Mário Pontes,* O Jornal do Brasil.

A peddler in a fair in the interior of Pernambuco in the early 1960s. Note the booklets strung along the cords stretched from one post to another. Courtesy Roberto Benjamim.

Left: Pedro Oliveira, repentista *or on-the-spot composer from Juazeiro do Norte, Ceará. The singer is playing a rustic violin known as a* rabeca. *Courtesy Tânia Quaresma.*

Overlooking the fair in Caruaru, Pernambuco, some two and a half hours from Recife. Every Saturday the city is transformed into a marketplace as farmers surge in from the countryside to sell their foodstuffs and livestock and to buy everything from rubber sandals to the sugar candy known as alfenim. Long known as a "gateway to the sertão," thanks to its position between the coastal area and the backlands, Caruaru still boasts one of the region's larger weekly markets. Only at dusk do the stands fold and the sweepers appear as the city reverts to a series of winding streets. Courtesy Tânia Quaresma.

*This is the main street of a small town in the interior of Pernambuco, but
the picture could have been taken almost anywhere in the Northeast.
Courtesy Tânia Quaresma.*

A face in the fair. This and the following five illustrations show the sort of people who surround the poet in the marketplace and then take home his wares. Note the range in age and ethnic background. Courtesy Tânia Quaresma.

VII. "I Sing for Everyone": The *Folheto* in the Eyes of the Poet[1]

natural question arises in reading through the preceding case studies. To what degree do these three *folhetos* and other stories reveal a set of largely impersonal patterns and to what degree are they the voice of a particular individual, community, or nation?[2] This chapter and the next present some of the views expressed by popular poets and by their readers on the nature and meaning of the *literatura de cordel*. They are meant both to allow these persons to speak for themselves and to situate the question to which the final chapter will return.

To be sure, authors never speak of a six-step pattern and would no doubt scratch their heads or laugh at terms such as "*DR*" and "*DW*." Nevertheless, the *folheto*'s dependence on a series of literary givens is evident to them in their own terms. "Even though I have written ten myself, I don't like these stories," asserts one quite special poet-singer, Patativa,

> because the *folheto* author translates instead of creating. He talks about some noble prince or some awful giant who swallows people whole when I want to say that farmers where I live earn less than the price of a cup of coffee for a whole pound of cotton.[3]

1. Given the difficulties in translating from Portuguese to English, the meaning of the verb *sing* in this study is not always identical. The "singing" here refers both to the chanting recitation that the poet does in the marketplace to drum up business and to his activities in general. Thus, when the poet Joel Borges said to me, "Canto para todo mundo" (literally, "I sing for everyone"), he was referring specifically to his reading aloud of certain texts in the local fair as an example of his obligation to please the public (Sítio Cruzeiro, Pernambuco, May 18, 1978).

2. The question of impersonal form versus individual and community involvement is, to be sure, a familiar problem. Clearly, any art form will be both. For a discussion of the culture-bound nature of any art form, see Robert A. Hall, *Cultural Symbolism in Literature* (Ithaca: Cornell University Press, 1963); and Dorothy Lee, *Freedom and Culture* (Englewood Cliffs, N.J.: Prentice-Hall, 1959).

3. Antonio Gonçalves da Silva (Patativa), Serra de Sant'Ana, April 11, 1978. Aside from the ten *folhetos* which he has written, Patativa (the name refers to a kind of songbird) is also the author of three books of *caboclo* poetry and has achieved considerable fame as a poet-singer. For an overview of the poet, see *Patativa de Assaré*, ed. J. de Figueiredo Filho (Fortaleza: Universidade Federal do Ceára, 1970).

Patativa's reference to translation instead of creation emphasizes the *cordel*'s more obvious limits and at least its superficial conservatism. However, it does not necessarily follow that because most *folhetos* reveal a common generative pattern, tied in turn to a broader vision of how things ideally ought to function, that they allow no room for creation or have little or nothing to do with daily life. The *cordel* author sees his art as both a money-making venture and a vocation. Although he perceives himself as a spokesman committed to expressing the views of others, he can never escape his sense of himself as a particular individual singled out by "inspiration" to lead his fellow men. This awareness often leads him to express dissatisfaction with his public's insistence on hearing a particular message. And, yet, much as he may rail at his audience for its "credulity" (by which he really means "obstinacy" in most cases), he still sees himself as part of that larger community. Asked if they consider themselves *matutos* ("bumpkins" or "country folk"), most poets say something like, "Why, of course. What else could I possibly be?"[4]

Author and audience alike actively nurture a whole mythology concerning the *literatura de cordel*. Among its major tenets are "Poetry is a gift; it comes from the cradle"; "The poet learns his craft from no one; he learns everything alone"; "The poet is the voice of the people"; and "The best poet is the one who knows fastest how to please."[5]

As should be evident from the brief sketches of the poets in our three case studies, such statements are only partially true. Nevertheless, such assertions provide an important illustration of the twin concepts of poetry as both an almost supernatural mission and a demanding job. One *cordel* author sums up this essential duality succinctly when he says that "poetry is a kind of trade like any other, except of course that it is a trade in mysteries."[6]

As suggested in Chapter 1, the word "poetry" provides a convenient umbrella for the related and yet quite separate activities of (1) writing and (2) production and marketing. Poets themselves refer to the act of composition more specifically as *inspiração* ("inspiration"), *a visita da Musa* ("the visit of the muse"), *traduzir a estória em versos* ("translate the story into poetry"), or simply *versejar* ("put into verse"). Most *cordel* authors

4. This close identity of poet with the community is typical of other kinds of storytellers who may be nonprofessionals or semiprofessionals. See, for instance, Linda Dégh, *Folktales and Society: Story-Telling in a Hungarian Peasant Community*, tr. Emily M. Schlossberger (Bloomington: Indiana University Press, 1969).

5. For some interesting comparisons in which the artist emerges as mediator, explicit or tacit, between collective and individual striving for expression, see *The Traditional Artist in African Societies*, ed. Warren L. d'Azevedo (Bloomington: Indiana University Press, 1973).

6. Olegário Fernandes, Caruaru, Pernambuco, January 14, 1978.

take great pride in invention. Nevertheless, this creative moment represents only a fraction of the time occupied by that broader term *poesia*, a full-time occupation comparable on many fronts with bread baking or carpentry. As one poet explains,

> An art is something that you know how to do and I do not know how to do. There is the art of making furniture, of building walls, of driving a car. Then there is the art of making a *folheto*. The only difference between it and those other arts is that it can't be learned. Anyone can drive a car if he works at it, but not everyone can be a poet. However, the divine part, the inspiration, is only the beginning. After that, the poet has to break his back like anyone else, believe me.[7]

Cordel authors make no attempt to disguise the fact that they write for money. On the contrary, they call attention to their need to make a living, typically appealing to their listeners to reward their efforts by buying a copy of their stories as in the following conclusion to José Pacheco's *Great Debate Between Lampião and Saint Peter*, in which both the poet's pride in his favored status and need to make a living are clear.

Poeta tem liberdade	The poet has the freedom
Sagrado dom da natura	to write about whatever
Conforme a literatura	inspires him
Escreve o que tem vontade	as a sacred gift of nature.
Também a propriedade	Property, however,
Precisa o dono ter	always has an owner,
Pelo menos vou dizer	and so I tell you
Se meu espírito não mente	in all honesty
Poeta também é gente	that the poet has to eat
Também precisa comer.	like any other human being.[8]

The practical difficulties of being an author are often stressed by popular poets. One points out that "a house painter can pick up his brush any time he feels like it, but a writer has to wait until the muse is good and ready." Although "both poet and painter work to satisfy the person who pays them," the poet is not so lucky as the painter because people always need their walls painted, and they can go for months without reading a single page."[9]

Financial interest is not always the writer's only motive, but it is definitely one of his principal incentives. "The purpose of the *folheto*," says

7. Olegário Fernandes, Caruaru, Pernambuco, March 17, 1978.
8. José Pacheco, *Grande Debate Entre Lampião e São Pedro* (n.p., n.d.).
9. Francisco de Souza Campos, São Lourenço da Mata, Pernambuco, March 1, 1978.

one poet bluntly, "is to provide the children's dinner."[10] "I like to write, but no one wants to work for nothing," another author asserts, "so I love poetry and I love money. You could say that those were my two passions." Asked to define "necessity," he says,

> Well, look, suppose I am a poet and I need money. So I set about imagining the trials of some beautiful princess, or perhaps I decide to marry off Saint Peter. No, of course Saint Peter never got married, but if I need the money badly enough, then you can be sure that his days as a bachelor are numbered![11]

Although poetry is a welcome source of income, it is also, thanks to "inspiration," a very special kind of job. As many educated observers have pointed out, the popular artist is often first and foremost an artisan. In some ways, the *cordel* writer resembles a basket maker who seeks to turn out the most beautiful basket possible in accord with a series of set measurements. He may, perhaps, weave a slightly different pattern into the straw or give the handle an unexpected, whimsical twist. But because his first concern is to please the would-be buyer, he does not give a great deal of thought to the essential nature of baskets or worry too much about whether the user will be carrying potatoes or eggs. This sort of detachment allows *cordel* authors to turn out *folhetos* for opposing candidates without the slightest qualm. Some writers actually specialize in "two-sided" *folhetos*, in which they carefully celebrate the victory of *A* ("Hurrah, the best man won!") while lamenting the defeat of *B* ("Ah, that fine fellow of a loser put up such a good fight!").[12]

In similar fashion, a writer who never goes to church may write a *folheto* denouncing people's laxness in their religious duties. One *cordel* author sees no contradiction in the fact that the *folheto* "is one way, life another." According to him, this is the way things should be since "whoever sells something has to make whatever he sells in accord with what the customer wants." A fellow poet, who "does not consider himself

---

10. José Soares, Prazeres (Recife), Pernambuco, January 17, 1978.

11. José Costa Leite, Condado, Pernambuco, February 18, 1978.

12. The poet who explained this process to me was Olegário Fernandes (Caruaru, Pernambuco, March 18, 1978). For an illuminating example of two *folhetos* admittedly quite distant in time, which reflect radically different viewpoints, see José Francisco Soares, *A Vitória de Arraes ou a Vingança de Zé Ninguém* (1962), and his *Feitos da Revolução e Reformação Política* (1977). Excerpts appear in Maurício et al., *Arte popular*, pp. 1–2. For a brief but suggestive discussion of the differences between folk and erudite art, see Roman Jakobson and Petr Bogatyrev, "On the Boundary Between Studies of Folklore and Literature," in *Readings in Russian Poetics*, ed. Ladislav Matejska and Krystyna Pomorska (Cambridge, Mass.: MIT Press, 1971), pp. 91–94.

a religious man," writes prophecies "because this is art and art is something that a person does to make a living. It has absolutely nothing to do with what he believes."[13]

The idea that the group is more important than the individual underlies many writers' assertions. Thus, at least one writer compares the poet with a circus clown "because his duty is to please others even if his children are sick or if his mother died yesterday." And, yet, although the poet routinely adjusts his verses to fit his public's needs and desires, this willingness to please has limits, and there are certain stances that he will not take no matter how much money is offered. "Once," a prominent figure within the tradition confides,

> I really needed money, and a man came around here offering me a small fortune if I would write a pornographic *folheto*. Well, I tell you, I thought about it for two whole days and nights, but in the end I told him no because I just wouldn't have felt right. It would have gone against something in myself.[14]

The balance between what a poet will and will not say becomes more evident in discussions about which side ought to win in a particular contest. To a certain extent, the poet is at the service of his immediate audience. "Obviously, if I am singing here in Rio, I am not going to let the *carioca* lose to a *paulista*, and if I am in São Paulo, I am not going to let the *carioca* win," a Rio-based poet-singer explains. Nevertheless, he admits that the question of a contest between a rich man and a poor man poses other difficulties. "The rich man can win and he can lose depending on whether he got rich robbing others or as a reward for his good deeds." Granted, letting the rich man win is "a little like killing off the hero in a love story," but it is still possible "because all rich men were once poor." "Now, evil," he continues,

> that's another matter. You might like to be rich, but you wouldn't like to be bad, I mean really bad, would you? Aha, I didn't think so! Well then, evil never wins because nobody likes it and besides, the world just isn't made that way.[15]

The urge to please all of his readers all of the time does not strike the poet as hypocritical. A good poet must have "a certain clarity of thought,

13. Manuel d'Almeida Filho, Aracaju, Sergipe, June 7, 1978; Caetano Cosme da Silva, Campina Grande, Paraíba, March 4, 1978.
14. Olegário Fernandes, Caruaru, Pernambuco, May 27, 1978; Manuel Camilo dos Santos, Campina Grande, Paraíba, March 6, 1978.
15. Antonio Curió, Rio de Janeiro, December 17, 1977.

an ability not only to rhyme *princesa* with *beleza* but to get to the very heart of things." Above all, he must be in tune with his public. Thus, one successful vendor considers the best poet to be the writer "who has the most psychology, who knows what a person is thinking almost before he does." According to him, the secret of the marketplace is "not to sing loud or well but to give the listener exactly what he wants." He himself takes great pride in humoring drunks into silence, improvising incidents which do not exist within the story, and coaxing reluctant buyers to lay out the same amount of money for an eight-page *folheto* as for a thirty-two-page *romance*. "Which is better, I ask them, a little piece of tender meat or a big plate of stew?"[16]

Although the writer clearly manipulates his public in many ways, he is apt to insist loudly that his mission is to fulfill its wishes. "A good poet," one Southern transplant asserts, "is he who gives people the most pleasure." "I don't have an opinion," says Rodolfo Coelho Cavalcante, "other than the opinion that people want to hear." Still another claims that everyone knows the difference between a good and a bad poet. A good poet knows how to rhyme well and to tell new and surprising stories. The difference between a good and a very good poet is, however, more difficult to measure since "it is the public not the poet who knows."[17]

This much-touted loyalty to the reader does not mean that writers do not attempt to perfect an individual style. Although they may profess to do so in order to better serve their public, many have a strong sense of their craft. True, the concepts of originality and plagiarism differ in the popular sphere from those in the educated sphere. Although the term *plágio* is usually restricted to the theft of words rather than of ideas, almost all popular poets recognize a qualitative difference between an "invented" and a "translated" story. They agree that some stories, such as folktales or movie plots, are communal property, which any author is free to "perfect" so long as he does not copy another's version word for word. And yet the writer who reworks an existing *folheto* is less esteemed by his fellows than another who spins a tale from his own imagination. Thus, while one present-day poet expresses admiration for the powers of expression of the great Recife poet-printer João Martins de Ataíde ("He could say so much by just hinting!"), he asserts that he was not as great as his predecessor Leandro Gomes de Barros "because he never thought up his own plots." "Look," a fellow writer declares,

16. João Alexandre, Juazeiro do Norte, Ceará, April 9, 1978; Joel Borges, Bezerros, Pernambuco, March 30, 1978.
17. Cícero Vieira da Silva (Mocó), Duque de Caxias, Rio de Janeiro, January 2, 1978; Rodolfo Coelho Cavalcante, Salvador, Bahia, June 5, 1978; Antonio Curió, Rio de Janeiro, December 17, 1977.

> if you want a *folheto* about that matchbox, I can have it for you tomorrow. But if you want a real story, something with ideas, not just a description, you are going to have to wait because they take much longer, they are a lot more work.[18]

Not all popular poets share the same sense of craftsmanship. There are a number, however, who think of poetry as "a march toward perfection." "The true poet," José de Souza Campos explains, "tries to make his words worthy of his thoughts and vice versa."[19] Manuel d'Almeida Filho, whom most contemporary poets regard as today's leading *cordel* author, admits that he takes real pleasure in "a well-made verse, an image you can almost see." His concern for form is as well-developed as any university-educated writer's. "I have written some books [*folhetos*] that I think are good," he says,

> but I have written others that I can't stand because when I look back at them I find all sorts of errors. Once, for instance, I called Paris a seaport and had to go back and redo the whole verse. Another time I wrote *resgatar* in place of *regatear*, and two editions came out before I realized my mistake.[20]

Although not all writers share this particular author's high standards, their apologetic references to their lack of study or of time to polish their work often hint at a similar concern. Almost all become incensed at typographical errors. Then, too, most actively seek to develop themselves as poets. According to a writer in Juazeiro do Norte, a poet may like one kind of *folheto* better than another, but a poet worthy of the name must be able to write all kinds—love, adventure, humor, prophecy—because "poetry is much more than just doing what you like; it is being able to do whatever is necessary."[21]

Money is important to the poet not only for practical reasons but also as proof of public favor. "My *folheto Daniel and His Friends Fighting over a Princess* paid for that refrigerator," says its author with obvious pride. Eagerness to write a best seller has as much to do with the desire for fame as fortune. "The *folheto*, you must understand," adds another veteran

---

18. Manuel d'Almeida, Aracaju, Sergipe, June 7, 1978; José Francisco Borges, Bezerros, Pernambuco, January 20, 1978. For a discussion of degree of creativity within a given tradition, see Gregory Gizelis, "A Neglected Aspect of Creativity of Folk Performers," *Journal of American Folklore*, 86 (1973): 167–72.

19. José de Souza Campos, Recife, Pernambuco, February 5, 1978.

20. Manuel d'Almeida Filho, Aracaju, Sergipe, June 7, 1978.

21. Expedito Sebastião da Silva, Juazeiro do Norte, Ceará, April 8, 1978.

writer, "is not only a question of money but of one's name circulating, the satisfaction of being sought after by strangers, of arriving in a strange city where everybody knows your stories."[22]

A poet-singer from Pernambuco asserts that even if he were to strike it rich in the national lottery, he would not stop writing or singing "because fortune is very good but fame is even better." In fact, he goes on to assert, fame is the most important thing in the world because "even if a person loses everything, if he has a name, then he will be able to get everything back." The desire for immortality is not limited to educated authors. "How happy I would be if I could think that people would still remember me after I had died!" one poet-printer exclaims. "Really, there is nothing in this whole world which would please me more, not even a mountain of money."[23]

Not only does the *folheto* poet feel an obligation to write what his audience expects, but he often finds the idea of recording his own thoughts and experiences distasteful. "Is there any relationship between my own life and my poetry?" asks the author of some twenty stories. "No, I don't think so because the public doesn't want to know these things." "If I myself don't like to think, let alone write, about my life," a poet-singer in the small city of Timbaúba says, "why would someone else want to read about it?" Another writer asserts that only one of his twenty-odd *folhetos* (*The Poor Man's Sufferings*) failed to sell well because people said that they "already knew too much about suffering."[24]

As a group, poets emphatically reject the suggestion that one's individual joys and sorrows could be worthy of note. "If I were to write only to please myself and not the public, well then why write?" a publisher's assistant asks.

> I don't need the money because I am a printer, not a vendor. I write because I like inventing stories for others. For myself? I think that's silly. What would be the point?[25]

"You want me to write something that has to do with me alone?" scoffs an author who has been writing for some two decades.

22. Manuel d'Almeida Filho, Aracaju, Sergipe, June 7, 1978; Delarme Monteiro, Olinda, Pernambuco, January 17, 1978.

23. José Severino Barbosa (Guriatã do Norte), Olinda, Pernambuco, April 28, 1978; Olegário Fernandes, Caruaru, Pernambuco, April 28, 1978.

24. Gerson Araújo de Lucena, Campina Grande, Paraíba, March 5, 1977; Severino Borges Silva, Timbaúba, Pernambuco, March 2, 1978; José Soares da Silva (Dila), Caruaru, Pernambuco, May 12, 1978.

25. Expedito Sebastião da Silva, Juazeiro do Norte, Ceará, April 8, 1978.

> Now why would I do that, what interest would that have? Do you think that people really care whether I lose my land or sweetheart? Forget it! They'd be happy: "Great, he's lost his farm," they'd say." Look, the people who buy *folhetos* have no interest in the poet's problems. Why should they? What I have suffered, they too have suffered and someone else is suffering right now. So why talk about it when talking does no good?[26]

The fact that poets consciously exclude the details of their own lives from their stories does not mean that they regard their work as fantasy. In order to write, the poet "must have been sick and gotten well, must have laughed and cried in order to make his audience feel weak and then strong, laugh and then burst into tears." "Above all," says a poet-singer,

> a poet must know how to suffer for other people. He must write with his soul. For instance, I have never been in the South, but I can imagine what it must have been like to travel to São Paulo in one of those terrible trucks that workers from here have to ride all crowded up in, and so I sat down and wrote a *folheto* all about it.[27]

Many *cordel* authors admit at least roundabout links between their own experience and their stories. There is a marked tendency for a poet's first *folheto* to be rooted in an immediate circumstance. One author describes how he used to live near a marketplace where he saw herb vendors with big baskets full of cures for nonexistent diseases. "Watching those charlatans day after day," he says, "gave me the idea for a *folheto* about an old man who seeks a potion to make him young again so that he can marry a sixteen-year-old girl."[28] Another writer offers this explanation for his first story.

> In Surubim once, I saw a young man beating an old woman. So I approached them and asked the man why he was hitting the old lady. The woman spoke up and told me that she had just sold one of her pigs for 80 *milreis* and that her son now wanted half the money. So I said, "Boy, don't act that way with your mother! Have you no shame?" And then I went on, but I still felt so angry that when I got home I sat down and wrote *The Son Who Beat His Mother and Turned into a Pig*.[29]

According to a poet in Rio de Janeiro, the *folheto* is nothing other than "a more perfect vision of things which the poet has seen and heard." He admits, however, that the writer "has to invent a good deal."

26. Olegário Fernandes, Caruaru, Pernambuco, March 18, 1978.
27. João Alexandre, Juazeiro do Norte, Ceará, April 9, 1978.
28. Delarme Monteiro, Olinda, Pernambuco, January 17, 1978.
29. Antonio Lourenço da Silva (Antonio Canhotinho), Campina Grande, Paraíba, March 9, 1978.

> For example, in that *folheto* of mine called *The Sufferings of a Northeasterner*, well, I was single when I wrote it, but I still told everything as if I had a wife and children because somehow that made it seem more real.[30]

The question of "truth" in the *cordel* is essential and in no way simple. Poets make no effort to pretend that the magic birds or princesses they write about are real. However, they readily admit that a good story must have a number of "ornaments." Nevertheless, the poet does not "lie"; rather he "exaggerates," and a good *folheto* must have the appearance of truth. One poet-astrologer explains that

> a *folheto* must have a basis in reality; it must be something that could have happened. In the case of *The Arrival of Lampião in Hell*, the basis is that Lampião killed a lot of people, and for this reason plenty of persons think that he must have gone to hell. Of course he didn't go to either heaven or hell, but that doesn't matter. What matters is that people believe that he did.[31]

Another poet refers to his *folheto* about a son who murdered his mother because of a quarrel over a cassava root. Although he admits that nothing of the sort ever happened, "there are children who murder parents, and parents who murder children." The *folheto* itself was based on a rumor that the poet heard on the street. Once he had published his story, the rumor grew until people claimed that they had actually seen the murdered mother buried up to her waist in the earth. According to the poet, "Things are always this way: once you have a rumor to work with, you can say anything you like." However, if there is no kernel of fantasy to develop, "it does no good to write since the *folheto* will not sell."[32]

The question of the *folheto*'s reality is complicated by the poets' own sense of mission. Many state that when they do not write, they "feel nervous" or begin to drink. *Cordel* authors reject the idea of writing without publishing. Most, however, admit that they would continue to write even if they could not see their stories in print. "I feel sick when I write a story and see it lying in the drawer, but I will only leave off writing when I die," a poet of many years asserts. According to another, younger author, "Only God" can stop an author from inventing stories because "it is not poets themselves who choose to write; they write because they have to."[33]

Despite their largely matter-of-fact attitude toward their work, poets tend to think of poetry (better read as "inspiration") as something serious. "A person may buy a story for amusement just like a sack of peanuts or a

30. Cícero Vieira da Silva (Mocó), Duque de Caxias, Rio de Janeiro, January 2, 1978.
31. Vicente Vitorino de Melo, Caruaru, Pernambuco, March 17, 1978.
32. Olegário Fernandes, Caruaru, Pernambuco, January 14, 1978.
33. Severino Cesário da Silva, Recife, Pernambuco, January 12, 1978.

roll of tobacco," says a particularly successful author, "but the *folheto* is much more because although its language must be simple, its message is profound."[34] "Though I myself sang plenty when young, I have never liked the art of the *repentista*," asserts a writer in Campina Grande, "because it relies on speed, not real feeling. The *folheto*, no, it is a child of the intellect which no wind can blow away." According to another author, poetry is "a philosophy that the reader has to feel."[35]

Cordel authors' descriptions of inspiration frequently allow for an element of magic. This makes poetry a special force, which comes from both within and without. Sometimes the poet will compare himself with a medium who transmits a message from another world or, more specifically, from God. Expressions such as *a poesia baixou em mim* ("poetry came down into me") or *a poesia me descobriu* ("poetry discovered me") point to an outside force. The concept of visitation emphasizes the poet's identity as a chosen person. "Poetry called me, all I did was answer," a singer who is also an author says.[36] "Poetry is like love," asserts a writer who specializes in prophetic *cordel* stories, "because no one can control her; she comes and goes at will." José de Souza Campos claims that poetry "has her moons." His brother Francisco adds that inspiration may come and go without warning so that "while sometimes I pass whole months without writing a single word, other times I have to scribble verses on a scrap of paper, or scratch them with a stick into the mud."[37]

The association of poetry and astrology in Brazilian as in much European chapbook literature is no coincidence. *Cordel* publishers often choose company names recalling the "star" of inspiration, such as Luzeiro da Norte (North Star) and Estrella da Poesia (Star of Poetry). Poet Manuel Camilo dos Santos, owner of the once powerful Estrella press, explains that the star with the number seventeen within it, which he still stamps on all of his *folhetos*, is the wise men's star. "I chose the name *estrella* spelled with two 'l's," he explains, "because it means 'inner light,' 'dominion,' 'elevation,' and the words of counsel 'Free yourself from your errors and passions.'"[38]

Even those poets who have no interest in astrology may prefer to write during the new moon, waiting to release their booklets until after it has begun to wane. A writer may express relief that the public "favors his star," or he may explain a *folheto*'s sluggish reception with the assertion

34. José Costa Leite, Condado, Pernambuco, February 18, 1978.

35. Manuel Camilo dos Santos, Campina Grande, Paraíba, March 6, 1978; Severino Cesário da Silva, Recife, Pernambuco, January 12, 1978.

36. Severino Borges Silva, Timbaúba, Pernambuco, March 2, 1978.

37. Antônio Caetano de Souza, Recife, Pernambuco, February 27, 1978; José and Francisco Souza de Campos, São Lourença da Mata, Pernambuco, March 1, 1978.

38. Manuel Camilo dos Santos, Campina Grande, Paraíba, March 6, 1978.

that "his star was dim." Occasionally, stories themselves may be compared to stars. Thus one elderly author notes with satisfaction that the *folhetos* he wrote as a young man and which are still found in fairs throughout the interior have become "like stars that will shine long after my death."[39]

Poets readily admit that the raw material for their stories is everywhere: "in that woman yawning in the window, in a house that is crumbling, in a man who was strong yesterday and is old and tired today." The writer "sees the same thing that everyone else sees but only better." Thus poetry itself is "the ability to perceive." As such, it is not only an exterior force but an interior potential. "Inspiration boils up within me when I least expect it," explains one author, "but if I do not write, my vision evaporates like steam."[40]

"I was nine years old when I discovered within me the ability to sing," a writer in Campina Grande says. Some authors actually speak of another person who lives somewhere within them. This writer claims to have spent his life with two women, his wife, and "my companion, my inspiration, my means of livelihood, my favorite pastime, and my true love, poetry."[41]

Regardless of where the individual may localize inspiration, he sees his talent as a special gift. A number of writers, many of whom tend to live in the conservative countryside or in the still highly traditional city of Juazeiro do Norte, express this sense of vocation in religious terms. According to a writer who has spent many decades in Juazeiro do Norte, the poet can be "a prophet, a counselor, or simply a poet." The writer sees himself as,

> not exactly a prophet, but I have visions of the future. Of course, sometimes it is hard to know when a particular vision comes from God and when it comes from my own head. In any case, I consider my poetry a form of counsel. Of course, I don't *only* counsel, but I do try to advise and help my readers because that is my duty as a poet.[42]

Even those *cordel* authors who do not define their art in religious terms speak of mysterious powers that permit the poet to act not only as a spokesman for a particular public but as a mouthpiece for unseen realities. Writing is thus nothing less than "concretizing a vision," or "latching onto something which did not previously exist." One individual writes above

39. Manuel Tomás de Assis, Olivedos, Paraíba, April 4, 1978.
40. Caetano Cosme da Silva, Campina Grande, Paraíba, March 4, 1978.
41. José Clementino de Souto (José Alves Sobrinho), Campina Grande, Paraíba, March 3, 1978.
42. João Quinto Sobrinho (João do Cristo Rei), Juazeiro do Norte, Ceará, March 9, 1978.

all "to pass on what I have learned, to share what the voice inside me has allowed me to perceive."[43]

Clearly, this rather exalted sense of mission must necessarily collide at times with the poet's own desire to make a living and his readers' often mundane demands. Despite real loyalty to his public, the poet also reveals a certain impatience and sometimes actual fear of his would-be buyers. Part of this ambivalence stems from continuing anxiety about his ability to make a living. If a new *folheto* fails to sell, his family may go hungry. Then too, the poet's impatience may also reflect a certain skepticism about many of the principles that his stories illustrate.

Although most poets tend to be better off than subsistence farmers or unskilled laborers, they must live with constant insecurity. As many note, when the poet is working, all is well, "but when he gets sick, he goes hungry, he suffers all manner of abuse because he has no document, and he does not enjoy even the few pennies that the farmer who belongs to a syndicate can claim." Proud as they are of their calling, writers are well aware of its risks. "I have two grandsons who could be poets," a veteran author says, "but thank God they have other talents as well because it is better not to have to depend on poetry for a living, better not to have to spend one's life wandering from fair to fair."[44]

No poet likes to admit that one or another of his *folhetos* has had a bad reception. All claim that the public likes them, that they understand their readers' wants. Nevertheless, the more one talks with *cordel* authors, the more one perceives a certain degree of bewilderment and insecurity. Even the best-established authors cannot be sure that a story will "take," just as even the most seasoned vendors have days in which people will not buy, no matter what. This constant uncertainty accounts for jokes such as the following:

A. Well, I've written a new *folheto*.
B. Really? What kind?
A. Oh, it's a great mystery.
B. You don't say. What's so mysterious?
A. Ah, no one knows who's going to publish it. Look, I am the author and even I'm not sure![45]

Some poets make a habit of testing potential publications on their friends and families. "When I want to see if a *folheto* is any good, I get my daughter to read it out loud," a respected poet says. "Only when I listen to it as if I were not the author can I tell whether it will sell." Other

43. Manuel Camilo dos Santos, Campina Grande, Paraíba, March 6, 1978.
44. Joel Borges, Bezerros, Pernambuco, January 21, 1978; João Quinto Sobrinho (João do Cristo Rei), Juazeiro do Norte, Ceará, March 9, 1978.
45. José Costa Leite, Condado, Pernambuco, February 18, 1978.

writers actually read a manuscript version of their *folheto* in the market-place to gauge audience reaction before committing it to print. "The author," explains another leading poet, makes himself "into two persons, writer and reader, and if the reader doesn't like the writer's story, then out it goes because you can be sure that the *folheto* will not be a success."[46]

Even the most reliable tests, however, have been known to fail. Perfect in theory, the poet's judgment may prove fallible in practice, and though experience improves one's probability of guessing right, there is always an element of chance. One writer, for example, recalls the time when he gave two *folhetos* to a printer but wanted only one to be published. When the man printed the wrong one by mistake, the poet was furious. Since the damage had been done, however, he decided to try to sell it. "You know," he says, "I ran out of copies of the first *folheto* in a matter of a few days, but that second *folheto*, the one I thought would sell, took years to get rid of. In fact, I still have copies around the house—imagine!" The same uncertainty holds true in the case of the marketplace. Vendors report that it is possible to read a *folheto* that gets almost no response, then read the same booklet later in the day with great success. "Sometimes," one notes, "a badly written story will sell well while a really good one, a classic, will sell only one or two copies. No one understands it, and if they say they do, don't you believe them!"[47]

The apparent fickleness of a public that treats the poet "like a woman who is young and beautiful one day, ugly and out of favor the next," puts the poet, who has a good deal at stake, on the defensive, increasing his sense of distance from his readers. Although the writer rushes to insist that there is no difference between him and members of his audience, his superior education and experience necessarily set him apart from the masses from which he originally came. Because the poet normally reads, travels, and comes in contact with many kinds of people, his vision of the world tends to be wider than that of most subsistence farmers or factory workers. The mass media is changing this situation somewhat, but there is a difference between experiencing something first hand and hearing about it on the radio. It is therefore not surprising to hear the poet express a certain irritation with his buyers' vision of the world. "The *matuto*," one author says, with a trace of impatience, "only wants a pretty story. He wants to know that the young man fought for the princess and then married her. He wants jokes and blows and sweet 'I love you's'; he does not want to think."[48]

46. Manuel d'Almeida Filho, Aracaju, Sergipe, June 7, 1978; Delarme Monteiro, Olinda, Pernambuco, January 17, 1978.

47. Manuel Camilo dos Santos, Campina Grande, Paraíba, March 6, 1978.

48. Antonio Curió, Rio de Janeiro, December 17, 1977. Joel Borges, Bezerros, Pernambuco, January 21, 1978.

As already suggested, the poet's desire and obligation to please his audience make him perfectly capable of writing something he half-believes or actually thinks untrue. Therefore, while he is clearly gratified by the public's acceptance, he may still poke fun at its supposed gullibility. One experienced vendor insists that a farmworker's response to the most clearly fictional situations is frequently to say "Oh, yes, that happened in that house down the road apiece," or "Now I remember, I think that my grandfather once said. . . ." According to him, many buyers "firmly believe what they have heard and go about spreading the poet's wildest fantasies as if they were the most solemn truth."[49]

To be sure, almost all fiction implies a tacit acceptance of a story's "truth" on the part of both writer and reader, and the willingness to agree to the preposterous is not confined to *cordel* buyers. As the most startling reversals can be accepted as real within the boundaries of the *cordel* as within any other kind of story, the poet's apparent scorn is often mixed with pride. ("Look, I'm such a good storyteller that everyone believes me!") There are cases, however, in which poet and public may not be in agreement on the truth of the story's underlying message. "I don't believe in this business about the hairy leg," the author of a *folheto* on the subject says flatly, "but people like to pretend that such a thing exists. If I say that the hairy leg is waltzing up and down the railroad tracks, you can be sure there will be people who refuse to take the train."[50]

Moralistic whoppers such as the hairy leg tale are not an overly serious matter. Many people believe such tales in the same way one "believes" a horror movie, and the poet himself may change his tune on a dark night near the deserted tracks. Rather, a more interesting problem arises when authors express doubt concerning the moral implications of the six-step pattern, which they themselves perpetuate. Over and over again, one finds *cordel* authors casually denying their own most fervent claims. "I don't believe that Frei Damião [a religious leader whom many view as the successor to Padre Cícero] works miracles," one writer states, "and even though I once wrote a *folheto* all about his power to make sick people well again, I don't think that he cures anyone." Another author points out that women who watch television soap operas often get so angry when the seductress tries to ruin the hero's love affair that they are "capable of swallowing the television set." "Well," he says, "you see, it's the same thing with the *folheto*: people want to see good battle evil and then feel happy when good wins." A fellow author agrees that the public always wants the poor man to triumph, and so

49. Manuel Miguel da Silva, Caruaru, Pernambuco, February 18, 1978.
50. José Costa Leite, Condado, Pernambuco, February 18, 1978. For further consideration of ritual reversals, see Victor Turner, *Dramas, Fields, and Metaphors: Symbolic Action in Human Society* (Ithaca: Cornell University Press, 1974).

I make the *folheto* turn out that way even though I think that it is ridiculous. Everyone knows that the poor man always loses; what does he have going for him? Nothing! Only in a story can a rich man lose.[51]

The poet seldom regards these contradictions cynically. He is apt to be sincere in his belief that his opinion is one thing, the *folheto* another. Nevertheless, he cannot help experiencing a sporadic pull between what he writes and what he believes. "Although I write about the Devil as if he existed, I think that he is really just a figment of each person's imagination," one writer says. "No, no! Hell is right here among people who stab each other, rob and lie, and we ourselves invent the devil and then stick him on the street." Another author affirms in similar fashion that "the man who is sitting in the shade talking with a friend, sipping cool water, is in heaven while the man whom the police are beating is right smack in hell."[52] "I have written a number of *folhetos* about miracles," asserts a poet in Pernambuco,

> simply because I have to. Look, if the priest were to say that some saint up there on the wall had no value, the church would empty in a flash. Well he and I both have to keep on saying that Frei Damião is a powerful saint, etc., etc., if we want to count on these people's support.[53]

To be sure, poets vary. There are some who put more faith in the principles that the *cordel* champions than others do. More conservative poets may regard much of what they write about, like the end of the world or local miracles, as fact. Others, however, tend to be more independent thinkers, and the great majority of poets express doubt about one or another position that they have taken at some time in their own stories. "The world ends for the person who dies," a seasoned poet says.

> I write *folhetos* that talk all about the fires and the floods that are coming because if I don't, then I'll lose money, but I myself know that the world is going to keep on as always no matter what some preacher says.[54]

Another well-known writer admits that he too has written about the day of judgment, but "no one really knows what is going to happen; no one

51. José Costa Leite, Condado, Pernambuco, February 18, 1978; Manuel d'Almeida Filho, Aracaju, Sergipe, June 7, 1978; José Camilo da Silva (Miné), São Lourenço da Mata, Pernambuco, January 9, 1978.
52. Caetano Cosme da Silva, Campina Grande, Paraíba, March 4, 1978. Olegário Fernandes, Caruaru, Pernambuco, March 18, 1978.
53. José Costa Leite, Condado, Pernambuco, February 18, 1978.
54. Severino Borges Silva, Timbaúba, Pernambuco, March 2, 1978.

can rent you an apartment up there in heaven for you to use after you die."[55] A poet now in his sixties voices skepticism about the notion of destiny. "I used to believe in it," he says,

> but then I began to notice that some stones in the road crumble more easily while others are hard and sharp. And some flowers wilt a lot faster than others. So if there are differences like these among the stones and flowers and no one ever talks about their *sina*, why then should things change all of a sudden when the subject is man?[56]

And yet, despite the existence of very real differences, the poet's occasional impatience with his readers comes less from an uncomfortable consciousness of himself as an individual as from his deep identification with the readers whom he feels ought to be as dissatisfied as he is with conventional explanations. Necessity leads the *cordel* author to proclaim his willingness to offer his poetic services to whoever wants to pay him. "If you want to charter an airplane, then we'll go sing up on a cloud," says a group of writers clustered about a table in the Northeastern quarter of São Paulo. However, if one asks the same people why they do not sell their *folhetos* to tourists in the city's Praça da República, they immediately change their tune. "Ah, we don't like to go there. This place may be poor, but it is ours and we feel at home."[57]

The poet can protest his public's stubborn insistence that all turn out as forecast precisely because he considers himself part of the group he is criticizing. "I am a member of the *povo*, and the *povo* doesn't change," Rodolfo Coelho Cavalcante says. "People listen to whatever messiah comes along; they believe the same old things. Their way of thinking has not changed."[58]

Asked whether they consider themselves *matutos*, most poets, like buyers, answer in the affirmative. "I am a *matuto*; I would say that hanging on the cross," says a writer who believes that the *folheto*'s days are numbered. "Furthermore, that's the way all *matutos* are; they don't want to be anything else."[59]

"I am a domesticated *matuto*, but a *matuto* just the same," Apolônio Alves dos Santos asserts. A fellow poet in the Northeast claims that he was born "with both feet in the mud. How could I write *folhetos*, how

55. Manuel d'Almeida Filho, Aracaju, Sergipe, June 7, 1978.
56. Manuel Camilo dos Santos, Campina Grande, Paraíba, March 6, 1978.
57. These comments came from a conversation involving Guriatã do Coqueiro, Firmino da Paz, and José Francisco de Souza at the Recanto dos Poetas, Braz, São Paulo, on December 13, 1977.
58. Rodolfo Coelho Cavalcante, Salvador, Bahia, June 5, 1978.
59. Caetano Cosme da Silva, Campina Grande, Paraíba, March 4, 1978.

could I please my customers if I were not a *matuto*?" he asks.[60] To be sure, these responses often sound more than a little strident, not unlike the kind of bragging that is ultimately a defense. Effectively barred from official society, *folheto* writers may claim that its advantages do not interest them in any case. Nevertheless, it is certain that despite their need to protect their own self-pride, *folheto* authors feel a deep loyalty to the persons for whom they have always written. "I am a Joe No One," one of the best-known writers asserts,

> and everyone likes me because I am just like them. There is no difference whatsoever between us, and still I can write *folhetos*. If I were a university graduate, if I had studied in some school, that would be something else. But I am no better than they are, and I still manage to write. Furthermore, they understand me. An educated person's writing is too fine, too pretty; it makes them feel silly and uncomfortable.[61]

Even in those rare cases in which he does not consider himself a *matuto*, the poet tends to express respect for values associated with the term. "A *matuto*," one such writer says, "is any good person who lives up to his word." A person born in the city can still be a *matuto* since attitudes are more important than place of residence or occupation in determining one's identity. Similarly, an individual born in the countryside is a *praciano* or "city dweller" if he rejects the countryman's way of doing things. "I was born in the city," explains one popular poet, "but I follow the same rhythm as other people who have always worked out in the fields." [62]

These and similar comments suggest that *cordel* writers like their readers do not necessarily reject their marginal status. While most educated Brazilians would regard the term *matuto* as derogatory, the poet and his public respond to the question with grins and a large dose of defiant pride. Often they contrast the *matuto* with the university graduate, who "may know a good deal, but when the hour comes for saddling a wild horse, his knowledge is worth nothing."[63]

"I pass the day pouring rum and selling biscuits, so I am not a great *repentista*," one individual says.

> But I am a poet and I write like a *matuto* because I was born and grew up in the fields. I really wouldn't want to be anything else though. How many educated people are there who are not capable of doing what we poets who know little more than our ABC's can do?[64]

60. Apolônio Alves dos Santos, Rio de Janeiro, January 1, 1978.
61. José Soares, Prazeres (Recife), Pernambuco, January 17, 1978.
62. Luiz de Souza Campos, Recife, Pernambuco, March 29, 1978.
63. José Costa Leite, Condado, Pernambuco, February 18, 1978.
64. José Gonzaga dos Passos, Olinda, Pernambuco, March 28, 1978.

According to a number of poets, the *matuto* is often smarter than the city dweller because he is less vain. While the city dweller sits around listening to the radio and television, the *matuto* is "working, thinking, imagining, not wasting his energy in foolish daydreams that do no one any good."[65]

As indicated earlier, the *literatura de cordel* has begun to attract widespread interest. Poets are clearly flattered by this new attention as well as increasingly dependent upon the additional money it brings in. Nevertheless, they often express a certain amount of distrust of their new admirers. "I am against these congresses, these festivals," a *cordel* author says. "They do nothing for the poet and are organized by people who are interested in their own well-being."[66] "I sing for everyone," affirms a poet-singer. "I sing in universities and lecture halls; I sing in theaters as well as fairs. But believe me, it's the little guy who keeps the bread on my table, who buys one or two *folhetos* every Sunday and who is still going to do so long after these important people have gotten interested in something else."[67] Part of the poet's hesitancy in regard to persons not born within the tradition stems from a feeling that they do not really understand his art. "They all ask the same questions," one Recife-based author remarks. "I wish I had one of those tape recorders so that I could just press the button when they come around."[68]

For many poets, singing for students in high schools, where high-level official support for folklore has made the subject an increasing part of the social studies curriculum, is not the same as singing for a gathering in the countryside. "You have the impression of performing for people who don't really have any idea of what you are doing," many say, "and so you don't really try to do your best." "I have contracts with three different tourist agencies," a *repentista* who also writes *folhetos* asserts,

> and when I sing for them, I earn plenty. In the countryside, the pickings are usually meager, but you know, I still like to sing for those farmers who will walk five miles in the rain to hear you. They don't have the money to buy bread, and somehow they still find a few coins for the poet because poetry

65. Olegário Fernandes da Silva, Caruaru, Pernambuco, March 17, 1978.
66. Manuel d'Almeida Filho, Aracaju, Sergipe, June 7, 1978.
67. José João dos Santos (Azulão), Engenheiro Pedreiro, Rio de Janeiro, November 15, 1977.
68. Severino Marquês de Souza Júnior (Palito), Olinda, Pernambuco, January 17, 1978. It is worth adding here that when I then asked the poet whether he would prefer not to talk to me, given the attitude he had just expressed toward interviews, he exclaimed, "Oh no! Didn't you come all the way from the United States just to talk to me?" Clearly, these and all comments in this chapter necessarily reflect to some degree the fact that the poet was either speaking to, or in the presence of, a foreigner, a female, and a member of another social class. Nevertheless, the fact that the same sentiments keep coming up again and again with very different authors suggests that they have a certain validity.

is almost the most important thing in the world for them, and so I feel I have to sing much better for them than for the professor who can't tell one verse from another and will applaud no matter what.[69]

Many authors insist that "the popular poet learns from his customers." One cites an experience with the *folheto The Devil's Castle* by João José da Silva, explaining that the story involves a young man who arrives at a castle on horseback, then leaves the horse outside while he enters and fights to rescue a princess. "I'll never forget one time," the poet says, "that I finished reading that story and a *matuto* demanded, 'And what about the horse, did they just leave him tied up outside?' He was right, of course; the poet had simply forgotten, and that's the sort of thing that happens all the time."[70]

Poets also take obvious satisfaction in the certainty that they know better than anyone else how to please their traditional public. "Only the popular poet knows how to season the *matuto*'s spiritual food with the salt of suffering and the pepper of humor so that he will keep on coming back for more," Rodolfo Coelho Cavalcante says.[71] Even the most successful "new-style" *repentistas* echo many of the same sentiments. According to one of the most successful young performers, "*matuto*-style poetry is more appealing, more beautiful, and even easier to sing." Although he clearly enjoys the fame and money that middle-class competitions carry with them, he still asserts that "the poet rediscovers who he is in singing for the *povo*."[72]

Because of the existence of various "schools" or associations as far back as the early nineteenth century, popular poets have long had a collective sense of self. Given their loyalty to their public, they have identified in turn with a larger socioeconomic group. Though this identification is certainly a form of class consciousness, it tends to have an existential rather than ideological cast. Less a result of clearly delineated political ideas than of their perception of their inferior status, most poets reveal a strong sense of solidarity with their readers. "I feel sorry for the poor man," one poet, who prefers to remain unidentified, explains,

and even if I were to become rich, I would still like poor people better. Me, I write for the Christs. Do you know what a Christ is? It is someone who works for another person. Well, then, I write for him, and the only reason I don't talk more about his sufferings is that the others, the bosses, would kill me if I did.

69. Aniceto Pereira de Lima (Sinésio Pereira), Olinda, Pernambuco, February 28, 1978.
70. Manuel d'Almeida Filho, Aracaju, Sergipe, June 7, 1978.
71. Rodolfo Coelho Cavalcante, Salvador, Bahia, June 5, 1978.
72. Geraldo Amáncio Pereira, Juazeiro do Norte, Ceará, April 5, 1978.

A fellow writer explains that a *matuto* is "a poor person, someone who knows what suffering is." Asked if rich people do not suffer with the loss of a child, a personal failure, or sickness, he replies, "Oh no, no, suffering is what the father of a family feels when he sees his children go hungry. That other isn't suffering; it is simply life."[73]

Although poets are hesitant to talk about social problems, most have no illusions about their own and their readers' disadvantageous position. "The worker is always there, defenseless on the ground, and the employer is always there, standing over him with a gun," one writer comments matter-of-factly; "it has been that way since the beginning of time. The employer relies on the money which he has paid the judge, the police, the senator, and the worker can only call on God because he has nothing with which to defend himself. Haven't things changed? Of course not. Things never change for people like us."

The *cordel* author's loyalty to the *folheto* is bound up with his sense of himself as part of this larger group. Thus while printmaker José Francisco Borges realizes that he could make a good deal more money if he were to leave Bezerros for São Paulo, he insists on remaining in the Northeast. "The *folheto*," he explains,

> taught me all I know. When I left the fields, the hoe, all that more brutish way of life, it was to write stories, not to make prints for museums and rich people's living rooms. I make prints now because they bring me money, but I make *folhetos* because I like them. I even miss the fair with those long hours in the sun and terrible water. It was like going to war! But I miss it, yes, because I was born in the harness, and the person who is born there never gets used to the saddle, no matter how long he may ride.[74]

While bent on making a living, most poets think of the *folheto* not just as a means but a way of life. Although not one would refuse a bulging wallet, a number, like Borges, have, nevertheless, passed up opportunities to earn more money because they would have demanded substantial changes in their way of life. Health, proximity to family members, and continued inspiration continue to be as important as wealth to most poets. One poet presently living in Rio de Janeiro expresses a frequent viewpoint when he asserts:

> Look, the house I am living in stinks, and if I could, I would leave it tomorrow for something better. But I wouldn't go to Copacabana or any of those fancy places. If I could, I'd have a good solid house in the country-

---

73. Francisco de Souza Campos, São Lourenço da Mata, Pernambuco, March 1, 1978.
74. José Francisco Borges, Bezerros, Pernambuco, March 30, 1978.

side with plenty of room where I could live in peace with my family. I am not a rich man, and I don't want to live with rich people. They are different from me; I don't understand them.[75]

The poets' attachment to their traditional readers does not mean that they are unaware of their rapidly changing role. "To tell you the truth," says one young author a little sadly, "I don't have much hope of the *cordel* ever returning to what it was. I was born twenty years too late." "The big problem with these professors," comments another, older writer, "is that they want the *folheto* to keep on as it has always been. Everything else changes, but the *cordel*, no. How come?"[76]

Poets are decidedly matter-of-fact about the tradition's uncertain future. "Look," says one, "if I had been born today, I would never have become a *folheto* author; I would have been, who knows, a journalist." "Sure the *cordel* is dying," says another, "so is the almanac, and all I hope is that they both last long enough for me to retire!"[77]

Despite their awareness of the *cordel*'s current problems, few authors would abandon the *folheto* to become, say, a television or comic strip writer, were that possible. "Soap operas come from the mind of a single person," points out an author in Juazeiro do Norte, "but the *folheto* is different because it may come from God himself." A fellow writer seconds this position by emphasizing the difference between *cordel* stories and others found in comic books. "Look," he says,

> you read a *folheto* about a girl who turns into a serpent after beating her mother. Well, maybe she didn't really become a serpent with fangs and scales and all, but it is certain that she was acting just like a real monster, wouldn't you agree? In comic books, no, people turn into snakes for no good reason. So I could never write those kinds of stories. To me, they make no sense.[78]

The poet's sense of obligation to the muse of poetry remains strong within many who have written all their lives. "Stop writing *folhetos* to write comic books?" asks one of these individuals rhetorically,

> Oh no, I couldn't do that! I have an obligation. To whom? To poetry. I always asked God to show me a way that would allow me to stop being the

75. Cícero Vieira da Silva (Mocó), Duque de Caxias, Rio de Janeiro, January 2, 1978.

76. Manuel d'Almeida Filho, Aracaju, Sergipe, June 7, 1978.

77. Manuel d'Almeida Filho, Aracaju, Sergipe, June 7, 1978; Vicente Vitorino de Melo, Caruaru, Pernambuco, March 17, 1978.

78. João Quinto Sobrinho (João do Cristo Rei), Juazeiro do Norte, Ceará, March 9, 1978; Antonio Curió, Rio de Janeiro, December 17, 1977.

slave of others, and He gave me the ability to write. The *cordel* saved me from that dead end in which I was living, so I couldn't leave it now no matter what.[79]

In reality, the author typically feels a double obligation to his gift and to the people whom this talent serves. "How much better it would have been," declares one writer, "if there had been *cordel* authors back there in Egypt so that we would now know how they made those mummies, or why they built the sphinx."[80]

Folheto writers may see themselves as the extension of a community, which, while it is changing, may still look to him for guidance, insight, and the humor which makes a hard life easier to bear. "The thing you have to understand about our work is this," remarks a veteran of the tradition,

> We poets count on silent poets, people who understand what the author is trying to say. These persons may be unable to write a word, let alone a story, but without them there would be no *folhetos*, and every author knows that.[81]

79. Olegário Fernandes da Silva, Caruaru, Pernambuco, March 18, 1978.

80. Manoel Caboclo e Silva, Juazeiro do Norte, Ceará, April 4, 1980.

81. Severino Cesário da Silva, Recife, Pernambuco, January 12, 1978. The poet gives a particularly apt description of what, in folklore scholarship, could be termed "active" versus "passive" bearers of a tradition. The classic formulation of these two types of transmitters is in C. W. von Sydow, "On the Spread of Tradition" in *Selected Papers on Folklore*, ed. Laurits Bødker (Copenhagen: Rosenkilde & Bagger, 1948), pp. 11–43.

VIII. "The Poet Sings to Please Us":
The *Folheto* in the Eyes of the Public

The most common answer to the question "Why do you like *folhetos*?" is that they are "good stories." People speak of the ones they like best as "funny," "beautiful," and "exciting." One construction worker defines a good story as "one that says all the things a person wants to hear." Poetry itself is "rich" and "special" because it takes time and effort to write and "not everyone, you know, has a way with words."[1]

Not all persons surrounding a poet in a fair or market are necessarily enthusiastic about the *cordel*. Some are passersby who have stopped to rest a moment. Others are simply there accompanying a *folheto*-buying friend. Such individuals often evince little or no interest in poetry, claiming that "there is nothing to it." They would rather be soccer players or television and movie stars than authors of any sort.

The majority of persons in a given audience, however, express admiration for popular poets. Most agree with the authors themselves that "poetry is not a question of wanting to write but of being born a writer." "To be a poet," one buyer says, "you have to know things that other people don't."[2] Another claims that he would like to be a poet because "it is a

---

1. Rio: LM, 27, Caratinga, Minas Gerais, 1977. Information about each speaker quoted in this chapter will be footnoted in the following manner: Place of interview, occupation, age, birthplace (city and state), date of arrival in city of interview. Thus, the place of the interview is given first. (In the case of Rio de Janeiro, where interviews were conducted in two separate sites, I have indicated which of these applies by the use of the abbreviation "FSC" for the fair of São Cristóvão and "LM" for the Largo do Machado.) The person's occupation and age then follow. If the individual's birthplace is different from the place of the interview, I have indicated this fact together with the date of arrival in the initial city. Unless otherwise indicated, all respondents are men. It is also worth noting that in some cases age is approximate; that is, persons often said to me, "Look, I'm not really sure when I was born, but my official identity card says that I am thirty-four years old." In our first example, the speaker is a twenty-seven-year-old male from Caratinga, Minas Gerais, who arrived in Rio de Janeiro in 1977, and who was interviewed in the Largo do Machado. Because the information that he is a construction worker has been given in the text, it is not repeated here. Any other information provided in the text, such as age or birthplace, will not be repeated in the footnotes.

2. Rio: FSC, bricklayer, 36, Campina Grande, Paraíba, 1977.

kind of work that requires a lot of thought, and although people like me work very hard, what we do is different."[3]

Most people believe that a child is born with his own calling (once again, the *sina*), with which it would be wrong to interfere. Nevertheless, except for a few who complain that poets don't have a steady job or "aren't really serious," they agree that it is good to have a poet or "artist of the word" in the family. Members of the audience note that a poet must be intelligent, have a good memory, and show skill with words and meter. He should also have a marked ability for invention. Thus one regular buyer remarks,

> I think that the *folheto* is a little like a song. And whom do you admire more—the composer or the singer? I admire the composer because anyone can sing, but not everyone can write. I myself am capable of reading one of these stories out loud in a good voice, but I admire the poet because he, not I, has the gift of creation.[4]

According to most people, a poet must have a knowledge of both books and the world. He must "know what is important and be good at talking with people, getting along with everyone no matter who or where."[5] The public clearly shares the poet's feeling that a good writer seeks to please his readers. "The poet always knows how to make people happy," claims one buyer. "That is his biggest job."[6]

"What is a good poet?" one sixty-six-year-old farmer from Bezerros demands. "He is someone who sings to please us, who can write a story someone like me who has spent his life chasing cows can understand." Not all persons who buy *folhetos* put great store in them. Some claim, "They are just to make you laugh, to pass the time of day." Even for these individuals, however, *cordel* stories have a certain meaning. Few people, for example, treat them in the same casual manner as they would a newspaper or magazine. Instead, an impressively high percentage either set aside the booklet in a special place once they have read it or pass it on to a friend.

Some persons prefer *folhetos* with comic book covers to the standard type with a photograph or woodcut because they find them more "modern" or more "elegant." Others, however, like these newer versions because they last longer than flimsier editions. These individuals may be proud of the collections they have inherited from a relative or built up over the

3. Rio: LM, doorman/chauffeur, 20, Campina Grande, Paraíba, 1977.
4. Recife: straw hat vendor, 28.
5. Rio: LM, soldier, 41, Fortaleza, Ceará, 1956.
6. Rio: LM, sandwich maker, 20, Fortaleza, Ceará, 1975.

years. "How do I know that I have exactly thirty-seven *folhetos* at home?" asks one buyer. "Well, how do you think I know? I've counted them, of course."[7]

Another individual explains that ever since his wife threw out all his stories during a particularly thorough house cleaning, he has been upset. "I haven't had the heart to buy a single new *folheto* after she did that stupid thing," he says.[8] It is common for persons to buy a fifth or sixth copy of a favorite story because "when something is really good, you want to share it, and *folhetos* like *John Cricket* make everybody happy."[9]

Then too a large number of individuals memorize whole or parts of *folhetos*. These persons may enjoy radio, television, and magazines, but they tend to forget the titles and plots of stories associated with the mass media almost immediately. They can, however, often remember long sections of *folhetos* that they learned years ago. Some who are capable of memorizing a thirty-two-page story "almost word for word" after two or three readings cannot recall the name of the movie they saw last night. "What for?" one such person demands. "Do you suppose that I am going to ask to see that film again?"[10]

Part of a *folheto*'s appeal undoubtedly lies in its identity as a group experience.[11] Though the rising literacy rate means that more individuals are free to read at will, a sizable percentage continue to read *folhetos* in small groups at least part of the time. Whereas those with limited schooling may prefer group readings because they need help in deciphering the story, many of the more educated buyers are also voicing a preference for this group experience. "I understand better when I read alone, but it is much better to read with others," one says.[12] "My friends and I all know how to read, but we like to get together because reading a *folheto* all by oneself is cold and lifeless," another declares.[13]

In some instances, group members take turns reading. It is more common, however, for a single individual to read aloud. Many of these persons take as much pride as poets in their presentation. As one says, "When I read, the whole neighborhood appears on my doorstep: old people,

7. Recife: cake vendor, 36.

8. Rio: LM, construction worker, 47, Recife, Pernambuco, 1975.

9. Recife: construction worker, 24.

10. Rio: LM, gardener, 26, Catolé da Rocha, Paraíba, 1975.

11. See Robert A. Georges, "Toward an Understanding of Storytelling Events," *Journal of American Folklore*, 82 (1969): 313–28. Also useful here is *Ritual, Play, and Performance: Readings in the Social Sciences/Theatre*, ed. Richard Schechner and Mady Schuman (New York: Seabury Press, 1976).

12. Rio: LM, construction worker, 27, Caratinga, Minas Gerais, 1977.

13. Rio: LM, bricklayer, Ferreiros, Pernambuco, 1969.

young people, men, and women. I sing for whomever wants to listen, and almost everybody does!"[14]

A significant percentage of readers and listeners prefer oral presentation because they feel that it aids in memorization. One young man claims that "it's much better to read *folhetos* with others because the group encourages the reader, and he gets better and better as time goes on, and that makes the verses stick in your mind.[15] As this remark suggests, listening is by no means a necessarily passive experience. Even illiterate members of the group may actively participate by interjecting comments, clapping, hissing, laughing, or otherwise indicating pleasure or disapproval.[16]

In fact, group readings may become such noisy affairs that some persons prefer to go through the *folheto* alone. "I like to read with others, but only if they listen to the person who is singing. Otherwise it's much better to find a quiet corner where you can concentrate," one says.[17] In this case, the person may pretend that he is performing before a group. "It is true that *folhetos* exist to be sung," one buyer says, "but it isn't always easy to get a group together, and so those times I can't find anyone to listen, I just imagine I am the poet reading out loud in the fair."[18]

Many persons regard group readings as not only an effective and particularly enjoyable form of storytelling but an affirmation of both an individual and collective past. "The *folheto* is above all a memory," an old woman from Bezerros says. "And while I suffered a lot in the past, I still like to hear those old stories." Some regard the *folheto* as a kind of document. As one house painter says, "Things are better today than they used to be, but still, looking back, you get a picture of the past that makes you think."[19]

Persons far from their childhood home are especially apt to value the *folheto* as a record. "I don't ask my sons and daughter to stay away from comic books or movies," one emigrant to Rio says; "after all, we live in the heart of Brazil. However, I would like them to know something about how their parents lived."[20] Some individuals reveal a heavy dose of nostalgia.

14. Rio: FSC, carpenter, 47, Lagoa Grande, Paraíba, 1974.
15. Rio: LM, cook, 20, Fortaleza, Ceará, 1975.
16. The role of the audience has not been lost on folklore scholars. For a summary of work on the subject see Robert A. Georges, "From Folktale Research to the Study of Narrating," in *Folk Narrative Research: Some Papers Presented at the VI Congress of the International Society for Folk Narrative Research* (Helsinki: Suomalainen Kirjallisuuden Seura, 1976), pp. 159–68.
17. Rio: LM, waiter, 21, Montes Claros, Minas Gerais, 1975.
18. Rio: LM, key grinder, 53, Maceió, Alagoas, 1975.
19. Rio: FSC, 42, Bom Jardim, Pernambuco, 1971.
20. Rio: FSC, cement mixer, 38, Itabaiana, Paraíba, 1956.

> In the past, there was always someone who used to recite one or another story when we got together to clear the brush from the pasture land. So I like to hear *folhetos* because they make me remember my friends back there in Caruaru when we were all carefree and young.[21]

Those persons who have made the most successful transition to city life are often the most apt to reminisce. Although many indicate no desire to return to the Northeast, they still think of it as home. Thus, one buyer notes that he likes to read with others because

> I grew up in the countryside, and we learned a lot of *folhetos* by heart just listening to them over and over again when there was nothing else to do. Those old stories remind me of all those long hot mornings with a deep blue sky above us, and so, I like to hear them because they remind me of where I was born.[22]

Sometimes people single out one or another story as particularly Northeastern. Especially in the South, they may favor tales about specifically regional figures that remind them of particular experiences. "My grandmother served Lampião coffee on a silver tray, and so I like *folhetos* about him because it is almost like reading about somebody I knew."[23]

Within Rio, a liking for *cordel* stories may be a form of self-affirmation. Although there are natives of the city (*cariocas*) who buy *folhetos*, some Northeasterners insist that no Southerner could possibly appreciate them. In this case, the *folheto* not only unites but effectively excludes. "Where I work," one buyer says,

> we all read *folhetos* together except for two fellows from here who only talk nonsense. Their life is samba, the beach, soccer. How could *they* understand a story like *The Gambler Soldier*?[24]

Individuals may acknowledge the *folheto*'s supposedly limited appeal with either reluctance or defiance. "It's very fine to be an author in the North," another says, "but here it isn't because these people know nothing about poetry and so don't support him."[25] This same sense of the *folheto* as a familiar tradition pervades people's explanations of why they prefer a live poet to the growing number of recordings available especially in the South. As in the case of comic book covers, some individuals have prac-

21. Recife: railroad maintenance man, 39, Caruaru, Pernambuco, 1963.
22. Rio: FSC, construction worker, 64, João Pessoa, Paraíba, 1954.
23. Rio: LM, machine operator, 20, Campina Grande, Paraíba, 1964.
24. Rio: FSC, watchman, 44, Montes Claros, Minas Gerais, 1965.
25. Rio: LM, orderly in mental hospital, 26, Sobral, Ceará, 1970.

tical reasons for their preference for recordings. They may argue that the quality of the voice is better, that the listener can play the tape or record at will instead of waiting for market day to hear a story, that the singers themselves tend to be better, and that recordings guarantee that the story will continue uninterrupted from beginning to end. "Nothing," one buyer notes, "is worse than not knowing how the hero finally got to marry the rancher's daughter."[26] In each case, the emphasis is not upon the record in and of itself but on its function as a more effective vehicle for a given message. Interestingly enough, at least one buyer favors records above live performances because they are "more visible."[27]

Despite the drawbacks of live performances, close to half of all respondents in Rio and more in the Northeast prefer them. The idea that a man only really becomes a poet when surrounded by listeners is a common theme. People often favor a live performance for much the same reasons that they form groups to rehear *cordel* stories. "Each poet is different," one buyer remarks. "That means that the *folheto*, even when it is an old story, always seems new because no two poets read exactly the same way, and you notice things with one that you didn't with the other."[28]

Another buyer remarks that he likes to hear the poet in the fair much better than on a record because "on a record, who is the poet singing for? Certainly not me!" Aside from being expensive, records are "artificial, only words."[29] "The *folheto* is much better when the poet reads it aloud because he says lots of funny things that make you understand the story," a ten-year-old Rio schoolgirl adds.

While most people do not regard *cordel* stories as anything profound or unusual, their very familiarity tends to enhance their appeal. Many individuals emphasize that these tales deal with persons much like themselves. Not only the language of the *folheto* but the problems it poses are well known. Buyers' comparisons of *cordel* to other kinds of stories often emphasize this sense of identification. A nineteen-year-old farmer from Bezerros says, "The *folheto* is clumsy and the magazine is much better looking, much more modern, but I still like *folhetos* because I guess that I too am sort of clumsy." Another buyer points out that *cordel* stories often have a more immediate quality. "I prefer the *folheto* to comic books because I am more inside the story. I feel almost as if those things the poet talks about could be happening to me," he says.[30]

As already mentioned, many *cordel* buyers enjoy radio and television broadcasts, magazines, and movies. Poets themselves often point out that

26. Rio: LM, cashier, 26, Patos, Paraíba, 1967.
27. Rio: FSC, construction worker, 49, Umbuzeiro, Paraíba, 1976.
28. Rio: LM, factory worker, 21, Serra Madureira, Acre, 1974.
29. Rio: LM, bus driver, 27, Remédios, Minas Gerais, 1967.
30. Bezerros: ice cream vendor, 30.

a person who reads comic books or watches films on television will not necessarily stop buying *folhetos*. The similarities which some authors perceive between their own work and that of television and magazine writers are apparent to many members of their public. As one buyer comments, "The soap opera is like the *folheto* because you can see the seeds of what is going to happen from the very beginning."[31] "There is really not much difference between the *folheto* and a soap opera," says another. "In fact, they are like sisters. The only difference is that the stories you see on television are always pure invention."[32] According to still another, "the *folheto* was the soap opera of the past and is still good for Sundays when there is hardly anything on the television."[33]

Although some persons see little or no difference between the *cordel* and, say, comic book stories, others point out a number of dissimilarities. Indeed, the great majority of *folheto* buyers, when asked if they would prefer a *folheto*, a magazine, or a comic book, opted for the *folheto*. Some individuals who prefer *folhetos* to other kinds of reading matter emphasize its relationship to them.

> Would I rather read "Donald Duck" or a *folheto*? Well, I don't know. I like both. I think Donald Duck is great. And if I really had to choose? Oh then I guess I'd take something like *Lampião in Hell* or *The Princess of Go-and-Don't-Come-Back*. O, yeah, sure, in that case, I'd stick with my roots.[34]

Other persons emphasize the *cordel*'s perennial nature. Although no one uses the word "art," their comments suggest that they see the *folheto* as far more than entertainment. *"Folhetos* are good because you can keep them,"* one such individual says. "My friends and I write down the best parts in a little notebook, and then when we have children, we will be able to show them what their mothers thought when they were young."[35] "You can read a magazine once, but a *folheto* you can read four, five, ten times," asserts another. "So to my way of thinking you get more for your money."[36]

> I'm crazy about magazines. I have a whole collection of love stories. Of course, they're not like those old, old stories that go back to the beginning of the world. The people in magazines are like the people you see on television. You really can't expect that you will ever see them again. But the people in *folhetos* are easier to remember. It's as if you'd known them for a long time, understand?[37]

31. Recife: cake vendor, 37.
32. Recife: railroad maintenance worker, 39, Caruaru, Pernambuco, 1967.
33. Recife: construction worker, 24.
34. Rio: LM, unemployed, 27, Cajazeiras, Paraíba, 1973.
35. Rio: LM, maid (F), 24, Belém, Pará, 1975.
36. Caruaru: farmer, 30.
37. Rio: LM, maid (F), 30, São Luís, Maranhão, 1972.

Buyers may perceive *folhetos* as somehow more "serious" or "authentic" than soap operas or comic books. It is common for people to contrast the *cordel*'s supposed "reality" with the media's more "artificial" nature. The perception of such differences does not necessarily imply that the individual has a preference. He or she will often like both for different reasons. One buyer notes, for instance, that "the *folheto* is a way of feeling while the soap opera is just a story, but I think that both are good."[38]

For other persons, however, such differences are qualitative as well.

> I don't know why, but I just don't feel attracted to magazines. I like them, but I don't understand them as well as I do the *folheto*. For one thing, they are harder to read. For another, the stories themselves seem more complicated. I guess that I never really believe that they could happen.[39]

Sometimes the *folheto* buyer will indicate out-and-out dislike for other kinds of stories. This dislike is most commonly directed toward comic books and, above all, soap operas. While few people object to news broadcasts, a number indicate an almost violent dislike for those enormously popular serialized stories known in Brazil as *novelas*. Though few persons would agree with the doorman who considers television "the work of the Devil,"[40] a significant minority of buyers express distaste for soap operas. Not infrequently, the motives for their dislike reveal conflicting values. The wall painter who dismisses *novelas* as "all lies" and who feels that "those actors could be talking Chinese"[41] clearly views the world from another, more traditional perspective.

Some of the most interesting comments made by buyers concern the existence or nonexistence of the "mysterious peacock," a magical bird which gives its name to the title of a particularly well-known *folheto*, which has, significantly, gone on to inspire a soap opera. Originally written by José Camelo de Melo Resende shortly after World War I, the story was rewritten by João Melquíades Ferreira; it is this second version which most people know.[42] The tale focuses on a young man, Evangelista, who falls in love with the well-guarded and very beautiful daughter of a noble Greek. Paying a scientist to devise a flying machine that will allow him to visit the lovely maiden, the hero persuades her to elope with him. With

38. Rio: LM, bus driver, 27, Remédios, Minas Gerais, 1967.
39. Rio: FSC, construction worker, 32, Recife, 1975.
40. Rio: FSC, 27, Timbaúba, Pernambuco, 1975.
41. Bezerros: wall painter, 52.
42. João Melquíades Ferreira, *O Pavão Misterioso* (Juazeiro do Norte: Tipografia São Francisco, 1951), *Literatura popular em verso: Antologia*, I (Rio de Janeiro: Fundação Casa de Rui Barbosa/MEC, 1964), pp. 57–64 (hereafter cited as *Antologia*). The "theft" of the original written by José Camelo de Melo Resende triggered a bitter debate among popular poets which continues even today.

her father in hot pursuit, the young couple flies off into the sky within the trusty aluminum peacock. Once married and living in Evangelista's native Turkey, they are forgiven by the heroine's mother, her father having died of chagrin.

The idea of a flying peacock is present in other folk literatures and is not a recent or specifically Brazilian contribution; also the tale is clearly influenced by the invention of the airplane.[43] Charged with a sustained lyricism, it is a *folheto* classic that continues to sell thousands of new copies a year. *Folheto* buyers often mention the peacock in discussions about *cordel* stories. Thus, one individual does not like soap operas because they are lies whereas stories, "like the 'mysterious peacock'" are different. "Now, the peacock didn't really exist," he explains, "but that story is still true because there was a young man who did everything anyone could do to save that beautiful princess and that is really what that *folheto* is all about."[44]

Considerations of the peacock inevitably raise the kinds of question about the *folheto*'s relationship to its readers' experience discussed in the last chapter. The poet's claim to offer "examples of purest reality" is not lost on the buyer. Even if he takes them with a grain of salt, he is apt to respond to a certain urgency within these tales. Thus, while a given individual may enjoy comic books or magazines, he tends to see the *folheto* in a somewhat different light. "The people in comic books never existed, but those in the *folheto* are different," one buyer asserts. "I like comic books, but I have to admit that they are just to kill time while the *folheto*, no, it teaches many things," says a thirty-three-year-old watchman from Caruaru, Pernambuco.

For those persons who insist that all *folhetos* are fact, the *cordel* functions within the realm of faith.[45] "Those stories are true, though of course the person who doesn't believe in Jesus also doesn't believe in the poets," says one sixty-year-old farmer from Bezerros. "The mysterious peacock not only existed in the past; he exists today," one Recife-based buyer insists.[46]

These persons who interpret all *cordel* stories literally are, however, a small minority. It is far more common for buyers to assert that different

43. See F675.1, "King makes a wooden peacock for son," in Stith Thompson, *Motif-Index of Folk Literature: A Classification of Narrative Elements in Folk-tales, Ballads, Myths, Fables, Medieval Romances, Exempla, Fabliaux, Jest-books, and Local Legends*, rev. ed. (Helsinki: Suomalainen Tiedakatemia, 1956), III, 193.

44. Recife: watchman, 37, Sertânia, Pernambuco, 1960.

45. See Clifford Geertz, "Ethos, World-View, and the Analysis of Sacred Symbols," in *Every Man his Way*, ed. Alan Dundes (Englewood Cliffs, N.J.: Prentice-Hall, 1968), pp. 301–14.

46. Recife: breadfruit vendor, 23, Bom Jardim, Pernambuco, 1973.

folhetos contain varying degrees of fact. Most perceive some difference between news stories and *romances*, and most find some fictional stories "truer" than others. According to one buyer, some *folhetos* are fact "because you can tell the poet about where you work and what you do, and he will go home and write a story all about you," but others are fiction because they are "just ideas." For another, all *cordel* tales are clearly fiction. "I know that they are fantasy because I myself wrote a story called *The Man Named Joe Goat*, and there was never a man like the one I talked about."[47]

The majority of persons, however, view *cordel* stories in general as a blend of fact and fantasy. "They are real things dressed in fiction," one construction worker explains.[48] Another claims that "the poet starts with one word that soon becomes fifty."[49] "Part of what the poet says is true, and the other part is to make the story rhyme," still another says.[50] The *folheto* is thus "neither all true nor all false but a mixture and for that reason is a lot better."[51] The poet "puts together in one story a little bit of everything; news, legend, films, history, and so there's something for everyone and no one feels left out."[52]

Interestingly enough, differences in age, birthplace, and schooling seem to have little influence on people's responses to the question of whether or not the mysterious peacock or other comparable figures in well-known *cordel* stories really existed. In Rio de Janeiro, for instance, two otherwise quite different groups of buyers gave almost identical answers to the question of the peacock's existence, with approximately two-thirds of each group answering in the affirmative. The only significant difference occurs between persons who like and others who dislike soap operas. A computer breakdown of responses suggests that the more enthusiastic a buyer is about the latter, the more he or she tends to deny the existence of the peacock and the "truth" of the *cordel* in general. Conversely, the more the buyer insists that the peacock was or is a real bird, the more likely he or she is to reject soap operas. There does not, however, appear to be any similar correlation involving comic books, magazines, movies, radio programs, or newspapers.

A "yes" response to the question of the peacock's existence does not mean that the speaker expects to find a magic bird in every tree. If one were to ask most persons in another context whether they had ever seen a

47. Rio: FSC, warehouse worker, 26, Brejo, Maranhão, 1973.
48. Rio: FSC, 51, Mamanguape, Paraíba, 1948.
49. Rio: FSC, carpenter, 53, Sapé, Paraíba, 1952.
50. Recife: messenger boy, 16.
51. Recife: taxi driver, 34, Gravatá, Pernambuco, 1969.
52. Rio: LM, construction worker, Esperança, Paraíba, 1970.

magic peacock, they would undoubtedly say "no." Even when referring specifically to the *cordel*, the great majority of persons qualify their responses to suggest that such a creature *might* have existed, that it existed long ago and far away, and/or that other people *say* that it existed or exists.

Although the term "metaphor" is never used, the concept is clearly present. A number of persons describe the *folheto* as a *verdade enfeitada*, a "decorated" or "embellished" truth. "The poet starts out with the truth and then helps out a little," one buyer explains.[53] "The mysterious peacock is like an enchanted airplane" for another.[54] "There was some bird, but whether or not he was mysterious, that I don't know!" yet another buyer exclaims.[55]

As poets themselves point out, the notion of potentiality is crucial. Though the event which the *folheto* describes may not have ever happened, it is considered true if it *could* have happened or *might* happen in the future. A *cordel* story is thus "more or less something that seems possible, a picture that the poet sees in his mind."[56] "I don't know if the story of the mysterious peacock is true," an itinerant barber says, "but I suppose that there could be a bird like that one somewhere because the world is a lot bigger than the little part of it we know."[57]

Quite often, people will attempt to prove a particular story's truth through reference to their own or others' experience. Such statements reaffirm their faith in the *cordel*'s essential reality and once again suggest the *folheto*'s communal nature.

> My mother told me that she saw the peacock when she was a little girl. That was in the backlands of Paraíba. No, I don't know how he got there from Turkey. Maybe some rancher read the story and sent someone there to buy him.[58]

Even when the speaker has doubts, he is apt to trust in the experience of others, particularly when these are friends or close relations. Thus, another Southern transplant says, "Look, I know that it sounds a little strange, but my grandmother told my mother that that peacock lived right there in the Borborema Mountains. . . . Yes, that's what she told us, so I guess it must be true."[59] Although most such assertions rest on hearsay, some persons find parallels in their own lives and in other stories. "I once

53. Rio: FSC, carpenter, 57, Guarabira, Paraíba, 1946.
54. Rio: FSC, warehouse supplyman, 26, Brejo, Maranhão, 1973.
55. Recife: Xerox copy worker, 20.
56. Rio: LM, welder, 20, Banho Azul, Minas Gerais, 1973.
57. Recife: 37, Campina Grande, Paraíba, 1968.
58. Rio: FSC, waiter, 22, São Benedito, Ceará, 1976.
59. Rio: LM, waiter, 20, Crato, Ceará, 1977.

knew a girl who suffered just like the heroine in one of these *folhetos*," one buyer asserts. "She had never read the story, but believe me, what happened to her was just like what happened to that other, and so I think that those stories must be true."[60]

Many persons have been touched at least peripherally by people or events recorded in *folhetos*. "Lampião?" asks one old man in typical fashion,

> sure thing, I knew him. When I was just a boy he rode through where I lived. My uncle even had a knife that once belonged to him. Now if he went to hell like the poet says, I'm not sure but a lot of the things he says about him are the truth, I guarantee it.[61]

When people have no direct observation with which to compare or document the *folheto*, they may point to others' belief (not actual experience) as proof of its veracity. "Of course the peacock existed; that story is very well known" is a typical response. "Did the peacock exist?" asks one buyer. "Well, I've heard he did, and he must have because people wouldn't talk so much about something that wasn't true."[62] "Did the peacock exist?" another repeats. "Why, of course. Ask anybody here!"[63]

The speaker frequently makes use of the story's built-in escape hatches, arguing that the event occurred "but somewhere else" and/or "very long ago." Such comments suggest that people perceive *cordel* tales as qualitatively different from simple statements of fact. The fact they are removed in time and space simply emphasizes their otherness.

> The mysterious peacock existed. He just wasn't Brazilian.[64]

> The story of the peacock is a legend, that is, he existed but a long time ago. What is a legend? Oh, it's something that happened back in that time when there were still witches and kings.[65]

> Ferrabras and Oliveiros? Oh yes, they were real people, but they lived at least a hundred years ago along with Charlemagne and princess. . . . I don't remember her name now, but there was a princess and they all lived together over there in Paris. Where is Paris? Why everybody knows that Paris is in France.[66]

60. Recife: plumber's assistant, 18, Iguaraçu, Paraíba, 1975.
61. Bezerros: farmer, 68.
62. Recife: electrician, 33, Campina Grande, Paraíba, 1977.
63. Rio: LM, doorman, 30, Santa Quitéria, Ceará, 1977.
64. Recife: bus driver, 23.
65. Rio: LM, factory worker, 40, Sergipe, Aracaju.
66. Recife: watchman, 37, Sertânia, Pernambuco, 1974.

The fact that the *folheto* recounts something that took place "somewhere else" may actually make it more meaningful to some buyers. For a number of persons, *cordel* stories provide a comforting assurance that some things do not change. These individuals may insist that "that story of the peacock dates back more or less to the beginning of the world." "Ever since I was a child, I've heard that story, so how could it not be true?" one elderly farmer in Bezerros demands. "I'm very old, but it is even older than I."

Logically, if sometimes surprisingly, those stories which people are most apt to question are those which appear closest to everyday experience. Persons who insist that the mysterious peacock and Donzela Teodora existed may shrug their shoulders when asked about a more contemporary argument between a peddler and a market tax collector in a nearby town. In the same manner, buyers may question or deny certain exploits of a flesh-and-blood bandit such as Antônio Silvino or Lampião while continuing to swear by Aladdin's magic lamp. "All *folheto* stories are true," one individual says,

> except that story of Cancão de Fogo because the poet says that he was from Limoeiro. I'm from there myself and I never heard of anybody who had known him. Now the Donzela Teodora, she existed. Where? Oh, I forget. Somewhere in France or Greece.[67]

Tales about familiar persons and places may come too close to reality for comfort. When this happens, the buyer tends to deny the specific instance in order to keep believing in the *cordel* as a whole. One woman does not believe the story of the peddler and the tax collector because "no poor person could talk back to the police like that and get away with it." However, "a lot of other stories are a hundred percent true."[68]

Conversely, a buyer may deny the truth of the *cordel* in abstract terms, then affirm the reality of a particular *folheto*. The same person who asserts that all *folhetos* are "pure fantasy" may do an about-face when questioned more specifically about the Gambler Soldier or the mysterious peacock. "The *folhetos* are all make-believe, that's for certain, pure invention. The peacock? Ah well, *he* existed. Now that story is a fact."[69] This tendency to believe in one or another personage despite doubts about the *cordel* in general suggests a recognition of the fictional nature of the writing process together with a more immediate identification with those problems which *folheto* heroes and heroines confront.

67. Rio: FSC, mechanic, 44, Limoeiro, Pernambuco, 1959.
68. Recife: prostitute (F), 16, Garanhuns, Pernambuco, 1972.
69. Rio: FSC, construction worker, 30, Fortaleza, Ceará, 1977.

> Are those stories true? No, no, no! Those things all happened, sure, but in the poet's head. Well now, that story of the peacock is a little different. I think that he existed. That Genoveva too, poor thing, how she suffered![70]

There are, to be sure, buyers who deny the truth of all *cordel* stories. The great majority of those who respond with a flat denial are very often, however, from regions of Brazil other than the Northeast. While some Northeasterners may doubt the truth of most or all *folhetos*, they are more apt to express this disbelief in indirect or interrogatory terms. Even those who most clearly dismiss one or another story as unadulterated fiction are apt to do so with a wink, a smile, an embarrassed laugh, or a silent movement of the head.

Significantly, the term "lie" is seldom used in reference to the *folheto*. Many persons employ it freely in talking about comic books or soap operas, but most are hesitant to apply it to the work of popular poets. Persons are more likely to express doubt about *folhetos* in a more roundabout manner. One buyer asserts, for instance, that *folhetos* "are, perhaps, all fantasies."[71] "Those stories are all made up, don't you think?" asks another. "I mean, did *you* ever see a bird like the poet describes?"[72] "The *folhetos* are true, but some are a lot truer than others, and I don't think that the peacock is one of those," still another says.[73]

When people express skepticism about the truth of a particular story, they frequently temper their denial with expressions of admiration for the poet or for poetry in general. At times, their comments are almost apologetic, suggesting that they may feel disloyal or even guilty about their doubt. One young man calls *folhetos* "all lies; there's no two ways about it," but is quick to add, "but, Virgin Mary, they are really beautiful whoppers!"[74] Not infrequently, such persons will attempt to change the subject. "Look, to be honest with you, I doubt that that peacock ever existed," says one buyer, "but you have to admire the poet's imagination. The story of the mysterious peacock? No more than pure invention. Hey, I've memorized the first ten stanzas. Listen and I'll sing them!"[75]

This reluctance to write off the peacock as "just a story" reaffirms many people's feeling that the *folheto* is part of their own history. Individuals who have grown up with these tales may find them truer than scientific reports. This position is obvious in the following interchange.

70. Rio: FSC, pumpman, 26, Recife, Pernambuco, 1974.
71. Rio: LM, waiter, 21, Belo Horizonte, Minas Gerais, 1977.
72. Recife: watchman, 32, Condado, Pernambuco, 1959.
73. Bezerros: farmer, 27.
74. Recife: carpenter, 16.
75. Recife: watch repairman, 24, Bonito, Pernambuco, 1969.

Interviewer: Tell me, I've been wondering about something. That mysterious peacock, did he really exist?

Respondent. Oh yes. That is, the poet invented a few details and exaggerated here and there in order to make the story better, but the peacock existed, you can rest assured. [pause] Now you tell me something. Do you think that a man really went to the moon?

Interviewer: Why yes, I think so. Didn't you see the pictures in the newspapers?

Respondent: Oh sure, my daughter has a television set in her house, and I watched the whole thing from beginning to end. But you know, I have my doubts about it. How do you know that someone didn't fake those pictures? Somebody could have made up the whole thing! A man way up there on the moon, walking around among the stars and all? Come on now! I don't have much of an education, but still, I'm no fool who believes everything that people tell me.[76]

Hesitancy in denying the magic bird's existence may also reflect more or less conscious recognition of its symbolic nature. Most *folheto* buyers see no more reason to demand concrete proof of the mysterious peacock's reality than they would of a biblical figure such as Jonah's whale. This is not to suggest that buyers regard *cordel* stories, which they know are the work of men, in the same way as they do tales that most believe to be the work of God. Despite the fact that one might argue that the *folheto* functions within a "sacralized" universe, the mysterious peacock is clearly not a sacred figure. Nevertheless, most buyers have been familiar with both bird and whale since childhood. In their own way, both are intimately associated with principles which most readers regard, or claim to regard, as solemn truth.

The peacock, as many buyers point out in their own words, is essentially a particularly appealing reiteration of an important point. It is difficult if not impossible to divorce such reiterations or symbols from the larger reality that they represent, particularly when they have played a major role in an individual's formative experience. To say that the peacock or whale is a lie necessarily implies that the proposition that courage and faith ultimately triumph over adversity—is also false. For many persons, the underlying messages of the *folheto* are unquestionably true. To reject the vehicle of their expression as fantasy, no matter how blatantly fictive, therefore, makes little sense, especially since this rejection may threaten these guiding principles.

Furthermore, because the *folheto* tradition is intimately associated with a particular community, to deny the peacock is tantamount to casting doubt

76. Recife: fruit vendor, 60, Bom Jardim, Pernambuco, 1952.

upon the judgment of one's friends and relatives. It is also to question those moral premises on which one would at least like to believe that one's own most crucial decisions are based. Because the *folheto* actually encourages the reader/listener to define both the quality and intensity of the story's truth for himself through a series of disclaimers, expressions of uncertainty on the part of the narrator ("I'm just saying what I heard"), and a series of distancing techniques, he can frequently sidestep this problem. The *folheto* thus allows him to avoid compromising his sense of objective reality at the same time that he reads his own situation into the text.

The *Folheto* in the Eyes of the Poet and His Public: A Summary

Clearly, different buyers see the *folheto* differently. Also, not all poets view their work in exactly the same way. Nevertheless, it is possible to abstract a number of common themes. One can actually go through this chapter and the last one and match up statements point by point. Though people's perspective may vary, poets and buyers generally have similar expectations. Above all, they see the writer's role in much the same way. Both groups feel responsible for the *folheto*'s success. Each has a good idea of how the creative process functions and what the *cordel* is all about.

Those discrepancies which do exist tend to arise within the shifting area of what is "real" and seldom concern the mechanics of how a particular story functions. Though poets themselves frequently throw up their hands at their readers' supposed ignorance, they are usually not expressing impatience with an inability to grasp the concept of a metaphor. While many readers assert that the peacock existed, their affirmations are of a qualitatively different nature from a statement such as "the sky is blue." The truth of the *folheto* is perceived as relative. The stories themselves function within a limited, recognizably special sphere.

Furthermore, most writers and buyers share an understanding of how symbols work. "The poet tells about something that isn't true but has the appearance of truth," says one writer. However, *cordel* authors reject the notion that their stories are "lies" with the same force as most buyers. "But poetry doesn't deceive anyone," another explains.

> It says something that everyone knows very well isn't true. The fellow who sells those remedies which he claims will cure an incurable disease is a liar, but the poet doesn't make anyone sick; in fact, he makes people feel better.[77]

77. Olegário Fernandes da Silva, Caruaru, Pernambuco, March 18, 1978; Severino Borges Silva, Timbaúba, Pernambuco, March 2, 1978.

A similar point is made by a *cordel* author and *repentista*, who points out that

> every detail in a story can be invented, and the idea can still be true. You take a *folheto* like *Alípio and His Faithful Dog*. Well, there was no such boy and no such dog, and those things the author describes never really happened. And yet what he says about friendship is absolutely true.[78]

Although some buyers believe everything that the poet says, these are a small minority. Rather, most tensions or misunderstandings that arise between *cordel* authors and their public have to do with the *folheto*'s underlying message, not with individual symbols, but with the larger six-step sequence into which these symbols fit. For many buyers, a *folheto* is not a *folheto* if it does not respect this sequence, which is, to be sure, not perceived in the same terms that I have used here. The one time a well-known author decided to let a character who had killed the heroine's father marry her at the end of his story, a vendor came to him and said that he would have to change the last three stanzas right away because a man who had been standing there listening to him got so angry that he ripped up a whole stack of *folhetos* and threw them on the ground. "I had thought that I could get away with it," the poet says, "but then I saw I couldn't, so I changed the end and made a lot of money."[79]

The fact that people insist on the presence of this six-step pattern with its underlying world view does not necessarily mean that they apply it themselves to their own lives. A seasoned writer makes this clear when he remarks,

> I have to say that the bikini is against God, against the church and against I-don't-know-what-else because if I don't say this, then nobody is going to buy the story. I myself have nothing against bikinis, and the people who buy the *folheto* go to the beach no matter what. Still, if I don't talk this way, if I don't try to scare them, then I might as well throw my copies in the woods.[80]

"I don't think that people really believe these stories," one of his fellows adds, "but I do know that they want to hear them over and over." As a poet from Campina Grande says succinctly, "the *folheto* buyer doesn't want life as it is but as it could be."[81]

It is difficult to gauge anything so subjective as "belief." Probably many

78. João Alexandre, Juazeiro do Norte, Ceará, April 9, 1978.
79. José Costa Leite, Condado, Pernambuco, February 18, 1978.
80. Manoel Caboclo e Silva, Juazeiro do Norte, Ceará, April 5, 1978.
81. Manuel d'Almedia Filho, Aracaju, Sergipe, June 7, 1978; Gerson Araújo de Lucena, Campina Grande, Paraíba, April 4, 1978.

buyers are much like one woman in the Sant'Ana Hills who responded to the question of whether she believed in destiny (*sina*) with a firm "Of course I do! Sometimes." It is certain, however, that people want to see good win and evil lose. The poet's problem does not stem from the necessity of implementing patterns that he learns from experience but rather from a certain reluctance to tamper with a message which most people think comes from God.

As suggested in chapter seven, the poet himself believes that his primary goal is to please his public and that the best writer is therefore the most popular. Nevertheless, he also believes that inspiration is a special, even divine force. Were this not the case, there would be no obstacle whatsoever to his rearranging his ideas in that neat six-step sequence. Because, however, poetry implies a charge, a privileged vision, it is somewhat harder for him to relinquish his own concept of the way a story should be written.

We have seen that the essential pull within the poet is between his role as a spokesman and his own individuality. It is not, however, as the educated observer might assume, a tension between a sense of obligation to speak for others and a desire to speak for himself. Most popular poets are not overly concerned with recording the particulars of their own experience. Though some do write biographies from time to time, most show little interest in recording the details of an ill-fated love affair or describing the people and places they have known.

Rather, the real and very powerful conflict that many poets feel from time to time involves two sets of obligations: on one hand, his duty to his public; on the other, his duty to poetry and the superhuman forces with which it is associated. The irritation which many poets periodically express in regard to their public arises not only from the very real problems involved with making a living in a fluctuating market but also from the frustrating necessity of altering a vision with which they feel they have been honored. In brief, the apparently clear-cut role of spokesman is complicated by the poet's perception of himself as a recipient of important messages which are destined for a group that may not really want to hear them.

Most poets admit that if they did not have to worry about the marketplace, they would write quite different kinds of stories. In most cases, however, these *folhetos* would not be about themselves or everyday experience but about more spiritual matters: the nature of the world and man's place within it. As one poet says,

> If I could write anything without worrying about whether or not it would sell, I would write about the Bible, about religion, though not the kind you learn from priests. But people do not want this. The *matuto* likes a story

about the end of the world, with lots of fire and brimstone, but a book about ideas, no. A religious *folheto* either has to have something about the sufferings of Christ, or the poet has to throw in the Devil in order for it to sell.[82]

Authors who have printed *folhetos* at their own expense testify to the force of this pull between the poet's sense of himself as a spokesman of the people and as a mouthpiece of other, higher powers. The ideas which poets express within these individually financed works are usually quite different from those of established religious groups, most notably the Roman Catholic church. One *cordel* author tells of seeing the name "Jesus" spelled out in letters of fire in the sky, then writing a *folheto*, "which, of course, I gave away to buyers as a gift."[83] "I have stories which I have given away free," another says.

> It is possible for a poet's own thoughts to coincide with what he writes. I, for instance, like to write adventure stories and they sell well. But when I want to write something of a more spiritual nature, not religion exactly but sort of a reflection about the world and the people in it, I have to do it without thinking of the money because that's not what readers want.[84]

"Jesus said, 'Give freely what ye so freely received,'" asserted eighty-year-old Manuel Tomás de Assis less than a week before his death,

> and I received the gift of poetry without asking; therefore it is my duty to share it with others. The materialists say that a mango tree is a mango tree and that is all there is to it. But the poet knows that this life is full of hidden meanings, and where other people see a mango, he sees many mysteries.[85]

The *cordel* author's desire to share his recognition of these "mysteries" may prompt sporadic tensions. Nevertheless, poet and public share a common universe. The desire to please as well as the conviction that writing is above all a service are firmly ingrained. As the *folheto*-buying community becomes more heterogeneous, the familiar six-step pattern may no longer satisfy either its readers or its writers. The kinds of changes that the poet will be able to make and the nature of his future role are still not clear. For the moment, however, the dynamics of the tradition are much as they have always been. "If someone asked me, 'Did the mysterious peacock really exist?'" says one author bluntly, "I would tell him that he didn't, but you know, I have been a poet forty years now, and no one has ever asked."[86]

82. Olegário Fernandes da Silva, Caruaru, Pernambuco, January 17, 1978.
83. Antonio Caetano de Souza, Recife, Pernambuco, February 27, 1978.
84. Francisco de Souza Campos, São Lourenço da Mata, Pernambuco, March 1, 1978.
85. Manuel Tomás de Assis, Olivedos, Paraíba, July 3, 1978.
86. José Costa Leite, Condado, Pernambuco, February 18, 1978.

IX. Stories on a String: The Brazilian *Cordel*

Folheto readers and writers are united by far more than a common vision of the mysterious peacock or a sense of what a *cordel* story ought to do. Most live in similarly difficult circumstances, and although poets may be better off than many of their customers, they too usually have to struggle for survival. "There is a difference between necessity and hunger," explains one popular poet, as casually as he might explain any other point of information. " 'Necessity' is when you don't have anything to eat for a day or two, and 'hunger' is 'necessity' after the third day."[1]

There is presently considerable debate among educated Brazilians about the nature of the relationship between *folhetos* and their readers' daily life. In the most general terms it is possible to distinguish between those who see this form of popular poetry as "a reflection of the dominant ideology" and others who find it a unique expression of the most fundamental concerns of the Northeastern masses.[2] Naturally, still other persons take a third stance or position somewhere between these two extremes.

Representatives of the first group usually argue that the *folheto* is a hangover from the Middle Ages, which has survived in the Northeast because of the region's backwardness. They see *cordel* tales of kindhearted kings and loyal retainers as a more or less obvious sanction of the status quo. In their eyes, the stylized treatment of violence in these stories provides an effective means of neutralizing and absorbing resentments, which should, by rights, explode.[3] Members of the second group, who may or may not acknowledge the *cordel*'s more reactionary aspects, insist that these stories represent the voice of the people. According to them, the *folheto* speaks both to and for the masses. Its long history of best sellers testifies to its appeal among large numbers of persons who have for decades managed to find a spare coin for these stories.

1. Joel Borges, Sítio Cruzeiro, Pernambuco, May 18, 1978.

2. Most of the persons who have written on the *cordel* have tended to see it as an expression of the *povo*. Recently, however, there has been a new trend toward envisioning the *cordel* as the expression of values largely foreign to its readers and writers. See, for instance, Antônio Fausto Neto, *A ideologia da punição* (Petrópolis: Vozes, 1979).

3. This containment theory, once popular among folklorists, has increasingly lost ground in favor of the view of folklore as a more all-encompassing cultural and behavioral system. See Richard Bauman, "Quaker Folk-Linguistics and Folklore" in *Folklore: Performance and Communication*, ed. Dan Ben-Amos and Kenneth Goldstein (The Hague: Mouton, 1975), pp. 259–63.

Although this debate is often suggestive, its participants cannot solve the questions they raise. As evident in the last two chapters, poets and their customers may provide valuable clues about the *folheto*'s relationship to their own lives, but they cannot provide any definite solutions. Rather, if there are answers, these must come from a comparison between patterns found within the society at large with others apparent within a series of individual texts. Rather than deciding that the *cordel* is alienating because some stories feature benevolent kings or relevant because others star backlands bandits who speak a Portuguese just like that spoken by subsistence farmers in Paraíba, it is necessary to examine its underlying six-step sequence within a larger framework.

Ever since colonization in the sixteenth century, Brazilian society has been highly stratified. Although different writers divide and label these layers in various ways, the mass of *folheto* readers and writers will normally fall into the least privileged of these slots.[4] The rural, agricultural system to which the majority of poets and buyers are, or at one time were, related is characterized by a series of horizontal and vertical exchange ties. These ties, which may be found in varying forms in other Latin American and Mediterranean communities, are generally referred to as "dyads" because they occur almost exclusively between pairs and do not bind larger groups. Thus, "*A*'s tie to *B* in no way necessarily binds him to *C*, who is also tied to *B*," and although *A* may have a contractual relationship with *C* as well as *B*, "this does not give rise to a feeling of association or group."[5] Normally, these pacts or contracts fall into two basic types. *Colleague contracts* bind people of equal or approximately equal socioeconomic status, who exchange the same kinds of goods and services. *Patron-dependent contracts* are both vertical and asymmetrical. This means that they unite persons of significantly different socioeconomic status, who exchange different kinds of goods and services. They may also unite human and superhuman beings. Given that these networks outlined by social scientists who have worked in northeastern Brazil recall, albeit imperfectly, other patterns found within the *folheto*, it is worth looking at them in somewhat more detail.[6]

4. Seven such schemes are summarized in convenient chart form in Forman, *The Brazilian Peasantry* (New York: Columbia University Press, 1975), p. 70.

5. George M. Foster, "The Dyadic Contract in Tzintzuntan, II: Patron-Client Relationship," *American Anthropologist*, 65 (1963): 1281.

6. For a discussion of the dyadic contract in particular and the notion of social exchanges in general, see Peter Blau, *Exchange and Power in Social Life* (New York: John Wiley, 1964); George Foster, "The Dyadic Contract," *American Anthropologist*, 63 (1961): 1280–94; George Foster, "The Dyadic Contract: A Model for the Social Structure of a Mexican Peasant Village," *American Anthropologist*, 63 (1961): 1173–92; Bertram Hutchinson, "The Patron-Dependent Relationship in Brazil: A Preliminary Examination," *Sociologia Ruralis*, 6 (1966): 3–30; John Duncan Powell, "Peasant Society and Clientelist Poli-

Close horizontal ties (colleague contracts) are not uncommon among subsistence farmers in the Northeast.[7] These ties are strongest among individuals within a single household, who tend to act as a unit within the larger community. While similar bonds may be established among household members and more distant relatives and neighbors, in these cases ties do not reflect well-defined, inherent rights and duties. Instead, they grow out of mutually agreed upon terms, which remain subject to either dissolution or change.

Transactions involving equals or near-equals are not regarded on a purely material, tit-for-tat basis. The word frequently used for such exchanges, *vizinhar*, which means literally "to neighbor," stresses the emotional as well as economic nature of these ties. Nevertheless, although the generalized character of this kind of alliance implies a certain flexibility as to the timing and nature of repayment of favors, these must definitely be repaid.

Horizontal exchanges customarily involve common necessities such as beans, corn, and manioc flour. One partner may make an outright request for aid, or if his situation is apparent, the needed article may simply arrive on his doorstep. While more expensive presents such as meat must always be returned in kind, these smaller gifts may be repaid with an equivalent present, for example, lima beans for rice. Labor exchanges between approximate equals is also fairly routine. If a worker is still clearing his land when his neighbors are ready to burn their fields, he may request help from persons with whom he already has some form of tie. Finally, persons of more or less equivalent social status may borrow or lend each other

tics," *American Political Science Review*, 64 (1970): 411–25; Eric R. Wolf, "Kinship, Friendship, and Patron-Client Relationships in Complex Societies," in *The Social Anthropology of Complex Societies*, ed. Michael Banton (London: Tavistock, 1966), pp. 1–22; and Forman, *The Brazilian Peasantry*, especially Chapter 3, pp. 38–86. For a pertinent contrast, see also James C. Scott, "Patron-Client Politics and Political Change in Southeast Asia," *American Political Science Review*, 66 (1972): 91–113; and James C. Scott, "The Erosion of Patron-Client Bonds and Social Change in Rural Southeast Asia," *Journal of Asian Studies*, 32 (1972): 5–37.

7. This description relies heavily on Forman, *The Brazilian Peasantry*; and on Allen Johnson, *Sharecroppers of the Sertão* (Stanford, Ca.: Stanford University Press, 1972). I have also found helpful the titles listed in footnote 6, above, and Clóvis Caldeira, *Mutirão: Formas de ajuda mútua no meio rural* (São Paulo: Companhia Editora Nacional, 1965); Billy Jaynes Chandler, *The Feitosas and the Sertão of Inhamuns: The History of a Family and a Community in Northeast Brazil, 1700–1930* (Gainesville: University of Florida Press, 1972); Kalervo Oberg, "The Marginal Peasant in Brazil," *American Anthropologist*, 67 (1965): 1417–27; Bernard Siegel, "Social Structure and Economic Change in Brazil," in *Economic Growth: Brazil, India, China*, ed. S. Kuznets, W. E. Moore, and J. J. Spengler (Durham: University of North Carolina Press, 1955), pp. 388–411; and the work of Gilberto Freyre, exemplified by *The Masters and the Slaves: A Study in the Development of Brazilian Civilization*, tr. Samuel Putnam (New York: Knopf, 1956).

small amounts of money. These debts, clearly favors, which may once again cement or establish more far-reaching bonds, are quickly repaid.

Vertical (patron-dependent) bonds also imply definite rights and obligations. Although they involve two persons of unequal social status, they too are only formed when both parties are willing and may be dissolved by either party. Such asymmetric or lop-sided relationships are particularly common among subsistence farmers and landowners, each of whom gives and receives quite different benefits. Whereas the former seek to guarantee a certain degree of security, the latter strive for economic and political power.

Landless farmers include squatters (*moradores* or *camaradas*), tenant farmers (*rendeiros*), and sharecroppers (*meeiros*). In some parts of the Northeast, the patron-dependent relationship was originally a largely non-economic device designed to permit the integration of a sizable number of ambulatory workers into a preexisting social framework, thereby protecting its stability. With time, however, most of these tenants came to have definite obligations. New taxes on rural property levied by some state governments toward the beginning of the twentieth century encouraged landowners to seek new sources of income. At the same time the increasing demand for agricultural products made it advisable to maximize the yield. Therefore, owners began to require new or increased payment for the use of their land, forcing farmers to contribute a set portion of their labor and/or produce.[8]

The rights and obligations of subsistence farmers vary from region to region and from landowner to landowner. Tenants may, for instance, be expected to give the farm a set number of work days each week. They may also be required to hand over a share of their own harvest. Usually, this percentage ranges from a quarter to a half. For example, the landowner may claim a third of each farmer's manioc flour and one-half of his cotton. In some cases, he will also insist on buying the remainder of his harvest for a price slightly below the going market rate. Some landowners also demand that farmers provide a certain amount of free labor upon request.

In return for his cooperation, the farmer gets to use a portion of the owner's land. He may or may not also receive a house, access to the local water supply, and the right to firewood from surrounding fields and forests. In cases where the owner is interested in promoting a particular crop, such as cotton, he may furnish his tenants with seed. Usually, the farmer is permitted to grow small amounts of food exclusively for his own use.

Like horizontal exchange ties, these vertical bonds are calculated to provide not only material but important psychological support. Thus the

8. See Chandler, *The Feitosas and the Sertão of Inhamuns*, pp. 134–45.

good landlord offers the farmer not only certain material advantages but guarantees him protection and continuing support. A good boss is not only an employer, but a counselor, judge, makeshift banker, and, as one writer puts it, "a sort of lay deity."[9] He routinely makes use of his elite status to defend "his" workers from outside interference, shielding them, for instance, from brushes with the law. By demanding that his tenants lead more or less exemplary lives, he assures a certain degree of order in their lives. Routinely evicting troublemakers (thieves, heavy drinkers, and persons who dare to question his authority), he also serves as arbiter in feuds involving members of the farm community.

Most farmers are well aware of the high price for these guarantees. They know, for example, that they are buying back their own corn and beans in company stores at inflated prices. Nevertheless, if they are understandably bitter about these practices, they see no alternative means of insuring the security which they value above all else. As one *cordel* poet points out casually in private conversation,

> The poor man has nothing, he goes hungry, he goes barefoot and has no right to own anything. He cannot fight with Joe Blow who is standing over him at three in the morning telling him that it is harvest time and he cannot sleep. Poor thing, if he so much as yawns, he endangers his family's dinner.

The instability of most workers' lives is, as a number of anthropologists have pointed out, no figment of their imagination. They are dependent on others for survival because they do not own the land on which they grow their crops. Also, they must continually face the threats of insects, blight, and drought. Despite minimal advances made in the early 1960s, most farmers have no effective insurance against illness, and retirement benefits are scant. In the face of these and other seemingly inscrutable or monolithic forces, they see no recourse but alliance with one or another more powerful individual. Thus, according to Forman, "throughout his life the Brazilian peasant *submits* to a series of acknowledged dis-equal relationships in which he *obligates* himself in a variety of ways." Born of necessity, this behavior is sanctioned by "a set of general propositions about submissiveness to authority and obligation to meet debts which are reinforced by ideas from a variety of domains, above all the religious."[10]

9. Hutchinson, "The Patron-Dependent Relationship," p. 15.
10. Forman, *The Brazilian Peasantry*, p. 76. To be sure, there have been a number of revolts against the status quo, indicating that the workers' submission has never been total. These movements have tended to be expressed as sporadic uprisings, as messianic movements, and as support for bandits. See, for instance, Roderick J. Barman, "The Brazilian Peasantry Reexamined: The Implications of the Quebra-Quilo Revolt, 1874–1875," *Hispanic American Historical Review*, 57 (1977): 401–24; Maria Isaura Pereira de Queiroz, *O*

This system can continue despite its obvious drawbacks and contradictions because it is accepted by both members of the pact. While neither partner may have much confidence in the other as an individual, both remain faithful to time-honored notions of how such relationships ought to function. Thus, while subsistence farmers tend to move about frequently, their high degree of mobility does not affect the strength or nature of these more abstract bonds. No matter who the boss, the worker owes him faithful service; regardless of his dependents' identity, the landlord sees them as guarantors of both his wealth and reputation among the peers with whom he jockeys for political and economic power.

As already suggested elsewhere, changes in the traditional Northeast market system have fostered a noticeable shift from patron-dependent to patron-client relationships. Growing industrialization requiring a greater urban work force has led employers in both city and countryside to compete for cheap, reliable wage labor, and workers to vie in turn for the best of these new jobs. Nevertheless, these changes are in no way total, and in many regions the centuries-old patterns sketched here remain strong.

Turning back to the *cordel* now, we see that the *folheto* is no mechanical repetition of this larger, very general social network. If certain vertical alliances underlie many stories, the links between these and most people's experiences remain indirect. This is partly because, as Althusser suggests, the ideological manifestations evident in art forms are not merely the passive reflection of a particular political and economic reality.[11] Rather, they are normally a far more complicated representation of largely imaginary relationships between men and the circumstances in which they find themselves. *Cordel* stories deal with values as much as or more than facts, acting not as a mirror but as a purposely distorted lens designed to create a particular vision.[12]

---

messianismo no Brasil e no mundo (São Paulo: Dominus Editora, 1965); and René Ribeiro, "Brazilian Messianic Movements," in *Millenial Dreams in Action*, ed. Sylvia L. Thrupp (The Hague: Mouton, 1962), pp. 55–79; Rui Facó, *Cangaceiros e fanáticos*, 4th ed. (Rio de Janeiro: Civilização Brasileira, 1976); and Amaury Guimarães de Souza, "The Cangaço and the Politics of Violence in Northeast Brazil," in *Protest and Resistance in Angola and Brazil*, ed. Ronald Chilcote (Berkeley: University of California Press, 1972), pp. 109–31. For an overview of peasant political movements in Brazil, see Shepard Forman, "Disunity and Discontent: A Study of Peasant Political Movements in Brazil," *Journal of Latin American Studies*, 3 (1971): 3–24.

11. Louis Althusser, "Ideologie et appareils idéologiques d'état: Notes pour une recherche," *La Pensée*, 151 (1970): 3–38.

12. See George Foster, "Treasure Tales, and the Image of the Static Economy in a Mexican Peasant Community," *Journal of American Folklore*, 77 (1964): 39–44. Also useful in considering the relationship between literature and reality is Benjamin N. Colby, "The Analysis of Cultural Content and the Patterning of Narrative Concerns in Texts," *American Anthropologist*, 75 (1966): 374–88.

Furthermore, *folhetos* do not simply record events but play an active role in shaping these. The *cordel* story tends to mold its raw material at the same time that it is molded. Thus, popular poet Manuel Camilo dos Santos' autobiography, written for his own pleasure, rather than commercial gain, casts him as a *folheto* hero. Battling "sickness and persecution, loss and affliction, suffering and hardship" in a manner wholly foreign to the way he describes his life in conversation, the author becomes, largely despite himself, a model of *firmeza* the minute he begins to write. The fact that the same writer may turn out *cordel* stories, which reflect one world view, and *canções* or songs for the radio, which clearly reveal another, is yet another proof of the power exerted by the actual form.[13]

Then, too, not only poets have shaped their lives according to literary molds. The noted outlaw Antônio Silvino was, for instance, an amateur *repentista*. His first run-in with the man whom he was to murder in revenge for the death of his own father occurred during a poetic contest between the two. Once denounced by the authorities, the bandit went on to construct his public image around ideal models of the renegade found in the *cordel* while at the same time providing *folheto* authors with fuel for new stories. Even President Getúlio Vargas may have had an eye upon popular traditions when he chose August 24 for his dramatic suicide. His sense of timing was not lost on the many *cordel* poets who began their accounts of his death by solemnly confronting their readers with this new "proof" that the devil runs wild on St. Bartholomew's Day.[14]

And yet if the *cordel* is much more than a simple mirror, it is certain that the six-step sequence characterizing most *folhetos* bears a profound relationship to the community which these stories serve. The concept of a pact and the stress upon *firmeza* which underlie this pattern are only the most obvious indications of the *cordel*'s debt to a larger context.[15] As

13. I am grateful to Manuel Camilo dos Santos for showing me a manuscript of his *A Vido de um Poeta* in an interview in Campina Grande, Paraíba, on March 6, 1978.

14. There is a reference to Silvino singing the *desafio* in Gustavo Barroso, *Almas de lama e de aço* (São Pãulo: Melhoramentos, 1930), pp. 81–82. I am grateful to Linda Lewin for supplying this information; see her "Oral Tradition and Elite Myth: The Legend of the 'Good' Thief Antonio Silvino in Brazilian Popular Culture," paper read at Popular Dimensions of Brazil: A Symposium; in the *Journal of Latin American Lore* 6 (1980): 5–53. According to Stanley Robe ("The Devil and Saint Bartholomew," paper read at American Folklore Society meetings, Salt Lake City, October 22, 1978), the belief that the devil roams over the earth on Saint Bartholomew's Day, August 24, in various parts of Spanish America and in Spain goes back to the ancient Romans, who thought that the gates to the nether regions were opened on certain days to permit the souls of the dead to flee. One of these days was August 24, designated the feast of Saint Bartholomew in the eighth century. Thus, the escape of the devil from captivity appears to have been equated with the release of pagan souls from Hades.

15. See Linda Dégh, "Some Questions of the Social Function of Story-Telling," *Acta Ethnographica*, 6 (1957): 91–146. For further suggestions on an artwork's relationship to

evident in the *folhetos* presented in this study, *cordel* stories rely on a series of two-way ties, which, while highly stylized, are not unlike those described by social scientists. In the case of *HR* tales, this alliance is horizontal. Though the equal or near-equal participants in this sort of *peleja* exchange insults rather than beans, money, or labor, they do so in accord with definite rules, which guarantee that there will be no irreversible loss or gain. The *peleja* itself is nothing other than a special exercise in generalized reciprocity involving a series of carefully chosen words. If *X* lists all the planets, *Y* must rattle off the constellations. If *A* suddenly changes the meter from a *décima* to a *sextilha*, *B* must follow suit. As in other kinds of horizontal exchanges, these participants have certain rights and duties toward each other, which each makes a conscious decision to honor so long as the *peleja* lasts. The pact can be broken if either lapses into prose or steps beyond implicit bounds with certain kinds of insults, which will be met not with a verbal but a violent, physical response. Both parties must be satisfied before the contest can end in a draw.

HW, *DR*, and *DW* stories feature a series of unequal one-to-one exchanges recalling other vertical relationships found in the society at large. *DR* and *DW* tales, which account for the majority of *folhetos*, inevitably cast the inferior member of the alliance as their protagonist. Regardless of whether this individual is a king or fisherman, his position vis-à-vis the other, divine partner is inferior. The rich and powerful hero may therefore play the same role as the subsistence farmer, who is always on the botton in everyday life.

The story itself can usually be seen as a trial, which the protagonist may either pass or fail. If the individual is humble but courageous and steadfast in his obligations to the superior partner, he or she passes and is suitably rewarded. If he or she manifests rebelliousness in the form of deceit, unwillingness to render service, or cowardice, punishment ensues. Only very rarely is there any sort of middle road. When the superior partner is not God, he or (rarely) she serves as His representative, often acting as judge. The landowner who stubbornly denies the poor but virtuous young man his lovely daughter may therefore hand her over once her suitor has proven himself, thereby admitting him into the ranks of the powerful and wealthy.

In *HW folhetos*, the errant authority figure is chastised through shame and/or material loss. As previously indicated, these persons are small-time shopkeepers, soldiers, tax collectors, priests, and other persons more

---

the community to which it belongs, see Alan Dundes, "Texture, Text, and Context," *Southern Folklore Quarterly*, 28 (1964): 251–65; and Clifford Geertz, *The Interpretation of Cultures* (New York: Basic Books, 1973), especially Chapter 8, "Ideology as a Cultural System," pp. 193–233, and Chapter 6, "Ritual and Social Change: A Javanese Example," pp. 142–69.

closely related to the middle sector than the ruling elite. Thus, while the poet ridicules these figures for failing to live up to their obligations, their downfall represents a somewhat muted criticism of the status quo. Indeed, the inferior partner often gives his nouveau riche or petty bourgeois ally his comeuppance precisely because he does not know how to act like a true authority figure. As Forman explains, while workers tend to admire and respect old-style patrons, they often "despise and fear those of their peers who shoulder them aside and now look back mockingly."

Cordel stories not only offer paradigms for different sorts of exchanges but also provide a series of detailed role models. King Vrixadarba in José de Souza Campos' *The King, the Dove, and the Sparrowhawk* is, as we have seen, a walking model of *firmeza*. Interestingly enough, he also satisfies all of the requirements for a good landlord outlined by anthropologists.

A comparison of the major characteristics outlined by Johnson in his study, *Sharecroppers of the Sertão*, with a half-dozen stanzas from José's story reveals a striking similarity between the king and ideal landowner.[16] Though presented as "the great king of Benares," Vrixadarba would be equally at home on a *fazenda* in Pernambuco or Ceará. His concern for his dependents' material and spiritual welfare insures not only his own prosperity but their security. In the following comparison, the stanzas from the *folheto* do not follow in the same order as the original, and the emphases are mine.

IDEAL TRAIT	FOLHETO
First, a landlord should be a powerful man, holding an elite position in society. After all, one of his ideal qualities is the ability to protect his dependent workers; and the more powerful and important he is, the better he can do this.	*He was beloved by everyone* *in his beautiful nation.* Poor men respected him, *rich men listened to him* because of his just nature and good heart.
Second, a landlord must have a quality expressed by the Portuguese word *moral*. By this the *moradores* [tenants] mean that he insists upon and receives deference, respect, and obedience. . . .	The kings of other nations came to visit him, and he never appeared tired of receiving whoever arrived. *His ministers followed* *his every order.*
Next, a good landlord assumes responsibility for the health and well-	*His chief interests were* *looking out for the poor,*

16. Johnson, *Sharecroppers of the Sertão*, pp. 125–27.

being of his workers and their families.

A good landlord also makes money and food available to the *moradores* during the very difficult period just before the harvest begins, and during the periodic drought years.

In the same vein, a good *fazendeiro* is reliable—especially when he says he will loan money to a *morador*, or pay him what he owes him.

Finally, a good landlord is willing to spend the money and effort to make his *fazenda* beautiful and something to be proud of.

cultivating his lands,
keeping an eye on his wealth,
counseling members of every social class,
and getting along well with the nobles.

Finding themselves in difficulty,
thousands of creatures call on me
and encounter help
in my strong arm.
I would give my fortune
to save a life.

"Be calm, divine bird—
no one will rise against you,
I have promised to protect you
from all evil
and the king of Benares
keeps his word."

He cared for his animals,
and admired the crops in the fields,
expressing gratitude for the good fortune
bestowed by protective hands.
He smiled to see the fauna of
the beguiling birds.

This example, while particularly clear, is in no way unusual. José's king represents the ideal authority figure, but other *folhetos* portray equally exemplary workers. Although, for instance, the fisherman in Apolônio Alves dos Santos' *Serginho* story appears only briefly, he does everything a model worker should. First, he has all the right sentiments, which cause him to be "suffused with grief" upon discovering the body of the murdered child. His willingness to walk "almost ten miles" to the nearest police station where he proceeds to report the tragedy proves both his respect for authority and his capacity for sacrifice. Thus, one personage commands, while the other exhibits deference, but both are clearly models of *firmeza*. Villains such as the sparrowhawk and Radio Joe are the epitome of *falsidade*.

The reader who takes the trouble to count the number of times the word *firmeza* and *falsidade* or their synonyms appear in a given *folheto* will be suitably impressed. The preoccupation with loyalty may be seen as part of a larger concern for stability. Not surprisingly, *folheto* actors fear deception more than death. In the old story of *Rose White, or the Fisherman's*

Daughter, for example, the heroine wavers in marrying the handsome young hero "because you are rich / and may therefore leave me / to love a rich woman / abandoning me without the least feeling / and I prefer to die / rather than have that happen."[17]

The poet not only champions *firmeza* while decrying *falsidade* but seeks above all to set up a sort of moral cause and effect. His characters are therefore embodiments of good and evil, which the six-step sequence then puts into play. If steps 1 (cause) and 6 (effect) are often essentially illustrations of one or both qualities, steps 2, 3, 4, and 5 portray a contest in which they reveal themselves through action. At heart, a *cordel* story is a moral question whose answer becomes evident through a largely ritual narrative process.

The fact that the reader knows that good will triumph does not diminish his interest in the particulars of the struggle, which serves to reaffirm a spiritual order, of which most persons find little proof in daily life. These individuals may take consolation in the poet's assurance that, in the *folheto* if nowhere else, "falsehood never helps anyone / and honor and loyalty are always rewarded." By attributing natural disasters to men's and women's errant behavior rather than mere chance or even fate, the *cordel* implies that its readers have at least limited control over their lives. Thus, though ephemeral suffering may afflict the good man, he is sure to pull through just as the villain is equally sure to meet a fitting, and usually violent, end. Moreover, in insisting that the universe is closed ("when one laughs, another cries"), the poet further limits the play of chance. Given many readers' chronic insecurity, the notion that both good and evil are finite and that human life has been "measured out beforehand" in accord with one's own conduct does not cause dismay but rather a certain relief. The *folheto* appeals to the buyer largely because it offers him a world at once familiar and happily different from the one he knows.[18]

The obvious relationship between certain valuative aspects of *cordel* stories and the oppressive social system in which these stories play a part has led some observers to dismiss them as a form of alienation. Many have suggested that they function like certain religious principles, as a tool of the elite. There is no doubt that, on an explicit level, the *folheto* reinforces poor people's sense of impotence and obligation to superiors, legit-

17. Luís da Costa Pinheiro, *História de Rosa Branca ou a Filha do Pescador* (Juazeiro do Norte, 1976).

18. James L. Peacock addresses this problem of the relationship between an art form steeped in certain values which people do not find corroborated elsewhere and the realities of everyday life in his *Rites of Modernization: Symbolic and Social Aspects of Indonesian Proletarian Drama* (Chicago: University of Chicago Press, 1968). His last chapter, "Symbolic Action and Society: Rites of Modernization," pp. 234–55, has particular relevance to this section.

imizing and thus perpetuating their inferior position. *Folheto* heroes make no attempt to change the society that would exclude them, choosing instead to trick or battle their way through its locked and gleaming doors. By willfully glossing over the contradictions all too apparent in day-to-day relationships, the *cordel* provides false hope. In attributing human suffering to some preordained *sina*, the *folheto* limits the options of the chronically oppressed to patient suffering. Its tendency to champion harmony at any cost has prompted writers like Gramsci to assert that such popular art forms "substitute and at the same time nurture the common man's tendency to fantasize," leading him to "sleep with open eyes." Mandrou concludes his study of French chapbook literature of the seventeenth and eighteenth centuries with the affirmation that these booklets represent "above all, an evasion." [19]

And yet despite its more reactionary aspects, the *folheto* resists reduction to a moral, religious, or political tract. The reliance of these stories on symbols not only allows but often obligates them to deal on not just one but several levels with their readers' poverty and humiliating impotence. If, on one hand, the author provides a convenient rationale for suffering, on the other, he strings together stories full of hidden, when not largely unconscious, meanings. Routine statements of principle are interspersed with bursts of rage and passion. Solemn moral lessons reveal glints of individual as well as collective dreams. Beneath the frozen surface of the most pious stories, one glimpses obscene gestures, the sudden clenching of a fist.

Although the principles reiterated time and again in *folhetos* are fundamental to their understanding, these statements represent only one aspect of a more comprehensive whole. The most superficially conservative *folhetos* may thus contain within them oppositions that explain much of their appeal as well as their artistic force. Often as a result of the pull between a poet's desire to say what people want to hear and his own flights of fantasy ("inspiration"), these contradictions are not recognized on a conscious level by either reader or writer. Some of these discrepancies do not appear odd to them. Others, potentially threatening to either their concept of how things ought to be or to their material security, are summarily dismissed.

The poet, for his part, tends to brush aside all questions relating to these undercurrents. "What does the story mean? It means just what it says." But these tales are not just *what* the author says; they are also *how* he says this. If a prince explicitly praises brotherhood, his words must certainly

---

19. Antonio Gramsci, *Arte e folklore* (Rome: Newton Compton Editore, 1976), p. 180; Robert Mandrou, *De la culture populaire aux 17ᵉ et 18ᵉ siècles* (Paris: Stock, 1964), p. 163.

be noted. If he does so with his foot upon an enemy's neck, this is just as, if not more, important.[20]

The complex nature of the *cordel*, and indeed popular art in general, makes it more elusive than many critics suggest. Bollème's reply to Mandrou's judgment of French pamphlet literature reveals a particular sensitivity to its multiplicity. "Escapist literature?" she asks.

> Yes, that idea has been frequently expressed. But [this literature is escapist] to the extent that it is a substitute for action, a mode of projection, of projecting oneself into a multitude of other actions, to the extent that the discourse is a discourse which distances itself from reality, a magic discourse which is always a prescription against, a prescription for: for repelling death, fear, misery, and which, if it creates another world also attempts at the same time and through this very process to improve and conquer this one.[21]

If underlying tensions characterize the *cordel* in general, they are certainly obvious in the three examples presented in this study. Although a number of these points have already been noted, it is worth mentioning them once again in order to make their common features clearer. In his *The King, the Dove, and the Sparrowhawk*, for example, José de Souza Campos champions the ideals of hierarchy and order. His king is not only a supreme authority upon whom his dependents can rely but a model of patient resignation. His exemplary treatment of the dove who begs his protection apparently proves beyond a doubt that while "the just suffer on earth," they are "accepted by God."

And yet a genuine question triggers this rather routine affirmation. In fact, the *folheto*'s first few stanzas are strongly tinged with doubts which an apparently rote request for inspiration cannot wholly mask. Although José worries that his request for "an easier existence" may be a sin, he admits to feeling "exhausted by the struggle." Although he does assert that "the truth" continues to defend him, this is only after completing a lengthy catalogue of ills. Before finally declaring that right is on his side, he complains about his health, his family obligations, and his financial woes. "The epoch itself defies me," he notes unhappily.

His initial response to these problems is closer to revolt than pious resignation. "I have a desire to one day / give poverty a swift kick," José says, "take on new courage, / put an end to hesitation, / embrace elegance / and assure myself wealth." Only after this detailed unburdening, a far

---

20. See Mary Douglas, *Implicit Meanings: Essays in Anthropology* (London: Routledge & Kegan Paul, 1975).

21. Geneviève Bollème, *La bibliothèque bleue: Littérature populaire en France du XVIIᵉ au XIXᵉ siècle* (Paris: Juilliard, 1971), pp. 24–25.

cry from the patient resignation he will prescribe in the ensuing story, does an inner voice command him to recount "the blessed fate" of the virtuous monarch.

The act of telling the story apparently answers his initial question. He deciphers the tale in the last stanzas of the *folheto* for both the reader and himself. "That sparrowhawk," he asserts, "was one / of Satan's angels, / and the divine little dove / was the dove of peace / who came to earth to demonstrate / the ways of the just." His doubts, however, may not have totally vanished. "Jehovah, holy name," the poet concludes with telltale emotion, "seed of greatest good, / just and gracious ruler / and unifier, / watch over my life! / *I love you and no one else*" (emphasis mine).

A somewhat different kind of moralistic overkill characterizes Apolônio Alves dos Santos' account of the Serginho murder. In this case, the poet carefully lays the ground for his final plea for justice by introducing the kidnapping in the very first stanza as "the blackest crime / which has ever occurred in our nation." The bereaved parents' suffering not only unites the community of Bom Jesus but draws in the audience as well. By painting the murderer as both a cold-blooded and unrepentant villain, the poet rouses the reader's ire to the degree that by the end of the story most individuals are ready to rush out into the streets to lynch Radio Joe with their own hands. Tellingly, the final stanzas are not a prayer for the dead child's soul but a plea for retribution. Just as the sparrowhawk's punishment provides an ominous warning in José de Souza Campos' story, so Apolônio ends by censuring the villain. "I beg Divine Justice / of the Omnipotent Judge," declares the poet. "May He severely punish / the murderous monster / who bathed his evil hands / in the blood of an innocent child."

This denunciation of a particular murder reflects a more generalized sense of contained rage at injustice pervading the *cordel*. The reader who wonders if this story may not be a fluke has only to look through other *folhetos* by this author and by others. In *The Northeasterners in Rio and the Deserted Northeast*, for example, Apolônio directs his anger in similar fashion at a group of landowners who, if they are not outright murderers, are as heartless as Radio Joe. Once again he gives a detailed account of the sufferings of the upright and courageous victims, declaring that "there are many heads of families / who live by renting themselves out." These persons "continue to work, hungry / sick and self-sacrificing / in order to give their children / a shrunken, bitter bread." [22]

22. Apolônio Alves dos Santos, *Os Nordestinos no Rio e o Nordeste Abandonado* (Rio de Janeiro: Ministério de Eduçãcao e Cultura, 1978). It is interesting to note that the original title referred to the Northeast as "failed" (*fracassado*) instead of "abandoned" (*abandonado*) but that Apolônio changed it out of fear that his compatriots would take offense and thus not buy the *folheto*.

As in the *Serginho* story, the villain, identified as "the accursed sugar mill owner," is fully conscious of his misdeeds. In both cases, the victim is ultimately not an individual or family but an entire community in whose name the poet goes on to call for vengeance. Thus, this *folheto* ends with a cryptic allusion to the reversals promised at the end of the world ("much salt [tears], few words") followed, as in the *Serginho* tale, with a call to God not only to look over the faithful but to blast their enemies.

Finally, in the case of Rodolfo Coelho Cavalcante's *Tereza Batista*, the author, like José and Apolônio, identifies with the underdog. Despite her dubious identity as a prostitute, Tereza becomes a symbol for all those who suffer. The unfortunate circumstances in which she lives do not stop her from playing a role structurally similar to that of King Vrixadarba or Serginho's grieving parents. Admitting that "society" forces Tereza to follow a path which she would not have otherwise chosen, Rodolfo insists that she respond not with patient resignation but by making "the world suffer as much / as it inflicted suffering on her."

Tereza's success in hitting back at those who would compromise her prompts "even no-goods" to weep on the day of her death. Ultimately, it is this capacity for vengeance, not the heroine's sweetness or compelling beauty, which makes her a candidate for sainthood, whose "familiar name / and grievous drama" live on in the populace's heart. Like José, who admits that he is "worn out" and "disheartened," Rodolfo is "tired of battle." He sees in Tereza not only the will and ability to act but a rare and, therefore, all the more precious glimmer of hope for people like himself.

Even these few examples should illustrate how, in terms of values, the *cordel* may be reduced to a half-dozen propositions, each of which invites if not demands qualification. The following list suggests both the most important explicit statements made by popular poets and typical contradictions apparent in their stories.

1. *Spiritual things are more important than material concerns*, BUT *cordel* stories inevitably reveal a recurring and powerful interest in money. Granted, kings who "wouldn't give a poor man a penny if asked" are punished, and a person who "only has eyes for gold" is sure to meet an unhappy end. As the story of *The Balloon of Destiny or the Maiden on the Enchanted Isle* makes clear, money isn't everything. ("Why should I marry a princess just because she has three kingdoms and a duchy to boot?" the handsome young Durval demands of his parents.) Be this as it may, no *folheto* hero treks off into the world without first providing for his family in concrete terms. In *The Prisoner of Black Rock Castle*, for instance, Rodolfo jumps on the train to adventure only after making sure that his mother will be "well provided for / with money and good food, /

lacking nothing." Though billed as a highly spiritual experience, love is typically expressed in material terms. Thus, in *Rose White or the Fisherman's Daughter*, the poet feels justified to assert that "no love was ever as pure as Vitoriano's" on the basis of the hero's speed in dashing off to a furniture store to buy "an expensive piano and the most regal-looking crystal mirror" for the woman he wants to marry.[23]

Furthermore, spiritual relationships are frequently expressed in economic terms. In the above-mentioned *Black Rock Castle* story, the poet assures his readers that "Jesus paid Rodolfo / for all that he had suffered." Similarly, the hero, obligated to "pay back" either a right or wrong, proclaims that God is his bondsman (*fiador*). In *Juvenal and the Dragon*, the poet insists that "evil never gets anyone anything / but honor and fidelity / are always paid back in full." This means that although virtue is ostensibly its own reward, few purehearted heroes and heroines fail to live comfortably ever after. Thus, the farmboys who become king not only proclaim their desire to serve the community but invite "poor people for miles around" to the palace where they dance in the streets and "eat cakes for a whole week." Long-suffering protagonists such as Mariana in *Mariana and the Sea Captain* do not pray for their dead husbands' errant souls or thank God for their own delivery but instead rush home to pocket the tyrants' ill-gotten money.[24]

2. *Christ is our earthly guide whose teachings we must faithfully follow*, BUT the *folheto* has little use for so fundamental a Christian concept as forgiveness. To be sure, *cordel* stories routinely cast saints as actors. As is evident in *The King, the Dove, and the Sparrowhawk*, where the monarch has a vision of the cross, they are full of religious images and fervent prayers to Christ and the Virgin Mary.

However, *cordel* stories are, as we have seen in Apolônio's *Serginho*, full of cries for vengeance. In *The Death of Alonso and the Vengeance of Marina*, for example, Alonso's murderer, Braulino, spends a stanza or so reflecting on how he would prefer to forget his father's request for his victim's blood since "revenge is madness." Nevertheless, since he has promised to get back at Alonso, he stabs him just as soon as he finishes

23. João Martins de Ataíde, *O Balão do Destino ou a Menina da Ilha*, 2 vols. (Juazeiro do Norte, 1977), I, 11; João Martins de Ataíde, *O Prisioneiro do Castelo da Rocha Negra* (Juazeiro do Norte, 1976), p. 4; Pinheiro, *História de Rosa Branca*, p. 19.

24. Ataíde, *O Prisioneiro*, p. 46; João Martins de Ataíde, *Juvenal e o Dragão* (Juazeiro do Norte, 1978), p. 1; José Bernardo da Silva, *Mariana e o Capitão do Navio* (Juazeiro do Norte, 1976), *Literatura popular em verso: Antologia*, I (Rio de Janeiro: Fundacao Casa de Rui Barbosa/MEC, 1964) (hereafter cited as *Antologia*), p. 153. ("Mariana quando soube / disse para o capitão: / o negro Jorge morreu / partimos do Indostão / porque na riqueza dele / eu quero passar a mão.")

this brief soliloquy. The next twelve pages recount a particularly gory struggle between Braulino and Marina, in which the heroine asserts that the former's life is her inheritance, and his blood her gold, death itself being incapable "of making me forget my desire for vengeance."[25]

In reality, the *cordel* is full of examples of unmitigated violence. Usually, the high-minded victim's revenge is every bit as heinous as the original crime. In *The Monster, the Indian, and the Child*, for instance, the hero cheerfully chops off the fingers of the culprit's hand one by one "to make him realize / that there is a just God in Heaven." In *Evil in Return for Good*, a title ironically reminiscent of the New Testament injunction to turn the other cheek, Rosa invites a suitor who once jilted her to a wedding banquet. Although she has agreed to forgive him and become his wife, her promise turns out to be a ploy, which has the desired effect of driving him mad.[26]

Finally, pleas for forgiveness, while present, are usually singularly unconvincing. "I beseech you once more to pardon your brother," the long-suffering Alzira says to her husband, "a weak and sordid spirit / full of deceit, / a soul without conscience, / a body without heart!"[27]

3. *The world is divided into the good, who provide positive, and the bad, who provide negative models*, BUT some of the most memorable characters in the *cordel*, as in so much of literature, are rogues and villains. Although the godly live happily ever after and sinners roast in hell, this does not make at least some miscreants any less appealing. Few persons, for example, can remember anything about the suitably virtuous heroine of the previously mentioned *Mariana and the Sea Captain*, except her name, which they would probably also forget were it not part of the title. They are, however, full of information about Mariana's would-be suitor, the villainous black president, whose misdeeds they recount in much detail with obvious relish.

Then too, while the poet carefully undercuts roguish protagonists by making them physically unattractive children, an antihero such as Cancão de Fogo has plenty to say about a number of hallowed ideals. "Honor," he proclaims, "is nothing but a ridiculous trick / because the capitalist / never heeds the honorable person / and if you set honor on a scale in the marketplace / you will see that you get nothing for it." Thus, though no one wants to emulate a snub-nosed brat, the popularity of these stories indi-

25. Leandro Gomes de Barros, *A Morte de Alonso e a Vingança de Marina* (Juazeiro do Norte, 1975), p. 22.

26. Manuel d'Almeida Filho, *O Monstro, o Índio e o Menino* (Juazeiro do Norte, n.d.), p. 10; Leandro Gomes de Barros, *O Mal em Paga do Bem* (Juazeiro do Norte, 1976), p. 30.

27. Leandro Gomes de Barros, *Os Sofrimentos de Alzira* (Juazeiro do Norte, 1976), p. 22.

cates something quite other than outrage or disapproval of their antics.[28]

4. *Because the group is more important than the individual, love is less important than honor*, BUT many of the most successful *folhetos* are romantic adventure stories. Although solemnly asserting that "the roots of the tree of love are honor," the poet usually finds a way to satisfy the demands of both. In *Between Love and the Sword*, for instance, duty apparently poses an irremediable obstacle to love, but some careful footwork allows both to triumph in the end. Thus, in a plot worthy of a Golden Age honor play, a young man, José, is forced to murder his beloved's father but is forgiven by her when he attempts to take his own life to satisfy her ensuing thirst for vengeance.[29]

Even when honor triumphs over love, however, the poet often permits himself lyric passages, which undercut this end. For instance, while the author denounces the hero for his lack of courage in the last few pages of *Romeo and Juliet*, his preceding descriptions of the young lovers all but negate this final censure. "Romeo," he explains (too convincingly for his own good), "thought no more / of the oath which he had sworn to his aged father / because love is the droplet of water / which, when it falls upon our soul / causes the desire for vengeance / to fade like smoke." Few readers will find themselves impervious to the farewell in which the hero takes leave of the city surrounded by blue mountains where he "leaves his dreams," assuring Juliet that while he himself must go, "my heart remains with you."[30]

5. *Authority commands respect and loyal service*, BUT all hell breaks out in the *folheto* from time to time. It is true that parents, kings, and landowners are usually easily forgiven. Thus, Eduardo, in *A Night of Love*, who has suffered all his life because of his illegitimate birth, assures his errant though suitably repentant mother that she need not ask his pardon. Similarly, the once-perfidious Rosina in *The Tale of the Greek Slave* is pardoned by her stepdaughter, going on to live in model fashion "for her husband, castle, and nothing else."[31]

Instances of forgiveness, however, usually reflect quite special circumstances, such as direct blood ties. In other *folhetos*, authority may ultimately triumph, but is not necessarily sacrosanct. In the *Argument Between a Market Tax Collector and a Meat Vendor*, for example, a female

28. Leandro Gomes de Barros, **A Vida de Cancão de Fogo e o Seu Testamento* (Juazeiro do Norte, 1975), *Antologia*, p. 424.

29. José Camelo de Melo Resende, *Entre o Amor e a Espada* (Juazeiro do Norte, 1976), p. 1.

30. João Martins de Ataíde, *Romance de Romeu e Julieta* (Juazeiro do Norte, 1966), p. 28.

31. João Martins de Ataíde, *Uma Noite de Amor* (Juazeiro do Norte, 1974), p. 30, João Martins de Ataíde, *Romance do Escravo Grego* (Juazeiro do Norte, 1977), p. 48.

peddler, who refuses to pay a new tax, confronts the authorities who threaten to impound her store of cows' hooves and sheep's intestines. Incensed, the old woman and her cronies fall upon the soldiers responsible for keeping order, attacking them with animals' hooves. When a priest attempts to dissuade them, they invade the church. In the end, a new mayor suspends the tax, and the peddlers go about their work in peace. Nevertheless, before calm descends, the poet has filled three of his eight pages with a description of the women's rampage amidst a series of plaster saints. Although some persons would argue that the *folheto* merely endorses the status quo by giving vent to hostile feelings which it then smoothes over, it is not certain that the final, pacific stanza can balance all that has gone before.[32]

Similarly, though *Midnight in the Cabaret* begins and ends with a denunciation of the derelicts whom the poet then allows to speak, their individual statements betray his disapproving introduction. The thief robs to feed his starving children; the gambler has to rely on games of chance to feed his aged mother; the prostitute has become "a human spittoon" after being seduced and abandoned at the age of fourteen. "It was the courts who sealed my fate," explains the man who murdered to avenge his daughter's honor, "and only when an honest man / comes to rule this world / will truth descend / and will money cease to be / synonymous with justice." Thus, although the poet dutifully interjects periodic jabs at these supposed sinners, it is difficult for the careful reader to see them as anything but victims.[33]

6. *One has no control over one's destiny*, BUT the poet and his public know exactly how any given story will turn out. "The future is veiled / like a snowy horizon," the poet may say, but if the exact manner in which good will win out is often unclear, its ultimate triumph is certain. Although "life and destiny / are mysteries of Nature," no *folheto* writer allows the villain to ride away with the lovely princess or the courageous young man to fail. Instead, he starts his tale with an assertion of principles: "Who reads this story / from beginning to end / will see that falsehood / always fails," or "Don't confide / in money and power / and therefore go about doing evil / and everything that you please / because the person who thinks this way / will surely suffer tomorrow."[34]

Fate provides a convenient motive and explanation but is not a true unknown. There is really no chance, for instance, that the young monarch in *The Prince Who Was Born Destined to Die by Hanging* is going to end

32. Manuel de Assis Campina, *Discussão entre um Fiscal e uma Fateira* (n.p., n.d.).
33. João Martins de Ataíde, *Meia Noite no Cabaret* (Juazeiro do Norte, 1974), p.7.
34. Ataíde, *O Balão do Destino*, p. 1.

up dangling from a tree.[35] Instead, fate provides the limits within which the poet works, as well as a degree of short-term suspense. It is not only a handy motivation but a necessary explanation of why a virtuous protagonist should suffer. Significantly, the ways of destiny never run counter to the six-step pattern and indeed confirm it by providing the necessary test situation (step 2).

In reality, the concept of destiny is an intimate part of a larger idea of limited good found in many peasant societies. The idea that not only material goods but emotions exist in short supply is a constant throughout the *cordel*. Love, for instance, must always be first love since were it not, some of the available store would have been exhausted. The concept of limited good is also responsible for repeated insistences on the interrelatedness of all beings. Because life "is one great whole," it follows that "when one rises, another falls, / when one dies, another lives / and when one smiles, another suffers." Thus, one does indeed have some control over one's destiny, if only by making sure that one beats out all other contenders for whatever is at stake. Though insisting on "life's grand design," the poet manipulates the pieces which constitute it through a series of ritual reversals aimed at insuring the poor but deserving man's inevitable triumph.[36]

Looking back over the preceding propositions as a whole, we can see that the *folheto* is in no way simple. Students of Brazilian popular culture have tended to view *cordel* stories as a source of information, entertainment, and moral and religious instruction. Some have also underlined the importance of "the aesthetic element," by which most mean the poet's pleasure in creation. As art in the fullest sense, however, the *cordel* encompasses and transcends these narrower goals. Despite their highly programed nature, many stories are profoundly ambiguous. If *folheto* authors obey time-honored guidelines in a more or (usually) less conscious manner, they also admit their dependence on a poetic "star," which remains beyond their control.

The fact that a recognizable six-step scheme underlies and in part defines the *cordel* tradition does not mean that it, like so many other forms of folk and popular culture, allows no room for individual creation or specific communal concerns. Although *folhetos* are predictable from many viewpoints, the poet remains free to incorporate a variety of unexpected

35. João Martins de Ataíde, *O Príncipe que Nasceu com a Sina de Morrer Enforcada* (Recife, n.d.).

36. See George Foster, "Peasant Society and the Image of Limited Good," *American Anthropologist*, 67 (1965): 293–315.

or contradictory elements. So long as he respects certain fundamentals, he can embroider or undercut at will. Thus, during a conversation I had with Olegário Fernandes about a new *folheto* he was writing, he told me about three-quarters of the story before stopping in midstream. "So what happened next?" I asked, but he refused to say. "You told me last week that you always know how a *cordel* story is going to end," he informed me. "Well, if you're so smart, then here's your chance to show it!"[37]

The *folheto*'s variety and often surprising freedom explains more than any other factor its continued survival in the midst of rapid change. Able to incorporate a two-thousand-year-old Buddhist parable, a local news event, or a recent best-selling novel with equal ease, the poet continues to write stories that mean something to the people who read them, that touch them in a way that other forms of entertainment do not. For all his interest in making a meager living, the *folheto* author does not toss them off in the same spirit as a writer of pulp novels. The reader does not throw away a *cordel* booklet he has finished reading like the Sunday supplement but hands it to a friend or slips it into a special drawer. The petty official flips through a stack of *cordel* stories with impatience, trying to pinpoint what annoys him in these "ingenuous" tales of saints and dragons. Were the *folheto* not full of disguised and yet transparent meanings, were it not imbued with what Miguel Arraes, former governor of Pernambuco, once called "the science of life's suffering," it would not have this power to console, inspire, and disturb.[38]

Today the world's most vital heir to a rich tradition once encompassing most of Europe, these stories on a string are also a peculiarly regional and now national phenomenon. Faithful to a particular pattern that distinguishes them in part from other representatives of the same heritage, they elude the very structures upon which they rely. A cry for justice as well as a steady murmur of oppression, the *cordel* is first and foremost poetry. "You know," says Rodolfo Coelho Cavalcante,

> I've learned a lot from reading all these books by scholars. But when they start talking about us poets as descendants of medieval minstrels marching around Europe with those funny hats and bells, then I have to disagree. They say that the *folheto* was born somewhere in Portugal, but I say that it's Northeastern, that it was invented right here. No, sir, the *cordel* has its roots in the very soil on which you and I are standing. Really now, I ask you, what could be more Brazilian?[39]

37. Olegário Fernandes, Caruaru, Pernambuco, May 19, 1978.
38. Miguel Arraes, "O que é o MCP," 1961. "MCP" stands for Movimento de Cultura Popular or "Popular Culture Movement." The quotation is reproduced but not further identified in Ivan Maurício, Marcos Cirano, and Ricardo de Almeida, *Arte popular e dominação*, 2nd ed. (Recife: Editora Alternativa, 1978), p. 96.
39. Rodolfo Coelho Cavalcante, Salvador, Bahia, June 5, 1978.

Appendices

Appendix A: Notes on Artists, Writers, and Other Educated Persons Interviewed

The persons listed below, many of whom are quoted in this study, have all demonstrated one or another kind of concrete interest in the *cordel* tradition. I have noted only those individuals with whom I had serious recorded conversations or who sent me written responses to a standard questionnaire. Thus, while I benefited from brief exchanges with a number of other persons (Jorge Amado, Carybé, Gilberto Freyre, etc.) their names do not appear here.

Most interviews were conducted in people's offices or homes. Whenever possible, I asked the individuals to fill out a two-page form beforehand so that I could prepare more specific questions before interviewing them in person. However, I also had a number of on-the-spot conversations in cars, in restaurants, and in back-stage dressing rooms.

Although the persons listed here are associated primarily with the arts, they represent a variety of personal backgrounds and occupations. The reader will find here the name of Antônio Houaiss, the Brazilian translator of James Joyce's *Ulysses*, as well as those of Mário Lago, a soap opera writer, and Eduardo Hoornaert, a priest.

There are persons missing from this list (poet João Cabral de Melo Neto, filmmaker Glauber Rocha, comic strip designer Jô Oliveira, playwright Alfredo Dias Gomes, etc.) whom I would have liked to interview. However, the names included here should give some sense of the *cordel*'s present audience.

Despite the fact that some of these individuals know a great deal about popular poetry, I did not set out to talk to "experts." Rather, I was interested in interviewing almost anyone who had some demonstrated connection to the tradition, whether this was an article, a series of *cordel*-related paintings, or an extensive collection of *folhetos*. Some of these persons have a deeper relationship with the tradition than others, but few if any would call it their primary concern.

Each entry begins with the person's name, followed by one or more general self-designated occupational labels such as "professor," "actor," or "dentist." The date and place of the interview or where the questionnaire was completed follow. Should this place be different from the person's present residence, I have consistently noted this fact. As with popular poets (Appendix B), almost all of these interviews took place in either the Rio de Janeiro-São Paulo area or in a limited section of the Northeast. (See map, page xvii.) Finally, I have included a brief description designed to emphasize the heterogeneity as well as common features of the group. Cross-references to this appendix as well as to Appendix B are indicated by a single (Appendix A) or double (Appendix B) asterisk before the person's name.

A brief note on Portuguese alphabetization may be in order. In every case, the very last name is considered first, then the very first name is used, then the second, and so on (for example, João Pereira de Andrade would be listed before Joaquim Alves Andrade). The only names which do not count are family indicators such as *Filho*, *Júnior*, *Maior*, *Neto*, and *Sobrinho* ("son," "junior," "senior," "grandson," and "nephew").

Aderne, Isa. Graphic artist. November 22, 1977, Rio de Janeiro.
Born in Cajazeiras, Paraíba, Isa Aderne began designing *folheto*-like blockprints in the 1960s. Many of these prints are stylized treatments of specifically Northeastern themes, such as the puppet plays called *mamulengo* and local saints like St. Joseph of the Rains. She presently works with a program sponsored by *Paulo Grisolli's Department of Culture geared to acquaint children with a series of popular traditions. Her current interests include photography and films.

Alencar, Edigar de. Journalist, writer. November 18, 1977, Rio de Janeiro.
A native of Ceará, Edigar de Alencar works for the Rio daily *O Dia (The Day)*. He is the author of some fifty articles and *crônicas* (a journalistic genre closely associated with Rio de Janeiro) about the *literatura de cordel*. The author of a number of books of poetry, he has also written studies on Carnival and the history of the samba.

Almeida, Átila de. Mathematician. March 4, 1978, Campina Grande, Paraíba.
Professor of mathematics at the Federal University of Campina Grande, Átila de Almeida became interested in the *cordel* some twenty years ago when his father, *Horácio de Almeida, asked him to collect "all the *folhetos* he could find." The author of a number of short stories, he has published a comprehensive dictionary of popular poets and singers with *repentista* **José Alves Sobrinho. He has also devised a system of dating procedures for *folhetos*.

Almeida, Horácio de. Lawyer, historian. October 31, 1977, Rio de Janeiro.
Born in Areia, Paraíba, Horácio de Almeida is one of a small number of historians who have written specifically about his native state. With the help of his son *Átila de Almeida, he has assembled a collection of over 3,500 *folhetos*, many not duplicated elsewhere. He wrote an introduction to the work of the popular poet Leandro Gomes de Barros published by the Casa de Rui Barbosa *folheto* research center.

Almeida, Mauro William Barbosa de. Student. December 13, 1977, Campinas, São Paulo.
Presently completing a master's degree in social sciences (anthropology and sociology) at the University of São Paulo, Mauro Barbosa became interested in the *cordel* over ten years ago. His concern for the *folheto* grew out of "an interest in ideological questions related to the lower classes." He is co-author with *Ruth Terra of a morphological analysis of the thirty-two page *romance*.

Altino, José. Graphic artist. April 4, 1977, João Pessoa, Paraíba.
A printmaker who relies heavily on the *folheto* tradition, José Altino has recently returned to the Northeast from Rio de Janeiro "because here I can watch and talk

to popular artists; here I am close to all that which nourishes my work." Associated with the Federal University of Paraíba, he is particularly concerned with the effects of a new middle-class public on the popular poet.

Andrade, Carlos Drummond de. Poet. October 20, 1977, Rio de Janeiro.
Originally from Minas Gerais but long a resident of Rio, Carlos Drummond de Andrade is Brazil's most outstanding contemporary poet. His work has been translated into at least a dozen foreign languages. During the time that he worked in the Radio Ministry of Education, he periodically bought *folhetos* at the entrance to the nearby Dom Pedro II railway station, building up an indexed collection of some 363 titles. The author of a half-dozen *crônicas* based on the *cordel*, he is interested first and foremost in these stories as poetry.

Arantes Neto, Antonio Augusto. Anthropologist. December 14, 1977, Campinas, São Paulo.
Professor of anthropology at the Federal University of Campinas, Antonio Augusto Arantes recently completed his doctorate at Cambridge University on "Some Sociological Aspects of the *Literatura de Cordel*." Admitting a certain fondness for the *cordel* as literature, he is interested above all in "the ideology which is expressed in it as well as in other forms of popular art."

Araújo, Iaponi Soares de. Painter. November 23, 1977, Rio de Janeiro.
Born on a cattle ranch in Rio Grande do Norte, Iaponi Araújo's enthusiasm for the *cordel* dates back to the early 1960s when he helped organize a museum of popular art in the state capital of Natal. Although stylistically quite separate from actual *cordel* blockprints, his paintings, which have been exhibited in many parts of Brazil, utilize a number of *folheto* themes and figures such as Saint Severino and José de Souza Leão.

Araújo, Nélson de. Researcher. June 9, 1978, Salvador, Bahia.
A member of the African Traditions Research Center of the Federal University of Bahia, Nélson de Araújo has actively studied a number of popular art forms. As part of a survey of popular theater in and around Salvador, he conducted a series of interviews with popular poet **Rodolfo Coelho Cavalcante, who worked for many years as an itinerant circus clown.

Baccaro, Giuseppe. Administrator, merchant. January 18, 1978, Olinda, Pernambuco.
An Italian by birth, Giuseppe Baccaro came to Brazil as an art merchant. He heads the foundation known as the Casa da Criança (Children's House Foundation) in Olinda, which also houses a technically unrelated Poets' Association. The foundation has bought a large number of unpublished *folheto* manuscripts within recent years.

Batista, Sebastião Nunes. Researcher. November 12, 1977, Rio de Janeiro.
The son of noted popular *cordel* author and poet-singer Francisco das Chagas Batista, Sebastião Nunes Batista was born in the state of Paraíba. Presently completing a university degree, he still identifies closely with popular poets. The owner of approximately two thousand *folhetos*, he has edited an anthology of

popular poets sponsored by Shell Oil and the José Augusto Foundation. He frequently collaborates on projects for the Casa de Rui Barbosa *folheto* research center.

Bello, Roberto. Psychologist. November 13, 1977, Rio de Janeiro.
Currently studying for his doctorate in psychology, Roberto Bello has accumulated close to two thousand *folhetos*. The author of a prize-winning essay on the wise hero in the *literatura de cordel*, he believes that these stories are necessarily complex "because our subconscious is in no way innocent or simple." He has never set foot in the Northeast but considers the *folheto* to be part of the heritage of all Brazilians.

Benjamin, Roberto. Professor. March 27, 1978, Recife, Pernambuco.
A specialist in the field of communications, Roberto Benjamin heads the Folklore Research Center at the Rural University in Recife. A tireless fieldworker, he has authored a number of studies of journalistic *folhetos* and is presently involved in research on the African-influenced Carnival street players known as *maracatus*.

Bezerra, João Clímaco. Administrator. November 15, 1977, Rio de Janeiro.
Born in Lavras da Mangabeira near Juazeiro do Norte in the state of Ceará, João Clímaco Bezerra is a journalist, professor of psychology, and writer, as well as an advisor to the National Confederation of Industry. He has written a number of stories and novels with a distinctly regional flavor. Once the owner of one of Brazil's largest *folheto* collections, he abandoned the *cordel* in dismay after termites destroyed several decades of work.

Borges, Francisca Neuma Fechine. Professor. May 11, 1978, João Pessoa, Paraíba.
Acting coordinator of the new Library of Popular Literature in Verse at the Federal University of Paraíba, Neuma Borges is preparing a master's thesis on the literary sources of the *cordel*. The library, which is associated with the Casa de Rui Barbosa, hopes to foster both national and international exchange.

Brandão, Theo. Researcher. December 1, 1977, Rio de Janeiro. Home: Maceió, Alagoas.
Author of a number of varied studies of the *cordel*, Theo Brandao is presently applying the classificatory tale types devised by folklorists Stith Thompson and Antti Aarne to a number of *folhetos* and orally transmitted stories. Owner of some of the oldest existing wax cylinder recordings of popular poets, he has an extensive *folheto* collection that is housed in the museum within the Federal University of Alagoas that bears his name.

Calasans, José. Historian. June 9, 1977, Salvador, Bahia.
A professor of history at the Federal University of Bahia, José Calasans has written a number of articles on popular poems about Antônio Conselheiro, leader of the backlands rebels whom the federal government was hard pressed to quell at Canudos in 1897.

Callado, Antônio. Novelist, writer. November 17, 1977, Rio de Janeiro.
A journalist and internationally known literary figure, Antônio Callado is the

author of the play *Celebration in the Cananéia Sugar Mill* (*Forró no Engenho Cananéia*), which reveals the impact of Northeastern popular poetry. The play was written after the author went as a reporter to Pernambuco in order to investigate the Peasant Leagues, a grassroots attempt at agrarian reform. Although Callado was born in the South, he considers the Northeast the most "Brazilian" part of the country and sees the *cordel* as a testimony to its inhabitants' creative force. "How ironic," he exclaims, "that the poorest part of the country should be the richest in terms of art!"

Campos, Maximiano. Administrator, writer. March 16, 1978, Recife, Pernambuco.
The brother of the late Renato Carneiro Campos, who was the author of one of the first studies on the ideology of the *folheto*, Maximiano Campos draws on the *cordel* and other popular traditions in his short stories and novels. Presently employed by the Joaquim Nabuco Research Institute founded by writer Gilberto Freyre, he retains vivid memories of his childhood on the family sugar plantation.

Cavalcanti, Manuel. Actor. October 1, 1977, Rio de Janeiro.
Long active in both film and theater, Manuel Cavalcanti grew up in Maceió, the capital of Alagoas. He is a poet and novelist and the owner of approximately two thousand *folhetos*, which he dusts from time to time with great care "because they are my memories."

Cavalcanti, Newton. Graphic artist. October 24, 1977, Rio de Janeiro.
Born in Pernambuco, Newton Cavalcanti grew up in the state of Bahia where his father, "not a poet, but a politician," was elected president of the Northeastern Minstrels' Society. The artist's interest in the *literatura de cordel* as well as various indigenous Brazilian myths is evident in his oil paintings, watercolors, chalk sketches, blockprints, lithographs, and designs for postal stamps. For him, the *folheto* is an assurance that Brazil "continues to exist" and that "we Brazilians are still ourselves and not, thank God, someone else."

Chaves, Xico. Poet. November 18, 1977, Rio de Janeiro.
Xico Chaves works in the audio-visual division of the state's Division of Cultural Affairs. A poet, he customarily prints his work in the *folheto* or broadside form both because this reduces publication costs and because he finds the form aesthetically appealing. A member of a group of young writers called Gypsy Cloud (*Nuvem Cigana*) devoted to poetry in oral performance, he has filled his home with popular "art objects" including Amazon Indian masks and baskets and a six-foot loaf of bread. "I thought," says the author, "that it was pretty, and now, even if I wanted to eat it, it has gotten much too stale!"

Correia, Marlene de Castro. Professor. November 10, 1977, Rio de Janeiro.
The daughter of a Northeasterner, Marlene de Castro Correia grew up in Rio de Janeiro. She teaches Brazilian literature at the Federal University of Rio de Janeiro and has written several articles on linguistic aspects of the *folheto*. One, entitled "The Poetic Flavor of the *Literatura de Cordel*" ("O Sabor Poético da *Literatura de Cordel*") was adapted to music by a group of Rio samba musicians.

Diégues Júnior, Manuel. Administrator. November 9, 1977, Rio de Janeiro.
Presently director general of the Department of Cultural Affairs for the national
Ministry of Education and Culture, Manuel Diégues was born in Alagoas. He is
professor of cultural anthropology at the Catholic University of Rio de Janeiro
and director of the Latin American Center for Research in the Social Sciences.
The author of a number of books and articles on the Northeast, he has also written
a detailed preface to a volume of *folheto* studies published by the Casa de Rui
Barbosa research center.

Diniz, Stênio. Graphic artist. April 4, 1978, Juazeiro do Norte, Ceará.
The grandson of popular poet and publisher José Bernardo da Silva, Stênio Diniz
grew up surrounded by *folhetos*. A young artist who now participates in shows
throughout Brazil, he has organized a successful artisans' collective in Juazeiro.
He continues to work in the *cordel* press now owned and managed by his mother
and has designed a large number of *folheto* covers. Although his brilliant T-shirts
and Afro hair style give him a distinctly cosmopolitan appearance, he retains a
deep sense of himself as a Northeasterner.

Dumoulin, Annette, and Terezinha Guimarães. Pastoral workers. April 3,
1978, Juazeiro do Norte, Ceará.
These two nuns do both social work and research in what many Northeasterners
still regard as the holy city of Juazeiro do Norte. The home of famed religious
leader, Padre Cícero, canonized by one Brazilian branch of the Roman Catholic
church within the last decade, Juazeiro attracts a steady stream of pilgrims. With
the support of the city's Father Murilo, the two women have done extensive interviews among these people. Although they are not interested in the *cordel* per
se, their first-hand knowledge of many forms of popular culture has enriched this
study.

Fausto Neto, Antônio. Professor. May 11, 1978, João Pessoa, Paraíba.
Professor of social sciences at the Federal University of Paraíba, Antônio Fausto
is the author of a study on the *literatura de cordel*. His central argument is that
"while the *folheto*'s language is truly popular, its content is not."

Fernandes, Francisco Ciro. Graphic artist. December 1, 1977, Rio de Janeiro.
Born in Uiraúna, Paraíba, to subsistence farmers, Ciro Fernandes had little formal
education. After emigrating to Rio de Janeiro, he began working for an advertis-
ing firm, going on to design a series of blockprints with Northeastern themes. He
soon became interested in the Rio-based *cordel* poets, for whom he has designed
a number of *folheto* covers which mingle popular and more sophisticated motifs.

Galvão, Gilberto. Student. November 12, 1977, Campinas, São Paulo.
A student of literature at the University of São Paulo, Gilberto Galvão also works
as a journalist and has written on subjects such as the poet-singer Patativa for
national publications. His interest in the *cordel* dates back over a decade. Owner
of a collection of over one thousand *folhetos*, he sees the *folheto* as above all "the
register of that which the Northeastern masses are thinking."

Grisolli, Paulo Affonso. Administrator. November 17, 1977, Rio de Janeiro.
Director general of the state of Rio de Janeiro's Department of Culture, Paulo
Affonso Grisolli is also a playwright, journalist, and television writer. He has
instituted a program of "cultural packages" designed to give new support to popular traditions within the state. His department recently celebrated National Book
Day with a program devoted to the popular poets, going on to print five *folhetos*
by each of the five participating authors.

Gullar, Ferreira. Poet, journalist. November 24, 1977, Rio de Janeiro.
Born José Ribamar Ferreira in São Luís, capital of the state of Maranhão, Ferreira
Gullar has recently returned to Brazil after a long period of exile. Now a writer
for the newspaper *O Estado de São Paulo*, his political views remain firm. During
the early 1960s, he published two long poems heavily influenced by the *literatura
de cordel*, *Who Murdered Aparecida? (Quem matou Aparecida?)* and *John Good-
Death, Brave Man Marked Out to Die (João Boa-Morte, Cabra Marcado Para
Morrer)*. He describes his present poetry as "the search for a way to create a
poetry based on popular art forms without simply copying these."

Houaiss, Antônio. Translator, writer. November 22, 1977, Rio de Janeiro.
The son of Lebanese immigrants, Antônio Houaiss has always been deeply involved in cultural affairs. A former diplomat and member of the Brazilian Academy of Letters, he has translated James Joyce's *Ulysses* into Portuguese. His
interest in the *folheto* as a linguistic and literary phenomenon began when he
worked on the catalogue for the Casa de Rui Barbosa collection in the late 1950s.
A small collection of *folhetos* given him by the father of poet João Cabral de
Melo Neto is now housed in the Casa de Rui Barbosa library.

Hoornaert, Eduardo. Priest. May 18, 1978, Recife, Pernambuco.
Author of a number of books and articles on popular religion, Father Eduardo
Hoornaert, a Belgian, has lived in the Northeast since 1958. Interested in the
cordel as "an expression of the oppressed," he has been active in reform-minded
Roman Catholic movements centered in Recife, home of internationally known
bishop Dom Helder Câmara.

Jorge Neto, Nagib. Writer, administrator. June 17, 1978, Recife, Pernambuco.
Best known for his short stories in which the *literatura de cordel* plays a major
role, Nagib Jorge Neto is fond of parody and social satire. Born in the state of
Maranhão, the author retains a strong feeling for the popular traditions associated
with his childhood. Formerly a journalist, he now works for a state development
agency.

Lago, Mário. Writer. November 15, 1977, Rio de Janeiro.
Author of sambas, soap operas, and popular songs, Mário Lago is enthusiastic
about the skill of the Northeastern poet-singer. His book *Chico Nunes of Alagoas*
tells the story of one such poet whom he met on a trip to the Northeast. A television writer, he has worked with at least one series based in part on the *literatura
de cordel*.

Lamas, Dulce Martins. Professor. October 20, 1977, Rio de Janeiro.
Professor of Brazilian musical folklore at the Federal University of Rio de Janeiro, Dulce Martins Lamas directs a research center for studies in the history of Brazilian music. She is the author of an essay on the music of the Northeastern poet-singers.

Leonardos, Stella. Poet, writer. November 17, 1977, Rio de Janeiro.
A translator as well as a writer, Stella Leonardos has published plays and prose pieces in addition to a number of volumes of poetry, which reflect her interest in the medieval ballad tradition. Secretary-general of the Brazilian Writers' Union of Rio de Janeiro, she is presently working on a book inspired by the *literatura de cordel*.

Lessa, Orígenes. Writer. November 15, 1977, Rio de Janeiro.
Born in the state of São Paulo, Orígenes Lessa spent part of his childhood in São Luís de Maranhão. One of the first writers of his generation to indicate an interest in the *cordel*, he published his first article on Northeastern popular poetry in 1954. Owner of one of the most extensive *folheto* collections in the world today (approximately five thousand titles), he is the author of a book-length study of President Getúlio Vargas as a protagonist in the *literatura de cordel* as well as a number of novels and short stories.

Lima, Jairo. Playwright. May 31, 1978, Recife, Pernambuco.
Jairo Lima grew up in the interior of Pernambuco. Author of two plays which draw heavily upon the *literatura de cordel*, *Cancão de Fogo* and *Lampião in Hell*, he takes pride in his success among a largely popular audience. Presently employed by a public relations firm, the author remains intensely interested in the relationship between "popular" and "erudite" art.

Marinho, Luiz. Playwright, banker. May 31, 1978, Recife, Pernambuco.
The author of a number of plays which draw on Northeastern traditions, Luiz Marinho has had an interest in popular culture for many decades and is most concerned with the linguistic aspect of the *folheto*.

Martins, Sílvia. Art gallery owner. March 22, 1978, Recife, Pernambuco.
Owner of the decade-old Nega Fulô Gallery (the name comes from a poem by Jorge de Lima), Sílvia Martins is proud of her "twenty-five years with popular art." The gallery specializes in pieces by regional artists, offering its customers paintings, sculptures, and ceramics, as well as a small number of *folhetos*. Together with two sociologist friends, Flávia Martins and Letícia Duarte, the owner has written a book entitled *Popular Sculptors from Bahia to Maranhão*, which includes interviews with 130 artists.

Maurício, Ivan. Publisher, journalist. June 21, 1978, Recife, Pernambuco.
Co-author of the book *Popular Art and Domination* (*Arte popular e dominação*), a case study of popular culture in Pernambuco between 1961 and 1977, Ivan Maurício believes that "documenting popular art does not mean saving it from anything." He asserts that for the urban masses, on whom his study concentrates,

popular art and "official" culture are not separate but exist in "a dialectical relationship."

Meier, Marlyse. Professor. December 11, 1977, Campinas, São Paulo.
Professor of literature at the universities in São Paulo and Campinas, Marlyse Meier became interested in the *cordel* after embarking on a study of the influence of Italian popular theater on eighteenth-century French drama. A course on Northeastern popular poetry with literary critic Manuel Cavalcanti Proença sharpened her sense of the affinities between the *folheto* and these European sources. She is presently researching the figure of Charlemagne in Northeast Brazilian popular poetry.

Melo, Veríssimo de. Researcher. November 1, 1977, Rio de Janeiro. Home: Natal, Rio Grande do Norte.
Adjunct professor within the Federal University of Rio Grande do Norte and founder of the Luís da Câmara Cascudo Museum, Veríssimo de Melo is the author of some sixty books and essays on folklore. The owner of an ample *folheto* collection, he has written a study of Northeastern popular poetry entitled *Poet-Singer* (*Cantador de viola*).

Mendonça, Luiz. Director, actor. October 15, 1977, Rio de Janeiro.
Director of the theatrical company Arrival (*Grupo Chegança*) and himself an actor, Luiz Mendonça has long had an interest in popular art forms including not only the *folheto* but the samba, the *pastoril* dance, and the festival known as *Bumba-meu-Boi*. Though his company performs a variety of plays, it specializes in texts based on Brazilian traditions and has done at least three plays related to the *literatura de cordel* within the last few years.

Mesquita, Samira Nahid de. Professor. November 4, 1977, Rio de Janeiro.
Professor of Brazilian literature at the Federal University of Rio de Janeiro, Samira Nahid de Mesquita describes her interest in the *cordel* as "both esthetic and ideological." She sees the *folheto* as a confirmation of "the necessity of poetry" regardless of economic conditions.

Nascimento, Braulio do. Administrator, scholar. November 16, 1977, Rio de Janeiro.
Director of the National Institute of Folklore, originally known as the Campaign for the Defense of Folklore, Braulio de Nascimento is an internationally known scholar with many distinguished contributions in the field of Luso-Brazilian balladry. He has also written a number of articles on the *literatura de cordel* and maintains a collection of some eight hundred *folhetos*.

Noblat, Ricardo. Journalist. March 1, 1978, Recife, Pernambuco.
A young journalist recently promoted to chief of the Salvador (Bahia) office of the Brazilian news magazine, *Veja*, Ricardo Noblat has written extensively about popular poets and poetry for a variety of publications. He is presently finishing a book intended as a general introduction to the *folheto*.

Nutels, Berta. Not stated. November 21, 1977, Rio de Janeiro.
The daughter of the late Noel Nutels, a multifaceted doctor known for his pioneer use of the *folheto* in public health education, Berta Nutels was kind enough to describe her father's work to me. His extensive collection of both *cordel* stories and indigenous artifacts remains in the Nutels' home in Rio de Janeiro.

Peregrino, Umberto. Professor, writer. November 16, 1977, Rio de Janeiro.
Born in Natal, Rio Grande do Norte, Umberto Peregrino is a retired general. Former director of the Army Library and the National Book Institute and today a professor at the Federal University of Rio de Janeiro's School of Communications, he is also a short story writer and journalist. Presently completing an extensive survey aimed at ascertaining the current state of the *folheto*, he has an extensive collection of the literature. He aims to turn his house situated on a hill above Rio de Janeiro into a center for the study and preservation of popular poetry.

Pereira, José Tarcísio. Bookstore owner. March 17, 1977, Recife, Pernambuco.
Owner of Recife's biggest bookstore, the Livro 7, with branches in Maceió and Campina Grande, José Tarcísio Pereira sells a small selection of *folhetos* as well as books. In 1974 and 1975, Livro 7 sponsored seminars on the *literatura de cordel* in which both popular poets and researchers were invited to participate. One edition of a literary magazine was published in *folheto* form. According to Tarcísio, current enthusiasm for the *cordel* reflects a more general interest in sociolinguistics and patterns of communication.

Pimentel, Altimar Alencar de. Administrator, writer. May 10, 1978, João Pessoa, Paraíba.
Related to the Batista family long known for its array of popular poets, Altimar Alencar de Pimentel studies popular art forms "perhaps to make up for the fact that I am not capable of writing *folhetos*!" Committed to making the Federal University of Paraíba a leader in folklore research, he is particularly interested in oral storytelling and puppet plays.

Pinheiro, Nevinha. Writer. November 22, 1977, Rio de Janeiro.
An employee of the National Institute of Folklore, Nevinha Pinheiro was born in the interior of Paraíba. She is presently completing a novel entitled *The Crucifixion of the Devil*, based on a series of themes taken from the *cordel* as well as other popular art forms.

Pinto, Aloysio de Alencar. Musician. November 18, 1977, Rio de Janeiro.
Composer of numerous musical pieces based in part on Northeast blindmen's songs, the poetic exchanges called *desafios*, and *benditos* or laments for the dead, Aloysio de Alencar Pinto works for the federal Department of Cultural Affairs. Born in Fortaleza, Ceará, he has been interested in the *literatura de cordel* since childhood and has directed a series of *folheto* recordings for the National Institute of Folklore.

Pontes, Mário. Journalist, writer. October 31, 1977, Rio de Janeiro.
A native of Novas Russas, Ceará, Mário Pontes works for the *Jornal do Brasil*. He has written articles for various journals on topics such as the presence of the

devil in the *folheto* and utopian aspects of the *cordel* tradition. As a child, he looked forward to the frequent visits of poet-improvisers and observes with a certain melancholy that the *cordel* today is "less and less a way of life and more and more the subject for university theses, most of them, by the way, idiotic."

Pontual, Roberto. Art critic. November 14, 1977, Rio de Janeiro.
Art critic for the *Jornal do Brasil* and author of an encyclopedic *Dictionary of Graphic Arts in Brazil*, which includes "popular" as well as "erudite" artists, Roberto Pontual became interested in the *literatura de cordel* after noting its influence on a number of contemporary artists. A native of Pernambuco, he is intrigued above all by "deep mythic structures" visible in reworkings of *cordel* material by nonpopular artists.

Proença, Ivan Cavalcanti. Writer. November 1, 1977, Rio de Janeiro.
The son of noted literary critic Manuel Cavalcanti Proença, who was coordinator of the catalogue of the Casa de Rui Barbosa *folheto* collection, Ivan Cavalcanti Proença is interested in not only the *folheto* but Brazilian popular music, American jazz, and soccer as forms of cultural expression. He has written a book about the underlying ideology of the *cordel* and is a professor of Brazilian literature at the Federal University of Rio de Janeiro.

Quaresma, Tânia. Filmmaker, photographer. November 13, 1977, Rio de Janeiro.
After working several years for a television station, Tânia Quaresma won a grant to study cinema in Germany. Her film *Cordel: Song and Improvisation* (*Cordel: Canção e Repente*) is a vivid, sensitive introduction to the popular culture of the Northeast. She is co-founder of a company, Trindade, dedicated to promoting a series of young Brazilian composers.

Queiroz, Rachel de. Writer. December 4, 1977, Rio de Janeiro.
The first woman member of the Brazilian Academy of Letters, Rachel de Queiroz is known for her regional novels, her literary *crônicas*, and her participation in numerous cultural activities. Born in the interior of Ceará, she still returns periodically to her family home. She has written an essay about the famous *repentista* Blind Aderaldo for the Casa de Rui Barbosa anthology.

Quinteto Armorial. Musicians. March 6, 1978. Campina Grande, Paraíba.
This group of musicians is composed of Antônio José Madureira, Antônio Carlos Nóbrega de Almeida, Edilson Eulálio, Fernando Torres Barbosa, and Antônio Fernandes. It is part of a larger movement associated with writer *Ariano Suassuna. Its members, who are interested in a variety of art forms, devote considerable time to informal fieldwork in specifically regional themes. The group's leader, Antônio José Madureira and its violinist, Antônio Carlos Nóbrega de Almeida, are composers as well as musicians. The members, who have made three records, have toured Brazil and visited the United States.

Quinteto Violado. Musicians. June 10, 1978, Recife, Pernambuco.
Like the Quinteto Armorial, this group of musicians—Luciano, Fernando, Toinho, Márcio and Zé da Flauta—utilizes folk and popular traditions while ap-

pealing to an essentially urban, middle-class audience. The Quinteto Violado has, however, a somewhat more cosmopolitan and commercial orientation than the Armorial group, and its music reveals the influence of contemporary Brazilian and American composers. Its members have made a number of highly successful records, staged shows in major cities throughout Brazil, and conducted an officially sponsored tour of the Pernambucan interior aimed at the very people from whom much of their raw material is taken.

Rocha, Pericles. Painter. November 21, 1977, Rio de Janeiro.
Pericles Rocha's canvases are full of fantastic serpents, headless mules, and enchanted birds. A native of Maranhão, the artist's fondness for the legends he heard as a child and for various regional festivals such as the *Bumba-meu-Boi* is evident throughout his work.

Samico, Gilvan. Graphic artist. March 8, 1978, Olinda, Pernambuco.
A printmaker and painter associated with the regional, folk-inspired movement known as the *Movimento Armorial*, Gilvan Samico turns out prints and canvases whose titles recall *folhetos*. His style reflects the influence of popular printmakers who, in turn, have happily reincorporated elements of his work.

Santos, Nélson Pereira dos. Filmmaker. November 25, 1977, Rio de Janeiro.
Head of Regina Films, Nélson Pereira dos Santos is one of the foremost filmmakers in Brazil today. Like fellow director Glauber Rocha, he draws heavily on popular traditions, including the *literatura de cordel*. His movie *Ogum's Amulet*, for instance, is narrated by a blind poet-singer. The son of a São Paulo tailor, the filmmaker explains his interest in the *folheto* as part of a more ample "attempt to create a language founded on the way in which the Brazilian people really speak and feel."

Santos, Vital. Playwright. June 3, 1978, Recife, Pernambuco.
The author of a number of plays based on popular motifs, Vital Santos' most recent work is *The Sun Struck the Earth and the Wound Spread* (*O Sol feriu a terra e a chaga se alastrou*), which was performed by *Luiz Mendonça's theater company on a special tour of Recife and Fazenda Nova. A native of Caruaru, Vital has worked from time to time with the *Quinteto Violado.

Sarno, Geraldo. Filmmaker. November 24, 1977, Rio de Janeiro.
Born in the interior of the state of Bahia, Geraldo Sarno is best known for his documentaries of Northeasterners and the Northeast. Among those which deal specifically with popular poetry are *Backlands Newspaper* (*Jornal do Sertão*), *The Verse Contest* (*A Cantoria*), and *Monday* (*Segunda-Feira*), which includes a sequence devoted to the sale of *folhetos* in the weekly open-air market. Despite the *cordel*'s "superficial conservatism," he finds it "a special form of protest and self-assertion."

Silva, Francisco Pereira da. Playwright, librarian. October 27, 1977, Rio de Janeiro.
Having spent his childhood in Campina Maior, a small town in the backlands of Piauí, Francisco Pereira da Silva identifies strongly with various popular art

forms. He has used pieces of the *literatura de cordel* in his plays *The Awaited One* (*O Desejado*) and *The Ballad of Vilela* (*Romance do Vilela*). The first deals with a cowman and a wild bull, the second with the great-great-grandfather of the Northeastern outlaws (*cangaceiros*). The writer, who works in the National Library, denies that he is a folklorist. "If the Northeast is present in my plays, it is because it lives within me," he declares.

Silva, Osório Peixoto. Writer. October 17, 1977, Rio de Janeiro. Home: Campista, Rio de Janeiro.
Although Osório Peixoto Silva was born in the South of Brazil, the *literatura de cordel* is present throughout his fiction. *The Ururau of Lapa and Other Stories* (*O Ururau de Lapa e Outras Estórias*) is the most recent example of his use of popular material. Formerly a journalist, he is a member of a poets' cooperative called UNI-VERSO and takes special pleasure in listening to the tales and legends told by local fishermen and sugar cane cutters.

Siqueira, José Cutsino de. Radio superintendent. March 19, 1978, Campina Grande, Paraíba.
Superintendent of the Caturité Radio in Campina Grande, José Cutsino de Siqueira has no particular personal interest in regional traditions. Because, however, his station runs a daily poet-improviser program, "Rough and Ready Guitarists" ("Os Bambas da Viola"), he has been forced to learn a good deal about Northeastern popular poetry. He explains that the public for his radio program is so enthusiastic that "if we miss one day, they send us letters or nag the boss's wife to call us so that it won't happen again."

Soares, Vital. Musician. November 1, 1977, Rio de Janeiro.
Born in Taperoá in the interior of Paraíba, Vital Soares is a song-writer, musician, poet, and playwright. He has made records, performed in shows, and written music for the soap opera *Saramandaia* based in part on the *folheto The Mysterious Peacock*. He has also published a study in *cordel* format of one particularly controversial popular poet entitled *Zé Limeira, Surrealist of the Poor*. According to him, "erudite" art is "nothing other than 'popular' material decked out in fancy clothes."

Souto Maior, Mário. Researcher. January 16, 1978, Recife, Pernambuco.
A member of the Folklore and Anthropology Section within the Joaquim Nabuco Institute for Social Science Research, Mário Souto Maior has published a large number of articles on various folk and popular traditions. He has collaborated on a two-volume anthology of *folhetos* and has written various articles about these stories in verse.

Souza, Arlindo Pinto de. Publisher. December 13, 1977, São Paulo.
Head of the São Paulo publishing company known as the Luzeiro, Arlindo Pinto de Souza estimates that he prints four hundred thousand *folhetos* with characteristic glossy covers a year. The company also publishes recipe books, joke collections, and how-to books—typing, the art of writing love letters, etc. The son of a Portuguese immigrant who imported miscellaneous pamphlet literature from Lisbon, the publisher got into the *cordel* business when he discovered the story

of the rogue *Cancão de Fogo*. As he explains, "I read it, liked it, and soon enough I was a *cordel* publisher just like any other."

Souza, Liêdo Maranhão de. *Folheto* collector, dentist. January 18, 1978, Olinda, Pernambuco.
Born in the center of Recife near the São José market, Liêdo Maranhão de Souza, who has been collecting *folhetos* for over a decade, boasts one of the largest and most varied collections in Brazil today. He has also collected extensive biographical information on a large number of popular poets. His publications include various articles, a series of photographs of the São José market, and an anthology of *folhetos* aimed at providing a "popular" classification system of the *literatura de cordel*.

Suassuna, Ariano. Writer. January 15, 1978, Recife, Pernambuco.
Internationally known novelist, playwright, poet, and professor of aesthetics, Ariano Suassuna is the founder of the *Movimento Armorial*, a movement which seeks to give new impetus to contemporary Brazilian art by the conscious inclusion of folk and popular motifs. First head of the Federal University of Pernambuco's Cultural Extension Center and then as secretary of education and culture for the city of Recife, he actively sponsored a variety of artistic activities related to regional traditions. While his critics lift an eyebrow at the *Armorial* ballet, circus, orchestra, and tapestry collective, his supporters argue that he has instituted new directions in not only Northeastern but Brazilian art.

Teatro da Criança do Recife. Actors. May 10, 1978, Recife, Pernambuco.
Suzana Costa, Fábio Coelho, Lau Chagas, Paulo Estevam, and Paulo de Castro, members of the Children's Theater of Recife, perform primarily for young viewers. They have also dramatized a series of *folhetos* by contemporary popular poets such as **João José da Silva and **Olegário Fernandes da Silva.

Tejo, Orlando. Writer. June 7, 1978, Recife, Pernambuco.
Author of a book about the much-disputed popular poet, Zé Limeiro, Orlando Tejo denies claims that the poet was a figment of the collective imagination. "These people just don't want to believe that an uneducated man could compose such strange, original verses, but he certainly did," the writer says.

Terra, Ruth Lêmos. Writer, professor. August 4, 1978, Rio de Janeiro. Home: São Paulo.
Presently associated with the University of São Paulo, Ruth Terra has written a number of articles on the *literatura de cordel*. One, done in collaboration with *Gilberto Galvão, applies the structural approach of Vladimir Propp to the *cordel* tradition. Like many younger Brazilian academics with an interest in popular culture, the author calls for new approaches to problems such as *cordel* classification.

Trigueiros, Osvaldo. Administrator. May 12, 1978, João Pessoa, Paraíba.
Professor of folklore at the Federal University of Paraíba, Osvaldo Trigueiros heads a new field work division aimed at collecting folk and popular material in

the state. A native of the small city of Patos, he is particularly interested in popular sculpture and in journalistic *folhetos*.

Vasconcellos, Francisco José Ribeiro de. Lawyer, folklorist. November 1, 1977, Rio de Janeiro.
A lawyer by profession, Francisco Vasconcellos' interest in folk and popular traditions prompted him to publish a journal *Encounter with Folklore* (*Encontro com o Folclore*) between 1964 and 1972. Aside from *folhetos*, he is particularly interested in popular religious manifestations, ceramics, and Carnival celebrations.

Appendix B: Notes on Popular Poets Interviewed

The following persons, all of whom are associated in some way with popular poetry, supplied information used in this study. Although I learned a good deal from casual exchanges, I have noted only the names of those persons with whom I had longer, usually tape-recorded conversations. The great majority of interviews were conducted in either Rio de Janeiro and São Paulo or in the traditional Northeast heartland of the *folheto*: Pernambuco, Paraíba, and southeastern Ceará. While there are a few key *folheto* authors missing from the list (I would, for instance, have liked to talk to Joaquim de Sena, Natanael de Lima, and João de Barros), most of the more important contemporary *cordel* authors can be found among these names.

In each case, I have first identified the person as a *folheto* author or *repentista* (poet-improviser), printmaker, wholesaler, *editor* (legal owner of *folhetos* authored by others), vendor, printer, almanac writer (literary astrologer), or "other" occupation subsequently described. If several labels are separated by commas (for example, *repentista*, author), this means that the first activity is decidedly more important than any other to the person in terms of time or money. If separated by hyphens (*repentista*-author), the activities are of more or less equal weight. The term "other" refers to a steady supplementary occupation rather than the odd jobs which many poets take from time to time to add to their earnings.

In the case of writers, who are my major interest in this study, I have given the approximate number of *folhetos* which they state they have published in parentheses after the word "author." (Naturally, most poets have written more stories than they have printed.) After the occupational label, I have given the individual's place and year of birth. (The reader should note that a person listed as born in "Juazeiro" may actually have been born in the countryside surrounding the city.) In the case of authors now living in the South, I have also given the dates of their arrival there. I have then noted the date and place of tape-recorded interviews, from which the great majority of the quotations by poets used in this study have come. Although I had sustained contact with a number of persons in the Rio and Recife areas, only the dates of actual recordings are noted. In the few cases where the place of recording is not the person's home city, I have noted this fact.

A short, descriptive paragraph follows this initial identification. More detailed biographical information on both writers and singers and a full listing of *folheto* authors' works can be found in Átila de Almeida and José Alves Sobrinho's *Dicionário bio-bibliográfico de repentistas e poetas de bancada* and Sebastião Nunes Batista's *Antologia da literatura de cordel*. I have limited myself to one or two distinguishing characteristics designed to create a sense of the individual and thus the range as well as common features of the group. Since the great majority of these writers come from a subsistence agriculture background, have had a year or less of schooling, and wrote their first *folheto* before the age of thirty, I have noted only exceptions to these norms. Cross-references are noted by one (Appendix A) or two (Appendix B) astericks.

KEY

Line 1: Name. Occupation(s) and, if author, approximate number of published *folhetos* in parentheses.
Line 2: Birthplace and Birthdate. For Northeastern authors now living in the South, the date of arrival in the South.
Line 3: Date and place of tape-recorded interview(s).

Alexandre Sobrinho, João. *Repentista*, author (20).
Sant'Ana de Ipanema, Alagoas, 1920.
April 9, 1978, Juazeiro do Norte, Ceará.

Long associated with poet-singer radio programs, João Alexandre has written *folhetos* as short as two pages as well as numerous *canções* or songs. He has lived in Juazeiro since the age of eight when his parents fled the countryside for fear of the bandit Lampião.

d'Almeida Filho, Manuel. Author (130), vendor-wholesaler.
Alagoa Grande, Paraíba, 1916.
June 7, 1978, Aracaju, Sergipe.

Cited by many fellow poets as the leading contemporary *cordel* author, Manuel d'Almeida is the author of classics such as *Florisberto and the Black Sorcerer* (four hundred thousand copies) and *Vicente, King of Thieves* (well over half a million). He is chief advisor to the São Paulo-based Luzeiro press in *cordel*-related matters.

Areda, Francisco Sales. Author (115), other.
Campina Grande, Paraíba, 1916.
January 21, 1978, Caruaru, Pernambuco.

Although Chico Sales presently earns his living as a peddler, he is the author of *cordel* best sellers such as *The Death of Getúlio Vargas* and *The Prince John-Without-Fear and the Princess of the Isle of Diamonds*. Internationally known playwright *Ariano Suassuna based his *Rogues' Trial* in part on the popular poet's *folheto The Man Who Owned the Cow and the Power of Fortune*.

Assis, Manuel Tomás de. Author (100)-vendor-other.
Alagoa Nova, Paraíba, 1899–1978.
March 7, April 4, July 3, 1978, Olivedos, Paraíba.

A prime example of an old-style, deeply religious *cordel* author, Manuel Tomás de Assis remained a farmer despite his frequent travels. After making the rounds with his *folhetos*, he always returned to his plot of land outside the small town of Olivedos. Up until a week before his death, he read his stories aloud in the fairs around his home. One of the earliest poet-reporters, his first *folheto* dealt with the march of the revolution-minded Prestes Column through the Northeast in 1926.

Azevêdo Filho, Teófilo. Other, author (10).
Birthplace and birthdate unknown.
December 15, 1978, São Paulo.

Although best known for his performances in nightclubs with a sophisticated samba group, "Teo" Azevêdo has recently turned to the *cordel* as an additional source of income, turning out *folhetos* on a new electric press.

Azulão. *See* José João dos Santos.

Barbosa (Guriatã do Norte), José Severino. *Repentista*, author (60), vendor.
Bom Jardim, Pernambuco, 1936.
April 28, 1978, Olinda, Pernambuco. Home: Bom Jardim, Pernambuco.

Although the bulk of Guriatã's income comes from his activities as a poet-singer (he regularly appears on radio programs), he continues to write *folhetos* as well as songs. These include not only journalistic stories and *pelejas* but also more obviously fictional accounts such as *The Prophecy of a Traveler and the Mysterious Old Man*. His dream is to travel through Amazonas "singing and selling *folhetos*."

Barbosa Filho, José. *Coquista*.
Santa Rita, Paraíba, birthdate unknown.
September 18, 1978, Rio de Janeiro.

The *coco* is a type of popular poetry improvised to the beat of tambourines, associated more with the coastal region of the Northeast than with the interior. José Barbosa performs with **Mariano Isidro every Sunday in the São Cristóvão fair from dawn to midday where the public "barely allows us the time for a coffee break." The two singers are frequent guests in "culture classes" staged in various high schools and have had their music taped "by a professor who came here all the way from Indiana in the United States of North America."

Barreto, José Praxedes. Other, author (6).
Birthplace and birthdate unknown.
November 17, 1977, Rio de Janeiro.

Known as "the poet-cowboy," Zé Praxedes Barreto has worked for various radio and television shows over the past twenty years. Originally from Rio Grande do Norte, he has written songs and hymns as well as *folhetos* about tourism, the 1964 "revolution," and the theft of St. Sebastian's arrows.

Batista, Abraão Bezerra. Other, author (80), printmaker.
Juazeiro do Norte, 1935.
April 6, 1978, Juazeiro do Norte, Ceará.

Abraão Batista started writing *folhetos* some ten years ago. Since then, he has written a good number of journalistic stories, many with a strong vein of social criticism (for example, *The Failed Industrialist or the Fly-by-Night Senator from Pernambuco*). He has a college education and works as a pharmacist. Popular poets seldom like his stories but often admire his woodcuts. Before his political views began causing him trouble, he worked as a journalist and as a university professor.

Borges, Joel. Author (1)-vendor-printmaker-other.
Correntes, Paraíba, 1943.
January 20, March 30, March 31, 1978, Sítio Cruzeiro, Pernambuco.

A farmer and jack-of-all trades, Joel Borges works off and on for his cousin **José Francisco Borges as a printer's assistant, often taking time out to sell *folhetos* on the weekend. Although he entered the trade at age thirty-one, later than most poets, he has written five *folhetos*, of which only one has been published.

Borges, José Francisco. Author (50)-printmaker-printer-wholesaler-editor.
Bezerros, Pernambuco, 1935.
January 1, March 30, July 18, 1978, Bezerros.

An internationally known printmaker, José Francisco Borges has had his work exhibited in the Smithsonian and the Louvre. Nevertheless, he continues to work as a one-man printer, turning out *folhetos* that sell at regular prices. He specializes in "examples" such as that of the girl who sold her hair and was made to visit hell or the woman who turned into a vampire after baring her shoulders.

Caldas, João Bandeira de. *Repentista*, author (10).
Jotobá de Piranhas, Paraíba, 1944.
April 13, 1978, Juazeiro do Norte, Ceará.

A regular performer on his brother **Pedro's daily radio program, João Bandeira has written a number of journalistic *folhetos*. He has been a poet-singer from an early age.

Caldas (Daudeth Bandeira), Manoel Bandeira de. *Repentista*.
Jotobá de Piranhas, Paraíba, 1945.
January 16, 1978, Olinda, Pernambuco. Home: Juazeiro do Norte, Ceará.

A member of the famed Bandeira family, Daudeth frequently participates in festivals and congresses. According to him "a show is very different from a live performance, but today a poet-singer has to do a little bit of everything."

Caldas, Pedro Bandeira de. *Repentista*, author (100).
São José de Piranhas, Paraíba, 1938.
April 15, 1978, Juazeiro do Norte, Ceará.

A true entrepreneur among popular poets, Pedro Bandeira runs a highly successful radio program in which various other members of his family regularly participate. At one time a mule driver, he and his wife presently study literature in the
local university.

Campos, Francisco de Souza. Author (20), other.
Timbaúba, Pernambuco, 1926.
March 1, 1978, São Lourenço da Mata, Pernambuco.

Like his brothers **José and Manuel, Francisco has been a poet-vendor since an
early age. As a young man, he spent a year in Aracaju where he learned a good
deal about poetry from **Manuel d'Almeida Filho. Self-conscious about his three
months of schooling, he took a correspondence course in Portuguese which he
failed by two points "and you know, I still feel bad about that. If I had had the
time to study harder, I am sure that I could have passed."

Campos, José de Souza. Author (12)-vendor.
Timbaúba, Pernambuco, 1920.
March 1, 1978, São Lourenço da Mata, Pernambuco. Home: Jaboatão, Pernam-
buco.

A veteran of Recife's São Jose market, José de Souza Campos sells his *folhetos*
in the adjoining plaza six days a week. On Sundays, he offers his wares in the
weekly market of nearby Limoeiro. Asked why he decided to become a poet, he
says, "I heard the vendors singing in the fair when I was a boy and found poetry
a marvel. It's been fifty long hard years now, but my opinion has not changed. I
come to the market every day not only because I have to earn a living but because
I am a poet and this is what poets do."

Campos, Luiz de Souza. Other, author (1).
Recife, 1949.
March 29, 1978, Recife, Pernambuco.

Presently a peddler of belts in the São José market, Luiz de Souza Campos began
selling *folhetos* at the age of five. The son of **José de Souza Campos, he has
written a half-dozen stories. "Look," he says, "this business of poetry is a night-
mare for the man who has to feed a family. But despite myself there are those
days when something almost forces me to write."

Canhotinho, Antônio. *See* Antônio Lourenço da Silva.

Carvalho, Elias de. Other, author (20), *repentista*, accordion player.
Timbaúba, Pernambuco, 1918. Rio, 1957.
December 2, 1977, Rio de Janeiro.

Although his *folhetos* have never sold well, Elias de Carvalho continues to turn out stories. He notes ruefully, "Others make money from their *folhetos*, but I pay for what I write!" His stories tend to be highly informational: *Birds of the World*, *ABC of the Human Body*, etc. He has earned his living for thirty years as a hospital aide.

Catapora. *See* Cosme Damião Vieira de Oliveira.

Cavalcante, Rodolfo Coelho. Author (1,500)-editor-wholesaler.
Rio Largo, Alagoas, 1919.
June 5, 1978, Salvador, Bahia.

President of three successive poets' organizations, Rodolfo Coelho Cavalcante devotes a good deal of his time to overseeing his present association's journal and to answering an incessant flood of letters. He has written a number of *cordel* best sellers, one of which, *The Girl Who Beat Her Mother and Turned into a Dog*, has sold close to half a million copies in twenty-nine successive editions.

Cícero. *See* João Severo da Silva.

Curió, Antônio. *Repentista.*
Birthplace and birthdate unknown.
December 17, 1977, Rio de Janeiro.

A frequent performer in Rio's Largo do Machado and São Cristóvão fair, Antônio Curió would like to return home if conditions permitted. "Here in the South," he says, "I earn a lot more money, but I feel I would be a better poet in the Northeast because the public there is more demanding."

Dila. *See* José Soares da Silva.

Dila, José Cavalcanti e Ferreira. *See* José Soares da Silva.

Guriatã de Coqueiro. *Repentista*, author.
Birthplace and birthdate unknown.
December 13, 1977, São Paulo.

One of the more successful *repentistas* in São Paulo today, Guriatã de Coqueiro began singing "on the afternoon of Holy Saturday of 1936." Responsible for a large number of records, he has also written a handful of *folhetos*, most of which are *pelejas*. Greatly respected by his fellow poets, his picture hangs on the back wall of the small restaurant known as The Poets' Hideaway (*O Recanto dos Poetas*) in the city's Northeast quarter, Braz. *Repentistas* often spend the afternoon here drinking and rolling cigarettes as they compose verses for each other and the two parrots who bob about in a cage above the aged refrigerator.

Guriatã do Norte. *See* José Severino Barbosa.

Isidro, Mariano. *Coquista*, other.
Santa Rita, Paraíba, birthdate unknown.
September 18, 1977, Rio de Janeiro.

Although illiterate, Mariano Isidro always wanted to be a poet. He learned his craft at an early age by watching and then imitating other *coquistas*. Like his partner, **José Barbosa Filho, he is a native of Santa Rita, Paraíba, and has been in Rio for the past sixteen years. At the end of a performance, the two men express their thanks for contributions in clever, funny counting rhymes, which inevitably prompt members of their audience to place yet another coin in the outstretched tambourine.

João do Cristo Rei. *See* João Quinto Sobrinho.

José, Antonio. *Repentista*, other.
Arapriaca, Alagoas, 1947.
December 13, 1977, São Paulo.

Born in the countryside of Alagoas, Antonio José has worked as a house painter, peddler, taxi driver, and construction worker in order to supplement his income as a *repentista*. Dressed in a striped hat, fringed shirt, and bright pink trousers, he no longer looks like a subsistence farmer.

Leite, José Costa. Printmaker-author (200)-vendor-editor-wholesaler-almanac writer.
Sapé, Paraíba, 1927.
February 18, 1978, Condado, Pernambuco.

With **José Soares da Silva and **José Francisco Borges, José Costa Leite is one of the best-known popular printmakers in Brazil today. Adept at reworking already existing *folhetos*, he has a number of stories which topped one hundred thousand copies. He has been writing almanacs for nineteen years and finds that they now sell better than ever "because, thank God, you can't find a schoolboy today who doesn't know the name of his astrological sign."

Lima (Sinésio Pereira), Aniceto Pereira de. *Repentista*, author (3).
Vertentes de Taquaritinga, Pernambuco, 1935.
February 28, 1978, Olinda, Pernambuco.

When Sinésio Pereira was a child, his father, who thought poetry was "irresponsible," broke the would-be singer's guitar, which he had hidden in a grain bin. His calling, however, survived the blow. Now vice-president of the Olinda Poets' Association, he performs regularly on the radio and in various officially sponsored festivals. As with many *repentistas*, the *folhetos* he writes are all *pelejas*.

Lucena, Gerson Araújo de. Other, author (14).
Santa Luzia, Paraíba, 1927.
March 2, 1978, Campina Grande, Paraíba.

The majority of Gerson Araújo de Lucena's *folhetos* were written before his conversion to Protestantism in 1966. Although he still writes stories from time to time, he earns his living, like his father before him, as a carpenter. His first *folheto* was based on the film version of Tarzan; his latest is a love story, "which isn't true but which is the kind of untruth which hurts no one."

Medeiros, Manuel. *Repentista*, other.
Birthplace and birthdate unknown.
November 14, 1977, Rio de Janeiro.

A poet-singer from Paraíba, Manuel Medeiros frequently sings with his countryman **Azulão. He can be found on weekends in both Rio's Largo do Machado and São Cristóvão fair.

Melo, Vicente Vitorino de. Almanac writer, author (12).
Limoeiro, Pernambuco, birthdate unknown.
March 17, 1978, Caruaru, Pernambuco.

Although successful as an author of *folhetos* such as *The Debate Between a Rum Guzzler and a Protestant* in 1951, Vicente Vitorino de Melo is best known for his annual almanacs. A serious astrologer who has done a good bit of reading on his own ("I even have a book about the stars in Spanish"), he continues to peddle his almanacs throughout the interior, charging approximately three dollars for a detailed personal astrological consultation.

Miné. *See* José Camilo da Silva.

Mocó. *See* Cícero Vieira da Silva.

Monteiro, Delarme. Author (100), other.
Recife, Pernambuco, 1917.
January 17, 1978, Olinda, Pernambuco.

Born in that part of Recife known as Campo Grande, Delarme Monteiro, unlike most poets, was never a subsistence farmer. Because his family was very poor, his mother hired him out as a beggar while he was still a child. He went on to become the chief printer's assistant to João Martins de Ataíde, once Recife's *folheto* king. Many *folhetos* which bear the latter's name were actually written by Delarme. Now troubled by cataracts, he works for *Giuseppe Baccaro's Children's House Foundation in Olinda, occasionally writing a *folheto* commissioned by Sears Roebuck or a local bank.

Moreira, Flávio Fernandes. Other, author (25).
Bom Jesus, Rio de Janeiro, 1937. Rio de Janeiro, 1955.
December 30, 1977, Rio de Janeiro (Duque de Caxias).

Although Flávio Moreira grew up in the state of Rio de Janeiro, he was familiar with *folhetos* from childhood. He wrote his first story, about the inexplicable murder of a popular townsman, at the age of fifteen. Most of his stories are contemporary, urban *folhetos* such as *The Busdriver's Drama*, *Umbanda in Verse*, and *The Fishes' Soccer Game*.

Mulatinha, Antônio da. *See* Antônio Patrício de Souza.

Oliveira (Catapora), Cosme Damião Vieira de. Other, author (6).
Itapiruna, R.J., 1939. Rio de Janeiro, 1953.
December 27, 1977, Rio de Janeiro (Duque de Caxias).

Long a clown in the Christmas celebrations known as the Folia dos Reis, Catapora memorized *cordel* verses to chant among other bits and pieces of poems as he danced from door to door. After running away from home at the age of fourteen, he continued these activities in Rio. Present official encouragement of various local traditions led him to begin writing *folhetos* such as *Black Beans*, a verse account of the shortage of this staple in Rio de Janeiro. His primary occupation is loading and unloading trucks.

Palito. *See* Severino Marquês de Souza Júnior.

Passos, José Gonzaga dos. Other, *repentista*, author (10).
Bezerros, Pernambuco, 1920.
March 28, 1978, Olinda, Pernambuco.

A shopkeeper by trade, José Gonzaga dos Passos feels strongly enough about poetry to attend the meetings of the Olinda Poets' Association. His most recent *folheto* was an appeal to the Brazilian government to increase the pensions of veterans of World War II. He himself enlisted as a young man in the Brazilian army because, "believe me, you don't need as much courage to be a soldier as you do to be a farmer."

Patativa. *See* Antonio Gonçalves da Silva.

Paz, Firmino da. *Repentista*, other.
Maceió, Alagoas, 1947.
December 13, 1977, São Paulo.

Now a frequent visitor to the Poets' Hideaway in Braz (São Paulo), Firmino da Paz grew up in the Northeast. Asked if he finds the Southern public different, he shakes his head and says, "No, same pot of beans."

Pereira, Geraldo Amáncio. *Repentista*, author (10).
Cedro, Ceará, 1946.
April 5, 1978, Juazeiro do Norte, Ceará.

One of the best-known young *repentistas*, Geraldo Amáncio Pereira has his own radio program, participates in scores of festivals, and has made a number of records. His *folhetos*, like those of most *repentistas*, tend to be brief accounts of news events or literary *pelejas*.

Pereira, Sinésio. *See* Aniceto Pereira de Lima.

Pimentel, Antônio. Printer.
Campina Grande, 1938.
March 6, 1978, Campina Grande, Paraíba.

Although Antônio Pimentel prints a range of items, he has a special fondness for *cordel* stories. Since he began his own business in 1975, he has overseen publication of over two hundred *folhetos*, some of which were sponsored by the Federal University of Paraíba in Campina Grande. Last year, he turned away ten titles for lack of time, "so from my point of view, at least, the *cordel* is doing well."

Pinheiro, Jair Gonçalves. Other, vendor.
Rio de Janeiro, 1937.
December 1, 1977, Rio de Janeiro.

A well-known figure in Rio's Largo do Machado, Jair Pinheiro became interested in the *folheto* during the time that he worked for a printing press called The Popular Tune ("A Modinha Popular") some twenty years ago. He specializes in those *cordel* stories with glossy covers published by the São Paulo-based Luzeiro company. Although he cannot depend on *folheto* sales for a living, he continues to offer his wares in the Largo every Saturday and Sunday night, "because it gives me tremendous pleasure to offer people stories which they will read from cover to cover."

Quinto Sobrinho (João do Cristo Rei), João. Author (150)-vendor.
Areia, Paraíba, 1900.
April 6, 1978, Juazeiro do Norte, Ceará.

João do Cristo Rei ("John of Christ the King") adopted his name as the result of a vow. He has lived in Juazeiro since 1927, becoming a *cordel* author on the suggestion of the city's spiritual leader Padre Cícero. Now eighty, his eyesight is failing, but he still periodically reads *folhetos* with an extraordinary booming voice at fairs.

Ribeiro, Edgley. Other, author (7).
Cajazeiras, Paraíba, 1951.
April 17, 1978, Juazeiro do Norte, Ceará.

Edgley Ribeiro, who works in a hotel, does all his *folheto* writing with his friend **Francisco Zénio. While still high school students, the two took a course in printmaking with *folheto* designer and artist *Stênio Diniz. Although Edgley remembers his mother reading *folhetos* to him as a child in Cajazeiras, his work is "not like those old stories."

Ricardo, José. Other, *repentista*.
Serra Branca, Paraíba, 1945.
January 24, 1977, Rio de Janeiro.

A resident of Rio for some ten years now, Zé Ricardo works as a butcher during the week. At nights and on weekends he sings in various locations in and around the city.

Rodrigues, Estêvão. Other, author (15).
Birthplace and birthdate unknown.
April 9, 1978, Juazeiro do Norte, Ceará.

Estêvão Rodrigues, who has always enjoyed writing verses, wrote his first *folheto* in 1974 on a whim. When his account of a sensational emasculation, revenge for a seduction in a nearby town, sold twenty-five thousand copies, he decided to write "a whole lot more." The poet, who has had almost six years of schooling, works as a laboratory assistant in the local ministry of health.

Santos, Apolônio Alves dos. Author (30)-vendor-wholesaler.
Guarabira, Paraíba, 1920. Rio de Janeiro, 1950.
December 22, 1977, Rio de Janeiro.

Apolônio Alves dos Santos sells his *folhetos* on weekend nights in the Largo do Machado as well as every Sunday in the São Cristovão fair. His work is a mixture of standard Northeastern themes and contemporary urban subjects. Presently dependent on *cordel* sales for an income, he has worked as a bricklayer and night watchman.

Santos (Zé Duda da Paraíba, Zé do Cabelo Ruim), José Herculano dos. *Repentista*.
Campina Grande, Paraíba, 1933.
October 24, 1977. Rio de Janeiro.

Zé Duda (also nicknamed Joe-with-the-Awful-Hair) is one of Rio's better-known poet-singers. He has performed in universities in not only Rio de Janeiro but Belo Horizonte and Brasília. Formerly head of his own radio program in Ceará, he misses the North, but "I've been here twenty years now and twenty years is a long time."

Santos, José Felix dos. Vendor, author (1).
Chão Grande, Pernambuco, 1954.
March 29, 1977, Recife, Pernambuco.

One of a small number of young poet-vendors, José Felix dos Santos has published one *folheto* entitled *The Prostitute's Life*. Still unmarried, he enjoys extended sales trips through the interior, but inevitably returns to Recife's central market. "I eat lots of vitamins," he says, "because the poet's life is very difficult, and he has to be strong."

Santos (Azulão), José João dos. Author (60)-vendor-*repentista*.
Sapé, Paraíba, 1932. Rio de Janeiro, 1949.
November 15, 1977, Rio de Janeiro (Engenheiro Pinheiro).

The best-known popular poet in Rio, Azulão (the name of a songbird, like "gu-riatã" or "patativa") is equally well known as a *repentista* and *folheto* writer. He has made a number of lecture tours and at least one record. He normally sings in shirtsleeves in the São Cristóvão fair on Sundays. On the days when the television crews arrive, however, he proudly sports a suit "because otherwise the people watching will think the poet is a hick." He has played in two television soap operas. Within his community, he is a leader of the folk festival called *Bumba-meu-Boi*.

Santos, Manuel Camilo dos. Author (150)-editor-wholesaler.
Guarabira, Paraíba, 1905.
March 6, 1978, Campina Grande, Paraíba.

Once the owner of an important *folheto* press with agents in every Northeastern city, Manuel Camilo dos Santos lost everything he owned in an unsuccessful bid for election to public office. A well-known poet distinguished by his lyric descriptions, he continues to write and sell *cordel* today. Originally a *repentista*, he began writing *folhetos*, "already an old man," at the age of thirty-five "because one can write alone without having to put up with anyone."

Silva, Antônio Alelúia da. *Repentista*, author (13).
Cupira, Pernambuco, 1926.
February 28, 1978, Olinda, Pernambuco.

Primarily a *repentista*, Alelúia sings on the radio as well as for local roundups. He has written a number of eight-page *folhetos* as well as various *canções*.

Silva (Patativa), Antonio Gonçalves da. *Repentista*, author (10).
Serra de Sant'Ana, 1909.
April 8, 1978, Juazeiro do Norte; April 11, 12, 1978, Serra de Sant'Ana, Ceará.

Well known as a *repentista*, Patativa (a bird's name) has a prodigious memory, which allows him to repeat hundreds of verses word for word. He is the author of not only *folhetos* but books of consciously regional-sounding (*caboclo*) poetry with a social message geared as much for an educated as a popular audience. He continues to tend his farm in the hills several hours from Juazeiro do Norte. Self-taught, he is familiar with the work of Camões, Machado de Assis, and Marx.

Silva (Antônio Canhotinho [Antônio Southpaw]), Antônio Lourenço da.
Other-author (10)-*repentista*.
Bonito, Paraíba, 1925.
March 9, 1978, Campina Grande, Paraíba.

Although Antônio Canhotinho makes his living as a salesman, he continues to attend the meetings of the local poets' association. The son of a subsistence farmer, he developed a liking for poetry at the age of twenty when a fellow factory worker recited a *folheto* to him. Formerly a poet-vendor, he has written a number of stories such as *The Triumph of Love and the Victory of Two Lovers* and *The Child Who Was Raised by a Tiger*.

Silva, Antônio Miguel da. Other, *repentista*.
Timbaúba, Paraíba, 1911.
October 23, 1977, Rio de Janeiro.

In "the long life which God has seen fit" to give him, Antônio Miguel da Silva has worked as a watchman, an airport maintenance man, and an employee of at least a dozen different firms in Rio de Janeiro. He left the Northeast some thirty years ago, "but I miss it because there people embrace and esteem poetry." Lamenting that his eyesight does not permit him to read as much as he once did, he notes, "this is a bad moment for such a thing to happen because today's poet-singer has to know everything that is happening in the world."

Silva, Caetano Cosme da. Author (120), vendor, other.
Nazaré da Mata, Pernambuco, 1927.
March 4, 1978, Campina Grande, Paraíba.

Author of a number of best sellers (for example, *The Assassin of Honor or the Madwoman in the Garden* and *Tears of Love or The Vengeance of a Condemned Man*), Caetano Cosme da Silva depends on sales of herbs for a living today since the *folheto* "is no longer interesting to anyone except professors." His brothers have all moved to São Paulo, but he is determined to stay in the Northeast "because for all its problems, there is more liberty."

Silva (Mocó), Cícero Vieira da. Other, author (50).
Campina Grande, 1936. Rio de Janeiro, 1963.
January 2, 1978, Rio de Janeiro (Duque de Caxias).

Although barely literate (his wife customarily writes down the stories as he dictates), many of his fellow poets consider Mocó the most talented *folheto* writer living in the South of Brazil. A fare collector on a municipal bus, which he reports has been held up as often as three times a month, he lives in one of the worst *favelas* (slums) in the working-class outskirts of Rio known as the Baixada Fluminense.

Silva, Edson Pinto da. Vendor, wholesaler.
Carpina, Pernambuco, 1922.
January 18, 1978, Recife, Pernambuco.

Edson Pinto da Silva, who has been selling *folhetos* since 1936, remains a central figure in the Recife *cordel* trade. He commissioned a sign that reads "*Literatura de Cordel*" some five years ago "after everyone started using the *folhete*'s new name." Father of a large family, he dreams of his eldest daughter's studying at a university.

Silva, Expedito Sebastião da. Author (110), other.
Juazeiro, 1928.
April 8, 1978, Juazeiro do Norte, Ceará.

Although Expedito Sebastião da Silva grew up in the city, he has always identified with the *folheto*-buying public. His eleven years of schooling, extraordinary for a *cordel* poet, has not made his style any less "popular." He began working for José Bernardo da Silva at the age of seventeen and continues to work for the press now owned by Zé Bernardo's daughter. He also writes short poems and sonnets, which he uses as filler or which he prints on the back of *cordel* covers.

Silva, João José da. Author (200), editor, wholesaler.
Vitória de Santo Antão, Pernambuco, 1923.
January 10, 1978, Recife, Pernambuco.

Once the owner of an important *cordel* press, the Luzeiro do Norte, which closed in the 1960s, the poet is presently an agent of the São Paulo-based Luzeiro. A vendor "at that time when there was no bus and the poet got to know the whole Northeast on foot," he retains the rights to some three hundred well-known *folhetos* by himself and other authors.

Silva (Cícero), João Severo da. Author (20)-vendor.
Ingá do Bacamarte, Paraíba, 1921–1978.
May 11, 1978, João Pessoa, Paraíba.

The best-known vendor in João Pessoa, Cícero was studying law at the Federal University at the time of his death. He was the author of a number of *canções* as well as *folhetos*.

Silva, Joaquim. Other, author (10).
Vitória de Santo Antão, Pernambuco, 1931.
June 2, 1978, Recife, Pernambuco.

Author of various moralistic *folhetos* ("writing has always been my favorite sport"), Joaquim Silva earns his living as a finance inspector. He enjoys improvising but has never worked as a poet-singer. One of his favorite topics is the evils of prostitution, "though you know," he says, "my stories are just stories and not always what I think."

Silva (Miné), José Camilo da. Author (10)-vendor.
Tanques de Orobó, Paraíba, 1942.
January 9, 1978, São Lourenço da Mata, Pernambuco.

One of the few younger poets who has succeeded in making poetry a full-time occupation, Miné uses a loudspeaker in chanting his verses aloud. Unmarried, he was twenty-three years old when he paid a prostitute to teach him to read. Before becoming a poet, he worked as a hired laborer.

Silva, José Gonçalves da. *Repentista*, author (2).
Várzea Alegre, Ceará, 1926.
March 8, 1978, Campina Grande, Paraíba.

President of the Association of Singers and Poets of Campina Grande, José Gonçalves da Silva takes pride in the fact that the city has donated the use of a building for the group's periodic meetings. Although primarily a poet-singer, he is also the author of two news *folhetos*.

Silva, José Rodrigues da. Vendor.
Birthplace and birthdate unknown.
March 8, 1978, Campina Grande, Paraíba.

A part-time *cordel* vendor for years, José Rodrigues presently has no other means of support. Optimistic about the *folheto*'s future, nevertheless, he admits that "yesterday these stories were like the single plate you could order in a wayside restaurant. Today, no, there are many eating places offering a whole range of dishes, and so it is normal that people should not want the same food all the time."

Silva (Dila, José Cavalcanti, e Ferreira Dila), José Soares da. Printmaker, author (30), other.
Bom Jardim, Pernambuco, 1937.
May 17, 1978, Caruaru, Pernambuco.

Known primarily as a graphic artist, Dila is also a *folheto* author. At least one of his stories, *The Pilgrim's Dream*, has topped the one hundred thousand mark. His fixation with the figure of the bandit Lampião has begun to exert an increasing impact on his work.

Silva, Manoel Caboclo e. Author (25)-printer-editor-wholesaler-almanac writer.
Juazeiro do Norte, 1916.
April 5, 1976, Juazeiro do Norte, Ceará.

After many years as a printer's assistant to José Bernardo da Silva, Manoel Caboclo e Silva acquired his own press. Although he started writing *folhetos* in 1940, he did not begin to sign his work until 1970. Born in the city, he grew up in the countryside where he taught himself to read at the age of fifteen with the aid of *folhetos* and the pamphlets enclosed in soap wrappers. His grandmother was a Brazilian Indian, thus the surname *Caboclo*.

Silva, Manuel Miguel da. Vendor.
Birthplace and birthdate unknown.
March 16, 1978, Caruaru, Pernambuco.

Though not an author, Manuel Miguel da Silva has spent a lifetime with the *literatura de cordel*. Unhappy with declining sales, he continues to sell *folhetos* in local fairs around Caruaru, "because this is what I've always done and what I'll always do."

Silva, Olegário Fernandes da. Author (100)-printer-printmaker-vendor-editor.
Caruaru, 1932.
January 17, 1978, March 18, 1978, Caruaru, Pernambuco.

Olegário Fernandes da Silva's first *folheto*, *The Minas Bull*, sold seven thousand
copies in one week. The story itself was about the dangers of tainted meat, but
the poet himself "ate meat every day that week—I still remember!" Best known
for his journalistic *folhetos*, he now owns two printing presses, "not bad for a
man who attended school for eighteen days, eh?"

Silva, Severino Borges. Author (120)-*repentista*.
Aliança, Pernambuco, 1919.
March 2, 1978, Timbaúba, Pernambuco.

Author of well over a hundred *cordel* stories, Severino Borges is one of the few
contemporary poets known equally as a *repentista* and as a writer. The majority
of his stories are thirty-two-page *romances*, but he has also written shorter *folhetos* such as an eight-page account of his trip to Amazonas sponsored by the State
Tourism Bureau of the city of Manaus. Having sold the bulk of his stories, he has
copies of few of his own works, but "that doesn't matter because a poet's wealth
is in his head, and he can always write new ones."

Silva, Severino Cesário da. Author (120), other.
Bezerros, Pernambuco, 1913.
January 12, 1978, Recife, Pernambuco.

Author of a number of *cordel* classics, Severino Cesário da Silva has made his
living as a civil servant and a barber. At present he is considering setting up a
folheto stand "even though vendors are like poets and make nothing. All they
make is friends, and sometimes they don't even make them!"

Soares, José Francisco. Author (300)-vendor.
Campina Grande, Paraíba, 1914.
January 17, 1978, Prazeres (Recife), Pernambuco.

Well known as a poet-reporter, Zé Soares has written a number of best sellers (for
example, *The Death of the Bishop of Garanhuns* and *The Renunciation of Jânio
Quadros*). The treasurer of the Olinda Poets' Association, he has two printmaker
sons, who design the covers for his *folhetos*. Besides *folhetos*, he sells second-
hand magazines and samba lyrics, which he himself transcribes from phonograph
records. (News of his death came as this book was going to press).

Souto (José Alves Sobrinho), José Clementino de. Other, author (14).
Picuí, Paraíba, 1921.
March 3, 1978, Campina Grande, Paraíba.

A *repentista* who began traveling through the interior at the age of thirteen, the
poet was forced to abandon singing in 1960 because of health problems. After
trying his hand at various occupations, he began writing *folhetos* and is presently

employed by the Federal University of Paraíba as a fieldworker in folk traditions and is co-author with *Átila de Almeida of a dictionary of popular poets and poetry.

Souza, Antônio Caetano de. Author (40)-vendor.
Jacuitinga, Alagoas, 1915. Home: Palmares, Pernambuco.
February 27, 1978, Recife, Pernambuco.

Best known for his fire and brimstone prophecies, Souza accepts much of what the *cordel* preaches on a more or less literal basis. Although now in his sixties, he sings *folhetos* in local fairs where he pays for the customary "floor" tax by writing *folhetos* for local politicians. He had only three months of schooling, "but fortunately for all of us *cordel* authors, poetry has absolutely nothing to do with how long a person has studied."

Souza (Antônio da Mulatinha), Antônio Patrício de. Author (30)-vendor-wholesaler.
Mulatinha, Paraíba, 1926.
March 9, 1978, Campina Grande, Paraíba.

Owner of the "Oriente" *folheto* depot, Antônio de Mulatinha has been a resident of Campina Grande since 1926. He usually "catches" three or four local fairs a week, supplementing his income by participating in *repentes* ("verbal duels") throughout the countryside. He began his poetic career with a *folheto* about a bus accident ("I went there myself to see and wrote everything down"), followed by another commissioned by the father of a murder victim.

Souza, José Francisco de. *Repentista*, author (10).
Lagoa Grande, Paraíba, 1937.
December 13, 1977, São Paulo.

One of the better-established poets in São Paulo's Northeastern district, Zé de Souza is a poet-singer who only began writing *cordel* stories after his arrival in São Paulo some ten years ago. Like many of his fellow poets, he has made a number of recordings for the Crazy Record Company. He sells his *folhetos* "in universities, in shows, and in the bars around here."

Souza, Paulo Teixeira de. Author (30), vendor, other.
Rio de Janeiro, 1928.
December 28, 1977, Rio de Janeiro.

Born in Rio's Leblon district before it became fashionable, Paulo Teixeira began writing *folhetos* only ten years ago at the suggestion of an employer. Formerly a baker, a construction worker, and a bookbinder, he now works as a janitor during the day. At night, he goes from bar to bar in Rio's southern district selling his *folhetos* "to both professors and construction workers; everybody likes my books."

Souza Júnior (Palito), Severino Marquês de. Other, author (30).
Recife, 1926.
January 17, 1978, Olinda, Pernambuco.

A native of Recife, Palito (the nickname "toothpick" emphasizes his thinness), was the son of a petty police officer. He spent fifteen years in a parochial school where he ran the printing press, then worked five years for ** João José da Silva. At present he is employed as a printer at the Casa de Criança in Olinda with **Delarme Monteiro.

Zénio, Francisco. Other, author (7).
Juazeiro do Norte, 1957.
April 7, 1978, Juazeiro do Norte, Ceará.

A student and aspiring erudite poet, Francisco Zénio and his friend **Edgley Ribeiro hope to make a career of *folheto* writing. They are interested in tapping the new "official" rather than the traditional *cordel* buyer and have been successful in getting small businesses to place ads on the back covers of their booklets.

Appendix C: A Socioeconomic Analysis of *Folheto* Buyers

The following table provides a breakdown of the responses of two hundred *folheto* buyers to a number of questions about themselves and their attitudes toward the *literatura de cordel*. These conversations took place between September 1977 and January 1978 in the Largo do Machado and the São Cristóvão fair, the two most important *folheto* markets in Rio de Janeiro.

A glance at the following table is enough to show that the Largo group tends to be younger, better educated, more media-oriented, and considerably more heterogeneous than the São Cristovão sample. Despite these differences, the two groups gave almost identical responses to certain questions, such as "Did the mysterious peacock really exist?"

Although this table should be largely self-explanatory, it is worth clarifying one or two points. For instance, the great majority of persons who have made more than one trip from their home state to Rio de Janeiro but who do not consider themselves city dwellers continue to divide their time between the South and the Northeast. Thus "more than one" usually means "dozens" of trips. It is also worth noting that those persons who prefer Rio to their home state are not necessarily those who plan to make the city their permanent residence, and vice versa. Finally, the occupational prestige ratings used here are based on a list compiled by Nélson do Valle ("Posição Social das Ocupações," 1972, unpublished manuscript) of some three hundred jobs weighted according to wages and requisite level of education. I am grateful to Philip Fletcher for calling this rating scale to my attention as well as for his help in programming the Stanford University computer.

It would be interesting to compare figures for *folheto* buyers in the South with those in the Northeast, but my interviews in Northern marketplaces do not lend themselves to quantitative analysis, as my formal sample, which is small (approximately one hundred buyers in the Northeast compared with two hundred in the Brazilian South) is divided between a large city (Recife) and small towns (for example, Bezerros) some two hours away. More important, because I was more interested in allowing these conversations to develop freely than in obtaining answers to a long list of questions, many interviews are incomplete in terms of the Rio questionnaire. By the time I got to the Northeast, I had had enough experience with *folheto* buyers to know more or less what to expect and was more interested in pursuing unexpected answers. I was also more disposed to challenge people's responses with, "Oh come on, you can't really believe that!" or "So-and-so just told me the opposite. How can you both be right?"

The following information, which comes from the earlier, more structured interviews, was not always easy to obtain. I am grateful to Azulão at the São Cristóvão fair and to Apolônio Alves dos Santos and Jair Pinheiro in the Largo do Machado for their help. All three explained to people that I had come from the United States to talk to them about *folhetos* because I lived in a country that had none and my friends had asked me to find out about them. Although few buyers would talk to me at first, as I returned to these places week after week, they became more willing to talk. Many wondered how a country as rich and important as the United States could have no *cordel* authors. At least a dozen told me that they wanted to answer my questions because they felt sorry for people who had no *folhetos* to read. "I'm sure that if you just explained to your own poets about these stories," one old man assured me, "that they could write others almost as good."

	Largo do Machado	São Cristóvão Fair
Number in sample		
Men	94	94
Women	12	0
Total number of respondents	106	94
Age		
Under 20	28.3%	3.1%
21–30	51.9	38.3
31–40	15.1	18.1
Over 40	4.7	40.5
Marital status		
Single	76.5	28.7
Married	22.6	69.2
Other	0.9	2.1
Years of schooling		
None	5.6	14.0
1–3	42.4	46.2
4–6	32.1	30.1
Over 6	19.9	9.7
Present occupation		
Construction	39.5	56.5
Nonconstruction	60.5	43.5
Occupational prestige		
Very low	37.6	26.8
Low	28.8	43.4
Medium	16.3	9.6
High	17.3	20.2

	Largo do Machado	São Cristóvão Fair
Birthplace		
Rural	54.7	69.1
Urban	45.3	30.9
State of birth		
Paraíba	12.3	52.1
Pernambuco	19.4	12.7
Ceará	15.1	13.8
Other Northeast	29.6	17.1
Rio (city or state)	12.3	3.2
Other non-Northeast	11.3	1.1
Initial arrival in Rio		
Month or less	11.5	5.4
Month–year	20.8	18.3
1–5 years ago	33.3	16.1
6–10 years ago	24.0	20.4
Over 10 years ago	10.4	39.8
Number of trips to Rio from home state		
One	59.3	17.3
More than one	38.4	67.9
Now settled here	2.3	14.8
Location of immediate family		
In Rio	14.1	33.0
Part in Rio	5.7	9.6
Elsewhere	78.3	54.3
Other (orphan, etc.)	1.9	3.1
Preference (Rio, home state)		
Rio	44.8	33.0
Good points to both	20.8	23.4
Birthplace if other	32.3	42.5
Don't know	2.1	1.1
Plans for future		
Staying in Rio	43.5	43.0
Undecided	33.3	16.1
Not staying	23.2	40.9
Number of folhetos *owned*		
None	7.8	12.8
1–10	49.5	52.1
11–30	32.0	24.4
Over 30	10.7	10.7

	Largo do Machado	São Cristóvão Fair
Content preference		
Traditional	63.2	50.5
Either	17.9	25.3
New	18.9	24.2
Cover preference		
Black and white (blockprint)	14.2	21.0
Either	24.5	22.5
Colored	61.3	56.5
Manner of reading		
Aloud	35.8	46.7
Either	23.6	14.9
Silently	40.6	38.4
Mode of reading		
Accompanied	34.9	56.4
Either	28.3	14.9
Alone	36.8	28.7
Memorize folheto		
Often	16.0	27.7
Sometimes	64.2	67.0
Never	19.8	5.3
After reading folheto		
Keep	74.5	79.7
Give away	16.0	16.0
Throw away	2.8	1.1
Other	6.7	3.2
Mysterious peacock		
Definitely existed	38.7	40.4
Probably existed	24.5	23.4
Probably didn't exist	18.9	14.9
Definitely didn't exist	16.0	20.2
Don't know	1.9	1.1
Frequency of radio listening		
Often	55.7	44.7
Sometimes	36.8	55.3
Never	7.5	
Frequency of television viewing		
Often	11.3	6.5
Sometimes	81.1	85.1
Never	7.6	8.4

	Largo do Machado	São Cristóvão Fair
Like soap operas		
Like	19.8	16.0
Like more or less	25.5	22.3
Don't like	54.7	61.7
Read newspapers		
Often	33.9	16.0
Sometimes	50.9	61.7
Never	15.2	22.3
Part of paper preferred		
News	38.8	40.4
Sports	31.1	23.4
Ads	7.5	9.6
Other	7.5	4.3
Don't read	15.1	22.3
Read magazines		
Often	12.2	4.2
Sometimes	60.4	42.6
Never	27.4	53.2
Read comic books		
Often	6.6	7.5
Sometimes	47.2	23.4
Never	46.2	69.1
Date of last movie attended		
Week or less	55.7	33.0
Week–month	19.8	11.7
Over a month	17.0	38.3
Never go	7.5	17.0
Remember name of last movie		
Yes	30.3	12.8
More or less	24.2	23.1
No	45.5	64.1
Prefer live or recorded poet		
Live	34.8	49.4
Record	27.4	24.3
Both	4.7	17.0
Neither	5.7	7.1
Don't know (unfamiliar)	27.4	2.2

	Largo do Machado	*São Cristóvão Fair*
Prefer folheto, *magazine, or comic book*		
Folheto	72.7	78.7
Magazine	13.2	10.6
Comic book	9.4	6.4
Like two or more	3.8	3.2
Other	0.9	1.1

Appendix D: Glossary

Although the following terms are defined within the text the first time they are used, many continue to reappear. I have therefore made a list of them, as well as various proper names which the reader unfamiliar with Brazil may find useful.

agregado. The collective term for subsistence farmers, which subsumes squatters (*moradores* or *camaradas*), tenant farmers (*rendeiros*), and sharecroppers (*meeiros*).

almanaque. "Almanac"; a kind of astrological guide providing a miscellany of moral and practical agricultural advice. A number of *cordel* authors publish *almanaques* along with their stories in verse. Poets such as Manoel Caboclo e Silva, José Costa Leite, and Vicente Vitorino de Melo annually publish these books, which may be seen as descendants of the centuries-old Iberian *Lunário Perpétuo.*

Associação Nacional de Trovadores e Violeiros (ANTV). A poets' union founded in 1955 by Rodolfo Coelho Cavalcante. The group, which included both *cordel* authors and poet-singers, lasted only three years but served as a model for later groups in various parts of Brazil.

Ataíde, João Martins de. Born in the countryside surrounding Ingá do Bacamarte, Paraíba, in 1880, João Martins de Ataíde bought the rights to the older poet Leandro Gomes de Barros' many stories from his widow, quickly becoming Recife's most important poet-printer. Although not the author of many of the stories on which his name appears, he wrote a number of *folheto* classics. His death in 1959 signaled the end of an era.

Barros, Leandro Gomes de. One of the first and in many poets' minds, the greatest *cordel* author of all time, Leandro Gomes de Barros, who was born near Pombal, Paraíba, in 1823, is said by some to have authored over a thousand stories. From an early age, he was associated with the poet-singers of Teixeira. Before his death in 1907, he wrote on almost every subject treated by present-day authors. His *folhetos* continue to go through many printings.

Batista, Francisco das Chagas. A poet-singer and author born in Teixeira, Paraíba, Francisco das Chagas Batista is known for a number of *folheto* classics. The owner of a printing press in the state capital of João Pessoa, he published a now-classic anthology of *cordel* authors and poet-singers three years before his death in 1930.

bendito. "Hallelujah"; a religious song sometimes published in *cordel* form. Performed orally, *benditos*, unlike the majority of *folhetos*, usually reveal little if any story line.

Bumba-meu-Boi. A traditional dramatic dance featuring a bull and a supporting cast of characters. This festival, which combines Afro-Brazilian and

Iberian elements, is associated above all with the Northeast. It is usually performed around Christmas and Carnival time.

caboclo. Acculturated Brazilian Indian or any Brazilian of mixed Indian and white blood. The term may also be applied to copper-colored mulattos with straight hair. It is used more widely to refer to any person from the backwoods.

canção (plural, *canções*). Literally "song"; refers here to the short compositions by poet-singers and sometimes *cordel* authors written for the radio. The lyrics are then printed on *folheto* presses and sold by *cordel* vendors in open-air markets and fairs.

cangaceiro. A kind of outlaw or bandit associated with the Northeast. The term is said to come from the word *canga* meaning "yoke," a reference to the manner in which *cangaceiros* slung their weapons across their backs. The most famous Northeastern *cangaceiros* of the twentieth century were Antônio Silvino and Virgolino Ferreira (Lampião).

cantador. Literally "singer"; refers here to those poet-improvisers known for their oral compositions and on-the-spot exchanges in verse. See *repentista*.

cantoria. A gathering characterized by the presence of *cantadores*, who engage in verbal dueling. Traditionally held in farmhouses, rodeos, and marketplaces, these matches are now also sponsored by official agencies.

capoeira. An Afro-Brazilian form of self-defense, which resembles a martial dance. Like the *folheto*, *capoeira* has become popular among members of the middle class.

carioca. A native or permanent resident of Rio de Janeiro.

Cascudo, Luís da Câmara. Perhaps the single greatest name in Brazilian folklore research, Luís da Câmara Cascudo, who, unfortunately, no longer grants interviews, has published numerous works on popular poets and singers. *Cordel* author Rodolfo Coelho Cavalcante's recent *folheto ABC of Câmara Cascudo* is a particularly fitting tribute to the folklorist's knowledge and love of Brazilian traditions.

chave. Those pauses in a poet's reading of the text when he encourages the audience to buy a copy of the story. The term *chave* means "key," and these breaks are indeed crucial to the vendor's success.

Cícero, Padre. A backlands priest who became a powerful political as well as spiritual leader after a series of events widely accepted as miracles in 1889, Padre (Father) Cícero Romão made the sleepy town of Juazeiro do Norte the region's most important city. The city is dominated today by an immense statue of the patriarch, who died in 1934 but whose memory continues to draw a steady stream of pilgrims from all over the Northeast.

conga. That percentage of the cost of the printed booklets that the author receives in return for the rights to his story; it is normally 10 percent but may vary.

Conselheiro, Antônio. Founder of the messianic community of Canudos in the interior of the state of Bahia, Antônio Conselheiro promised his backlands followers a new social and economic order on earth. The federal government, which considered the community's members rebels, sent four expeditions against Canudos before finally wiping it out in 1897.

coquista. The performer of a type of popular poetry improvised to the beat of the tambourine. The *coco* is associated more with the coastal region of the Northeast than with the interior, but *coquistas* resemble *repentistas* in their capacity for on-the-spot invention.

cordel. Short for *literatura de cordel* and used interchangeably with *folheto.* The *cordel* refers to the string on which these stories in verse were displayed in marketplaces. A Portuguese term, introduced by middle-class researchers, it has become popular with Brazilian *folheto* poets.

corrido. Found in various parts of Spanish America, the *corrido*, like the *literatura de cordel*, is descended from an older Iberian ballad tradition. *Corridos* are narrative poems set to music which generally fall into four-line stanzas (eight-syllable lines, consonantal rhyme scheme). The term comes from the verb *correr*, which means "to run," and refers to the form's relative brevity and avoidance of verbal flourishes.

cruzeiro. The Brazilian monetary unit, which replaced the *milreis* in 1942. In 1977–1978, the *cruzeiro* was worth approximately six cents. A *folheto* costs anywhere from three to ten *cruzeiros* depending on its length and the type of cover.

Cunha, Euclides da. Author of *Os Sertões* (*Revolt in the Backlands*), an account of the Canudos campaign published in 1902, Euclides da Cunha was a writer as well as soldier in the government forces. His book, which holds an honored place in Brazilian literature, was instrumental in awakening national interest in previously ignored forms of popular culture.

Damião, Frei. Considered by many Northeasterners to be the spiritual heir to Padre Cícero, Frei (Friar) Damião is credited by some with miraculous powers. Italian by birth, he has traveled the backlands for many years and is the subject of frequent *folhetos.*

desafio. Literally "challenge." The term refers to those contests in verse between two poet-singers (see *peleja*). The winner must demonstrate greater verbal skill and/or knowledge.

dom. The poetic gift, which readers and writers insist is inborn and cannot be learned.

editor (also *editor-proprietário*). The term for "publisher"; a person who is usually, but not necessarily, also a printer. *Cordel* authors may sell their stories to an editor who then becomes the legal owner. The going rate for a story varies anywhere from ten dollars to one hundred dollars cash, or the equivalent in booklets.

estrela. "Star"; refers here to the star of poetic inspiration.

exemplo. Literally "example"; refers to a *folheto* which offers an explicit moral lesson (for example, *The Example of the Girl Who Was Attacked by a Vampire for Wearing a Bikini When Her Mother Said She Shouldn't*).

ex voto. Payment to the saints or God for favors received, most often in the form of representations in wood or plaster of a body or part of the body which was ill and is now well.

falsidade. "Double-dealing" or "deceit." The opposite of *firmeza*, *falsidade* is the prime sin in the world of the *cordel*. Indicating a lack of loyalty to one's commitments, it endangers the social order.

favela. The term for a variety of fast-growing brush; it is also the word for those slums which tend to spring up and spread rapidly in Brazilian cities. Those popular poets who live in cities tend to inhabit *favelas*.

fazenda. The ranches or farmsteads frequently devoted to cattle raising in the Northeast.

feira. "Market" or "fair." There are different kinds of markets, but the most common has traditionally been the *feira de consumo* or weekly produce fair. In other Romance languages, the names for each of the five weekdays come from the Latin names for the gods, but Portuguese designates them as "second fair" (Monday), "third fair" (Tuesday), etc., indicating the importance of the *feira* as an institution.

firmeza. "Constancy"; the adjective *firme* means "durable" or "nonwavering"; *firmeza* is the ultimate virtue in the world of the *cordel*. People who exhibit it by living up to moral and social obligations are inevitably rewarded. The opposite of *firmeza* is *falsidade*.

folheto. The general term for "pamphlet" and used by *cordel* authors as a synonym for one of their stories. Technically, the *folheto* has eight or sixteen pages while the *romance* has thirty-two. In practice, *folheto* is used as a general term for stories of all lengths.

folheto de acontecimento. A news account in *cordel* form; *acontecimento* means "happening" or "event."

folheto de encomenda. A *cordel* story written at the request of a customer who generally provides the poet with a set of guidelines; *encomendar* means "to commission" or "order." Political candidates have always turned to popular poets for help at election time in the Northeast, but *folhetos* may also be ordered by businesses, civic organizations, government agencies, and church groups.

folheto de época. The same thing as a *folheto de acontecimento*; *época* means "epoch" or "time period." These news accounts are generally of intense but passing interest.

Fundação Casa de Rui Barbosa. A research institution named for the Bahian statesman who became finance minister toward the end of the nineteenth century under the Old Republic; the foundation has an extensive *cordel* library and has published a number of important research works on Northeastern popular poetry.

inspiração. Literally "inspiration"; refers to the act of writing, which popular poets distinguish from the numerous steps involved in printing and selling *folhetos*.

Instituto Nacional de Folclore. The Brazilian National Institute for Folklore, formerly known as the Campaign for the Defense of Folklore, acquired its new title in 1979. The institute coordinates documentation and dissemination of folk and popular traditions throughout the country.

Lampião (also spelled *Lampeão*). The most famous of the Northeastern bandits known as *cangaceiros*, Lampião ("light" or "lantern," a name taken by Virgolino Ferreira) was finally captured and beheaded by government forces in 1938. He and his companion Maria Bonita ("Pretty Mary") continue to make an appearance in the pages of the *cordel*, and there are readers who insist that the couple never died.

Lima, Silvino Pirauá. One of the great nineteenth-century poet-singers associated with the city of Teixeira, Silvino Pirauá Lima is said to have authored a number of the *cordel* stories attributed to Leandro Gomes de Barros. His presence within the tradition emphasizes the *folheto*'s ties to earlier poet-improvisers.

literatura de cordel. See *cordel.*

Luzeiro press. A São Paulo-based publishing company, the Luzeiro claims to be the biggest *folheto* printer today in Brazil. Specializing primarily in classic stories, the company, formerly known as Prelúdio, uses a glossy, comic book-like cover, editing out misspellings and generally standardizing texts.

matuto. "Backwoodsman," "bumpkin," "hillbilly"; generally regarded as a derogative term (*mato* means "woods") but often used by the people to whom it applies with defiant pride.

Mysterious Peacock. The title of a well-known *folheto* originally by José Camelo de Melo Resende, later rewritten by João Melquíades Ferreira. The story concerns a young man who falls in love with a lovely young woman who is kept a virtual prisoner by her father. Arranging for an inventor to supply him with a mechanical peacock that will allow him to visit the tower where the object of his affections lives, the hero persuades her to elope with him, and the two fly off in the peacock. Once married, they return when the heroine's mother sends word that her husband has died and that she wishes to make her son-in-law her heir.

nordestino. An individual from the Northeast, an area including the states of Alagoas, Ceará, Maranhão, Paraíba, Pernambuco, Piauí, and Rio Grande do Norte. The government development agency known as the SUDENE also considers Sergipe and parts of the states of Minas Gerais and Bahia as belonging to the Northeast. The region, known for its poverty, contains approximately a third of Brazil's 120 million people. Recife is the area's largest city.

oração. "Prayer"; one of the few usually prose compositions available in *cordel* form.

orgulho. "Pride"; a typical error in the *folheto* but not as grave as *falsidade*, *orgulho* implies an overstepping of one's social role.

patrão. "Boss" or "patron"; refers to an employer, often but not necessarily a landowner, with whom the worker establishes a necessary, if unequal, relationship.

paulista. A native or permanent resident of São Paulo.

peleja. Another term for the *desafio* or poetic contest, whose literal meaning is "battle" or "quarrel."

poesia. Synonymous with *inspiração*; refers more to the process of writing or to the poet's profession than to the written product or *folheto*.

poeta or *poeta de bancada*. The term used for the poet who writes instead of improvises. The *bancada* refers to the bench on which the poet sits to write.

povo. Literally "people" or "population" but often used to refer specifically to the common people as opposed to the elite. When the *cordel* poet says that he writes for the *povo*, he is referring to his own, generally lower-class, public.

praciano. "City dweller." The word, which comes from *praça* ("central square"), is used in opposition to *matuto* ("countryman") and generally carries a negative connotation.

Prestes, Luís Carlos. Known as "the Knight of Hope," Captain Luís Carlos Prestes led a column of persons dissatisfied with the prevailing political structure (which was to change through revolution in 1930) through the Northeastern backlands between 1924 and 1927. The column finally disbanded in Bolivia after a 14,000-mile trek, and Prestes returned to Brazil to become the leader of the Brazilian Communist party, founded a few years before. Various popular poets wrote about the Prestes column, and a few are still alive to reminisce about it.

quadra. The Portuguese term for "quatrain." In the Brazilian Northeast, the six-line stanza (*sextilha*) replaced the *quadra* or four-line stanza, frequently used in Portuguese *cordel* stories, in the early nineteenth century.

ramo. Literally "branch"; the term means "profession." Poets continually refer to poetry as *o ramo*. Difficulties are *espinhas* ("thorns") on the occupational branch.

repentista. Used as a synonym for *cantador*; it is related to the noun *repente* meaning "burst" or "gust" since these competitors in verbal duels must be able to think fast.

roda or *rodada*. The "wheel" or circle of people who surround the poet reading his verses at the fair.

romance. "Ballad," "romance," "novel," "story," "tale," or "fable." *Romances velhos* or *tradicionais* are those oral, anonymous ballads with obvious Iberian roots. In *cordel* terms, a *romance* is any story of thirty-two or more pages generally dealing with love and adventure.

sertão. The backlands or interior of the Northeastern states. Larger than France and Germany put together, the *sertão*, traditionally a cattle-raising area, grows green with the winter rains, then shrivels in the summer sun. Years without rain bring on disastrous droughts, which send its inhabitants fleeing toward the more humid coast. (These forced migrants are called *retirantes*.) One of the poorest regions of Brazil, the *sertão*'s new roads and the mass media have made it less isolated than in the past.

sesmaria. A land grant awarded to settlers of recognized position by the Portuguese crown. These persons were then supposed to serve as representatives of the imperial government. These holdings, some of which were enormous, began splitting up in the nineteenth century as a result of inheritance patterns and a shift in official land policy.

sextilha. The standard six-line, rhyming stanza used by *cordel* authors and poet-improvisers alike.

Silva, José Bernardo da. A poet-printer born in Alagoas, who later moved to Juazeiro do Norte. José Bernardo da Silva bought the rights to a number of stories from João Martins de Ataíde, who had in turn acquired these from Leandro Gomes de Barros. Although he died several years ago, Zé Bernardo's press, the São Francisco, continues to turn out a stream of *folheto* classics. His grandson, Stênio Diniz, is an artist and designer of *cordel* covers.

Silvino, Antônio. An early twentieth-century bandit second only in fame to Lampião.

sina. "Destiny" or "fate." The noun comes from the verb *assinar* meaning "to mark out" and is used to explain one's fortune or misfortune in this life.

Teixeira. A small city amidst the mountains of south central Paraíba; it has traditionally been a center for poet-singers. The school (*escola*) of Teixeira, a group of *cantadores* who emerged in the early nineteenth century, was responsible for making the six-line stanza or *sextilha* a standard poetic form.

toada. "Tune" or "air"; refers here to the chanting style that the poet uses to read his stories. The *toada* varies from poet to poet and from subject to subject.

tranca. Another word for *chave*; *trancar* means to "lock" or "close," and indeed these prose intervals serve to "tie things up" for the vendor, who uses them to communicate directly with his audience, coaxing them to buy his wares.

trancoso. A general term for folktale. Gonçalo Fernandes Trancoso was the author of a book entitled *Tales and Stories of Moral Counsel and Example*, published in Lisbon in 1585. Little by little, his name came to be used for any folk story.

trovador. Literally one who composes *trovas* or ballads.

vaqueiro. The term, which means "cowboy" or "herdsman," is used in the South of Brazil but is associated above all with the Northeast.

vaquejada. Roundup or rodeo. *Repentistas* frequently perform at these events.

Vargas, Getúlio. Born on a cattle ranch in the extreme south of Brazil in 1883, Getúlio Vargas governed Brazil for more than a generation. From 1930–1934 he served as chief of a provisional government, from 1934–1937 as the constitutional president elected by congress, from 1937–1945 as dictator, and from 1951–1954 as constitutional president elected by the people. His suicide in 1954 triggered a number of best-selling *folhetos*.

violeiro. Guitar player; a *cantador* who accompanies himself.

Zé. A common nickname for José.

Bibliography

The following bibliography has been divided for the sake of convenience into three principal sections. These are sources in English, sources in Portuguese and other foreign languages, and *folhetos* mentioned in this study.

The listings in all cases are as complete as possible. In the case of a small number of foreign language sources, I worked from photocopies for which complete bibliographical information proved impossible to obtain. Also, newspaper articles used in files maintained by an institute or by the newspaper itself were sometimes missing page and section numbers.

I have followed the standard alphabetizing procedure for each language. In Portuguese, where alphabetization is erratic, I have consistently used the last element of a compound surname. Thus, João Oliveira da Silva would precede Joaquim Bandeira da Silva. As is customary, the presence of terms such as *Filho*, *Júnior*, *Maior*, and *Neto* ("son," "junior," "senior," and "grandson") has not affected the alphabetical order. As always, initial indefinite articles (*o*, *a*, *os*, *as*) have been disregarded in alphabetizing titles, that is, *Literatura popular* would follow "O catolicismo no Brasil."

In the case of *folhetos*, I have given such information as exists. Those dates listed here refer to the editions to which I had access. The reader should be aware that *cordel* stories may go through dozens of printings and that many are actually much older than the date suggests. The reader should also realize that there may be multiple versions of a title by one or several authors.

Sources in English

Aarne, Antti, and Stith Thompson. *The Types of the Folktale*. 2nd rev. ed. Folklore Fellows Communications, No. 184. Helsinki: Suomalainen Tiedakatemia, 1961.

Abrahams, Roger. "Playing the Dozens." *Journal of American Folklore*, 75 (1962): 209–20.

Alencar, José de. *Iracema: The Honey Lips*. Trans. Isabel Burton. London: Bickers & Son, 1886.

Altman, Charles F. "Two Types of Opposition in the Structure of Latin Saints' Lives." In *Medieval Hagiography and Romance*, ed. Paul Maurice Clogan (*Medievalia and Humanistica*, n.s. 6). Cambridge: Cambridge University Press, 1975, pp. 1–11.

Amado, Jorge. *Tereza Batista, Home from the Wars*. Trans. Barbara Shelby. New York: Knopf, 1975.

Arantes Neto, Antonio Augusto. "Some Sociological Aspects of the *Literatura de Cordel*." Ph.D. dissertation. Cambridge University, 1977.

Armistead, Samuel G. "Edward R. Haymes, *A Bibliography of Studies Relating to Parry's and Lord's Oral Theory.*" *Modern Language Notes*, 90 (1975): 296–99.

Armistead, Samuel G., and Joseph H. Silverman. *The Judeo-Spanish Ballad Chapbooks of Yacob Abraham Yoná.* Berkeley and Los Angeles: University of California Press, 1971.

Ashton, John. *Chap-books of the Eighteenth Century.* London: Chatto & Windus, 1882.

Azadovskii, Mark K. *A Siberian Tale Teller.* Trans. James K. Dow. University of Texas Monograph Series, No. 2. Austin: Center for Intercultural Studies in Folklore and Ethnomusicology, 1974.

Babcock, Barbara A., ed. *The Reversible World: Symbolic Inversion in Art and Society.* Ithaca: Cornell University Press, 1978.

Baden, Nancy T. "Popular Poetry in the Novels of Jorge Amado." *Journal of Latin American Lore*, 2 (1976): 3–22.

Banfield, Edward. *The Moral Basis of a Backward Society.* Glencoe, Ill.: Free Press, 1958.

Barge, Ernest J., and Jan Feidel, trans. *The Warriors: Peleja Between Joaquim Jaqueira and Manoel Barra Mansa.* New York: Grossman, 1972.

Barman, Roderick J. "The Brazilian Peasantry Reexamined: The Implications of the Quebra-Quilo Revolt, 1874–1875." *Hispanic American Review*, 57 (1977): 401–24.

Bascom, William R., ed. *Frontiers in Folklore.* A.A.A.S. Selected Symposia Series, No. 5. Boulder, Co.: Westview Press, 1977.

Bauman, Richard. "Verbal Art as Performance." *American Anthropologist*, 77 (1975): 290–311.

———. *Verbal Art as Performance.* Rowley, Mass.: Newbury House Publishers, 1977.

Bauman, Richard, and Joel Sherzer, eds. *Explorations in the Ethnography of Speaking.* Cambridge: Cambridge University Press, 1974.

Bello, José Maria. *A History of Modern Brazil, 1889–1964.* 2nd ed. Trans. James Taylor. Notes by Rollie E. Poppino. Stanford, Ca.: Stanford University Press, 1968.

Ben-Amos, Dan. *Sweet Words: Storytelling Events in Benin.* Philadelphia: Institute for the Study of Human Issues, 1975.

———. "Two Benin Storytellers." In *African Folklore*, ed. Richard M. Dorson. Bloomington: Indiana University Press, 1972, pp. 103–14.

Ben-Amos, Dan, ed. *Folklore Genres.* American Folklore Society Publications, No. 26. Austin: University of Texas Press, 1976.

Ben-Amos, Dan, and Kenneth Goldstein, eds. *Folklore: Performance and Communication.* The Hague: Mouton, 1975.

Bettelheim, Bruno. *The Uses of Enchantment.* 2nd ed. New York: Vintage Books, 1977.

Bigsby, C. W. E., ed. *Approaches to Popular Culture.* Bowling Green, Ohio: Bowling Green University Popular Press, 1976.

Bishop, Elizabeth, and Emanuel Brasil, eds. *An Anthology of Twentieth-Century*

Brazilian Poetry. Middletown, Conn.: Wesleyan University Press, 1973.

Blau, Peter. *Exchange and Power in Social Life.* New York: John Wiley & Sons, 1964.

Bluestein, Gene. *The Voice of the Folk: Folklore and American Literary Theory.* Amherst: University of Massachusetts Press, 1972.

Boklund, Karin M. "On the Spatial and Cultural Characteristics of Courtly Romance." *Semiotica,* 20 (1977): 1–38.

Bouissac, Paul. *Circus and Culture: A Semiotic Approach.* Bloomington: Indiana University Press, 1976.

Brown, Walter J. *The Portuguese in California.* San Francisco: R & E Research Associates, 1972.

Burke, Peter. *Popular Culture in Early Modern Europe.* New York: New York University Press, 1978.

Burlingame, Eugene Watson, trans. *Buddhist Parables: Translated from the Original Pāli.* New Haven: Yale University Press, 1922.

Burns, E. Bradford. *A History of Brazil.* New York: Columbia University Press, 1970.

—————. *Nationalism in Brazil: A Historical Survey.* New York: Frederick A. Praeger, 1968.

Chandler, Billy Jaynes. *The Bandit King: Lampião of Brazil.* College Station: Texas A & M University Press, 1978.

—————. *The Feitosas and the Sertão of Inhamuns: The History of a Family and a Community in Northeast Brazil, 1700–1930.* Gainesville: University of Florida Press, 1972.

Chilcote, Ronald, ed. *Protest and Resistance in Angola and Brazil.* Berkeley and Los Angeles: University of California Press, 1972.

Clammer, J. R. *Literacy and Social Change: A Case Study of Fiji.* Leiden: Brill, 1976.

Colby, Benjamin N. "The Analysis of Cultural Content and the Patterning of Narrative Concerns in Texts." *American Anthropologist,* 75 (1966): 374–88.

Collison, Robert. *The Story of Street Literature: Forerunner of the Popular Press.* Santa Barbara, Ca.: Clio Press, 1973.

Coupe, William. *The German Illustrated Broadsheet in the Seventeenth Century: Historical and Iconographical Studies,* 2 vols. Baden-Baden: Heitz, 1966–1967.

Crane, Thomas Frederick. *The Exempla or Illustrative Stories from the Sermones Vulgares of Jacques de Vitry.* Publications of the Folklore Society, No. 26, 1890. Nedeln, Lichtenstein: Kraus Reprint Ltd., 1967.

Crawford, J. Wickersham. "*Echarse Pullas*: A Popular Form of *Tenzone.*" *Romanic Review,* 6 (1915): 150–64.

Crowley, Daniel J. *I Could Talk Old-Story Good: Creativity in Bahamian Folklore.* Berkeley and Los Angeles: University of California Press, 1966.

Cunniff, Roger Lee. "The Great Drought: Northeastern Brazil, 1877–1880." Ph.D. dissertation. University of Texas, Austin, 1971.

Curran, Mark J. *Introduction and Selected Bibliography of History and Politics in Brazilian Popular Poetry.* Tempe: Center for Latin American Studies, Arizona State University, 1971.

————. "The Politics of Culture." *Proceedings of the Pacific Coast Council on Latin American Studies*, 5 (1976): 11–25.

da Cunha, Euclides. *Revolt in the Backlands.* Trans. Samuel Putnam. 2nd ed. Chicago: University of Chicago Press, 1970.

d'Azevedo, Warren L., ed. *The Traditional Artist in African Societies.* Bloomington: Indiana University Press, 1973.

Dean, Warren. "Latifundia and Land Policy in Nineteenth-Century Brazil." *Hispanic American Historical Review*, 51 (1971): 606–25.

de Azevedo, Thales. *Social Change in Brazil.* Gainesville: University of Florida Press, 1963.

de Bono, Edward. *Lateral Thinking: A Textbook of Creativity.* New York: Harper & Row, 1970.

Dégh, Linda. *Folktales and Society: Story-Telling in a Hungarian Peasant Community.* Trans. Emily M. Schlossberger. Bloomington: Indiana University Press, 1969.

————. "Some Questions on the Social Function of Story-Telling." *Acta Ethnographica*, 6 (1957): 91–146.

Della Cava, Ralph. *Miracle at Joaseiro.* New York: Columbia University Press, 1970.

Dodson, Don. "Onitsha Pamphlets: Culture in the Marketplace." Ph.D. dissertation. Stanford University, 1974.

Douglas, Mary. *Implicit Meanings: Essays in Anthropology.* London: Routledge & Kegan Paul, 1975.

Dulles, John W. F. *Vargas of Brazil: A Political Biography.* Austin: University of Texas Press, 1967.

Duncan, Hugh D. *Symbols and Social Theory.* New York: Oxford University Press, 1969.

Dundes, Alan. *Analytic Essays in Folklore.* The Hague: Mouton, 1975.

————. "The Binary Structure of 'Unsuccessful Repetition' in Lithuanian Folktales." *Western Folklore*, 12 (1962): 165–74.

————. *The Morphology of North American Indian Folktales.* Folklore Fellows Communications, No. 195. Helsinki: Suomalainen Tiedakatemia, 1964.

————. "Texture, Text, and Context." *Southern Folklore Quarterly*, 28 (1964): 251–65.

Dundes, Alan, Jerry W. Leach, and Bora Ozkök. "The Strategy of Turkish Boys' Verbal Dueling Rhymes." *Journal of American Folklore*, 83 (1970): 325–49.

Forman, Shepard. *The Brazilian Peasantry.* New York: Columbia University Press, 1975.

————. "Disunity and Discontent: A Study of Peasant Political Movements in Brazil." *Journal of Latin American Studies*, 3 (1971): 3–24.

Foster, George. "The Dyadic Contract." *American Anthropologist*, 63 (1961): 1280–94.

————. "The Dyadic Contract: A Model for the Social Structure of a Mexican

Peasant Village." *American Anthropologist*, 63 (1961): 1173–92.

————. "Peasant Society and the Image of Limited Good." *American Anthropologist*, 67 (1965): 293–315.

————. "Treasure Tales, and the Image of the Static Economy in a Mexican Peasant Community." *Journal of American Folklore*, 77 (1964): 39–44.

Freyre, Gilberto. *The Mansions and the Shanties: The Making of Modern Brazil.* Trans. Harriet de Onís. New York: Knopf, 1963.

————. *The Masters and the Slaves: A Study in the Development of Brazilian Civilization.* Trans. Samuel Putnam. New York: Knopf, 1956.

Geertz, Clifford. *The Interpretation of Cultures.* New York: Basic Books, 1973.

————. "The Javanese Kijaji: The Changing Role of a Culture Broker." *Comparative Studies in Society and History*, 2 (1960): 228–49.

Georges, Robert A. "Structure in Folktales: A Generative-Transformational Approach." *The Conch*, 2 (1970): 4–17.

————. "Toward an Understanding of Storytelling Events." *Journal of American Folklore*, 82 (1969): 313–28.

Gizelis, Gregory. "Historical Event into Song: The Use of Cultural Perceptual Style." *Folklore*, 83 (1972): 302–20.

————. "A Neglected Aspect of Creativity of Folk Performers." *Journal of American Folklore*, 86 (1973): 167–72.

Goody, John Rankine. *Literacy in Traditional Societies.* Cambridge: Cambridge University Press, 1968.

Greenwald, Harold. *The Prostitute in Literature.* New York: Ballantine Books, 1960.

Greimas, A. J. ed., *Sign, Language, Culture.* The Hague: Mouton, 1970.

Gross, Daniel R. "Ritual and Conformity: A Religious Pilgrimage to Northeast Brazil." *Ethnology*, 10 (1971): 129–48.

Hall, Robert A. *Cultural Symbolism in Literature.* Ithaca: Cornell University Press, 1963.

Hamilton, Russell G. "Afro-Brazilian Cults in the Novels of Jorge Amado." *Hispania*, 50 (1967): 242–52.

Hawkes, Terence. *Structuralism and Semiotics.* Berkeley and Los Angeles: University of California Press, 1977.

Haymes, Edward R. *A Bibliography of Studies Relating to Parry's and Lord's Oral Theory.* Cambridge, Mass.: Harvard University Press, 1973.

Hølbek, Bengt. *Formal and Structural Studies of Oral Narrative: A Bibliography.* Copenhagen: Institut for Folkemindevidenskab, Kobenshavens Universitet, 1978.

Horton, Robin, and Ruth Finnegan, eds. *Modes of Thought.* London: Faber, 1973.

Hulet, Claude. "Two *Folheto* Versions of João de Calais." Paper read at the Second Symposium for Portuguese Traditions, University of California, Los Angeles, May 8, 1978.

Hutchinson, Bertram. "The Patron-Dependent Relationship in Brazil: A Preliminary Examination." *Sociologia Ruralis*, 6 (1966): 3–30.

Jakobson, Roman, and Petr Bogatyrev. "On the Boundary Between Studies of

Folklore and Literature." In *Readings in Russian Poetics: Formalist and Structuralist Views*, ed. Ladislav Matejeska and Krystyna Pomorska. Cambridge: MIT Press, 1971, pp. 91–94.

Jason, Heda. "Structural Analysis and the Concept of the 'Tale Type.'" *Arv*, 28 (1972): 36–54.

Johnson, Allen. *Sharecroppers of the Sertão*. Stanford, Ca.: Stanford University Press, 1972.

Johnson, John J., ed. *Continuity and Change in Latin America*. Stanford, Ca.: Stanford University Press, 1964.

Kirshenblatt-Gimblett, Barbara, ed. *Speech Play: Research and Resources for Studying Linguistic Creativity*. Philadelphia: University of Pennsylvania Press, 1976.

Lee, Dorothy. *Freedom and Culture*. Englewood Cliffs, N.J.: Prentice-Hall, 1959.

Levine, Robert M. *Historical Dictionary of Brazil*. Latin American Historical Dictionary Series, No. 19. Metuchen, N.J.: Scarecrow Press, 1978.

———. *Pernambuco in the Brazilian Federation, 1889–1937*. Stanford, Ca.: Stanford University Press, 1978.

Lévi-Strauss, Claude. *Structural Anthropology*. 2nd ed. Trans. Claire Jacobson and Brooke Grundfest Schoepf. New York: Basic Books, 1963.

Lewell, H. Ernest, ed. *The Cŕy of Home: Cultural Nationalism and the Modern Writer*. Knoxville: University of Tennessee Press, 1972.

Lewin, Linda. "Oral Tradition and Elite Myth: The Legend of the 'Good' Thief Antônio Silvino in Brazilian Popular Culture." *Journal of Latin American Lore* 5 (1980), 157–204.

Lipski, John M. "From Text to Narrative: Spanning the Gap." *Poetics*, n.s. 4 (1975): 191–206.

Lord, Albert B. *The Singer of Tales*. New York: Atheneum, 1976.

Lotman, Juri M. "On the Metalanguage of a Typological Description of Culture." *Semiotica*, 14 (1975): 97–123.

McDowell, John H. "The Mexican *Corrido*: Formula and Theme in a Ballad Tradition." *Journal of American Folklore*, 85 (1972): 205–20.

Maranda, Elli Köngas, and Pierre Maranda, eds. *Structural Analysis of Oral Tradition*. Philadelphia: University of Pennsylvania Press, 1971.

———. *Structural Models in Folklore and Transformational Essays*. The Hague: Mouton, 1971.

Matejska, Ladislav, and Krystyna Pomorska, eds. *Readings in Russian Poetics: Formalist and Structuralist Views*. Cambridge, Mass.: MIT Press, 1971.

Morse, Richard. "Some Themes of Brazilian History." *South Atlantic Quarterly*, 61 (1962): 159–82.

Mosher, Joseph Albert. *The Exemplum in the Early Religious and Didactic Literature of England*. New York: Columbia University Press, 1911.

Nariman, J. K. *Literary History of Sanskrit Buddhism*. 2nd rev. ed. Delhi: Motilal Banarsidass, 1972.

Neuberg, Victor E. *Chapbooks: A Guide to Reference Material on English, Scottish, and American Chapbook Literature of the 18th and 19th Centuries*. 2nd ed. London: Woburn Press, 1972.

Nist, John. *The Modernist Movement in Brazil*. Austin: University of Texas Press, 1967.

Norton, F. J., and Edward M. Wilson. *Two Spanish Verse Chapbooks: Romance de Amadis (c. 1515–19), Juyzio Hallado y Trobado (c. 1510): A Facsimile Edition with Bibliographical and Textual Studies*. London: Cambridge University Press, 1969.

Nunes, Maria Luisa. "The Preservation of African Culture in Brazilian Literature: The Novels of Jorge Amado." *Luso-Brazilian Review*, 10 (1973): 86–101.

Nutini, Hugo. *Ritual Kinship: The Structural and Historical Development of the Compadrazgo System in Rural Tlaxcala, and Its Comparative and Ideological Implication for Latin America*. Princeton, N.J.: Princeton University Press, 1980.

Oberg, Kalervo. "The Marginal Peasant in Brazil." *American Anthropologist*, 67 (1965): 1417–27.

Obiechina, Emmanuel N. *Onitsha Market Literature*. New York: Africana Publishing Corporation, 1972.

Paredes, Américo. "The Ancestry of Mexico's *Corridos*: A Matter of Definition." *Journal of American Folklore*, 76 (1963): 231–35.

―――. *"With His Pistol in His Hand": A Border Ballad and Its Hero*. Austin: University of Texas Press, 1958.

Paredes, Américo, and Richard Bauman. *Towards New Perspectives in Folklore*. Austin: University of Texas Press, 1971.

Pasqualino, Antonio. "Transformations of Chivalrous Literature in the Subject Matter of the Sicilian Marionette Theater." In *Varia Folklorica*, ed. Alan Dundes. The Hague: Mouton, 1978, pp. 83–100.

Peacock, James L. *Rites of Modernization: Symbolic and Social Aspects of Indonesian Proletarian Drama*. Chicago: University of Chicago Press, 1968.

Pedroso, Zophimo Consiglieri. *Portuguese Folk-Tales*. Trans. Henriquetta Monteiro. New York: B. Blom, 1969.

Pentikäinen, Juha. *Oral Repertoire and World View: An Anthropological Study of Marina Takalo's Life History*, Studia Fennica, No. 20. Helsinki: Suomalainen Tiedakatemia, 1978.

Pentikäinen, Juha, and Tuula Juurikka. *Folk Narrative Research: Some Papers Presented at the VI Congress of the International Society for Folk Narrative Research*. Helsinki: Suomalainen Kirjallisuuden Seura, 1976.

Péristiany, Jean G., ed. *Honour and Shame: The Values of Mediterranean Society*. The Nature of Human Society Series. Chicago: University of Chicago Press, 1966.

Pessar, Patricia. "Millenarian Movements in Rural Brazil: Prophecy and Protest." *Latin American Research Review* (in press).

Pittelkow, Ralf. "On Literature as a Social Phenomenon (Sociological Notes)." *Poetics*, 6 (1972): 7–28.

Poggioli, Renato. *The Oaten Flute: Essays on Pastoral Poetry and the Pastoral Ideal*. Cambridge, Mass.: Harvard University Press, 1975.

Poppino, Rollie E. *Brazil: The Land and the People*. 2nd ed. New York: Oxford University Press, 1973.

―――. "The Cattle Industry of the São Francisco Valley During the Colonial

Period." M.A. thesis. Stanford University, 1949.

———. "Princess of the Sertão: A History of Feira de Santana." Ph.D. dissertation. Stanford University, 1953.

Powell, John Duncan. "Peasant Society and Clientelist Politics." *American Political Science Review*, 64 (1970): 411–25.

Propp, Vladimir. *Morphology of the Folktale*. Rev. ed. Trans. Laurence Scott. Austin: University of Texas Press, 1969.

Purcell, Joanne, et al., eds. *Portuguese and Brazilian Oral Traditions in Verse Form/As tradições orais portuguesas e brasileiras em verso*. Los Angeles: University of Southern California Press, 1976.

Ribeiro, René. "Brazilian Messianic Movements. In *Millenial Dreams in Action*, ed. Sylvia L. Thrupp. The Hague: Mouton, 1962, pp. 55–79.

Riegelhaupt, Joyce F., and Shepard Forman. "Bodo Was Never Brazilian: Economic Integration and Rural Development Among a Contemporary Peasantry." *Journal of Economic History*, 30 (1970): 100–16.

———. "Market Place and Marketing System: Toward a Theory of Peasant Economic Integration." *Comparative Studies in Society and History*, 12 (1970): 188–212.

Robe, Stanley L. "The Devil and Saint Bartholomew." Paper read at American Folklore Society meetings, Salt Lake City, October 22, 1978.

Rodrigues, José Honório. *The Brazilians: Their Character and Aspirations*. Trans. Ralph Edward Dimmick. Notes by E. Bradford Burns. Austin: University of Texas Press, 1967.

Rogers, Francis Millet. *The Travels of the Infante Dom Pedro of Portugal*. Cambridge, Mass.: Harvard University Press, 1961.

Rosa, João Guimarães. *The Devil to Pay in the Backlands*. Trans. James L. Taylor and Harriet de Onís. New York: Knopf, 1963.

———. *Sagarana: A Cycle of Stories*. Trans. Harriet de Onís. New York: Knopf, 1966.

———. *The Third Bank of the River and Other Stories*. Trans. Barbara Shelby. New York: Knopf, 1968.

Schechner, Richard, and Mady Schuman, eds. *Ritual, Play, and Performance: Readings in the Social Sciences/Theater*. New York: Seabury Press, 1976.

Schramm, Wilbur, and Daniel Lerner, eds. *Communication and Change: The Last Ten Years—and the Next*. Honolulu: University of Hawaii Press, 1976.

Scott, James C. "The Erosion of Patron-Client Bonds and Social Change in Rural Southeast Asia." *Journal of Asian Studies*, 32 (1972): 5–37.

———. "Patron-Client Politics and Political Change in Southeast Asia." *American Political Science Review*, 66 (1972): 91–113.

Shanin, Teodor, ed. *Peasants and Peasant Societies: Selected Readings*. London: Penguin Books, 1971.

Shepard, Leslie. *The Broadside Ballad: A Study in Origins and Meaning*. London: H. Jenkins, 1962.

———. *The History of Street Literature: The Story of Broadside Ballads, Chapbooks, Proclamations, News-Sheets, Election Bills, Tracts, Pamphlets, Cocks, Catchpennies, and Other Ephemera*. London: David & Charles, 1973.

Shils, Edward. "Deference." In *Social Stratification: Sociological Studies*, ed. J. A. Jackson. Cambridge: Cambridge University Press, 1968.

Shirley, Robert. *The End of a Tradition*. New York: Columbia University Press, 1971.

Siegel, Bernard. "Social Structure and Economic Change in Brazil." In *Economic Growth: Brazil, India, China*, ed. Simon Kuznets, Wilbert E. Moore, and Joseph J. Spengler. Durham: Duke University Press, 1955, pp. 388–412.

Simmons, Merle E. "The Ancestry of Mexico's *Corridos*." *Journal of American Folklore*, 76 (1963): 1–15.

———. *A Bibliography of the Romance and Related Forms in Spanish America*. Bloomington: Indiana University Press, 1963.

———. *Folklore Bibliography for 1975*. (Philadelphia: ISHI, 1979).

———. *The Mexican Corrido as a Source for Interpretive Study of Modern Mexico, 1870–1950*. Bloomington: Indiana University Press, 1957.

Singlemann, Peter. "Political Structure and Social Banditry in Northeast Brazil." *Journal of Latin American Studies*, 7 (1975): 59–83.

Slater, Candace. "Folklore and the Modern Artist: The Northeast Brazilian *Movimento Armorial*." *Luso-Brazilian Review*, 16 (1979): 160–90.

———. "Joe Bumpkin in the Wilds of Rio de Janeiro." *Journal of Latin American Lore*, 6 (1980): 5–53.

———. "The Romance of the Warrior Maiden: A Tale of Honor and Shame." In *El romancero hoy: historia, comparatismo, bibliografía crítica*, ed. A. Sánchez-Romeralo et al. Madrid: Gráficas Condor, 1979, pp. 167–82.

Smith, Hilary Dansey. *Preaching in the Spanish Golden Age*. New York: Oxford University Press, 1978.

Smith, T. Lynn. *Brazil: People and Institutions*. 4th ed. Baton Rouge: Louisiana State University Press, 1971.

Soons, Alan. "Spanish Ballad and News-Relation in Chapbook Form: The Index of a Mentality." *Kentucky Romance Quarterly*, 20 (1973): 3–17.

Stein, Stanley. *The Brazilian Cotton Manufacture: Textile Enterprise in an Underdeveloped Area, 1850–1950*. Cambridge, Mass.: Harvard University Press, 1957.

Stewart, Susan. *Nonsense: Aspects of Intertextuality in Folklore and Literature*. Baltimore: Johns Hopkins Press, 1979.

Stolz, Benjamin A., and Richard S. Shannon, eds. *Oral Literature and the Formula*. Ann Arbor: Center for the Coordination of Ancient and Modern Studies, University of Michigan, 1976.

Suassuna, Ariano. *The Rogues' Trial*. Trans. Dillwyn F. Ratcliff. Berkeley and Los Angeles: University of California Press, 1963.

Swan, Charles, trans. *Gesta Romanorum*. London: George Bell & Sons, 1906.

Sydow, C. W. von. "On the Spread of Tradition." In *Selected Papers on Folklore*, ed. Laurits Bødker. Copenhagen: Rosenkilde & Bagger, 1948, pp. 11–43.

Thomas, Henry. *Early Spanish Ballads in the British Museum*. 3 vols. Cambridge: Cambridge University Press, 1927.

Thompson, Stith. *Motif-Index of Folk Literature: A Classification of Narrative Elements in Folk-tales, Ballads, Myths, Fables, Medieval Romances, Exempla, Fabliaux, Jest-books, and Local Legends*. Rev. ed. 6 vols. Helsinki:

Suomalainen Tiedakatemia, 1955–1958.

Tubach, Fredric C. *Index Exemplorum*. Folklore Society Communications, No. 204. Helsinki: Suomalainen Tiedakatemia, 1969.

Turner, Victor. *Dramas, Fields, and Metaphors: Symbolic Action in Human Society*. Ithaca: Cornell University Press, 1974.

Vincent, Jon S. "Jorge Amado, Jorge Desprezado." *Luso-Brazilian Review*, 15, Supplementary Issue (Summer 1978): 11–18.

Wagley, Charles. *An Introduction to Brazil*. Rev. ed. New York: Columbia University Press, 1971.

Webb, Kempton E. *The Changing Face of the Northeast*. New York: Columbia University Press, 1974.

Wilson, Edward M. "Tradition and Change in Some Late Spanish Chapbooks." *Hispanic Review*, 25 (1957): 194–216.

Wilson, William A. *Folklore and Nationalism in Modern Finland*. Bloomington: Indiana University Press, 1976.

Winner, Irene Portis, and Thomas G. Winner. "The Semiotics of Cultural Texts." *Semiotica*, 18 (1976): 101–56.

Wolf, Eric R. "Aspects of Group Relations in a Complex Society: Mexico." *American Anthropologist*, 58 (1956): 1065–78.

———. "Kinship, Friendship, and Patron-Client Relationships in Complex Societies." In *The Social Anthropology of Complex Societies*, ed. Michael Banton. London: Tavistock, 1966, pp. 1–22.

Wright, Will. *Sixguns and Society: A Structural Study of the Western*. Berkeley and Los Angeles: University of California Press, 1968.

Young, Jordan M. *The Brazilian Revolution of 1939 and the Aftermath*. New Brunswick: Rutgers University Press, 1967.

Zipes, Jack. "Breaking the Magic Spell: Politics and the Fairy Tale." *New German Critique*, 2 (1975): 116–35.

Zolbrod, Leon M. "Kusazōshi: Chapbooks of Japan." *Transactions of the Asiatic Society of Japan*, 3rd series, 10 (1968): 116–47.

Sources in Portuguese and Other Foreign Languages

Acevedo Hernández, Antonio. *Los cantores populares chilenos*. Santiago: Editorial Nascimento, 1933.

Aires, Felix. *O Piauí na poesia popular*. Rio de Janeiro: Artenova, 1975.

Albuquerque, Ulisses Lins de. *Um sertanejo e o sertão*. 2nd ed. Rio de Janeiro: José Olympio/INL, 1976.

Alegría, Fernando. *La poesía chilena: Orígenes y desarrollo del siglo XVI al XIX*. Berkeley and Los Angeles: University of California Press, 1954.

Alencar, José de. "O cantador nordestino e o épico português." *Ocidente: Revista Portuguesa de Cultura* (Lisbon), n.s. 83 (1972): 75–87.

———. *O nosso cancioneiro. Cartas ao Sr. Joaquim Serra*. Rio de Janeiro: Livraria São José, 1962.

———. *Obra completa*, ed. M. Cavalcanti Proença. 4 vols. Rio de Janeiro: J. Aguilar, 1960–1965.

Almanaque do pensamento. São Paulo: Editora Pensamento Ltda., 1978.

Almeida, Átila de, and José Alves Sobrinho. *Dicionário bio-bibliográfico de repentistas e poetas de bancada.* 2 vols. João Pessoa/Campina Grande: Editora Universitária/Centro de Ciências e Tecnologia, 1978.

Almeida, José Nascimento de. "Cantadores paulistas de porfia ou desafio." *Revista do Arquivo Municipal* (São Paulo), 13 (1947): 199–254.

Almeida, Renato. *A inteligência do folclore.* 2nd ed. Rio de Janeiro: Companhia Editora Americana/MEC, 1974.

Almeida, Ruy. *A poesia e os cantadores do nordeste.* Rio de Janeiro: Imprensa Nacional, 1947.

Althusser, Louis. "Idéologie et appareils idéologiques d'état: Notes pour une recherche." *La Pensée* (Paris), 151 (1970): 3–38.

Amado, Jorge. "Biblioteca do povo e coleção moderna." In Gilberto Freyre et al., *Novos estudos afro-brasileiros.* Biblioteca de Divulgacão Científica. Rio de Janeiro: Civilização Brasileira, 1937, II, 262–324.

————. "Coleção do povo." *Literatura* (Rio de Janeiro), 4 (1947): 45–47.

————. *Tereza Batista cansada de guerra.* São Paulo: Martins, 1972.

Amado, Jorge, et al. *Jorge Amado: Povo e terra.* São Paulo: Martins, 1972.

Andrade, Manuel Correia de. *Cidade e campo no Brasil.* São Paulo: Editora Brasiliense, 1974.

————. *A terra e o homem no nordeste.* São Paulo: Editora Brasiliense, 1963.

Andrade, Mário de. "O romanceiro de Lampeão." In *O baile das quatro artes. Obras completas de Mário de Andrade.* São Paulo: Martins/MEC, 1963, pp. 83–119.

Antologia da literatura de cordel. Vol. 1. Fortaleza: Secretaria de Cultura, Desporto e Promoção Social do Ceará, 1978.

Araújo, Aderaldo Ferreira de. *Eu sou o Cego Aderaldo.* Fortaleza: Imprensa Universitária do Ceará, 1963.

Araújo, Alceu Maynard. *Folclore nacional.* 3 vols. São Paulo: Melhoramentos, 1964.

Araújo, João Dias de. "Imagens de Jesus Cristo na literatura de cordel." *Revista de Cultura Vozes,* 68 (1974): 41–48.

Araújo, Nélson de. *Duas formas de teatro popular do recôncavo baiano.* Salvador: Edições O Vice Rey, 1979.

Araújo, Raimundo. *Cantador, verso, e viola.* Rio de Janeiro: Editora Pongetti, 1974.

Azevêdo, Carlos Alberto. *O heróico e o messiânico na literatura de cordel.* Recife: Edicordel, 1972.

————. "O realismo mágico na literatura popular de zona dos canaviais do nordeste." *Brasil Açucareiro* (Rio de Janeiro), 82 (1973): 43–46.

Azevedo, Luiz Heitor Correia de. "A arte da cantoria." *Cultura Política* (Rio de Janeiro), 4 (1944): 183–87.

————. "Instrumentos de música do cantador nordestino." *Cultura Política* (Rio de Janeiro), 4 (1944): 149–53.

Azzi, Riolando. *O catolicismo popular no Brasil: Aspectos históricos.* Petrópolis: Vozes, 1978.

Bandeira, Manuel. "Saudação aos cantadores do nordeste." *Jornal do Brasil* (Rio de Janeiro), September 12, 1959.

Baptista, Maria Edileuza. "A história do poeta-repórter que não foi agricultor, não deu para pedreiro e vive feliz escrevendo cordel." *Jornal do Commércio* (Recife), February 1, 1978, Section C, p. 8.

Barreto, Luiz Antônio. "A Bíblia na literatura de cordel: Primeira versão do 'Gênesis.'" *Revista Brasileira de Cultura* (Rio de Janeiro), 7 (1971): 137–55.

Barros, Manoel de Souza. *Arte, folclore, subdesenvolvimento.* Rio de Janeiro: Editora Paralelo, 1971.

Barroso, Gustavo. *Almas de lama e de aço: Lampeão e outros cangaceiros.* São Paulo: Melhoramentos, 1930.

————. *Ao som da viola: Folk-lore.* Rio de Janeiro: Livraria Editora Leite Ribeiro, 1921.

Bastide, Roger. *O candomblé na Bahia: Rito nagô.* Trans. Maria Isaura Pereira de Queiroz. São Paulo: Companhia Editora Nacional, 1961.

————. *Les Réligions africaines au Brésil: Vers une sociologie des interpénétrations des civilisations.* Paris: Presses Universitaires de France, 1960.

Batista, Francisco das Chagas. *Cantadores e poetas populares.* João Pessoa: Editora F. C. Batista Irmão, 1929.

Batista, Pedro. "Atenas de cantadores." *Revista do Instituto Histórico e Geográfico Paraibano* (João Pessoa), 6 (1928).

Batista, Sebastião Nunes. "Ainda o seu ao seu dono." *Encontro com o folclore* (Rio de Janeiro), 2 (1965).

————. *Antologia da literatura de cordel.* Natal: Fundação José Augusto, 1977.

————. *Bibliografia prévia de Leandro Gomes de Barros.* Rio de Janeiro: Biblioteca Nacional, 1971.

————. "Carlos Magno na poesia popular nordestina." *Revista Brasileira de Folclore* (Rio de Janeiro), 30 (1971): 143–70.

————. "A comunicação e a síntese na literatura de cordel." *Caderno de Letras* (Recife), 2(3) (1978): 39–53.

————. "O seu a seu dono." *Encontro com o Folclore*, 2 (1965).

Beltrão, Luiz. *Folk-comunicação: Um estudo dos agentes e dos meios populares de informação de fatos e expressão de idéias.* 2nd ed. São Paulo: Melhoramentos, 1971.

Benjamin, Roberto Câmara. "Breve notícia de antecedentes franceses e ingleses da literatura de cordel nordestino," *Revista Tempo Universitário*, 6 (1980): 171–188.

————. "Folhetos populares: Intermediários no processo da comunicação. *Comunicações e Artes* (São Paulo), 1 (1970): 113–30.

————. "Os folhetos populares e os meios de comunicação social." *Symposium* (Recife), 11(1) (1969): 47–54.

————. "Literatura de cordel: Expressão literária popular." *Brasil Açucareiro*, 76 (1970): 101–12.

————. "A religião nos folhetos populares." *Revista de Cultura Vozes*, 64 (1970): 21–24.

Benjamin, Roberto Câmara, and Edgar Grund. "Mito e verdade de um poeta popular." *Revista de Cultura Vozes*, 64 (1970): 5–20.

Benz, Richard Edmund. *Geist und Gestalt im gedruckten Deutschen Buch des 15. Jahrhunderts*. Mainz: Gutenberg-Gesellschaft, 1951.

Bertolli Filho, Cláudio. "Vida e morte na literatura de cordel." Unpublished paper. São Paulo, 1979.

Biderman, Sol. *Catálogo de literatura de cordel: Coleção da Faculdade de Filosofia, Ciências e Letras de Marília e da Library of Congress*. Marília: Ford Foundation, 1970.

Boiteux, Lucas Alexandre. *Poranduba catarinense*. Florianópolis: Comissão Catarinense de Folclore, 1957.

Bollème, Geneviève. *Les Almanachs populaires aux XVIIe et XVIIIe siècles: Essai d'histoire sociale*. La Hague. Mouton, 1964.

―――. *La Bible bleue: Anthologie d'une littérature "populaire."* Paris: Flammarion, 1975.

―――. *La Bibliothèque bleue: Littérature populaire en France du XVIIe au XIXe siècle*. Paris, Juilliard, 1971.

Borba Filho, Hermilo, ed. *Arte popular no nordeste*. Recife: Departamento de Turismo, 1967.

―――. *Fisionomia e espírito do mamulengo: O teatro popular do nordeste*. São Paulo: Companhia Editora Nacional, 1966.

Braga, Teófilo. *Contos tradicionais do povo português*. 2 vols. Porto: Livraria Universal, n.d.

―――. *O povo português nos seus costumes, crenças e tradições*. 2 vols. Lisbon: Livraria Ferreira, 1885.

―――. *Romanceiro geral*. 3 vols. Coimbra: Imprensa da Universidade, 1867.

Branco, Heloisa Castello. "Cordel, a literatura mais rica do mundo para um especialista da Sorbonne." *Jornal do Brasil*, December 16, 1977.

Brandão, Alfredo. "A poesia popular em Alagoas." *Revista do Instituto de Alagoas* (Sergipe), 22 (1943–1944): 7–17.

Brandão, Theo. *Folclore de Alagoas*. Maceió: Oficina Gráfica da Casa Ramalho, 1949.

―――. "Manoel Nenén: O cantador que faltou." *Boletim Alagoana de Folclore* (Sergipe), 4 (1959): 15–21.

―――. "Martelo Agalopado." *Boletim Alagoana de Folclore*, 3 (1958): 48–51.

―――. "Romances do ciclo do gado em Alagoas." In *Anais do primeiro congresso brasileiro de folclore*. Rio de Janeiro: Publicações do Ministério das Relações Exteriores, 1953, II, 113–49.

Bremond, Claude. *Logique du récit*. Paris: Edition du Seuil, 1973.

Brito, Mário da Silva. *História do modernismo no Brasil*. 2nd ed. rev. Rio de Janeiro: Civilização Brasileira, 1964.

Caballero Bonald, José Manuel. *Pliegos de cordel*. Barcelona: Seix y Barrel, 1963.

Calasans, José, *Os ABC de Canudos*. Cadernos Antônio Vieira, No. 3. Bahia: Comissão Baiana de Folclore, 1965.

―――. *Achegas ao estudo do romanceiro político nacional*. Bahia: Centro de Estudos Bahianos, n.d.

―――. *Ciclo folclórico do Bom Jesus Conselheiro*. Bahia: Tipografia Beneditina, 1950.

————. "A Guerra de Canudos." *Revista Brasileira de Folclore*, 6 (1966): 53–64.

————. *No tempo de Antônio Conselheiro: Figuras e fatos da campanha de Canudos*. Coleção de Estudos Brasileiros: Série Cruzeiro, No. 17. Bahia: Aguiar & Souza, n.d.

Caldas, Waldenyr. *Acorde na aurora: Música sertaneja e indústria cultural*. São Paulo: Editora Nacional, 1977.

Caldeira, Clóvis. *Mutirão: Formas de ajuda mútua no meio rural*. São Paulo: Companhia Editora Nacional, 1965.

Callado, Antônio. *Forró no Engenho Cananéia*. Rio de Janeiro: Civilização Brasileira, 1964.

————. *As indústrias da sêca e os Galiléus de Pernambuco*. Rio de Janeiro: Civilização Brasileira, 1960.

————. "Les Ligues paysannes." *Les Temps Modernes* (Paris), 23 (1967): 751–60.

Calmon, Pedro. *História do Brasil na poesia do povo*. Rio de Janeiro: Editora A Noite, n.d.

Camargo, Nara Pereira de. "Usos da forma de literatura de cordel." *Editorial* (São Paulo), 1 (1978): 21–36.

Campos, Eduardo. *Cantador, musa e viola*. Rio de Janeiro: Companhia Editora Americana/MEC, 1973.´

————. "Romanceiro do Padre Cícero." *Boletim da Comissão Catarinense de Folclore* (Florianópolis), 2 (1951): 30–33.

Campos, Renato Carneiro. *Ideologia dos poetas populares do nordeste*. 2nd ed. Recife: Instituto Joaquim Nabuco de Pesquisas Sociais/MEC, 1977.

Cândido, Antônio. *Os parceiros do Rio Bonito*. Rio de Janeiro: José Olympio, 1964.

Cantel, Raymond. "Les prophètes dans la littérature populaire du Brésil." *Caravelle: Cahiers du Monde Hispanique et Luso-Brésilien* (Toulouse), 15 (1970): 57–72.

————. "Les querelles entre protestants et catholiques dans la littérature populaire du nordest brésilien." In *Mélanges à la mémoire de Jean Sarrailh*. Paris: Centre de Recherches de l'Institut d' Etudes Hispaniques, 1966.

————. *Temas da atualidade na literatura de cordel*. Trans. Alice Mitika Koshiyama et al. São Paulo: Universidade de São Paulo, Escola de Comunicações e Artes, 1972.

Carneiro, Edson. *Candomblés da Bahia*. 2nd rev. ed. Rio de Janeiro: Editora Andes, 1954.

Caro Baroja, Julio. *Ensayo sobre la literatura de cordel*. Madrid: Editorial Revista de Occidente, 1969.

Carvalho, José Rodrigues. *Cancioneiro do norte*. 3rd ed. Rio de Janeiro: MEC, 1967.

————. "Folk-lore do Norte: Peleja do 'Bem-te-vi' com o 'Madrapolão.'" *Anuário Brasileiro Garnier* (Rio de Janeiro), 9 (1910): 272–77.

Carvalho, Murilo, et al. *Artistas e festas populares*. São Paulo: Editorial Brasiliense, 1977.

Carvalho Neto, Paulo de. *Folclore sergipano*. Porto: Museu de Etnografia e História, n.d.

Cascudo, Luís da Câmara. *Cinco livros do povo*. Rio de Janeiro: José Olympio, 1953.

———. *Contos tradicionais do Brasil*. 2nd ed. rev. Rio de Janeiro: Tecnoprint Gráfica, 1967.

———. "O folclore: Literatura oral e literatura popular." In *Introdução à literatura no Brasil*, ed. Afrânio Coutinho. Rio de Janeiro: Livraria São José, 1959, pp. 115–26.

———. *Motivos da literatura oral da França no Brasil*. Recife: n.p., 1964.

———. *Trinta estórias brasileiras*. Lisbon: Portucalense Editora, 1955.

———. *Vaqueiros e cantadores*. Porto Alegre: Livraria do Globo, 1939.

Catálogo da Coleção de Miscelâneas. 6 vols. Coimbra: Biblioteca de Coimbra, 1967.

"Cearenses fazem hoje o primeiro 'piquenique ecológico' do país." *Jornal do Commércio* (Recife), April 2, 1978, Section 3, p. 1.

Cocchiara, Giuseppe. *Storia del folklore in Europa*. 2nd ed. Torino: Edizioni Scientifiche Einaudi, 1954.

Coelho, Francisco Adolfo. *Contos populares portugueses*. Lisbon: P. Plantier, 1879.

Comblin, José. *Teologia da enxada: Uma experiência da Igreja no nordeste*. Petrópolis: Vozes, 1977.

Correia, Marlene de Castro. "O saber poético da literatura de cordel." *Cultura* (Brasília), 3 (1971): 49–54.

Cortázar, Augusto Raúl. *Guía bibliográfica del folklore argentino*. Buenos Aires: Imprenta de la Universidad, 1942.

Cossío, José María de. "Notas al romancero: Caracteres populares de la feminidad en 'La doncella que va a la guerra.'" *Escorial*, 6 (1942): 413–23.

Costa, Francisco Pereira da. *Folclore pernambucano*. Rio de Janeiro: Imprensa Nacional, 1908.

Coutinho, Edilberto. "Aproximações com a literatura de cordel e o cordel na literatura." *Cadernos Brasileiros* (Rio de Janeiro), 58 (1970): 45–52.

Coutinho Filho, Francisco. *Repentistas e glosadores*. São Paulo: A. Sartoris & Bertoli, 1937.

———. *Violas e repentes: Repentes populares em prosa e verso, pesquisas folclóricas no nordeste brasileiro*. 2nd rev. ed. São Paulo: Editora Leitura/ INL, 1972.

Curran, Mark J. *Literatura de cordel*. Recife: Universidade Federal de Pernambuco, 1973.

———. "A 'página editorial' do poeta popular." *Revista Brasileira de Folclore*, 12 (1972): 5–16.

Daus, Ronald. *Der epische Zyklus der Cangaceiros in der Volkspoesie Nordostbrasiliens*. Biblioteca Ibero-Americana, No. 12. Berlin: Colloquium Verlag, 1969.

Diégues Júnior, Manuel. "Cidade e vida urbana em folhetos populares." *Cultura*, 3 (1973): 59–67.

————. "A poesia dos cantadores do nordeste." In his *Estudos e ensaios folclóricos em homenagem a Renato Almeida*. Rio de Janeiro: Ministério das Relações Exteriores, Secção de Publicações, 1960, pp. 621–37.

————. "Poetas que nascem feitos." *Américas* (Washington, D.C.), 10 (1958): 29–32.

————. *População e propriedade da terra no Brasil*. Washington D.C.: Pan American Union, 1959.

Duarte, Manuel Florentino, et al. *Literatura de cordel: Antologia*. 2 vols. São Paulo: Global Editora, 1976.

Duchartre, Pierre. *L'Imagerie populaire russe et les livrets gravés: 1629–1885*. Paris: Grund, 1964.

"Estatutos da Associação Nacional de Trovadores e Violeiros." Mimeographed paper. Salvador, 1955.

"Euro Brandão recebe poetas e manifesto." *Diário de Pernambuco* (Recife), January 30, 1979, Section B, p. 8.

Facó, Rui. *Cangaceiros e fanáticos*. 4th ed. Rio de Janeiro: Civilização Brasileira, 1976.

Farias, João. "A cachaça na literatura de cordel." *Boletim da Comissão Fluminense de Folclore* (Vitória de Espírito Santo), 1 (1970): 23–25.

Fausto Neto, Antônio. *A ideologia da punição*. Petrópolis: Vozes, 1979.

Ferrari, Guido. *Per una semiotica del folklore*. Torino: G. Giappichelli Editore, 1978.

Ferreira, Jerusa Pires. *Cavalaria em cordel: O passo das águas mortas*. São Paulo: Hucitec, 1979.

Figueiredo Filho, J. de, ed. *Patativa de Assaré*. Fortaleza: Universidade Federal do Ceará, 1970.

Figueiredo Filho, J. F. "Revivendo o poeta José de Matos: Repentista do nordeste." *Encontro com o Folclore*, 14 (1970): 6–8.

Fortuna, Albertina. "Ciclos da literatura popular." *Boletim da Comissão Catarinense de Folclore*, 1 (1970): 12–13.

"Francês dá curso de cordel no Rio." *Tribuna da Imprensa* (Rio de Janeiro), July 24, 1976.

"Francês especialista de cordel ganha folhetos sobre Getúlio." *Jornal do Brasil*, March 10, 1972.

Franklin, Jeová. "O preconceito racial na literatura de cordel." *Revista de Cultura Vozes*, 64 (1970): 35–39.

Freitas, B., and T. da Silva. *Fundamentos da umbanda*. Rio de Janeiro: Editora Souza, 1956.

Freyre, Gilberto. "Manifesto Regionalista de 1926." *Boletim do Instituto Joaquim Nabuco* (Recife), 5 (1952): 21–43.

Galvão, Walnice. "Amado: Respeitoso, respeitável." In *Saco de gatos*. São Paulo: Duas Cidades, 1976, pp. 13–22.

García, Nicasio. *Contrapunto de Taguada con don Javier de la Rosa: En palla a cuatro líneas de preguntas con respuestas*. Santiago: Imprenta La Victoria, 1886.

García de Diego, Vicente. *Antología de leyendas de la literatura universal*. Barcelona: Editorial Labor, 1955.

García de Enterría, María Cruz. *Catálogo de los pliegos poéticos españoles del siglo XVII en el British Museum de Londres*. Pisa: Giardini, 1977.

———. *Pliegos poéticos españoles de la Biblioteca Ambrosiana de Milan: Homenaje a Antonio Rodríguez-Moniño*. 2 vols. Madrid: Joyas Bibliográficas, 1973.

———. *Sociedad y poesia de cordel en el barroco*. Madrid: Taurus Ediciones, 1973.

———. "Un memorial, casi desconocido, de Lope de Vega." *Boletín de la Real Academia Española*, 51 (1971): 139–60.

Garrett, Almeida. *Romanceiro*. 2 vols. Lisbon: Imprensa Nacional, 1875.

Gayangos y Arce, Pascual de, ed. "El libro de los enxemplos." In his *Escritores en prosa anteriores al siglo XV*. Biblioteca de Autores Españoles. Madrid: M. Rivadeneyra, 1860, vol. 51.

———. "El libro de los gatos." In his *Escritores en prosa anteriores al siglo XV*. Biblioteca de Autores Españoles. Madrid: M. Rivadeneyra, 1860, vol. 51.

Gramsci, Antonio. *Arte e folklore*. Rome: Newton Compton Editore, 1976.

Greimas, A. J. *Sémantique structurale*. Paris: Larousse, 1966.

Hardung, Victor Eugênio. *Romanceiro português*. Leipzig: F. A. Brockhaus, 1877.

———. *Histórias jocosas a cavalo num barbante*. Porto: Editora Nova Crítica, 1980.

Hoornaert, Eduardo. *Formação do catolicismo brasileiro, 1550–1800: Ensaio de interpretação a partir dos oprimidos*. Petrópolis: Vozes, 1974.

Huber, Edouard. *Sûtrâlamkâra: Traduit en français sur la version chinoise de Kumârajîva*. Paris: Ernest Leroux Editeur, 1908, II, 329–41.

Husseini, Maria Marta Guerra. "Literatura de cordel enquanto meio de comunicação no nordeste brasileiro." *Revista do Arquivo Municipal* (São Paulo), 188 (1976): 117–295.

Ishmael-Bissett, Judith. "Brecht e cordel: Distanciamento e protesto em 'Se correr o bicho pega.'" *Latin American Theatre Review*, 10 (1977): 59–64.

Joffily, Geraldo Ireneu. *Um cronista do sertão no século passado: Apontamentos à margem das "Notas sobre a Paraíba."* Campina Grande: Comissão Cultural do Município, 1965.

Julião, Francisco. *Que são as Ligas Camponesas?* Rio de Janeiro: Civilização Brasileira, 1962.

Koshiyama, Alice Mitika. *Análise de conteúdo da literatura de cordel: Presença dos valores religiosos*. São Paulo: Universidade de São Paulo, Escola de Comunicações e Artes, 1972.

Lago, Mário. *Chico Nunes das Alagoas*. Rio de Janeiro: Civilização Brasileira, 1975.

Lane, Federico. "Notas sobre as rabecas do Ribeirão Fundo." *Folclore* (São Paulo), 1 (1952): 81–94.

Lessa, Orígenes. *Getúlio Vargas na literatura de cordel*. Rio de Janeiro: Editora Documentário, 1973.

———. "Literatura de Feira." *Revista Esso* (Rio de Janeiro), 27 (n.d.): 13–16.

———. "Literatura popular em versos." *Anhembi* (São Paulo), 21 (1955): 60–87.

———. "Poesia de cordel: Ingénua ou mágica?" *Revista Shell*, 1970, pp. 17–20.

Libânio, J. B. *O problema da salvação no catolicismo do povo*. Petrópolis: Vozes, 1976.

Lima, Fernando de Castro Pires de. *Ensaios etnográficos*. Lisbon: Fundação Nacional para a Alegria do Povo, 1969, 2 vols.

————. *A mulher vestida de homem*. Coimbra: Fundação Nacional para a Alegria no Trabalho, 1958.

Lima, Jackson da Silva. "O boi no romanceiro tradicional." *Momento: Revista cultural da Gazeta de Sergipe* (Aracaju), 1(9) (1977): 5–20.

————. *O folclore em Sergipe: Romanceiro*. Rio de Janeiro: Livraria Cátedra/INL/MEC, 1977.

Lima, José Ossian. "Cordel e jornalismo." *Revista de Comunicação Social* (Universidade Federal do Ceará), 5 (1975): 22–40.

Lima, Rossini Tavares de. "Notas sobre o romance da donzela ou da menina que morreu de febre amarela." *Boletim Catarinense de Folclore*, 2 (1952): 69–79.

————. *Romanceiro folclórico do Brasil*. São Paulo: Irmãos Vitales Editores Brasil, 1971.

Linhares, Francisco, and Otacílio Batista. *Antologia ilustrada dos cantadores*. Fortaleza: Imprensa Universitária do Ceará, 1976.

Literatura de cordel. Lisbon: Biblioteca Geral da Fundação Gulbenkian, 1970.

Literatura popular em verso: Antologia. 4 vols. Rio de Janeiro: Fundação Casa de Rui Barbosa/MEC, 1964–1978.

Literatura popular em verso: Catálogo. Rio de Janeiro: Fundação Casa de Rui Barbosa/MEC, 1962.

Literatura popular em verso: Estudos. Rio de Janeiro: Fundação Casa de Rui Barbosa/MEC, 1973.

Littérature savante et littérature populaire: Bardes, conteurs, écrivains. Société Française de Littérature Comparée: Actes du Sixième Congrés National, Rennes 23–25 mai 1963. Paris: Didier, 1965.

Lopes, Antônio. *Presença do romanceiro*. Rio de Janeiro: Civilização Brasileira, 1967.

Lopes Neto, V. J. Simões. *Cancioneiro guasca: Coletânea de poesia popular rio-grandense*. Porto Alegre: Livraria Universal, 1910.

Lugones, Leopoldo. *El payador*. Buenos Aires: Ediciones Centurión, 1961.

Luyten, Joseph M. "A literatura de cordel como veículo de comunicação das populações marginais da cidade de São Paulo." Mimeographed paper presented to INTERCOM (Estudos Interdisciplinares da Comunicação). São Paulo, 1979.

Macêdo, Joaryvar. *Pedro Bandeira: Príncipe dos poetas populares*. Fortaleza: Imprensa Oficial do Ceará, 1976.

Macedo, Nertan. "Mitos nordestinos na poesia popular." *Brasil Açucareiro*, 70 (1965): 64–66.

Magalhães, Celso de. *A poesia popular brasileira*. Rev. ed. Introduction and notes by Braulio do Nascimento. Rio de Janeiro: Divisão de Publicações e Divulgação da Biblioteca Nacional, 1973.

Mandrou, Robert. *De la culture populaire aux 17e et 18e siècles*. Paris: Stock, 1964.

Maranhão (de Souza), Liêdo. "Clássicos do cordel." *Equipe* (Recife), 71(1–6) (1974): back covers.

———. "Cordel: Agentes e folheteiros." *Equipe*, 71(1) (1974): 3–6.

Marco, Joaquín. *Literatura popular en España en los siglos XVIII y XIX: una approximación a los pliegos de cordel.* 2 vols. Madrid: Taurus, 1977.

Marín, Francisco Rodríguez. *El Quijote y don Quijote en América.* Madrid: Librería de los Sucesores de Hermano, 1911.

Martins, José de Souza. "Música sertaneja: A dissimulação na linguagem dos humilhados." In his *Capitalismo e tradicionalismo.* São Paulo: Editora Pioneira, 1975, pp. 103–61.

———. "Viola quebrada." *Debate e Crítica* (São Paulo), 14 (1974): 23–49.

Martins, Wilson. *O Modernismo.* São Paulo: Editora Cultrix, 1965.

Maurício, Ivan, Marcos Cirano, and Ricardo de Almeida. *Arte popular e dominação.* 2nd ed. Recife: Editora Alternativa, 1978.

Medeiros, Coriolano de. *Folk-lore paraibano.* Rio de Janeiro: Livraria J. Leite, 1921.

Mello, José Leite de Vasconcellos Pereira de. *Romanceiro português.* 2 vols. Coimbra: Universidade de Coimbra, 1958–1960.

Melo Neto, João Cabral de. *Morte e vida severina e outros poemas em voz alta.* 2nd ed. Rio de Janeiro: Editora Sabiá, 1967.

Melo, Veríssimo de. *O ataque de Lampeão a Mossoró através do romanceiro popular.* Natal: Departamento de Imprensa, 1953.

———. *Cantador de viola.* Recife: Imprensa Oficial, 1961.

Mendoza, Vicente T. *El corrido mexicano: Antología.* Mexico City: Fondo de Cultura Económica, 1954.

———. *El romance español y el corrido mexicano.* 2nd ed. Mexico City: Fondo de Cultura Económica, 1959.

Menéndez-Pidal, Ramón. *Flor nueva de romances viejos.* 19th ed. Madrid: Espasa-Calpe, 1973.

———. *Poesía juglaresca y juglares.* 6th ed. Madrid: Austral, 1964.

———. *Romancero tradicional de las lenguas hispánicas: Español-portugués-catalán-sefardí.* Madrid: Gredos, 1957, 1963, 1969, 1971–1972.

Menezes, Cláudia. *A mudança.* Rio de Janeiro: Editora Imago/MEC, 1976.

Meyer, Augusto. *Guia do folclore gaucho.* 2nd ed. Rio de Janeiro: Editora Presença/MEC, 1975.

Monteiro, Clóvis. *A linguagem dos cantadores: Segundo textos coligidos e publicados por Leonardo Mota.* Rio de Janeiro: n.p., 1933.

Mota, Carlos Guilherme. *Ideologia da cultura brasileira (1933–1974): Pontos de partida para uma revisão histórica.* 3rd ed. São Paulo: Editora Ática, 1977.

Mota, Leonardo. *Cantadores: Poesia e linguagem do sertão cearense.* 3rd ed. Fortaleza: Imprensa Universitária do Ceará, 1961.

———. *Sertão alegre.* 3rd ed. Fortaleza: Imprensa Universitária do Ceará. 1963.

———. *Violeiros do Norte: Poesia e linguagem do sertão nordestino.* 3rd ed. Fortaleza: Imprensa Universitária do Ceará, 1962.

Moura, Abdalaziz de. *Frei Damião e os impasses da religião popular.* Petrópolis: Vozes, 1978.

Moura, Clóvis. *O preconceito de cor na literatura de cordel*. São Paulo: Editora Resenha Universitária, 1976.

Nascimento, Braulio do. "Arquetipo e versão na literatura de cordel." *Revista de Cultura Sergipana* (Aracaju), 1 (1977): 41–46.

———. *Bibliografia do folclore brasileiro*. Rio de Janeiro: Biblioteca Nacional/ MEC, 1971.

———. "Pesquisa do romanceiro tradicional no Brasil." In *Romancero y poesia oral: El romancero en la tradición oral moderna*, ed. Diego Catalán and Samuel G. Armistead. Madrid: Gráficas Condor. 1972, pp. 65–83.

———. "Um século de pesquisa do romanceiro tradicional no Brasil." *Revista Brasileira de Cultura* (Rio de Janeiro), 17 (1973): 37–54.

Nascimento, Luiz do. *História da imprensa de Pernambuco: 1821–1954*. Recife: Arquivo Público, Imprensa Oficial, 1962.

Nisard, Charles. *Histoire des livres populaires et de la littérature du colportage*. Paris: Amyot, 1854.

Noblat, Ricardo. "Ganhando status: Um simpósio universitário estuda o cordel." *Veja* (São Paulo), no. 529, October 25, 1978, p. 152.

———. "Literatura de cordel: O povo e o autor e o personagem." *Manchete* (Rio de Janeiro), 1(224) (October 4, 1975): 124–27.

Nordeste brasileiro: Catálogo da Exposição. Rio de Janeiro: Biblioteca Nacional, 1970.

Olímpio, Domingos. *Luzia Homem*. 5th ed. São Paulo: Melhoramentos, 1964.

Otaviano, Pe. Manuel. *Inácio da Catingueira*. Rio de Janeiro: n.p., 1949.

Paim, Antônio. *A filosofia da Escola do Recife*. Rio de Janeiro: Editora Saga, 1966.

Palmeira, Moacir. "Nordeste: mudanças políticas no século XX." *Cadernos Brasileiros* (Rio de Janeiro), 8 (1966): 67–78.

"Para professor francês, subvenção matará o cordel." *O Estado de São Paulo* (São Paulo), July 29, 1976.

Parain-Vial, Jeanne. *Analyses structurales et idéologies structuralistes*. Toulouse: E. Privat, 1969.

Passos, Claribalte. "A arte de xilogravura na terra do açucar." *Brasil Açucareiro*, 82 (1973): 39–42.

Pereira, Armando, et al. *A prostituição é necessária?* Rio de Janeiro: Civilização Brasileira, 1966.

Pereira, Thelmo de Jesus. "A expressão gráfica da literatura de cordel nordestina." *Remag: Revista Métodos de Artes Gráficas* (Rio de Janeiro), 15 (1965): 18–23.

Pinto, Alexina de Magalhães. "Poesias populares." *Anuário Brasileiro Garnier*, 8 (1910): 271–72.

Pinto, Aloysio de Alencar. "A voz do cantador." *Brasil Açucareiro*, 76 (1970): 71–73.

Piza, Flávio de Toledo. "Estudos sobre o romance do soldado jogador." *Revista do Arquivo Municipal* (São Paulo), 165 (1959): 71–121.

Placer, Xavier, ed. *Modernismo brasileiro: Bibliografia*. Rio de Janeiro: Divisão de Publicações e Divulgação, 1972.

Pontes, Mário. "O diabo na literatura de cordel." *Revista de Cultura Vozes*, 64 (1970): 29–35.

————. "A presença demoníaca na poesia popular do nordeste." *Revista Brasileira de Folclore*, 12 (1972): 261–85.

Pontual, Roberto. "Notas sobre a xilogravura popular." *Revista de Cultura Vozes*, 64 (1970): 53–59.

Proença, Ivan Cavalcanti. *A ideologia do cordel*. Rio de Janiro: Editora Imago, 1976.

Proença, Manuel Cavalcanti, et al. *Literatura de cordel*. São Paulo: Universidade de São Paulo, Departamento de Jornalismo e Editoração, 1971.

Queiroz, Maria Isaura Pereira de. *O campesinato brasileiro: Ensaios sobre civilização e grupos rústicos no Brasil*. Petrópolis: Vozes, 1973.

————. *O messianismo no Brasil e no mundo*. São Paulo: Dominus Editora, 1965.

————. *Sociologia e folclore: A dança de São Gonçalo num povoado baiano*. Salvador: Livraria Progresso Editora, 1958.

Ramos, Arthur. *O folk-lore negro do Brasil*. Rio de Janeiro: Civilização Brasileira, 1935.

Ramos, José. "Literatura de cordel." *MEC* (Rio de Janeiro), 3 (1959): 23–27.

Rego, José Lins do. "O poeta João Martins de Ataíde." In his *Poesia e vida*. Rio de Janeiro: Editora Universal, 1945, pp. 161–62.

Ribeiro, João. *O folk-lore: Estudos de literatura popular*. Rio de Janeiro: Jacinto Ribeiro dos Santos, 1919.

Rodrigues, José Daniel. *6 entremezes de cordel*. Lisbon: Editorial Estampa, 1973.

Rodrigues, Wilson W. "Poesia popular." In *Estudos de folclore luso-brasileiro*, ed. Mariza Lira. Rio de Janeiro: Laemmert, 1952, pp. 91–111.

Rolim, Maria Luiza. "Cantadores são perseguidos nas feiras do nordeste." *Diário de Pernambuco*, May 20, 1979.

Romero, Sílvio. *Cantos populares do Brasil*. 3rd ed. 2 vols. Rio de Janeiro: José Olympio, 1954.

————. *Contos tradicionais do Brasil*, 4th ed. rev. Rio de Janeiro: José Olympio, 1954.

————. *Estudos sobre a poesia popular do Brasil (1879–1880)*. Petrópolis: Vozes/Governo do Estado de Sergipe, 1977.

Rosa, João Guimarães. *Grande sertão: Veredas*. 10th ed. Rio de Janeiro: José Olympio, 1976.

————. *Primeiras estórias*. 8th ed. Rio de Janeiro: José Olympio, 1975.

————. *Sagarana*. 18th ed. Rio de Janeiro: José Olympio, 1976.

Salles, Vicente. "Guajarina, folhetaria de Francisco Lopes." *Revista Brasileira de Cultura*, 3 (1971): 87–102.

Sampaio, Albino Forjaz de. *Teatro de cordel*. Lisbon: Imprensa Nacional de Lisboa, 1922.

Santa Cruz, Luís. "O diabo na literatura de cordel." *Cadernos Brasileiros*, 5 (1963): 3–14.

————. *Os transportes no romanceiro popular brasileiro*. Rio de Janeiro: Ministério dos Transportes, 1970.

Souto Maior, Mário. "Antônio Silvino no romanceiro do cordel." *Revista Brasileira de Folclore*, 10 (1970): 45–53.

———. "Cantadores e vaqueiros." *Cultura*, 3 (1973): 68–77.

———. "Religião e cachaça: Discussão entre cantadores." *Brasil Açucareiro*, 36 (1968): 85–87.

———. "O sexo na literatura de cordel." *Ele e Ela* (Rio de Janeiro), 69 (1975): 59–62.

———. *Território da danação*. Rio de Janeiro: Livraria São José, 1975.

———. "A xilogravura popular na literatura de cordel." *Brasil Açucareiro* (Rio de Janeiro), 75 (1970): 45–53.

Souza, Liêdo Maranhão de. *Classificação popular de literatura de cordel*. Petrópolis: Vozes, 1976.

———. *O mercado, sua praça e a cultura popular do nordeste*. Recife: Prefeitura Municipal, Secretaria de Educação e Cultura, 1977.

Spalding, Walter. *Poesia do povo: Folclore*. Porto Alegre: Livraria do Globo, 1934.

Suassuna, Ariano. "Coletânea da poesia popular nordestina: Romances do heróico." *Revista do DECA* (Recife), 6(5) (1962): 11–27, and 6(7) (1964): 7–117.

———. "Notas sobre o romanceiro popular do nordeste." In *Ariano Suassuna: Seleta em prosa e verso*, ed. Silviano Santiago. Rio de Janeiro: José Olympio/INL/MEC, 1974, pp. 162–90.

———. *Vinte xilogravuras do nordeste*. Recife: Companhia Editora de Pernambuco, 1970.

———. *Xilogravura do nordeste*. Recife: Museu de Arte Popular, 1968.

Tavares Júnior, Luís. "O discurso fantástico na narrativa do cordel." *Revista Aspectos* (Fortaleza), 8 (1975).

Távora, Franklin. *O Cabeleira*. Rev. ed. Rio de Janeiro: Tecnoprint Gráfica, 1966.

Terra, Ruth Brito Lêmos, and Mauro W. B. de Almeida. "A análise morfológica da literatura popular em verso: Uma hipótese de trabalho." *Revista do Instituto de Estudos Brasileiros* (São Paulo), 16 (1975): 1–28.

Tinhorão, José Ramos. *Música popular: Um tema em debate*. Rio de Janeiro: JEM Editores, 1969.

Todorov, Tzvetan. *Grammaire du Décaméron*. Paris: Editions du Seuil, 1968.

———. *Poétique*. Paris: Editions du Seuil, 1968.

———. *Théories du symbole*. Paris: Editions du Seuil, 1977.

Trancoso, Gonçalo Fernandes. *Contos e histórias de proveito e exemplo*. Paris: Aillaud & Bertrand, 1921.

Tubach, Fredric C. "Struktur analytische Probleme: Das mittelalterliche Exemplum." *Hessische Blätter für Volkskunde*, 59 (1958): 25–29.

Valladeres, Clarivaldo Prado. "As raizes da cultura baiana na obra de Jorge Amado." *Jornal de Letras* (Rio de Janeiro) 13 (1961): 13.

Vasconcellos, Carolina Michaëlis de. *Estudos sobre o romanceiro peninsular: Romances velhos em Portugal*, 2nd ed. Coimbra: Imprensa da Universidade, 1934.

Vianna, Hildegardes. "A mulher vestida de homem." *Revista Brasileira de Folclore*, 6 (1963): 177–93.

Vilela, José Aloísio. "A vida dos cantadores." *Revista do Instituto Histórico de Alagoas* (Maceió), 25 (1947): 68–84.

Welter, J. Th. *L'Exemplum dans la littérature réligieuse et didactique du Moyen Age*. Paris: Occitania, 1927.

Xilógrafos nordestinos. Rio de Janeiro: Fundação Casa de Rui Barbosa, 1977.

Folhetos

Almeida Filho, Manuel d'. *Gabriela*. São Paulo: Editora Luzeiro, n.d.

———. *O Monstro, o Índio, e o Menino*. Juazeiro do Norte: Tipografia São Francisco, n.d.

Areda, Francisco Sales. *A Malassombrada Peleja de Francisco Sales Areda com o "Negro Visão."* N.P., n.d.

———. *As Prezepadas de Pedro Malazarte*. Recife: João José da Silva, n.d.

Ataíde, João Martins de. *O Balão do Destino ou a Menina da Ilha*, 2 vols. Juazeiro do Norte: Tipografica São Francisco, 1977.

———. *A Bela e a Fera*. Recife: n.p., 1944.

———. *Iracema, a Virgem dos Lábios de Mel*. Juazeiro do Norte: Tipografia São Francisco, 1978.

———. *Juvenal e o Dragão*. Juazeiro do Norte: Tipografia São Francisco, 1978.

———. *Meia Noite no Cabaret*. Juazeiro do Norte: Tipografia São Francisco, 1974.

———. *Peleja de Bernardo Nogueira e Preto Limão*. Juazeiro do Norte: Tipografia São Francisco, 1976.

———. *Peleja de João Athayde e Raimundo Pelado do Sul*. Juazeiro do Norte: Tipografia São Francisco, 1974.

———. *Peleja Entre Laurindo Gato e Marcolino Cobra Verde*. Juazeiro do Norte: Tipografia São Francisco, 1975.

———. *O Príncipe que Nasceu com a Sina de Morrer Enforcado*. Recife: n.p., n.d.

———. *O Prisioneiro do Castelo da Rocha Negra*. Juazeiro do Norte: Tipografia São Francisco, 1976.

———. *Romance do Escravo Grego*. Juazeiro do Norte: Tipografia São Francisco, 1966.

———. *Romance de Romeu e Julieta*. Juazeiro do Norte: Tipografia São Francisco, 1975.

———. *Sacco e Vanzetti aos Olhos do Mundo*. Recife: n.p., n.d.

———. *Uma Noite de Amor*. Juazeiro do Norte: Tipografia São Francisco, 1974.

———. *A Vida de uma Meretriz*. Recife: n.p., n.d.

Barros, Leandro Gomes de. *O Boi Misterioso*. Juazeiro do Norte: Tipografia São Francisco, 1976.

———. *O Encontro de Leandro Gomes com Chagas Batista*. Recife: n.p., n.d.

———. *O Mal em Paga do Bem ou Rosa e Lino de Alencar.* Juazeiro do Norte: Tipografia São Francisco, 1950.

———. *Os Martírios de Genoveva.* Recife: n.p., 1943.

———. *A Morte de Alonso e a Vingança de Marina.* Juazeiro do Norte: Tipografia São Francisco, 1976.

———. *Peleja de Manuel Riachão com o Diabo.* Juazeiro do Norte: Tipografia São Francisco, 1955.

———. *Os Sofrimentos de Alzira.* Juazeiro do Norte: Tipografia São Francisco, 1976.

———. *A Vida de Cancão de Fogo e o Seu Testamento.* Juazeiro do Norte: Tipografia São Francisco, 1975.

Batista, Antônio. *O Sonho do Pe. Cícero Romão Batista.* Juazeiro do Norte: Tipografia São Francisco, n.d.

Batista, Francisco das Chagas. *História da Imperatriz Porcina.* Recife: n.p., 1946.

Borges, José Francisco. *A Filha que Matou a Mãe pra Fugir com um Maloqueiro.* Olinda: n.p., n.d.

Borges, Severino. *A Escrava Isaura.* Recife: n.p., n.d.

Campina, Manuel de Assis. *Discussão Entre um Fiscal e uma Fateira.* N.p., n.d.

Campos, José de Souza. *As Bravuras de Zé Bobo e o Amor de Risomar.* Guarabira: n.p., n.d.

———. *O Caminho para o Mobral.* Recife: n.p., 1978.

———. *A Luta de Padre Cícero com o Diabo.* Recife: 1962.

———. *A Mocidade Hoje em Dia no Sistema do Quadrão.* n.p., n.d.

———. *A Paixão de Angelita e a Competência de Lino.* Recife: n.p., n.d.

———. *Peleja de José de Souza Campos com João Antônio de Barros.* Olinda: n.p., n.d.

———. *Peleja de José de Souza com Severino Milanez.* Olinda: n.p., n.d.

———. *O Rei, a Pomba e o Gavião.* Recife: n.p., 1978.

———. *Uma Peinha de Nada no Sistema de Quadrão.* Olinda: n.p., n.d.

———. *A Voz de Noé.* Olinda: n.p., n.d.

Cavalcante, Rodolfo Coelho. *Brasil Entrou, Alemanha Perdeu a Guerra.* Terezinha: n.p., 1942.

———. *E a Terra Brilhará Outra Vez: A Vinda do "Cometa Kohoutek."* Salvador: n.p., 1973.

———. *A Negra de um Peito só, Procurando Tu.* Salvador: n.p., 1973.

———. *Tereza Batista.* Salvador: n.p., 1973.

———. *O Vampiro na Feira de Santana.* Salvador: n.p., 1972.

Ferreira, João Melquíades. *O Pavão Misterioso.* Juazeiro do Norte: Tipografia São Francisco, 1951.

Gonçalves, Severino. *A Moça que virou Cobra.* N.p., n.d.

Leite, José Costa (José Parafuso). *O Encontro da Velha que Vendia Tabaco com o Matuto que Vendia Fumo.* N.p., n.d.

———. *O Papagaio Misterioso.* Condado: n.p., n.d.

———. *A Véia Debaixo da Cama e a Perna Cabeluda.* N.p., n.d.

Lima, João Ferreira. *O Casamento de Chico Tingolé com Maria Fumaça.* Juazeiro do Norte: Tipografia São Francisco, 1976.

Maciel, Laurindo Gomes. *Ah! Se o Passado Voltasse!* Juazeiro do Norte: Tipografia São Francisco, 1948.

Monteiro, Delarme. *Dr. Raiz e suas Ervas Milagrosas.* Recife: Universidade Federal de Pernambuco, n.d.

Moreira, Flávio Fernandes. *Umbanda em Versos.* Rio de Janeiro: Secretaria Estadual de Educação e Cultura, 1978.

Pacheco, José. *Grande Debate Entre Lampião e São Pedro.* N.p., n.d.

———. *Intriga do Cachorro e o Gato.* N.p., n.d.

Paula, Francisco Firmino. *História do Boi Leitão ou o Vaqueiro que não Mentia.* Guarabira: José Alves Pontes, 1973.

———. *Zé Matuto na Praça.* N.p., n.d.

Pereira Sobrinho, Manoel. *Arlindo, a Fera Homicida e os Mortos de Gravatá.* N.P., n.d.

———. *A Princesa do Reino da Pedra Fina.* São Paulo: Luzeiro, n.d.

Pinheiro, Luís da Costa. *História de Rosa Branca ou a Filha do Pescador.* Juazeiro do Norte: Tipografia São Francisco, 1976.

———. *História do Soldado Roberto e a Princeza do Reino de Canan,* 2 vols. Juazeiro do Norte: Tipografia São Francisco, 1951.

Quinto Sobrinho, João (João do Cristo Rei). *O Exemplo Interessante da Vida de Carolina.* Juazeiro do Norte: Tipografia São Francisco, n.d.

Resende, José Camelo de Melo. *Entre o Amor e a Espada.* Juazeiro do Norte: Tipografia São Francisco, 1976.

———. *História de Coco Verde e Melancia.* Juazeiro do Norte: Tipografia São Francisco, 1976.

Santos, Alípio Bispo dos. *O Filho que Chutou na Mãe e o Pé Ficou Redondo.* Salvador: n.p., 1978.

Santos, Apolônio Alves dos. *O Compadre Pobre e o Rico Ambicioso.* Guarabira: José Alves Pontes, 1973.

———. *O Grande Incêndio em Copacabana.* Guarabira: José Alves Pontes, 1955.

———. *O Herói Napoleão no Reino das Portas.* Guarabira: José Alves Pontes, n.d.

———. *O Mineiro que Comprou um Bonde no Rio de Janeiro.* Guarabira: José Alves Pontes, n.d.

———. *O Monstruoso Crime de Serginho em Bom Jesus de Itabapoana, Estado de Rio de Janeiro.* Guarabira: José Alves Pontes, 1977.

———. *A Mulher que Gostou dos Padres.* Guarabira: José Alves Pontes, 1971.

———. *Os Nordestinos no Rio e o Nordeste Abandonado.* Rio de Janeiro: Ministério de Educação e Cultura, 1978.

Santos, José João (Azulão). *Zé Matuto no Rio.* Rio de Janeiro: n.p., n.d.

Santos, Manuel Camilo dos. *Viagem a São Saruê.* Campina Grande: Estrella da Poesia, 1956.

Silva, Antônio Eugénio da. *O Cavaleiro Roldão.* Campina Grande: Estrella da Poesia, 1958.

Silva, Caetano Cosme. *O Assassino da Honra ou a Louca do Jardim.* Recife: João José da Silva, n.d.

———. *A Escrava Isaura.* N.p., n.d.

————. *Peleja Entre Caetano Cosme da Silva e Maria Lavandeira*. Recife: Luzeiro do Norte, n.d.

————. *A Praga de Gafanhoto no Sertão Paraibano*. N.p., n.d.

Silva, Galdino. *A Mulher que Pediu um Filho ao Diabo*. Salvador: n.p., n.d.

Silva, João José. *O Casamento do Macaco e a Onça*. Recife: n.p., n.d.

Silva, José Bernardo da. *História do Boi Mandingueiro e o Cavalo Misterioso*, 2 vols. Juazeiro do Norte: Tipografia São Francisco, 1951.

————. *Mariana e o Capitão do Navio*. Juazeiro do Norte: Tipografia São Francisco, 1976.

————. *Peleja de Ventania com Pedra Azul*. Juazeiro do Norte: Tipografia São Francisco, n.d.

Silva, Olegário Fernandes da. *Exemplo da Perna Cabiluda: Os Cinais do Fim da Era*. Caruaru: Jardim da Poesia, n.d.

Silva, Severino Borges. *A Princesa Maricruz e o Cavaleiro do Ar*. Recife: Luzeiro do Norte, n.d.

Soares, José Francisco. *Acabou a Gasolina? Ou a Gasolina Acabou?* Recife: n.p., 1977.

————. *O Choro de Leão e as Piadas de Fumanchú*. Recife: n.p., 1978.

————. *A Cobra de 2 Pés e a Porca que Deu Cria a um Cachorro*. N.p., n.d.

————. *O Divórcio no Brasil*. Recife: n.p., 1977.

————. *Os Estragos da Cheia 75*. Recife: n.p., 1975.

————. *Feitos da Revolução e Reformação Política*. Recife: n.p., 1977.

————. *O Fenômeno dos Fenômenos: O Rio de São Francisco Secando*. Recife: n.p., n.d.

————. *A Perna Cabeluda de Olinda*. Recife: n.p., 1976.

————. *A Perna Cabeluda de Tiuma e São Lourenço*. Recife: n.p., n.d.

————. *A Vitória de Arraes ou a Vingança de Zé Ninguém*. Recife: n.p., 1962.

Souza, Antônio Patrício de (Antônio da Mulatinha). *O Poema do Filho que Matou o Pai no Sítio Araçá Entre Arara e Serraria*. Campina Grande: n.p., 1977.

Index

Acrostic: device to identify author, 26, 95; as aid to establish property rights, 95

Afro-Brazilian culture: in historical development, xiii*n*1; influences on *cordel*, 16, 17; akpalô narrative tradition, 16; religious practices, 146

Agricultural system: stratification of society, 207. *See also* Fairs; Farmers; Market systems

Alencar, José de, author: use of *cordel* stories, xiv; studies of folk customs and poet-singers, 38; Indianism, 41

Alienation: educated observers' opinions on *cordel* values, 216–17

Almanac: as literary form, 85–86; *Almanaque do Pensamento*, 85–86, 86*n*5

Amado, Jorge, author: *cordel* elements in style and vocabulary, xiv; use of Northeast traditions, 145–47; blend of African and ballad strains, 146; Rodolfo Coelho Cavalcante's acquaintance with, 146; Amado's *Tereza Batista, Home from the Wars* (novel), structure and *cordel* elements, 144–47, 149, 152. *See also* Cavalcante, Rodolfo Coelho; *Tereza Batista*

Ambiguous behavior: atypical in *cordel*, 89

Andrade, Carlos Drummond de, poet, xvi

Andrade, Mário de, early modernist leader: studies of *cordel*, 38

Art, *cordel* as: distinctly Brazilian art form, xvii; as folk and as popular art, 2, 2*n*3, 7; present-day interest in, 39–47; complex nature of, 217–

19, 224–26. *See also* *Literatura de cordel*, art and culture

Art, popular graphic: on *cordel* covers, 3*n*4, 51, 188

Arts, popular: influence on *cordel*, xiv; research and interest in, 37–44; present-day impact of, 39–44; commercial organizations' interest in, 44–45; erudite literature using Northeast popular and folk traditions, 145*n*11; idealized representations versus social realities, 210–12, 215–20

Astrology: and poetry, 174–75; "star" in corporate names, 174

Ataíde, João Martins de: author and publisher, 24; six-step pattern of his *The Exploits of John Cricket*, 69

Audiences and publics: present composition, xiv, 37–47; *cordel's* traditional audience, 31–37; urban audiences, 32–34; migration from Northeast to cities, 32–34; poet's attitudes toward audiences, 178–86; audiences' attitudes toward poets, 187–89; audiences' attitudes toward *cordel*, 191–93, 200–202. *See also* Buyers of *cordel*; Appendix C, analysis of *folheto* buyers

Author: information on *cordel* booklets often incomplete or incorrect, 54–55

Authority: as *cordel* concept, 223–24

Azevêdo, Carlos Alberto: *cordel* classification system, 55

Azulão (José João dos Santos), *cordel* author, poet-singer, xvi, 49, 115–16

Backlands of Northeast Brazil. *See* Northeast Brazil

stratification of workers, 206; shifting relationships, 211

Firmeza (good): definitions, 71–73; in DR tales, 71–73; in *The King, the Dove, and the Sparrowhawk*, 90; in *The Monstrous Kidnapping of Serginho*, 120; in *Tereza Batista*, 156; the King as model landowner, 214; frequence of concept in *cordel*, 215–16. See also *Falsidade* (evil); Good and evil

Folhas volantes: Portuguese chapbooks, 8

Folheto. See *Cordel*; *Cordel* stories; *Literatura de cordel*

Folhetos de acontecimento: journalistic *cordel* stories, 127

Folhetos de encomenda: cordel written for specific purposes, 52

Folhetos de época: journalistic *cordel* stories, 127; sometimes written in anticipation of an event, 128

Folk art and folk literature: problem of definition, 2, 2n3

Folktales: contributions to *cordel*, 3; fusion with verbal dueling only in Brazil, 11; as basis for *cordel* stories, 14, 15

Food: Northeast audiences' concern with, 97–98; as *cordel* topic, 97–98

Forgiveness: seldom a *cordel* concept, 222

French influences: *littérature de colportage* (chapbooks), 9; government relations, effect on Luso-Brazilian literature and oral tradition, 9n18; scholars quoted on French pamphlet literature values, 217–18

Gambler Soldier theme, 9

Good and evil: as *cordel* concepts, 5, 90, 120, 216–17, 222, 223. See also *Falsidade*; *Firmeza*

Goulart administration: interest in popular culture, 44

Graphic artists, 49. *See also* Covers on *cordel* booklets

Gullar, Ferreira, poet: ties to *cordel*, xiv; on future of *cordel*, 46

Hairy leg: monster, as character in *cordel* stories, 77, 77n28, 78, 178

Historical and geographic development. See *Literatura de cordel*, historical development

HR tales: description, 60–62, 64–67; contests as pacts, 66; as back-and-forth, *peleja*-type exchanges, 67; least diverse of *cordel* plots, 67–68; horizontal social ties, 213. *See also* Six-step pattern

Humor: as teaching device in DW tales, 78

Hunger: often problem of cordel buyers, 97–98, 206. *See also* Food

HW tales: description, 59–62, 67–70; often include social satire, 67; as example, *John Cricket*, 69; as example, *Discussion Between a Bumpkin and a City Dweller* and *Joe Bumpkin in the Big City*, 69–70; vertical social relationships, 213–15

Iberian influences on *cordel*: ballad tradition, 5; chapbooks in sixteenth century, 6–9; effects of peninsular history on Brazilian literature, 9n18; variations of oral ballads today in Spain, Portugal and Sephardic Jewish communities, 5; traditional sex roles, 151–53. *See also* Chapbooks

Idealized representations versus reality: *cordel* characters and situations, 210–20

Identification of author, date, publisher: unreliability of information on *cordel* booklets, 54–55

Improvisers. *See* Poet-improvisers

Indianism: intellectual regional interest, 41

Indians: in Brazilian culture, xiiin1; contributions to *cordel*, 3; image in *cordel*, 16–17

Inspiration (*inspiração*): as act of

composition, 165; as influence on poet, 173–75

Insults: ritualized in verbal dueling, 67

Interviews, notes on. *See* Appendix A

"Invented" stories: compared with "translated," 168–70

Invocation: as *cordel* device, 94, 99

John Cricket: Brazilian folktale character, 15, 53; in HW six-step *cordel* pattern, 69

Journalistic *cordel*: exist alongside mass media, 35–36, 128–29; usually limited to specific region, 128; *The Monstrous Kidnapping of Serginho* as example, 127; usually DW accounts, 127–28; not more objective than other *cordel*, 130; goals differ from newspaper accounts, 130–33. See also *Folhetos de acontecimento*; *Folhetos de época*

Juglares: Iberian antecedents of *cantadores*, 10

Justice: demands for in *cordel*, 131–32

The King, the Dove, and the Sparrowhawk: discussion, 80–82; José de Souza Campos, author, 82–85; original source Buddhist parable, 85–87, 86n5; in present-day *Almanaque do Pensamento*, 86; comparison of parable and *cordel*, 86–98; six-step pattern, 87–88; examples of *firmeza* and *falsidade*, 90–91; divine qualities of King, 91; concept of destiny (*sina*), 92; language tone, 95–96; text of parable, 100–101; text of *cordel*, 102–11

Kubitschek administration: interest in folklore, 39

Lampião (Virgolino Ferreira): outlaw, 18n35, 73, 166, 191, 198

Language levels in *cordel*. *See* Vocabulary

Largo do Machado: Rio de Janeiro market, 114–15. *See also* Appendix C

Legal rights to *cordel* stories: ownership, 26, 95; unreliability of author, date and publisher on *cordel* booklet, 54–55. *See also* Acrostic

Leite, José Costa, graphic artist: blockprints for *cordel* covers, 49

Lenience: not a popular *cordel* concept, 74

Lessa, Orígenes, author: *cordel* classification system, 55

Lima, Jorge de, author: use of *cordel* traditions, xiv

Lima, Silvino Pirauá, poet-singer, 11

Literacy: low in rural areas in nineteenth century, 22–23; of present-day audiences, 34; prestige in past, 35; rise in national, 35, 189–90; campaign for adults, 84n4

Literary and oral sources of *cordel*, 1–18

Literary construction. See *Cordel* stories, literary construction

Literatura de cego: "blindmen's literature", 9

Literatura de cordel
—art and culture, influence on: present-day interest, xiv-xv, 1–3, 137–147, 181–86; distinctly Brazilian and expression of Northeast, 13–22
—historical development: literary forebears, 2–17; in colonial period and nineteenth century, 18–22
—origin of name, xiv-xv, 1n1
—social aspects of: as multifaceted national heritage, 41–43; present-day efforts to aid and preserve, 43–47; as affirmation of individual and collective past, 183–84, 189–94; likelihood of survival, 225–26
—sources and traditions: chapbooks, ballads, and others, 2–17; limited studies of before 1900, 3; comparison with pamphlet literature and oral traditions throughout world, 7–12
—three major steps: writing, printing, distribution, 25–28

85; toward educated audiences, 181–83; toward official support, 182
—backgrounds: racial origins, 17; sex, 22–23; homogeneity of backgrounds, 22–25; primarily Northeastern identity, 22–24
—*cordel's* changing role: poets' awareness of, 45–47, 185–86
—creative abilities: "*inspiração*", 167–68, 173–74, 202–205, 217–18
—literary standards: allegiance to special world view, 130–31; techniques of adjusting raw material to *cordel* values, 132–33, 173; strong sense of craftsmanship, 165–68; efforts to perfect individual style, 168–70; serious attitude and loyalty toward *literatura de cordel* tradition, 173–78
—numbers and locations of poets: today in urban centers as well as Northeast interior, 23–24; estimates of numbers today, 24–25; in greater Rio de Janeiro area, 114n4
—oral performances: at fairs, 29–30; chanting, 4, 29, 164n1; pressures of audiences, 168–70; buyers' opinions about live performances, 192–93
—poetry as occupation: includes writing, production and marketing, 22–30, 164–70; need for additional income, 24–25; printing and publication options, 25–28; writing conditions, 25; payment to poet for story, 25–27; dependence on publisher, 25–27
—poets of different times: famous *cordel* writers of early twentieth century, 10–11; style and approach of newer poets, 51–53
—poets and *cordel* buyers: unpredictability of story's success, 176–79; poet better educated and more experienced than buyer, 180–83
—problems related to: official support, 49–50; present-day interest, 185;

writing as occupation and as art, 164–86
—*sina* (destiny): *cordel* as sense of vocation, 175–76, 188–89
—tension between poet's creative abilities and his need to please buyers: conflict, 164–68, 175–78, 185–86; personal restrictions on self regarding topics, 168–73; money as proof of public favor, 170–71; insecurity about money and readers' approval, 175–79; poets who have printed *cordel* at own expense, 205
—see also *Cordel* stories; *Literatura de cordel*; individual topics; Appendixes B and D for names of individuals

Poets' associations and unions, 12, 12n23, 49–51, 143
Popular culture, interest in: parallels in eighteenth century Europe, 40–41
Popular poets. *See* Poets (*cordel* writers)
Portugal: government in Brazil, 111n1, 9n18
Portuguese chapbooks: and Brazilian *cordel*, 3–6, 7–9, 63–64 *See also* Iberian influences on *cordel*
Poverty in Northeast interior, 20–22
Povo (the common people): poets' identification with, 180
Press. *See* Printing presses
Princess Magalona theme, 9, 63
Printing presses: limited before Brazilian independence in 1822, 20–22; late arrival in Northeast, 20–22; introduction influenced by cotton wealth, 20–22; value of hand press to poet, 26–27; hand presses vanishing, 27–28; commercial presses, 27–28; corporate names of, 173
Production and distribution of *cordel*, 22–30
Proença, Manuel Cavalcanti: *cordel* classification system, 55

Sextilha: prevailing metrical pattern in *cordel*, 10

Sexual behavior: in *cordel*, 153*n*18, 155

Silvana-Delgadinha theme, 5

Silvino, Antônio, outlaw: one-time *repentista*, 212; *cordels'* effect on his image, 212; "good thief" theme, 212*n*14

Sina. See Destiny

"Sing": meanings in relation to *literatura de cordel*, 4, 164*n*1

Six-step pattern

—construction: underlies *cordel* stories, xv, 57–64; may be distorted by newer writers, 53; structural design, 57–64; steps and variations, 59–60; reasons for development in Brazil, 61–64; role of poet-singers, 63–64; outline of steps (diagram), 62

—in: *The King, the Dove, and the Sparrowhawk*, 87–88; *The Monstrous Kidnapping of Serginho*, 69–70, 117–18; *Tereza Batista*, 147–50

—significance: underlying world view, 202–204; necessary for buyer acceptance, 203; analysis of underlying societal framework, 206–26; two-way social ties, 212–13; characters exemplify good and evil, 216; predictable, but permits unexpected elements, 224–25

—types. *See* DR tales; DW tales; HR tales; HW tales

Soap operas: poets' attitudes toward, 185; audiences, 193–94

Soares, Dila, graphic artist: block-prints for *cordel* covers, 49

Soares, José Francisco, poet, 27, 50

Social change: effect on *cordel*, 32

Social contracts: implicit in *cordel*, 206–207

Social satire, HW tales as, 67–68

Social stratification in Brazil, 206–207; implications for *cordel*, 206–26

Sources of *cordel*, 1–15. See also *Lit-eratura de cordel*, sources and traditions

Southern *cordel*, 18

Souza, Liêdo Maranhão de: *cordel* classification system, 55

Spanish influences. *See* Iberian influences on *cordel*

Spiritual relationships: often expressed in economic terms, 220–21

"Star of inspiration": in printing press corporate names, 174

Students: as *cordel* audience, 32–34

Stylizing of events and characters: in folk art and in *cordel* stories, 122–23

Suassuna, Ariano, author: use of *cordel* themes, xiv, 145; *cordel* classification system, 55

Sultan's Revenge: as theme, 11

Sylphs: as example of imagery, 96–97, 97*n*9

Tales and Stories of Moral Counsel and Example: sixteenth-century collection of *exemplum*-related narratives, 14

Távora, Franklin, author: early user of *cordel*, 38

Teixeira, Escola do: nineteenth-century school of *cantadores*, 10

Tenzone: as troubadour antecedent of Brazilian verse dialogues, 3

Tereza Batista

—Jorge Amado novel: as source of *cordel*, 144–47; mingles African and ballad elements, 146; author's frequent use of *cordel* traditions, 147; construction of novel, 146–47

—Rodolfo Coelho Cavalcante *cordel*: analyzed, 147–158; six-step pattern, 147–54; as DR tale, 149–50; as DW tale, 150; nontraditional elements in, 154; example of *cordel* conservatism and flexibility, 157–58; text of *cordel*, 158–63

—comparison of novel and *cordel*: triple interchange of *cordel* and eru-

Designer: Richard Hendel/Eric Jungerman
Compositor: Graphic Composition, Inc.
Printer: Thomson-Shore, Inc.
Binder: John H. Dekker & Sons, Inc.
Text: Times Roman
Display: Neuland